Service Intelligence and Service Science:

Evolutionary Technologies and Challenges

Ho-fung Leung
The Chinese University of Hong Kong, China

Dickson K.W. Chiu
Dickson Computer Systems, Hong Kong

Patrick C.K. Hung
University of Ontario Institute of Technology, Canada

INFORMATION SCIENCE REFERENCE

Hershey · New York

Director of Editorial Content:	Kristin Klinger
Director of Book Publications:	Julia Mosemann
Acquisitions Editor:	Lindsay Johnston
Development Editor:	Christine Bufton
Publishing Assistant:	Keith Glazewski
Typesetter:	Keith Glazewski
Production Editor:	Jamie Snavely
Cover Design:	Lisa Tosheff

Published in the United States of America by
Information Science Reference (an imprint of IGI Global)
701 E. Chocolate Avenue
Hershey PA 17033
Tel: 717-533-8845
Fax: 717-533-8661
E-mail: cust@igi-global.com
Web site: http://www.igi-global.com/reference

Library of Congress Cataloging-in-Publication Data

Service intelligence and service science: evolutionary technologies and challenges / Ho-fung Leung, Dickson K.W. Chiu, and Patrick C.K. Hung, editors.
    p. cm.
  Includes bibliographical references and index.
  Summary: "This book presents the emerging fields of service intelligence and service science, positioning them as the most promising directions for the evolution of service computing, demonstrating the critical role such areas play in supporting service computing processes"--Provided by publisher.
  ISBN 978-1-61520-819-7 (hardcover) -- ISBN 978-1-61520-820-3 (ebook) 1. Software engineering. 2. Web services. 3. Artificial intelligence. 4. Service-oriented architecture (Computer science) I. Leung, Ho-Fung. II. Chiu, Dickson K. W., 1966- III. Hung, Patrick C. K.
  QA76.758.S4577 2010
  004.6'54--dc22
                                          2010012446

British Cataloguing in Publication Data
A Cataloguing in Publication record for this book is available from the British Library.

All work contributed to this book is new, previously-unpublished material. The views expressed in this book are those of the authors, but not necessarily of the publisher.

Table of Contents

Section 1
Basic Concepts and Theories

Rolv Bræk, Norwegian University of Science and Technology, Norway
Humberto Nicolás Castejón, Telenor GBD&R, Norway
Hien Nam Le, Norwegian University of Science and Technology, Norway
Judith E. Y. Rossebø, ABB Corporate Research, Norway

Li Li, Southwest University of China, China
Chengfei Liu, Swinburne University of Technology, Australia
Xiaohui Zhao, Swinburne University of Technology, Australia
Junhu Wang, Griffith University, Australia

Zhaohao Sun, University of Ballarat, Australia
Dong Dong, Hebei Normal University, China
John Yearwood, University of Ballarat, Australia

Section 2
Intelligent Technologies

Section 3
Applications and Case Studies

Detailed Table of Contents

Section 1
Basic Concepts and Theories

This section covers some basic concepts and theories of SISS, such as service composition and demand analysis.

Chapter 1

    Rolv Bræk, Norwegian University of Science and Technology, Norway
    Humberto Nicolás Castejón, Telenor GBD&R, Norway
    Hien Nam Le, Norwegian University of Science and Technology, Norway
    Judith E. Y. Rossebø, ABB Corporate Research, Norway

This chapter proposes a policy-based methodology for dynamic service composition and recommendation taking context into account, with a demonstration using a multi-media over IP service that considers security requirements, monitored threat levels, user locations, and preferences.

Chapter 2

    Li Li, Southwest University of China, China
    Chengfei Liu, Swinburne University of Technology, Australia
    Xiaohui Zhao, Swinburne University of Technology, Australia
    Junhu Wang, Griffith University, Australia

This chapter investigates transactional support for composing and scheduling Web services with different transactional properties in workflow constructs. The chapter also introduces the concept of connection point to derive the transactional properties of composite Web services and discusses the scheduling issue of composite Web services.

Chapter 3

Zhaohao Sun, University of Ballarat, Australia
Dong Dong, Hebei Normal University, China
John Yearwood, University of Ballarat, Australia

This chapter examines some fundamentals for demand analysis in Web services and proposes a demand-driven architecture and demand-driven Web service lifecycle for service providers, service requestors, and service brokers, respectively, in order to facilitate research and development of web services, e-services, service intelligence, service science, and service computing.

Section 2
Intelligent Technologies

This section covers some issues on intelligent technologies for SISS, such as ontology and data mining technologies.

Chapter 4

Manel Fredj, INRIA Paris-Rocquencourt, France
Apostolos Zarras, University of Ioannina, Greece
Nikolaos Georgantas, INRIA Paris-Rocquencourt, France
Valérie Issarny, INRIA Paris-Rocquencourt, France

This chapter deals with the dynamic maintenance of service orchestrations in the presence of unavailable services with a focus on the dynamic substitution of stateful services. It presents the SIROCO middleware platform based on ontology with some experimental evaluation of the first prototype, showing that SIROCO provides the necessary means for achieving dynamic maintenance with a reasonable expense on the execution of service orchestrations.

Chapter 5

Sietse Overbeek, Delft University of Technology, The Netherlands
Marijn Janssen, Delft University of Technology, The Netherlands
Patrick van Bommel, Radboud University Nijmegen, The Netherlands

This chapter studies the main concepts for integrated service delivery together with relationships, relational constraints, and interdependencies between the main concepts for integrated service delivery have been determined. An ontology was developed for integrated service delivery based on studying public domain knowledge from different viewpoints to support for organizations that wish to participate in integrated service delivery processes and monitor the execution of services.

Chapter 6

Hongwei Wang, Tongji University, China
James N. K. Liu, The Hong Kong Polytechnic University, China
Wei Wang, Fudan University, China

This chapter propose a six-element based ontological structure for semantic retrieval, and use description logic to semantically describe the atomic term, complex terms, instances, instances description, attribute assignment and axioms. The new structure is evaluated by the Gruber's criteria including explicitness and objectivity, consistency, extensibility, minimal encoding bias and minimal ontological commitment. Based on the new structure, the chapter proposes two reasoning mechanisms, together with conversion mechanisms and determining algorithms, which enable the reasoning for various relations in a specific area according to the rules made by domain experts. Finally, the chapter put forward four kinds of rules for information retrieval, and analyze the applications of the new structure in semantic retrieval.

Chapter 7

Edward Hung, Hong Kong Polytechnic University, Hong Kong

This chapter proposes a framework to develop different probabilistic data mining techniques by classifying uncertain data into different categories, in order to apply this directly on uncertain data and produce results that preserve the accuracy. This chapter also proposes a variety of definitions and approaches for different mining tasks on uncertain data with different properties. The advances in data mining application in this aspect are expected to improve the quality of services provided in various service industries.

Section 3
Applications and Case Studies

This section covers some contemporary applications and cases for SISS to demonstrate the applicability and potential of this emerging field

Juhnyoung Lee, IBM T. J. Watson Research Center, USA
Rama Akkiraju, IBM T. J. Watson Research Center, USA
Chun Hua Tian, IBM China Research Laboratory, China
Shun Jiang, IBM China Research Laboratory, China
Rong Zeng Cao, IBM China Research Laboratory, China
Siva Danturthy, IBM Global Services India, India
Ponn Sundhararajan, IBM Global Services India, India
Rakesh Mohan, IBM T. J. Watson Research Center, USA
Wei Ding, IBM China Research Laboratory, China
Carl Nordman, IBM Global Business Services, USA

This chapter presents a practitioner's tool, Business Transformation Workbench, for business transformation built on a component-based model, which implements a methodical approach that was devised to analyze business transformation opportunities and make business cases for transformation initiatives, thereby providing decision-support to the consultants. The Business Transformation Workbench has been instantiated with data from finance management domain and applied to address a client situation as a case study. An alpha testing of the tool was conducted with about dozen practitioners with 90% positive feedback. The tool is currently being piloted with customer engagements in a large IT consulting organization.

Vladimir Tosic, NICTA, Australia & The University of Western Ontario, Canada &
    The University of New South Wales, Australia
Rasangi Pumudu Karunaratne, The University of New South Wales, Australia
Qinghua Lu, NICTA, Australia & The University of New South Wales, Australia

This chapter research context specification for a management system performing various management activities and potentially used by mobile service-oriented systems. They model context properties analogously to QoS metrics because of their processing similarities. They built their solutions for specification of context properties and related management activities into two languages: the Web Service Offerings Language (WSOL) and WS-Policy4MASC, which increase usefulness of WS-Policy4MASC for management of mobile service-oriented systems.

Yong Zhang, Shandong University, China
Shijun Liu, Shandong University, China
Yuchang Jiao, IBM, China
Yuqing Sun, Shandong University, China

This chapter proposes a service-oriented approach to solve interoperability problem by providing an integrated platform, on which interoperability is considered as utility-like capability and delivered in the form of Software as a Service (SaaS). Each enterprise in a supply chain could establish the interoperation activities with other partners in this platform and thus they could efficiently collaborate. This is further illustrated with a case study on an automobile supply chain.

This chapter proposes a new car navigation system which enables the following three services: route search service with unspecified stopover points, route search service for traveling through sightseeing spots in consideration of sightseeing time, and quick response using dedicated hardware. The proposed car navigation system is implemented on a field programmable gate array, and its validity is verified by several evaluative experiments using actual map information.

This chapter deals with the process-oriented integration of product development and service documentation for technical customer services support in machine and plant construction. This chapter discusses the problem, as well as the solution on the basis of hybrid added value, the structure of the product service system, the IT-concept and the implementation of the service process modeling with a practical use case.

#### Chapter 13

This chapter explains how service quality is evaluated in online-oriented shopping. Because customer satisfaction is paramount, a service quality model incorporates customer satisfaction as an outcome. As this study is the first of its types focusing on service quality in the setting of "buy online, pickup in-store", traditional retailers can consider these findings as guidelines of advancing into the online world. As such, pure online retailers can benefit from these findings in understanding the impact of establishing a physical presence on service quality models and customer satisfaction.

Chapter 14

> *Liu Wenyin, City University of Hong Kong, China & CityU-USTC Advanced Research*
> *Institute, China*
> *An Liu, University of Science & Technology of China, China & City University of*
> *Hong Kong, China & CityU-USTC Advanced Research Institute, China*
> *Qing Li, City University of Hong Kong, China & CityU-USTC Advanced Research Institute, China*
> *Liusheng Huang, University of Science & Technology of China, China & CityU-USTC*
> *Advanced Research Institute, China*

This chapter proposes three insurance models for business Web services and enabling technologies, including quality description, reputation scheme, transaction analysis, etc. As such, the insurance of business Web services will help service competition and hence boost the development of more and more business Web services, and the software industry at large.

Preface

CHALLENGES AND OPPORTUNITIES FOR SERVICE INTELLIGENCE AND SERVICE SCIENCE

Introduction

The global economy and organizations are evolving to become service-oriented. There have recently been more and more research works on services provision, particularly with a cross-disciplinary approach. Beyond the Services Oriented Architecture (SOA), intelligence in computing is essential to achieve service excellence for the ever complicating requirements in the rapidly evolving global environment. This involves knowledge from various disciplines such as computer science, industrial and systems engineering, management science, operations research, marketing, contracts and negotiations; as well as culture transformation and integration methods based on beliefs, assumptions, principles, and values among organizations and humans. In this preface, we would also like to outline some challenges and opportunities for Service Intelligence and Service Science (SISS).

Challenges And Opportunities

As Zhang (2004) has pointed out, killer applications are required to drive Web Services researches. Since the publication of International Journal of Web Services Research (Zhang, 2004), basic researches for services have been steadily progressing. However, the big challenge of the engineering killer applications for intelligent services is still emerging based on the accumulating experiences of services deployment within and across organizations.

The current basis of services and most systems is the Web, which is ever evolving, towards Web 2.0, Web 3.0 (Lassila & Hendler, 2007), etc., so called Web x.0. Web 2.0 refers to a second generation of the Web, facilitating communication, information sharing, interoperability, and collaboration based on user-centered design. Virtual systems and virtual communities based on autonomous and peer-to-peer systems, in which a wide range of intelligent services and analysis are applicable, are therefore among the hottest research topics.

To scale up service provision, the Grid is a high-potential technology for the solution (Foster & Kesselman, 2004). Based on the Grid, concepts like software as a service (SaaS), communications as a service, utility computing, meta-services, and recently cloud computing have emerged (Hayes, 2008).

Such emerging system architectures and computing paradigms bring new power to massive intelligent systems and services, and provide opportunities in new application domains (such as aviation services).

However, they also bring ever increasing complexities that calls for innovations and standardization. In addition, social and legal issues of such emerging technologies and systems must not be ignored (Chiu, Kafeza, & Hung, 2009).

Recently, though there is still much debate on the scope of Web 3.0, key components of Web 3.0 include semantics and intelligence.

Agent based technologies is one of the most promising solution for the integration of systems and services in an intelligent context (He at al., 2003; Chiu, Cheung, & et al., 2010). Intelligent agents are considered as autonomous entities with abilities to execute tasks independently. Various technologies from artificial intelligence can be applied at services, agents, and systems level, including computational intelligence, soft computing, game theory, genetic algorithms, evolutionary computing, logics, machine learning, cybernetics, planning, optimization, and so on. Such intelligence is vital for excellence in service matchmaking, recommendation, personalization, operation, and monitoring (Chiu, Yueh, & et al., 2009). Further, ontology and semantics provides better understanding of the requirements for users and systems, as well as related trust, reputation, security, forensic, and privacy issues in order to provide a better foundation for intelligent system behaviors.

Example application areas include but not limit to service management, service marketing, relationship management, negotiations, auctions, and electronic marketplaces. Further, with increasing popularity of mobile and ubiquitous computing, location and pervasive intelligence for services (Hong et al., 2007) is also an active research area.

To empower systems and services with intelligence, knowledge acquired beforehand and during system execution is the key ingredient. Therefore, knowledge engineering is a key to excellence in systems and services, which includes knowledge modeling, architectures, acquisition, discovery, integration, and applications. Typical knowledge engineering services include content, multimedia, and metadata management, design management, engineering management, electronic education, and so on. As for knowledge application, they can be deployed for decision support and strategic information systems, integration of research and practice, and the management of service personnel and workforce, etc.

Book Content

This book intentionally seeks scientists, engineers, educators, industry people, policy makers, decision makers, and others who have insight, vision, and understanding of the big challenges in Service Intelligence for excellence in service provision. We also aim at helping in communicating and disseminating relevant recent research across disciplines, cultures, and communities. This book comprises of fourteen chapters that covers some novel practical issues of this emerging field. They can be divided into three categories or sections: (1) basic concepts and theories, (2) intelligent technologies, and (3) applications and case study.

Basic Concepts and Theories

The first section contains three chapters covering some basic concepts and theories of SISS, such as service composition and demand analysis.

Bræk et al. propose a policy-based methodology for dynamic service composition and recommendation taking context into account. They demonstrate their approach using a multi-media over IP service that considers security requirements, monitored threat levels, user locations, and preferences.

Li et al. investigate transactional support for composing and scheduling Web services with different transactional properties in workflow constructs. They introduce the concept of connection point to derive the transactional properties of composite Web services and discuss the scheduling issue of composite Web services.

Sun et al. examine some fundamentals for demand analysis in Web services. They propose a demand-driven architecture and demand-driven Web service lifecycle for service providers, service requestors, and service brokers, respectively, in order to facilitate research and development of web services, e-services, service intelligence, service science, and service computing.

Intelligent Technologies

The second section contains four chapters covering some issues on intelligent technologies for SISS, such as ontology and data mining technologies.

Fredj et al. deal with the dynamic maintenance of service orchestrations in the presence of unavailable services with a focus on the dynamic substitution of stateful services. They propose the SIROCO middleware platform based on ontology and present some experimental evaluation of their first prototype, showing that SIROCO provides the necessary means for achieving dynamic maintenance with a reasonable expense on the execution of service orchestrations.

Overbeek et al. study the main concepts for integrated service delivery together with relationships, relational constraints, and interdependencies between the main concepts for integrated service delivery have been determined. They develop an ontology for integrated service delivery based on studying public domain knowledge from different viewpoints to support for organizations that wish to participate in integrated service delivery processes and monitor the execution of services.

Wang et al. propose a six-element based ontological structure for semantic retrieval, and use description logic to semantically describe the atomic term, complex terms, instances, instances description, attribute assignment and axioms. The new structure is evaluated by the Gruber's criteria including explicitness and objectivity, consistency, extensibility, minimal encoding bias and minimal ontological commitment. Based on the new structure, they propose two reasoning mechanisms, i.e., terms-oriented and instances-oriented, for semantic retrieval application. They also propose conversion mechanisms and determining algorithms, which enable the reasoning for various relations in a specific area according to the rules made by domain experts. Finally, they put forward four kinds of rules for information retrieval, and analyze the applications of the new structure in semantic retrieval.

Hung proposes a framework to develop different probabilistic data mining techniques by classifying uncertain data into different categories, in order to apply this directly on uncertain data and produce results that preserve the accuracy. Hung also proposes a variety of definitions and approaches for different mining tasks on uncertain data with different properties. The advances in data mining application in this aspect are expected to improve the quality of services provided in various service industries.

Applications and Case Studies

The third section contains seven chapters covering some contemporary applications and cases for SISS to demonstrate the applicability and potential of this emerging field.

Lee et al. present a practitioner's tool, Business Transformation Workbench, for business transformation built on a component-based model, which implements a methodical approach that was devised to analyze business transformation opportunities and make business cases for transformation initiatives, thereby providing decision-support to the consultants. The Business Transformation Workbench has been instantiated with data from finance management domain and applied to address a client situation as a case study. An alpha testing of the tool was conducted with about dozen practitioners with 90% positive feedback. The tool is currently being piloted with customer engagements in a large IT consulting organization.

Tosic et al. research context specification for a management system performing various management activities and potentially used by mobile service-oriented systems. They model context properties analogously to QoS metrics because of their processing similarities. They built their solutions for specification of context properties and related management activities into two languages: the Web Service Offerings Language (WSOL) and WS-Policy4MASC, which increase usefulness of WS-Policy4MASC for management of mobile service-oriented systems.

Zhang et al. propose a service-oriented approach to solve interoperability problem by providing an integrated platform, on which interoperability is considered as utility-like capability and delivered in the form of Software as a Service (SaaS). Each enterprise in a supply chain could establish the interoperation activities with other partners in this platform and thus they could efficiently collaborate. They illustrate how two SaaS-typed applications interact with each other with a case study on an automobile supply chain.

Yoshikawa proposes a new car navigation system which enables the following three services: route search service with unspecified stopover points, route search service for traveling through sightseeing spots in consideration of sightseeing time, and quick response using dedicated hardware. The proposed car navigation system is implemented on a field programmable gate array, and its validity is verified by several evaluative experiments using actual map information.

Blinn et al. investigate process-oriented integration of product development and service documentation for technical customer services support in machine and plant construction. They discuss the problem, as well as the solution on the basis of hybrid added value, the structure of the product service system, the IT-concept and the implementation of the service process modeling with a practical use case.

Swaid and Wigand explain how service quality is evaluated in online-oriented shopping. Because customer satisfaction is paramount, a service quality model incorporates customer satisfaction as an outcome. As this study is the first of its types focusing on service quality in the setting of "buy online, pickup in-store", traditional retailers can consider these findings as guidelines of advancing into the online world. As such, pure online retailers can benefit from these findings in understanding the impact of establishing a physical presence on service quality models and customer satisfaction.

Liu et al. propose three insurance models for business Web services and enabling technologies, including quality description, reputation scheme, transaction analysis, etc. They believe that the insurance of business Web services will help service competition and hence boost the development of more and more business Web services, and the software industry at large.

Summary

The creation, operation, and evolution of the research and practice in Service Intelligence and Service Intelligence raise concerns that range from high-level requirements and policy modeling through to the deployment of specific implementation technologies and paradigms, as well as involve a wide (and ever growing) range of methods, tools, and technologies. They also cover a broad spectrum of vertical domains, industry segments, and even government sectors.

We are continuously seeking collaborations and carrying out various scholarly activities, including workshops, conference special tracks, and journal special issues on this topic. The *International Journal of Systems and Service-Oriented Engineering* (IJSSOE) (Chiu, 2010) of IGI has been established to provide a continuing forum for SISS and beyond. We also have edited a related special issue the *International Journal of Organizational and Collective Intelligence* (IJOCI).

REFERENCES

Chiu, D. K. W. (2010). Challenges and Opportunities for Web Services Research, Editorial Preface. *International Journal of Systems and Service-Oriented Engineering*, *1*(1), i–iv.

Chiu, D.K.W., Kafeza, E., and Hung, P.C.K. (2009) ISF special issue on emerging social and legal aspects of information systems with Web 2.0. *Information Systems Frontier.* doi:10.1007/s10796-009-9168-x

Chiu, D. K. W., Yueh, Y. T. F., Leung, H.-f., & Hung, P. C. K. (2009). Towards Ubiquitous Tourist Service Coordination and Process Integration: a Collaborative Travel Agent System with Semantic Web Services. *Information Systems Frontiers*, *11*(3), 241–256.

Chiu, D. K. W., Cheung, S.-C., Leung, H.-f., Hung, P. C. K., Kafeza, E., & Hu, H. (2010). Engineering e-Collaboration Services with a Multi-Agent System Approach. *International Journal of Systems and Service-Oriented Engineering*, *1*(1), 1–25.

He, M., Jennings, N. R., & Leung, H.-F. (2003). On agent-mediated electronic commerce. *IEEE Transactions on Knowledge and Data Engineering*, *15*(4), 985–1003.

Hong, D., Chiu, D. K. W., Cheung, S. C., Shen, V. Y., & Kafeza, E. (2007). Ubiquitous Enterprise Service Adaptations Based on Contextual User Behavior. *Information Systems Frontiers*, *9*(4), 343–358.

Lassila, O., & Hendler, J. (2007). Embracing "Web 3.0". *IEEE Internet Computing*, *11*(3), 90–93.

Zhang, L.-J. (2004). Challenges and Opportunities for Web Services Research, Editorial Preface. *International Journal of Web Services Research*, *1*(1), vii–xii.

Acknowledgment

The editing of this book is partially supported by the National Natural Science Foundation of China under Grants No.60873022 and No. 60903053.

Ho-fung Leung
The Chinese University of Hong Kong, China

Dickson K. W. Chiu
Dickson Computer Systems, Hong Kong

Patrick C. K. Hung
University of Ontario Institute of Technology, Canada

Section 1
Basic Concepts and Theories

Chapter 1
Policy–Based Service Composition and Recommendation

Rolv Bræk
Norwegian University of Science and Technology, Norway

Humberto Nicolás Castejón
Telenor GBD&R, Norway

Hien Nam Le
Norwegian University of Science and Technology, Norway

Judith E. Y. Rossebø
ABB Corporate Research, Norway

ABSTRACT

This chapter addresses concepts and methods to support dynamic composition of situated services. We focus mainly on service modelling and service design for execution environments that can support dynamic composition of situated services. In our approach, services are modelled using UML 2.x collaborations that are mapped to parts of a UML 2.x design model. Services are also associated with situations, that is, sets of properties that characterise the executing environment of the service. A policy-driven mechanism is proposed to enhance the service composition process. The policy model takes into account context situations and user preferences that can impact the performance and functionalities of the composed services. Within a given situation, executable services are identified and service composition policies used to determine their execution order. We demonstrate the approach using a multi-media over IP service that takes into account security requirements, monitored threat levels, user locations and preferences.

INTRODUCTION

Despite the considerable attention that services and service engineering have received in recent years, one has not yet arrived at a universal understanding of what a service is and what service composition and context adaptation entails. By "universal" understanding we mean a commonly agreed understanding that is not tied to particu-

DOI: 10.4018/978-1-61520-819-7.ch001

lar technologies such as web-services, protocol services or middleware services, but allows these as special cases within the wider domain of ICT systems.

As a step towards a universal understanding we venture to define "service" as *an identified functionality aiming to establish some desired goals/effects among collaborating entities.* This understanding is quite general and captures various common uses of the term "service", such as end-user services meaning functionality provided to end-users, protocol services meaning the functionality provided by a protocol layer to the layer above, component services meaning the functionality provided by a component to its environment across an interface. It is this latter understanding of service that is normally used in middleware such as CORBA, in web services and, to some extent, in the SOA paradigm.

Sometimes it is possible to make a distinction between a service provider that creates the effect and a consumer that makes use of it by means of an interface, but this is not always possible. In a two party call service directly established between two end-points, for instance, it is not so obvious who is the provider and who is the consumer. Both parties participate in creating the effect (i.e., the voice connection) and they both benefit from it. The definition above also covers this kind of peer-to-peer service. According to this understanding, services have several important characteristics:

A service is *functionality*; it is behaviour performed by entities.

A service implies *collaboration;* it makes no sense to talk about a service unless at least two entities collaborate (e.g. a client and a server).

Service behaviour is *crosscutting*; it implies coordination of two or more entity behaviours.

Service behaviour is normally *partial*; it is usually to be composed with other services to achieve complete system functionality.

It is the collaborative, crosscutting and partial nature of services that makes service engineering, in general, such a challenge. Ideally one wants to define services separately so they can be analyzed, understood and reused as separate entities; and then be able to compose them into well-functioning systems that can adapt to different context situations and individual preferences (Sanders, Castejón, et al. 2005; Papazolou, Traverso, et al., 2008). This can be achieved by separating service models from design models and implementations as illustrated in Figure 1.

Service models are used to precisely define and compose services. The new collaboration concept introduced in UML 2.0 (OMG, 2004) provides an excellent basis for service modelling. A collaboration defines a structure of *roles* (i.e. partial object behaviours) that cooperate with each other to achieve a common task or goal, so it closely corresponds to the concept of service as defined here. Moreover one may compose collaborations from smaller collaborations, representing sub-services, by means of *collaboration uses*.

Design models define design solutions as structures of interconnected parts having well-defined behaviour. UML structured classes with inner parts and state machines provide a good basis for design models. By binding the roles of service collaborations to parts in the design structure one defines the relationship between service models and design models. In general, a part will be able to participate in several services by playing different roles, and a service will involve roles played by several different parts. This illustrates that services and roles add a dimension of composition (and flexibility) on top of parts and classes.

Realizations are implementations that execute on different service platforms. Using state of the art MDE techniques, they may be automatically derived from service models and design models.

In previous publications (Castejón, Bochmann, et al., 2007; Kraemer, Bræk, et al., 2007) we have described methods and tools that enable precise definition of service models, automatic synthesis of design models from service models and automatic generation of executable implementations from design models, as well as formal analysis of

Figure 1. Service engineering overview

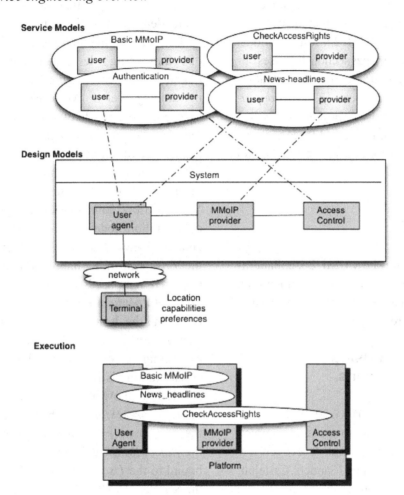

service models and design models. These works, however, do only consider static design models where the interconnections between the different structural parts are fixed. In practice, service invocation is normally dynamic and will often involve a structure of parts that are dynamically linked during the execution of a service. In addition, the parts of design models will in many cases represent domain entities such as users and terminals that are situated in a context, have limited resources and may have individual preferences that services and roles must adapt to. Service intelligence and situation-awareness emerge from the rules that govern role binding and role invocation in the individual parts, taking their situation and preferences

into account. In (Amyot, Becha, et al., 2008) we described an approach to next generation service engineering using service models as a basis for analysing tradeoffs and adaptation, as well as to perform dynamic adaptations to situations in a running system. In this chapter, we will explain solutions for dynamic service composition and adaptation to context situations and preferences using policies. The proposed policy-driven service composition approach aims at enhancing service composition by answering two questions: (1) in what situations can a given service be invoked?; and (2) given a situation, what service compositions might be performed?

The remainder of this chapter is organized as follows. The next section reviews previous work on service modelling using UML 2.x collaborations. The *Situation-aware services* section discusses our view on the concepts of situation and situation adaptation and the *Policy-based service adaptation* section introduces our policy-driven service composition approach. In the last three sections we discuss related work and future trends, and provide conclusions.

BACKGROUND

In this section we show how UML 2.x collaborations can be used to support service modelling, and how service behaviour can be specified using a collaborative choreography diagram.

Service Modelling Using UML 2.x Collaborations

UML 2.x collaborations (OMG, 2009) have been proposed as a powerful tool to structure complex service behaviour and give a high-level overview not provided by other notations (Sanders, Castejón, et al. 2005). In this section we briefly review the use of UML 2.x collaborations for service modelling. We exemplify the approach with a multimedia over IP case study that will be used as a running example throughout the rest of the chapter.

Service structure. At the early service modelling stages it makes little sense to identify the implementation level components that will participate in providing the service. One should rather focus on identifying actors[1] representing domain entities, such as users and user groups that are involved in the service (Bræk & Haugen, 1993). It does not make much sense to identify particular actors either, but to identify the properties and behaviour that those actors shall have, and specify these as roles. A service can then be understood as a collaboration between roles, to

be played by actors, that interact to accomplish some identified functionality.

UML 2.x collaborations describe structures of collaborating roles and are therefore suitable to model services. Figure 2(a) shows a basic multimedia over IP (MMoIP) service modelled as a collaboration between two roles, namely *mmoip_user* and *mmoip_provider*. An interesting feature of collaborations is that they can be defined in terms of other smaller collaborations by means of *collaboration uses*, as exemplified by the *SecureMMoIP* collaboration in Figure 2(b). This collaboration models a secure and news headlines-enhanced MMoIP service. To achieve this service the *BasicMMoIP* collaboration of Figure 2(a) has been composed with three other collaborations: *Authentication* and *AccessRightsCheck*, providing the desired security functionality; and *NewsHeadlines*, which provides news headlines as running text on the screen. Each of these sub-collaborations is represented as a collaboration use defining how its roles are bound to the roles of the *SecureMMoIP* collaboration. For example, the *mmoip_user* and *mmoip_provider* roles of the *BasicMMoIP* collaboration are respectively bound to the *User* and *ServiceProvider* roles of the *SecureMMoIP* collaboration by means of the *mmoip:BasicMMoIP* collaboration use.

Service behaviour. Crosscutting collaborative behaviour has traditionally been specified using Use Cases, interaction diagrams and other scenario oriented notations (Wang, Sørensen, et al., 2008). Such specifications tend to be incomplete, due to the large number of possible scenarios, so one normally needs to add behaviour detail later, during the design phase. Collaborations help to mitigate this problem:

Structural decomposition of complex collaborations naturally leads to sub-collaborations corresponding to interfaces and, further, to sub-collaborations triggered by independent initiatives taken by any of the two sides of the interface. This results in elementary sub-collaborations with behaviours that are comparatively simple and simple

Figure 2. Collaborations modelling (a) a basic MMoIP service and (b) a secure MMoIP service

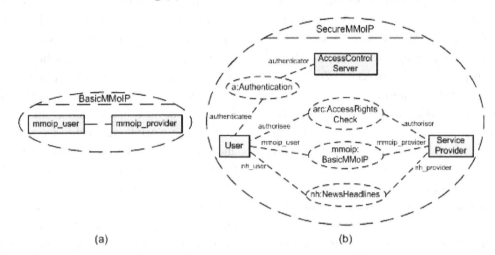

(a)   (b)

enough to be completely defined using UML 2.x interaction diagrams (Castejón & Bræk, 2006). One can also completely define the behaviour of each elementary collaboration as an activity, where the participating roles are represented by activity partitions.

The execution ordering of such elementary sub-collaborations can be fully described using activity diagrams where actions are call behaviour actions that invoke the behaviour of a collaboration use:

One can specify the *choreography*, or global ordering, of the sub-collaborations of a composite collaboration without localizing all control flow to composite roles or actors (Castejón & Bræk, 2006). An example is shown in Figure 3, where the choreography for the *SecureMMoIP* collaboration is presented[2]. This choreography specifies that, after both a successful authentication and a successful authorization, the basic MMoIP service is executed concurrently with the news headlines service.

When elementary collaborations are defined as reusable building blocks using activity diagrams, one can precisely define the ordering of

Figure 3. Choreography for the SecureMMoIP service collaboration

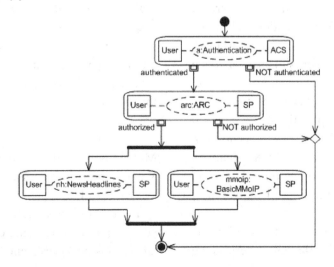

activities by linking the activities together in an enclosing activity diagram where all control flow is localized to composite roles and actors. This approach is supported by the Arctis toolset as explained in (Kraemer, Bræk, et al., 2009) and illustrated in Figures 10 and 11.

Design models and subsequent implementations may be fully automatically generated from the activity diagram describing the ordering of sub-collaborations (Castejón, 2008; Kraemer, Bræk, et al., 2009). Altogether this enables a shift in focus from design and implementation models towards service models. It is now possible to specify service behaviours with high precision and completeness, to analyze properties, to perform tradeoffs and to ensure service quality in ways unimaginable at the implementation level.

SITUATION-AWARE SERVICES

In this section we discuss the concept of situation as it is used in our service modelling approach. We exemplify the benefits of having situation-aware services, and address how and where situation adaptation can be achieved.

Situation

Context and situation are concepts that have been intensively discussed in the literature. Generally, context is defined as any information that can be used to describe the situation of an entity (Abowd, Dey, et al., 1999). However, situation has been differently defined and discussed. For example, in (Yau & Liu, 2006), a situation is considered as a set of contexts in applications over a period of time; while in (Holtkamp & Wojciechowski, 2007; Celentano, Faralli, et al., 2008) situations are user activities at a point in time that could have strong impact on the future behaviours of services or systems.

In our work we see the "situation" of a service as a set of properties that characterizes the executing environment of the service. We note that in a system providing several services, the environment of a given service will consist of any other running services, as well as the environment of the system itself. From the point of view of the *SecureMMoIP* service (see Figure 2(b)), for instance, the information about the authentication outcome originates within the service itself and does not characterize its environment. It is therefore not considered as part of the situation of the service. From the point of view of the *AccessRightsCheck* sub-service, however, the authentication outcome characterizes something happening in its environment (i.e., within the *Authentication* sub-service), so it is considered as part of its situation. The physical location of a user characterizes the system environment, so it is considered when determining the situation of both the *SecureMMoIP* service and the *AccessRightsCheck* sub-service.

Properties characterizing the situation of a service can be divided into two groups: *system level* properties, which describe the global situation of the system providing the service (e.g. current load level and level of monitored security attacks); and *actor level* properties, which describe the situation of a particular actor participating in a service (e.g. properties describing other active services involving the actor). Domain entities such as users, terminals and other beings that exist in real situations and have preferences will often be mapped into corresponding individual actors in the system that will maintain situation and preferences on their behalf. For an actor representing a user, for example, the location and agenda properties of that user would be part of the actor level situation properties of any service the actor participates in.

Consider, for instance, a system offering a MMoIP service directly connecting two users. We assume that each user is represented in the system by a UserAgent actor. The outcome of a call attempt clearly depends on the availability situation of the user being called, which is managed by his/her UserAgent. If available, a MMoIP

Figure 4. Relationship between situations and services

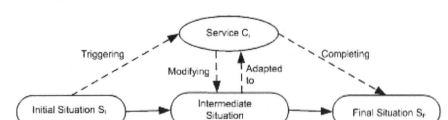

session can be established, but if unavailable (e.g. because the user is already involved in a MMoIP session with a third user), there may be a range of options for this situation such as simple rejection, call back when free or call forwarding. Which option to select may depend on the preferences of the called user, which, again, are managed by his/her UserAgent. This illustrates that the situation of a service depends on which other services or service instances are running (i.e. are active), and that is given by information held by the participating actors in the form of predicates. In general, the behaviour of services and roles may depend on the situation and also contribute to it (i.e. change it). Therefore there are mutual dependencies (interactions) between the roles that an actor plays and the situation of the same actor.

Following the above discussion, we define a situation of a service C as a tuple (Δ, P) where:

- is a set of services, or service instances, that are also active when C is running.
- P is a set of predicates, held by the actors of the system, that characterizes the execution environment of C both at the system level and actor level.

For each service an initial situation S_I and a final situation S_F can be identified (see Figure 4). The initial situation is a set of predicates over the service environment defining a pre-condition that should hold for the service to be initiated. The final situation is a set of predicates over the service environment that serves as post-condition

for the service execution. If the necessary initial situation for a service exists, the service is said to be *executable*. An executable service will be executed if it is *enabled* (i.e. the appropriate collaboration use has been reached in the service choreography) and its triggering event is observed in its environment. While being executed, a service may modify the situation properties, which may then affect the execution of other active services. Once the service execution is finished, the service's final situation is reached.

We illustrate the dependency between services and situations with help of the *SecureMMoIP* service presented in the *Background* section. This service starts with an authentication service (defined by the *Authentication* collaboration). In a static system, the authentication service will always be performed in the same way, what might be too inflexible. A more flexible system would allow the authentication procedure to be relaxed or strengthened depending on the current situation. That is, the most suitable authentication service may be executed depending on the situation (Rossebø & Bræk 2006):

A unilateral one pass authentication (UOPA) service may be used for low risk situations, such as when service requests come from users who have logged on to the network using a VPN solution.

A unilateral two pass authentication (UTPA) service may be used when a medium risk situation is identified, for example when user requests are coming from terminals located within a predefined geographical area (or trusted domain).

Figure 5. New Authentication collaboration with situation-dependent behaviour

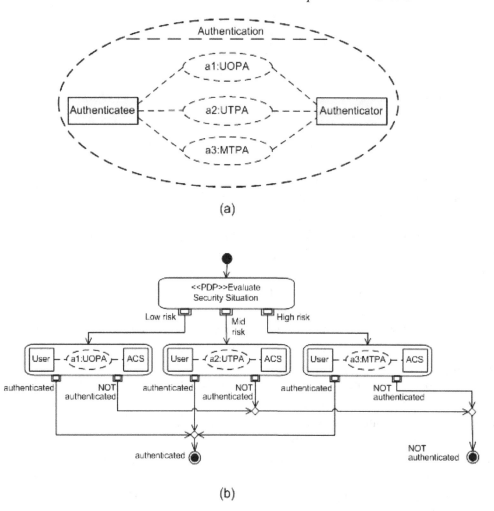

(a)

(b)

A mutual two pass authentication (MTPA) service may be used in high risk situations, for example when user requests come from a network address that has been identified as an un-trusted domain.

To specify the choice between authentication services we can refine the original *Authentication* collaboration as a composition of three sub-collaborations, each one of them describing an alternative authentication service (see Figure 5(a)). The behaviour of the new *Authentication* collaboration is then a situation-dependent choice between the three sub-collaborations, as shown by the choreography in Figure 5(b) (the meaning

of the *EvaluateSecuritySituation* activity will be explained in the *Policy-based service adaptation* section). According to that choreography, only one of the authentication alternatives becomes enabled depending on the evaluation outcome.

Table 1 illustrates the properties that characterize the situations related to the *SecureMMoIP* service. The user's physical location #UserPhysicalLoc (e.g., GPS latitude and longitude of Trondheim city) and logical location #UserLogicalLoc (e.g., a network domain) are actor level situation properties, while the #AccessTime and #MonitoredThreatLevel attributes are system level situation properties. Table 2 illustrates the

Table 1. Situation attributes of the SecureMMoIP service

Properties	Attributes	Descriptions
Actor level	#UserPhysicalLoc	Geographical location of users
	#UserLogicalLoc	IP address of service clients
System level	#AccessTime	Access time of users
	#MonitoredThreatLevel	Number of concurrent users accessing the service at #AccessTime

classification of situations in the *SecureMMoIP* service based on pre-defined values of situation properties. Besides the description of the different situations, a number of executable services has been identified (i.e. services that may be executed in each of the situations). However, at this point we do not specify the order in which these services will be executed, or whether all of them will indeed be executed. For example, in a low risk security situation, all three authentication services are executable. However, only one of these authentication procedures should be enabled and triggered for actual execution in a service session (as discussed in *Situation adaptation* section). In the *Policy negotiation in distributed systems* section, we will explain how composition policies can be used to govern the execution of services.

Figure 6 illustrates how situations and executable services evolve in the context of the *SecureMMoIP* service. In the figure, the $S_x/\{C_1,...,C_n\}$ notation denotes that services $C_1,...,C_n$ can be executed in the situation S_x. In the figure two situation decision points are identified, namely *EvaluaeSecuritySituation* and *EvaluateAccessRightSituation*. At these decision points it is possible to select between different executable subservices in order to meet the main service requirements or user demands. At the *EvaluateSecuritySituation* decision point the security situation is analyzed and, based on the actual situation, different authentication services (e.g., C_{UTPA}, C_{UOPA} or C_{MTPA}) may be selected for execution, as we discussed previously. If the authentication is successful, only the *AccessRightsCheck* service col-

Table 2. Situation specifications

Situation	Properties and triggered events	Executable services
Low risk security S_L	#UserPhysicalLoc = In(Trondheim) #UserLogicalLoc = In(ntnu.no) #AccessTime < 08:00 #MonitoredThreatLevel ≤ 50	C_{UTPA}, C_{UOPA}, C_{MTPA}
Medium risk security S_M	#UserLogicalLoc = In(trondheim.no) #AccessTime < 08:00 #MonitoredThreatLevel ≤ 50	C_{UTPA}, C_{MTPA}
High risk security S_H	#AccessTime > 08:00 #MonitoredThreatLevel ≥ 51 #UserLogicalLoc <> In(ntnu.no) OR In(trondheim.no)	C_{MTPA}
Authenticated S_{AU}	#User.Authentication = True	C_{ARC}
Normal service delivery S_D	#User.AccessRight = True	$C_{BasicMMoIP}$, $C_{NewsHeadlines}$
Limited service delivery S_{LD}	#User.AccessRight = False #MonitoredThreatlevel ≤ 50	$C_{NewsHeadlines}$

Figure 6. Situations of the Secure MMoIP service

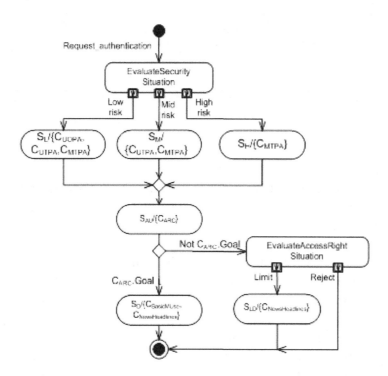

laboration may be executed. If such collaboration is executed and it achieves its goal, a situation where the user holds valid access rights is reached (i.e. normal service delivery situation, S_D). If it does not achieve its goal, a situation where the user does not hold valid access rights and the monitored threat level is less than a pre-defined minimum threshold may be reached (i.e., limited service delivery situation, S_{LD}). In the normal delivery situation both the *BasicMMoIP* and *NewsHeadlines* services are executable. In the limited delivery situation only the *NewsHeadlines* service may be executed. Note that this limited news service may be forced to abort if the number of concurrent users accessing the *SecureMMoIP* service increases. In that case the #MonitoredThreatLevel predicate would be updated and the situation would change.

Situation Adaptation

A large class of services involves state-full sessions among objects that are dynamically linked. Collaborations are well suited for defining the behaviour of sessions once the dynamic links are established. Setting up such links may be seen as dynamically binding roles to actors, here called *dynamic role-actor binding*. The UML notations and semantics do not directly support such dynamic role-actor binding. It is normally done using mechanisms in the runtime system.

It is clear that dynamic role-actor binding is an important point required in order to adapt the roles to the actor situations and preferences (Castejón & Bræk, 2006). In many cases the behaviour associated with dynamic role-actor binding is central to the service behaviour and to service intelligence. In dynamic role-actor binding there is normally an initiating actor and a requested actor. The initiating actor issues a request to the requested actor to play a given role. For example, in the *SecureMMoIP* service, when the Access Control Server (ACS) receives a request for authentication, the *authenticator* actor ACS may ask the client actor to play the role of *authenticatee* to perform a unilateral one pass authentication (UOPA) procedure. The response depends on the situation and preferences of the requested actor, and the two actors have to coordinate and agree before a role is bound to the requested actor. Reaching agreement may involve negotiation and possibly waiting for the situation to change (see the *Policy-based service adaptation* section). Thus an important class of situation adaptation and thus, service intelligence, is closely related with dynamic role-actor binding.

Once the process of dynamic role-actor binding is done, a session may proceed according to the role definitions until:

- Another dynamic role-actor binding needs to be performed;
- A point in the role behaviour is reached where the actor situation and preferences need to be considered in order to determine a choice between subsequent behaviours (i.e., policy decision points as explained in the *Policy-based service adaptation* section);
- A change occurs in the actor situation that calls for immediate interruption and adaptation of executing roles.

We may classify the two first initiatives as *role-pull* and the third one as *actor-push* (or *situation-push*). By suitably decomposing collaborations into sub-collaborations, the second point above can be made to coincide with transitions between sub-collaborations. Thus, the role-pull initiatives coincide with transitions in the global choreography of sub-collaborations of a composite service collaboration. The actor-push initiative may be completely unrelated to events of ongoing collaborations. If immediate action is required, then ongoing collaborations may have to be interrupted. This may be modelled using the interruption construct of activity diagrams. It therefore appears that given a set of elementary collaborations, both role-pull and actor-push initiatives can be treated on the level of activity diagrams defining the ordering of elementary collaborations and roles. In other words, situation dependency can be treated outside elementary collaborations, at the level of collaboration composition.

In summary, situation adaptation may be performed both:

- at the moment of establishing a service session, as part of the dynamic role-actor binding process;
- during the service session itself, by fine-tuning the composition of elementary collaborations.

In the next section we will explain how policies can be used to drive the situation adaptation.

POLICY-BASED SERVICE ADAPTATION

Decisions concerning adaptation to a given situation will in general, depend on the preferences and constraints of the individual actors. Rather than changing the functionality of pre-defined operations, policies define choices in behaviour in terms of the conditions under which such operations can be invoked. Applied to dynamic service composition, this means that policies may define choices in behaviour in terms of conditions under which roles can be dynamically bound to actors, and also, under which service roles can be dynamically composed together, rather than changing the specification of the service roles themselves. Thus, policies can be used to control the composition of services (i.e. to define the ordering of roles), while allowing to choose between alternative services with the same purpose or goals.

Figure 7. Two level policy-based service adaptations

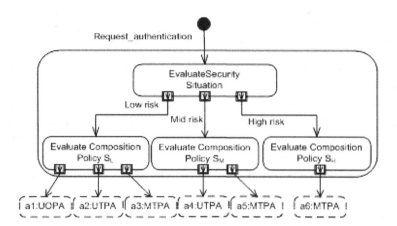

Our policy-based service adaptation is performed at two levels: situation adaptation and service collaboration adaptation (see Figure 7). Situation adaptation focuses on analysing the current situation in order to identify a set of compatible or equivalent services (Jørstad & Do, 2007) that are executable (see the *Situation* section). Service collaboration adaptation focuses on how elementary collaborations are composed based on the evaluation of composition policies. In Figure 7, the *EvaluateSecuritySituation* activity carries out a situation adaptation in which different security situations of the *SecureMMoIP* service (e.g., low risk, medium risk or high risk) are analysed and a set of executable services is identified. Which authentication collaboration that will be actually enabled is then determined with help of the *EvaluateCompositionPolicy* activities.

It is important to note that the changes in situations can strongly impact the service adaptation. For example, suppose that the *UOPA* collaboration is selected as authentication service in a low risk situation S_L. If the service situation changes from low risk S_L to medium risk S_M, then the on-going *UOPA* collaboration should be aborted and a new authentication collaboration, either *UTPA* or *MTPA*, should be invoked in situation S_M. In the case a collaboration *UTPA* is being executed in a low risk situation S_L, however, this authentication

procedure may continue to be executed in the new medium risk situation S_M.

Policy-Driven Service Composition

A composition policy is a set of policy rules specifying how a given set of service collaborations can be composed to obtain a given set of composite services. As such, a composition policy applies to a family of related services, where the number of possible services in the family depends on the choices governed by the policy rules. Choices are made to decide which collaborations will be composed in order to deliver the selected service.

To precisely support dynamic service composition, it is important to be able to specify, for each service in each situation, the conditions that must be satisfied, what triggers the transition from one service collaboration to another, and what the desired goals are. We have based our definition of policy rules on the *event-condition-action* rule paradigm of active database systems (Widom & Ceri, 1996), and have extended it with a service *goal G*. A policy rule is therefore of the following form:

If trigger T and condition C then action A and goal B.

Figure 8. Policy decision point for evaluation low risk security situation

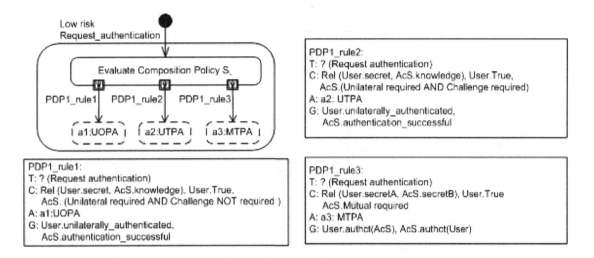

In a policy rule, the trigger *T* and condition *C* together define when the policy rule is applicable. The trigger is the sent or received event associated to a message sent to or from a composite role (e.g., User or Access Control Server). That role will then be the role discovering the trigger and responsible for enforcing the policy rule. For easier transformation from global to local policies (needed on the transformation from service to design models), the condition C is split in three parts, one condition for each of the two composite roles involved (e.g., in Figure 8, *User.True* and *AcS.(Unilateral required AND Challenge NOT required*) in PDP1_rule1), and one condition relating the roles (e.g., *Rel(User.secret, AcS.knowledge)* in PDP1_rule1). In this chapter, the semantics of these policy rules has been omitted; however, it has been clearly detailed in (Rossebø & Runde, 2008). The action *A* defines the collaboration use to be performed when the trigger event has occurred, given that the constraints in the condition *C* hold. The action also defines the necessary role bindings from elementary to composite roles. The goal *G* defines the desired result of the action when the policy is applied and is a Boolean predicate expressing when the goal is achieved from the perspective of the collaboration as a whole.

As explained in the *Background* section, in our approach UML 2.x collaborations provide a static structural overview of the separately specified collaborations and roles involved in a service composition. We allow for each of the sub-collaborations to be considered as a general pattern that may be further specialized. Choreographies and policy rules specify the dynamic composition of the behaviour associated with the sub-collaborations, showing the dependencies between the composed services. Up to this point, we have specified which specializations may be used statically. Further work should investigate the idea of specialization of a collaboration as a plug-in. With such an approach, the goal part of the policy rules becomes quite important. The idea would be that different collaborations could be considered for use in the service composition as specializations of a general pattern if the goal *G* of the collaboration is the same or at least as strong as the goal specified for the general pattern. For example, if the requirement is that unilateral authentication is achieved as a goal, (i.e., *User. unilaterally_authenticated* in both PDP1_rule1 and PDP1_rule2 as described in Figure 8), then a choice can be allowed between several unilateral and mutual authentication collaborations

Figure 9. Policy-driven service choreography for the SecureMMoIP collaboration

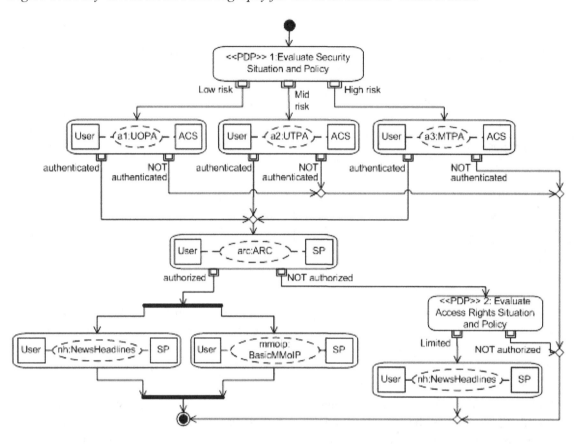

specialized differently with respect to algorithm, key length, etc. Each of those collaborations would be able to successfully fulfil the required goal of unilateral authentication. We note that while the goal is an important part of the policy rules as we have defined them, the use of goals to enable the plug-in of different collaborations in the overall choreography is not discussed in this chapter, but it is the subject of future work.

Figure 9 presents a policy-driven choreography diagram that can be understood as both a refinement and an extension of the static choreography in Figure 3, and is characterized by so-called *policy decision points* (PDPs). These are activities tagged with the <<PDP>> stereotype. At each PDP, situation and composition policies are evaluated, and an outgoing flow is chosen depending on the decision outcome. In Figure 9, a first situation

evaluation is carried out in PDP1 when a user sends a request for authentication. This request is the trigger event for situation and composition policy evaluations. Which outgoing edge to be taken will then depend on the conditions in the policy rules (e.g., collaboration uses *a1:UOPA* in low risk security situations or *a2:UTPA* in medium risk situations).

The policy-driven service choreography, along with the set of policy rules that apply at policy decision points, allows us to represent all the possible runs which allow achieving the overall goal for a family of services. This service consists of the selected collaboration uses to be composed, according to composition policy rules. Another service opportunity results when a different set of collaboration uses are selected based on the policy rules. The definition of a policy rule that

Figure 10. A distributed policy detection point

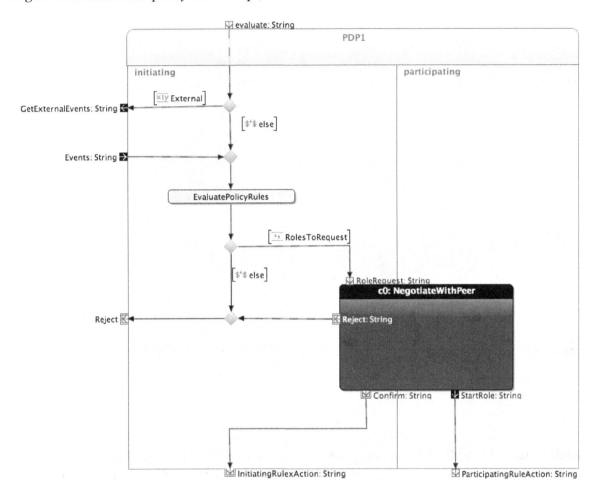

we have given above at the beginning of this section, is applicable for specifying policy rules at the service specification and design objects levels of abstraction, however, it may need to be refined at the implementation level, for example in order to specify ownership aspects of policies (Rossebø & Runde, 2008).

Policy Negotiation in Distributed Systems

In a distributed system involving several actors that may be in different situations and follow different policies, it is necessary to coordinate and negotiate among actors to ensure that coordinated policy decisions are made (i.e., situation adaptation choices). If not, actors may invoke incompatible roles. Such coordination can be considered a special kind of service and defined using collaborations in the same way as other services. Figures 10 and 11 define the behaviour of a distributed policy detection point with an inner coordination collaboration called *NegotiateWithPeer*. Both are defined as re-usable activity blocks using the Arctis tool (Kraemer, 2007; Kraemer, Bræk, et al., 2009). Using this tool the behaviour definition may be formally model-checked to ensure correctness and then be automatically transformed into executable state machines.

Figure 11. Policy negotiation in a distributed system

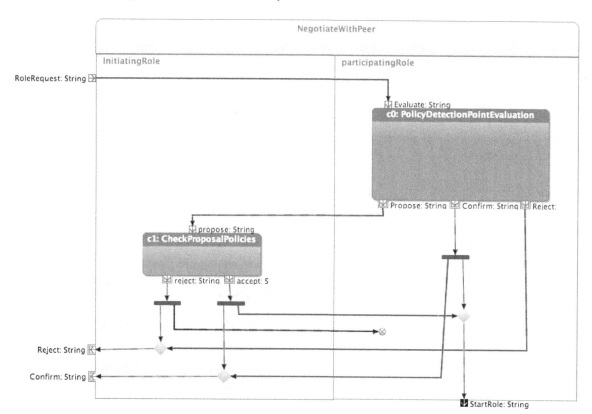

As described in Figure 10, the policy detection point is started when a token enters the evaluate pin. It may then optionally wait for an external trigger event before it evaluates policy rules local to the (actor playing the) initiating role. If one or more policy rules evaluate to true, the corresponding set of roles is given to the *NegotiateWithPeer* activity for coordination with the (actor playing the) participating role. This will either result in agreement of which service roles to enable or in a rejection if no roles may be agreed. In the case of the MMoIP service, the actors playing the *User* and *AccessControlServer* roles use the PDP collaboration to negotiate what authentication service should be performed (based on the situation of each actor). If both parties can agree on one authentication policy (e.g., UTPA in medium risk situation), then the *SecureMMoIP* service may be initiated. During the execution of services, if the

situation of either User agent or MMoIP service provider is changed, the policy negotiation can be re-invoked according to the overall choreography.

RELATED WORK

There are many proposals that discuss different mechanisms or methodologies to support the specification and composition of services (Papazoglou, Traverso, et al., 2008; Dustdar & Schreiner, 2005). However, there are still major limitations, for example, lacking of techniques to model service choices and support the dynamic service composition in different situations.

A taxonomy for multimedia service composition is discussed in (Nahrstedt & Balke, 2004). The authors distinguish three service composition cases: successive, concurrent and hybrid. A quality of service model is also discussed in relation to multimedia. An integrating metrics, which includes time, number of services, performance quality, content type and infrastructural support, is proposed in order to support the evaluation of service composition. However, this taxonomy does not consider situations in which services may or may not be composed together. The proposed taxonomy does not address the issues of service recommendation by policies or rules.

The problem of service selection in open and dynamic environments is studied in (Sensoy & Yolum, 2007). The authors propose an ontology-based service selection approach to capture and represent the context of requested and delivered services in detail. There are two main service selection mechanisms that are based on context-aware rating and experience rating. Our approach is similar to this approach in terms of describing the context of system level (or service providers) and actor level (or service clients) properties. The main advantage of our approach is the situation-based choices of service recommendation that may be further negotiated and benefit both service client and provider.

In (Celentano, Faralli, et. al, 2008) the authors propose a personal service composition model that is based on the situation. Situations are data values that describe a state of the user activity at different time stamps. In other words, a snapshot of the data instances is a situation. An activity is a partially ordered set of tasks which can be added or removed, and that evolves from an initial state to a final state. A task is a tuple of task name, task description, service events that can occur and task status. Services are independent processes that support the activities of users. For each situation, a service will be activated to serve the user requests. The proposed approach does however not address which services should be enabled in which situations to benefit user requests.

Policies for governing service execution are categorised and discussed in (Castejón & Bræk,

2005). However, the specification of rules for defining such policies is not addressed, and how policies are used to define the ordering of service roles is not discussed. An architecture for policy definition and call control policies is given in (Reiff-Marganiec & Turner, 2003). This work provides some high level ideas for defining policies to be used in enhancing and controlling features in the context of call control in telecommunication services. Use of policies at runtime to dynamically compose the roles executed by actors is however not addressed.

A model for service management for which policy rules define adaptive behaviour along with semantic expression of operational state has been proposed in (Lewis, D., Keeney, J., et al., 2006). A policy-driven framework for context-aware dynamic adaptation of services is presented in (Keeney & Cahill, 2003). Both of these works address the specification of mechanisms at the design model and implementation layers to enable dynamic adaptation at runtime. Our approach, however, focuses on the specification of adaptation mechanisms at the service model layer, early in the development process. In our recent work (Rossebø & Bræk, 2008; Rossebø & Runde, 2008), a policy-based service composition approach has been presented. In that approach, policies are the driving forces that support service composition. Policies are pre-defined rules that take into account the events which could have impact on the performance of service systems. The service systems will evaluate these rules to decide which service will be activated. With this method, policies are defined for collaborations where the detailed behaviour is specified using UML 2.x sequence diagrams. For each policy rule, the trigger part is an event which is clearly specified in a UML 2.x sequence diagram. This corresponds nicely to the idea of a situation presented in this chapter, for which an executable service will be executed if its triggering event is observed in its environment.

FUTURE TRENDS

At present, service-oriented computing and service-oriented architecture are providing a comprehensive approach for service development. Services are rapidly and separately designed, and then aggregated to efficiently meet the increasing demands of service clients. Our policy-driven service development approach is useful in terms of (1) supporting platform-independent service design by focussing on modelling the behaviours and interactions of service roles (via UML collaboration features); and (2) identifying different situations in which services can be composed and deployed early in the service development process.

The rapid growth of capacity and functionalities of computing devices and network technologies (e.g., mobile phones with 3G, WLAN, GPS and Bluetooth capabilities), has enabled a new service environment in which services must have the capacity to adapt to changes in the environment, that is, services must possess situation-awareness abilities. Furthermore, extra requirements of services (e.g., non-functional requirements like security or location) must also be taken into consideration. In our approach, we have addressed different situation properties like location and time to highlight the situation analysis and evaluation. Our approach can be extended to take care of any environment properties and non-functional requirements of services that can be measured and made available to the actors of a system. In terms of service design, in our approach, we focus on modelling interactive behaviours among service roles. These service roles will be bound to actors that actually perform these behaviours. Situation-awareness services then can be modelled as services whose behaviours adapt to the situations and preferences of the actors that participate in those services.

In the near future, development of services will be user-centric. This means that the service environments will advance toward ubiquitous and intelligent environments in which autonomic and adaptive services play vital roles. Users should be able to dynamically compose services in accordance with their service situations or goals, for example, when more suitable services become available or the locations of users or personal devices are changed. Our policy-driven service composition approach with dynamic role binding mechanism aims to support such personalized service compositions.

CONCLUSION

In this chapter, we have presented a policy-driven service choreography approach, which (1) takes into account different service situations and (2) expresses graphically the ordering and policy decisions, to support dynamic composition of services (i.e., collaborations). By declaring composition policies as part of the policy specification and providing a policy-driven choreography diagram that demonstrates how the service can execute according to the policy specification, the overall choreography becomes more flexible and adaptable. In this way, it is easier to provide information on how a set of re-usable services (which are designed as re-usable activity blocks) can be combined, while specifying rules for system behaviour in relation to service requirements such as availability requirements.

The policy management system for enabling dynamic composition in the runtime system is a separate management layer that sits on top of the deployed system. Services that have already been composed, implemented and deployed (designed according to the service and design model specifications) run uninterrupted and unchanged until an event triggers adaptation due to changes of service situations. At this point, there is a decision to adapt, by dynamically composing the service (changing which roles are invoked and ordering of roles).

REFERENCES

Abowd, G. D., Dey, A. K., Brown, P. J., Davies, N., Smith, M., & Steggles, P. (1999). *Towards a Better Understanding of Context and Context-Awareness* (pp. 304–307). Handheld and Ubiquitous Computing.

Almeida, J. P. A., Iacob, M.-E., Jonkers, H., & Quartel, D. A. C. (2006). *Model-Driven Development of Context-Aware Services* (pp. 213–227). Distributed Applications and Interoperable Systems.

Amyot, D., Becha, H., Bræk, R., & Rossebø, J. E. Y. (2008). *Next Generation Service Engineering. ITU-T Innovations in NGN Kaleidoscope Conference* (pp. 195-202). IEEE Computer Society.

Bastida, L. (2008). A Methodology for Dynamic Service Composition. *International Conference on Composition-Based Software Systems* (pp. 33-42).

Bræk, R., & Haugen, Ø. (1993). *Engineering Real Time Systems*. Hemel Hempstead: Prentice Hall.

Broll, G., Hubmann, H., Prezerakos, G. N., Kapitsaki, G., & Salsano, S. (2007). *Modeling Context Information for Realizing Simple Mobile Services* (pp. 1–5). Mobile and Wireless Communications Summit.

Castejón, H. N. (2008). *Collaborations in Service Engineering*. PhD thesis, Norwegian University of Science and Technology, Trondheim, Norway.

Castejón, H. N., Bochmann, G., & Bræk, R. (2007). Realizability of collaboration-based service specifications. *14th Asia-Pacific Software Engineering Conference* (pp. 73-80). IEEE CS.

Castejón, H. N., & Bræk, R. (2005). *Dynamic Role Binding in a Service Oriented Architecture*. International Federation for Information Processing 190.

Castejón, H. N., & Bræk, R. (2006). A collaboration-based approach to service specification and detection of implied scenarios. *5th Int. Workshop on Scenarios and State Machines: Models, Algorithms and Tools (SCESM'06)* (pp. 37-43). ACM Press.

Celentano, A., Faralli, S., & Pittarello, F. (2008). *The Situation Lens: Looking into Personal Service Composition* (pp. 165–174). ER Workshops.

Dustdar, S., & Schreiner, W. (2005). A survey on web services composition. *International Journal of Web and Grid Services*, 1-30.

Floch, J., & Bræk, R. (2000). Towards Dynamic Composition of Hybrid Communication Services. *International Conference on Intelligence in Networks* (pp. 73-92).

Hirakawa, M., & Hewagamage, K. P. (2001). Situated Computing: A Paradigm for the Mobile User-Interaction with Multimedia Sources. *Annals of Software Engineering*, *12*(1), 213–239. doi:10.1023/A:1013395612527

Holtkamp, B., & Wojciechowski, M. (2007). Experiences with Situation Aware Service Provision. *International Conference on Grid and Cooperative Computing* (pp. 863-870).

Jørstad, I., & Do, V. T. (2007). A Framework and Tool for Personalisation of Mobile Services Using Semantic Web. *International Conference on Mobile Data Management* (pp. 402-406).

Keeney, J., & Cahill, V. (2003). Chisel: A Policy-Driven, Context-Aware, Dynamic Adaptation Framework. *International Workshop on Policies for Distributed Systems and Networks* (pp. 3-14).

Kraemer, F. A. (2007). Arctis and Ramses: Toole Suites for Rapid Service Engineering. Norsk informatikkonferanse.

Kraemer, F. A., Bræk, R., & Herrmann, P. (2009). *Compositional Service Engineering with Arctis*. Telektronikk.

Lewis, D., Keeney, J., & Sullivan, D. O. (2006). *Policy-based Management for Resource-Specific Semantic Services*. Workshop on Distributed Autonomous Network Management Systems.

Nahrstedt, K., & Balke, W.-T. (2004). A taxonomy for multimedia service composition. In *Proceedings of the 12th Annual ACM International Conference on Multimedia* (pp. 88-95).

OMG. (2009). *UML 2.2 Superstructure Specification, formal/2009-02-02*. Object Management Group.

Papazoglou, M. P., Traverso, P., Dustdar, S., & Leymann, F. (2008). Service-Oriented Computing: a Research Roadmap. *International Journal of Cooperative Information Systems, 17*(2), 223–255. doi:10.1142/S0218843008001816

Reiff-Marganiec, S., & Turner, K. J. (2003). *A Policy Architecture for Enhancing and Controlling Features* (pp. 239–246). Feature Interactions in Telecommunications and Software Systems.

Rossebø, J. E. Y., & Bræk, R. (2006). A Policy-driven Approach to Dynamic Composition of Authentication and Authorization Patterns and Services. *Journal of Computers, 1*(8), 13–26. doi:10.4304/jcp.1.8.13-26

Rossebø, J. E. Y., & Runde, R. K. (2008). *Specifying Service Composition Using UML 2.x and Composition Policies* (pp. 520–536). Model Driven Engineering Languages and Systems.

Sanders, R. T., Castejón, H. N., Kraemer, F. A., & Bræk, R. (2005). *Using UML 2.0 Collaborations for Compositional Service Specification* (pp. 460–475). Model Driven Engineering Languages and Systems.

Sensoy, M., & Yolum, P. (2007). Ontology-Based Service Representation and Selection. *IEEE Transactions on Knowledge and Data Engineering*, 1102–1115. doi:10.1109/TKDE.2007.1045

Wang, A. I., Sørensen, C.-F., Le, H. N., Ramampiaro, H., Nygård, M., & Conradi, R. (2008). From Scenarios to Requirements in Mobile Client-Server Systems. In Tiako, P. F. (Ed.), *Designing Software-Intensive Systems: Methods and Principles* (pp. 80–101). Hershey, PA: IGI Global.

Widom, J., & Ceri, S. (1996). *Active Database Systems: Triggers and Rules For Advanced Database Processing*. Morgan Kaufmann.

Yau Stephen, S., & Liu, J. (2006). Incorporating Situation Awareness in Service Specifications. *International Symposium on Object-Oriented Real-Time Distributed Computing* (pp. 287-294).

ENDNOTES

[1] We use the term "actor" to denote a part in a design structure.

[2] This is an activity diagram where activity nodes have been adorned with the collaboration use being executed.

Chapter 2
Transactional Properties of Complex Web Services

Li Li
Southwest University of China, China

Chengfei Liu
Swinburne University of Technology, Australia

Xiaohui Zhao
Swinburne University of Technology, Australia

Junhu Wang
Griffith University, Australia

ABSTRACT

Web services have become a dominating technology for business integration. For operation reliability and robustness, transactional support is an important issue for Web service system design and development. Yet, most existing Web services protocols, like WS-BPEL which sticks to the compensation-based recovery strategy, only provide very limited supports for Web services in certain circumstances. As Web service systems are scaling up, more advanced transactional supports beyond traditional compensation-based solutions are required to catch up with the increasing complexity of composite Web services. This chapter looks into the problem of transactional support for composing and scheduling those Web services that may have different transactional properties. The transactional properties of workflow constructs, which are fundamental to the composition of Web services, are thoroughly investigated. The concept of connection point is introduced to derive the transactional properties of composite Web services. The scheduling issue of composite Web services is also discussed.

INTRODUCTION

Web services have been emerging as a promising technology for business process integration. Transactional support to business integration via

composing individual Web services is a critical issue. Several transaction relevant Web service standards have been proposed. Among them are WS-BPEL (Andrews et al., 2003), WS-Coordination (Cabrera et al., 2003), *Web Services Transactions Specifications*, 2005 (including WS-AT

DOI: 10.4018/978-1-61520-819-7.ch002

(Cabrera, Copeland, Feingold, Freund, Freund, Johnson et al., 2005) and WS-BA (Cabrera, Copeland, Feingold, Freund, Freund, Joyce et al., 2005)), and Web Service Choreography Interface (WSCI) (Arkin et al., 2002). These Web services protocols have been proposed to deal with this issue on a strong assumption that each Web service is compensatable for a recovery purpose. In other words, compensation is the basic mechanism adopted by all of these standards for backward recovery. However, it is arguable that Web services composition requires more transactional support beyond the compensation-based solution.

Investigating transactional properties of composed Web services is becoming more important in long-running systems as exclusively locking resources is impossible or impractical, given Web services are distributed and independent applications running on heterogeneous platforms. Intuitively, Web services infrastructures should provide comprehensive transaction support so that Web services can compose other Web services in a transactional manner. Unfortunately, the current Web services efforts (e.g., WS-BPEL, WS-Coordination, WS-Transaction) only provide limited support without giving much thought to the transactional features (Liu & Zhao, 2008). The need for transactional handling mechanism in complex Web services is obvious. Rather than assume that a Web service is compensatable for a recovery purpose, which is a very strong assumption in the business integration scenario, this chapter will discuss how to relax this constraint and provide a mechanism to derive transactional properties within composite Web services. The contributions of this chapter are twofold. First, we discuss transactional properties of atomic services (building blocks) in the presence of three transactional features. Second, we discuss how to derive transactional properties of a composite Web service based on these building blocks.

To this end, transactional features of workflow constructs will be studied followed by the discussion of composing Web services via these con-

structs in a Web service environment. Ultimately, transactional scheduling issues will be targeted to guarantee consistent outcomes and reliable business processes. As such, this chapter aims to contribute in deriving transactional properties and scheduling transactional business process for complex Web services on the basis of our previous work in (Li, Liu, & Wang, 2007).

WORKS ON WEB SERVICE TRANSACTIONS

Ensuring reliability of composite services is challenging. In addition to the latest release of WS-BPEL (the latest successor of the arguably de facto standard WS-BPEL 1.1) (Andrews et al., 2003), there are several other known proposals to extend the Web service with transaction-processing capabilities. They include the following emerged proposals, which define transaction protocols between composed services: the *Web Services Transactions Specifications*, 2005, the *OASIS Business Transactions TC*, 2004, the *Tentative Hold Protocol Part 1: White Paper*, 2001 and *Tentative Hold Protocol Part 2: Technical Specification*, 2001 from W3C, and the *OASIS Web Services Composite Application Framework (WS-CAF) TC*, 2004, which is designed to be used independently or together with other transaction protocols. The WS-CAF is the superset of WSC, WS-T, and WS-BA. Other main lines of research have attempted to extend some aspects of these proposals, or propose better strategies to cope with transactional issues in complex business activities. The following are some details.

Web Service Transaction Protocols

The current Web services specification, WS-BPEL, has been proposed to deal with transactional Web services. However, WS-BPEL only offers a limited support for recovery and there is no discussion of recovery actions (Vaculin, Wiesner,

& Sycara, 2008). Moreover, WS-BEPL is based on a strong assumption that each Web service is compensatable for a recovery purpose.

WS-Coordination (WS-C) and WS-Transaction (WS-T) specifications are two specifications that address the reliable, transactional coordination of Web services. They can be used individually, or in combination with BPEL to complement BPEL to provide mechanisms for defining specific standard protocol to transaction processing systems or other applications. They target the coordination of multiple Web services. In addition, they provide a Web service based approach to improve the dependability of automated long-running business transactions in an extensible and interoperable way. WS-Coordination provides a framework for coordinating the actions of distributed applications via coordination-context sharing. WS-Transaction leverages WS-Coordination by describing the coordination types that are used with the extensible coordination framework outlined in WS-Coordination specifications. WS-Transaction leverages WS-Coordination by defining two particular coordination types: "Atomic Transaction (AT)" and "Business Activity (BA)". WS-AtomicTransaction models short-running atomic transaction while WS-BusinessActivity models business transactions that are potentially long-lived. The protocols in WS-BusinessActivity depend on compensating transactions to handle exception and faults. It is important to note that the BA model derives from a specific industry requirement in the WS-BPEL specification. For example, WS-BusinessActivity's compensation model is based on open nested transaction. Hence, WS-BusinessActivity lacks equity between services as a parent scope has the ability to select which child tasks are to be included for a specific business activity. In doing so, parents direct the orchestration and impose their transactional semantics to children services. Furthermore, it seems that ATs and BAs may be sufficient for the current use cases that the specifications are aimed at. It is

generally accepted that other protocols may well be needed later.

The *OASIS Business Transactions TC*, 2004 aims at addressing business transactions in a loosely coupled Web service environment. An overview of Business Transactions Protocol can be found in work (Little, 2003). A comparison of Web service transaction protocols such as BTP and WS-C/T by Little & Freund, 2003 is available. W3C proposed the *Tentative Hold Protocol Part 1: White Paper*, 2001 and *Tentative Hold Protocol Part 2: Technical Specification*, 2001 to allow lock resources lock tentatively instead of exclusively. It allows multiple clients to hold the same resource temporarily. The THP is designed to exchange information between enterprises before a transaction begins. BTP attempts to solve a variety of different problems by only one model (atoms can be regarded as special case of cohesions, the cohesion model is essentially a superset of the atom model). This has the disadvantage of not allowing reasoning about an application's overall functionality and behaviour. It also has a potential problem of transaction interoperability between services implemented with different approaches. Tentative Hold Protocol, on the other hand, is likely to minimise compensation, but there is no guarantee on holding a resource and it must work with other protocols in practice.

Web Service Transaction Strategies

It is highly recommended that some mechanisms (e.g., concurrency control, error handling and recovery) to be proposed to relax ACID properties in a loosely coupled world. It is very common that business applications require transaction support beyond classical ACID transactions. An experimental study of the performance impact of different concurrency control algorithms is presented in work (Wu, Fekete, & Rohm, 2008). It points out that two-phase commit (2PC) locking and semantic locking by Weihl, 1988 perform equally in the setting environment.

The mechanism of compensation is originally proposed by Gray, 1981 and then widely used in advanced transaction models (ATMs) (Garcia-Molina & Salem, 1987; Mehrotra, Rastogi, Korth, & Silberschatz, 1992) and transactional workflows (Grefen, 2002) to maintain atomicity when the isolation property has to be relaxed. The compensation-based solution by Gray & Reuter, 1993 is well-known in semantically eliminating the effects of all the operations it has performed. Bhiri, Godart, & Perrin, 2005 proposed an approach by using accepted termination states (ATS) property as a correctness criterion to relax atomicity. Bhiri, Perrin, & Godart, 2005 proposes a transactional approach for reliable Web service compositions by ensuring the failure atomicity required by the designers. A set of transactional rules have been defined to assist designers to compose a valid composite Web service with regards to the specified ATS.

Zhao et al. present a reservation-based extended transaction protocol in work (Zhao, Moser, & Melliar-Smith, 2008). The proposed reservation protocol employs an explicit reservation phase and an explicit confirmation/cancellation phase. In this way, it avoids the use of compensating transactions but defines every task within a business activity to be executed in the above two phases as traditional short-running transactions.

A formal framework for Web service coordination with particular attention to Web transaction is presented in work (Guidi, Lucchi, & Mazzara, 2007). It aims to leverage the complexity of WS-BPEL in describing choreography for business processes.

Melliar-Smith & Moser, 2007 advocate a better strategy in coping with issues of complex business activities. Such issues could be long delays and long locked data when using the classical transaction strategy, or inconsistency when using the compensating transaction strategy. The proposed strategy describes an implicit protocol that can be hidden from the applications, and an explicit protocol that makes reservations of resources visible to the applications. The proposed strategy is compatible with existing business practices.

In addition to extend the existing strategies as shown above, a separate design layer dedicated to transactions is introduced by Schmit & Dustdar, 2005. A model-driven approach is used to tackle transactional guarantees.

Choi et al., 2008 criticise that early unlocked resources can spoil data integrity and cause incorrect outcomes. They propose a mechanism to ensure the consistent executions of isolation-relaxing WS transactions. The presented mechanism can detect inconsistent states of transactions effectively and then recovers them to consistent states. The authors validate the protocol in the developed prototype.

Schuldt, Alonso, Beeri, & Schek, 2002 also deal with the problems of concurrent control and recovery for transactional processes. However, no attempt has been made to handle these problems in the Web service environment. Our approach, however, is centred on deriving transactional properties of composite Web services to achieve the schedulability. Eventually, a desirable scheduling regarding the transactional properties can be achieved.

PRELIMINARIES FOR WEB SERVICE TRANSACTIONS

As self-contained modular programs, Web services can be discovered and invoked across the Internet, and thereby enable organisations to connect their applications and conduct collaborations across organisation boundaries independent of platforms or languages.

As the business collaboration scales up, more Web services are to be involved, and thereby create a complex cooperation structure and relationships between participating Web services. Consequently, the overall behaviour is more complicated than that of a single Web service. A popular way to analyse such complex services is to use classic workflow technologies to describe the relationships and structures. As specified in WS-BPEL, a complex Web service corresponds to a business process, which can be decomposed into a series of workflow fragments, such as wf_1, wf_2, ..., wf_n. Further, each workflow or workflow fragment can be represented as a composite Web service, and an activity of a workflow can be triggered by means of invoking a Web service. These terms may be used interchangeable in the following discussion.

The transactional properties of workflow activities are different from traditional ACID properties used in classic transition research. Characteristics such as long-running, business latencies, and network latencies may prevent Web services transactions from abiding to the strict ACID properties. In a long-running system, the transactional properties of an activity may reveal three features, viz. **compensatable** (c), **retriable** (r), and **pivot** (p), as mentioned in work (Mehrotra et al., 1992).

Compensatable. An activity is compensatable if it is able to offer compensation policies to semantically undo the original activity.

Retriable. An activity is retriable if it is able to offer forward recovery. In other words, activities with this property can guarantee a successfully termination after a finite number of invocations.

Pivot. An activity is pivot if it is neither compensatable nor retriable. On one hand, there is no guarantee that this type of activity can be executed successfully. On the other hand, a committed pivot activity cannot be rolled back.

Here, we treat a composite transactional Web service as a conglomeration of transactional Web services. In terms of workflow structures, we categorise composite Web services into the following classes:

- **Sequential Composite Services:** The activities within a sequential composite service are executed with a sequential dependency between them. As a result, the transactional property of an activity will be affected by those introduced previously (i.e. the properties of the preceding activities), especially the immediate preceding activities.

- **Concurrent Composite Services:** Different paths of concurrent composite services are allowed to execute simultaneously. Since there are no dependent restrictions between these paths, it leaves the room for the system to schedule these activities independently.

- **Alternative Composite Services:** One and only one path of alternative composite services will be executed.

- **Iterative Composite Services:** The activities within an iterative composite service are executed with repetition.

The transactional properties of composite Web services are subject to the composition structures and the transactional properties of the composed services. In next sections, we will discuss the influences from these factors.

TRANSACTIONAL PROPERTIES OF WORKFLOW CONSTRUCTS

It is a natural intention to schedule Web services in a transactional manner, i.e., preserving the maximal transactional properties for the composite Web service. We say that a composite Web service is schedulable if it can be treated as a unit of work. In this section, we focus on the scheduling of transactional workflows with the presence of transactional properties in $\{c, r, p\}$ for each individual Web service. $\vec{s}$ is used to indicate that the transactional property of a workflow is schedulable whilst $\tilde{s}$ is non-schedulable. In terms of the transactional properties in $\{c, r, \vec{s}\}$, we believe properties c and r are as much desirable than $\vec{s}$.

The transactional properties of a composite Web service can be derived from those of individual services given that they conform to $\{c, r, p\}$. Regarding the transactional properties, an activity's transactional property p neither supports forward nor backward recovery regarding scheduling, whilst r is able to be forward and c to be backward. In the following, we omit the activity itself but only illustrate its transactional property for simplicity. In other words, the notation $c \rightarrow r$ stands for two activities in a sequential routing, with transactional properties c and r, respectively. We are to discuss about the derivation of the transactional properties of a composite activity, according to different routing schemes, respectively.

Next, we are to discuss how the workflow structures influence the transactional properties, where some classic routing structures, viz., sequential, concurrent, alternative and iterative ones, are to reference.

1. Sequential Routing

Symbol $t_1 \rightarrow t_2$ ($t_1, t_2 \in \{c, r, p\}$) is defined to represent a sequential routing of two activities a_1 followed by a_2, and with transactional properties t_1 and t_2, respectively. The derived transactional property t of this sequential routing is shown in Table 1.

An important phenomenon is that sometimes having n times repetition of same transactional property will lead to the same transactional property as a whole. Take the sequential routing in a workflow as an example. Apparently, $c \rightarrow c \rightarrow c \ldots \rightarrow c$ will result in c which is schedulable undoubtedly. This rule is applicable to concurrent and alternative routings, too. Further, this rule also applies to the combination of $r \rightarrow r \rightarrow r \ldots \rightarrow r$ which leads to r in the end. As such, activities with the same transactional properties (i.e. $\{c, r\}$) are semantically equivalent to a single activity in terms of their transactional properties. Without loss of generality, these activities are eligible to be grouped and represented as c and r respectively.

Table 1. Transaction property of sequential routing

t_1	t_2	t
p	p	$\tilde{s}$
p	r	$\overrightarrow{s}$
p	c	$\tilde{s}$
r	p	$\tilde{s}$
r	c	$\tilde{s}$
c	p	$\overrightarrow{s}$
c	r	$\overrightarrow{s}$
c	c	c
r	r	r

2. Concurrent Routing

Symbol $\begin{pmatrix} t_1 \\ t_2 \end{pmatrix}$ ($t_1, t_2 \in \{c, r, p\}$) is defined to represent a concurrent routing of two activities a_1 and a_2 to be executed simultaneously. Given activities a_1 and a_2 have transactional properties t_1 and t_2, respectively, the derived transactional property t of this concurrent routing is shown in Table 2.

As mentioned in previous section, the scheduler may determine the execution order between the paths on site to achieve the best transactional property, as these paths execute independently. We discuss the possible scheduling cases as below.

- *Case* 1: A concurrent routing of $\begin{pmatrix} p \\ r \end{pmatrix}$ or $\begin{pmatrix} r \\ p \end{pmatrix}$. The schedulable feature $\overrightarrow{s}$ cannot be achieved unless an activity with transac-

Table 2. Transactional property of concurrent routing

t_1	t_2	t
p	p	$\tilde{s}$
c	c	c
r	r	r
p	r	$\overrightarrow{s}$
r	p	
p	c	$\overrightarrow{s}$
c	p	
r	c	$\overrightarrow{s}$
c	r	

tional property p is be executed before an activity with r.

- *Case 2*: A concurrent routing of $\begin{pmatrix} p \\ c \end{pmatrix}$ or $\begin{pmatrix} c \\ p \end{pmatrix}$. The schedulable feature $\overrightarrow{s}$ can be achieved only if an activity with transactional property c to be executed before an activity with p.

- *Case 3*: A concurrent routing of $\begin{pmatrix} c \\ r \end{pmatrix}$ or $\begin{pmatrix} r \\ c \end{pmatrix}$. The schedulable feature $\overrightarrow{s}$ can only be achieved only if an activity with transactional property c to be executed before an activity with r.

- *Case 4*: A concurrent routing of $\begin{pmatrix} r \\ r \end{pmatrix}$ and $\begin{pmatrix} c \\ c \end{pmatrix}$. The schedulable feature $\overrightarrow{s}$ can be achieved with r and c, respectively.

- *Case 5*: A concurrent routing of $\begin{pmatrix} p \\ p \end{pmatrix}$. The schedulable feature $\overrightarrow{s}$ cannot be achieved at all.

Cases 1, 2 and 3 indicate that a concurrent routing is schedulable under certain circumstances. It is called *conditionally* schedulable. On the contrary, scheduling in case 4 is called *unconditionally* schedulable.

3. Alternative Routing

Symbol $\left\langle \begin{matrix} t_1 \\ t_2 \end{matrix} \right\rangle$ $(t_1, t_2 \in \{c, r, p\})$ is defined to represent an alternative routing of two activities a_1 and a_2 with transactional properties t_1 and t_2, respectively. The derived transactional property t of this alternative routing is shown in Table 3.

We consider a single property (e.g. c, r and p) is more preferable than $\overrightarrow{s}$, which is obtained by scheduling properties c, p and r properly. The scheduling intends to preserve the transactional property from $\{c,r,p\}$ first. We conclude a priority order: $\{c, r\} \rangle\ p \rangle\ \overrightarrow{s} \rangle\ \tilde{s}$, for transactional properties.

Table 3. Transactional property of alternative routing

t_1	t_2	t
p	p	p
c	c	c
r	r	$\{r,c\}$
p	r	r
r	p	
p	c	c
c	p	
r	c	$\{r,c\}$
c	r	

Figure 1. Sequential composition – case 1

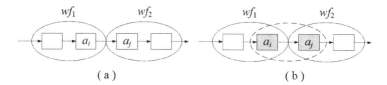

(a)　　　　　　　　　　(b)

4. Iterative Routing

Symbol $(t_1)^*$ $(t_1 \in \{c, r, p\})$ is defined to represent an iterative routing of activity a_1 with a transactional property t_1. The derived transactional property can be treated as those of a sequential routing with repetition.

In our discussion, the deriving transactional property of an iterative routing is treated as a special case of a sequential routing. More details on deriving the transactional properties of complex Web services are to be given in next section.

TRANSACTIONAL PROPERTIES OF COMPLEX WEB SERVICES

Last section discussed the derivation of transactional properties from workflow constructs. Complex Web services often own much complicated workflows underneath, which comprises various workflow fragments. Here, we reckon that it is wise to delay deciding the transactional property until the (transaction properties of) connecting services are known. For example, if two paths (alternatively) both have transactional property p, it is preferable to append a service with transactional property r, because the result composite service can obtain property $\vec{s}$ (see Table 1), which is better than $\tilde{s}$ according to the priority order $\{c, r\} \rangle p \rangle \vec{s} \rangle \tilde{s}$. Therefore, it is worth considering the transaction properties of the connecting services in order to well describe the transactional characteristics of the complex fragments. Based on this belief, we discuss about

the transactional properties of complex Web services in this section.

First, we assume that different workflow fragments are available, and the transactional property of each workflow fragment can be deduced from Tables 1, 2 and 3. Second, when combining these workflow fragments to serve for a complex Web service, the overall transactional property of the composite workflow is deducible, if each workflow fragment is schedulable. For two workflow fragments wf_1 and wf_2, we use $wf_1 \rightarrow wf_2$ to represent them in sequential routing, $\begin{pmatrix} wf_1 \\ wf_2 \end{pmatrix}$ for concurrent routing, and $\left\langle \begin{matrix} wf_1 \\ wf_2 \end{matrix} \right\rangle$ for alternative routing. A composed iterative routing is represented as $(wf_1)^*$.

Composing Sequential Routing

Given two schedulable workflow fragments wf_1 and wf_2 as shown in Figures 1(a) and 2(a), the corresponding composed Web services are shown in Figures 1(b) and 2(b), respectively. Attention is required that in some cases, the composed Web service may not be schedulable even if all its workflow fragments are schedulable. For example, suppose wf_1 is in the form of $(\ldots \rightarrow p)$ and wf_2 is with $(p \rightarrow \ldots)$. According to Table 1, it is apparent that $(\ldots \rightarrow p)$ and $(p \rightarrow \ldots)$ result in the composed Web service is non-schedulable, because $p \rightarrow p$ is non-schedulable (Table 1). In another case, if wf_1 is in the form of $(\ldots \rightarrow r)$, while wf_2 is with $(c \rightarrow \ldots)$. The composed Web service is non-schedulable, because $r \rightarrow c$ is non-schedulable (Table 1).

Figure 2. Sequential composition – case 2

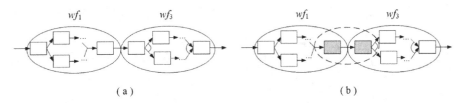

(a)   (b)

Therefore, further efforts are needed to determine whether the schedulable feature is decidable or not. Particularly, it is crucial to examine some connection points, for instance, those within the dotted circles as shown in Figures 1(b) and 2(b).

Connection Point. For two workflow fragments, wf_1 and wf_2, which are connected sequentially, the connection point is a time point after wf_1 finishes yet before wf_2 starts. Graphically, it is a point on the edge that connects two workflow fragments wf_1 and wf_2 in the process graph (e.g. Figure 1(b)).

Within a workflow fragment, a *connection point* has the same meanings but instead connecting two activities rather than two workflow fragments. The main purpose of introducing the *connecting point* is to facilitate the checking of transactional characteristics of the complex Web services.

Scheduling Bridge. Given that a sequential composition of two fragments wf_1 and wf_2 that are schedulable, a *scheduling bridge* consists of the last activity of wf_1, the *connection point* between wf_1 and wf_2, and the first activity of wf_2.

Safe Connection Point. Given that a sequential composition of two fragments wf_1 and wf_2 is schedulable, a *safe connection point* is a *connection point* such that the *scheduling bridge* is schedulable.

Lemma 1

It is clear that any *connection point* within a schedulable workflow fragment is a safe *connection point*.

Theorem 1

Given that two workflow fragments wf_1 and wf_2 that are schedulable, the sequential composition of wf_1 and wf_2 (i.e. $wf_1 \rightarrow wf_2$) is schedulable if and only if a *connection point* between wf_1 and wf_2 is a safe *connection point*.

Proof of Theorem 1

As the composed service is schedulable, the *connection point* between wf_1 and wf_2 is definitely a safe *connection point* according to *Lemma* 1.

Note that the *connection point* is safe. According to the definition of *safe connection point*, the *scheduling bridge* between wf_1 and wf_2 is schedulable. In order to prove that the composition of wf_1 and wf_2 is schedulable, all activities from both wf_1 and wf_2 should be considered.

1. Backward recovery: It is evident that the backward recovery is able to continue because any *connection point* within wf_1 is a safe *connection point*.

2. Forward recovery: Since wf_2 is schedulable, all *connection points* should be safe according to *Lemma* 1, it is certain that the forward procedure can be guaranteed to the end point.

Therefore, we can conclude that the sequential composition of wf_1 and wf_2 is schedulable.

Theorem 1 can be easily extended to more workflow fragments. In the sequential composition with a series of workflow fragments, such as $wf_1 \rightarrow wf_2 \rightarrow wf_3$, the *safe connection point* concept

Figure 3. Concurrent composition

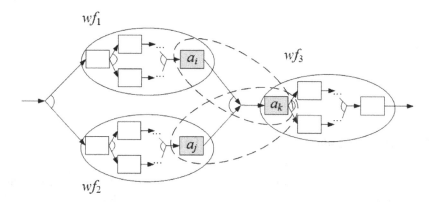

can also be used to determine whether the composition of these workflow fragments is schedulable or not. From above discussion, we can conclude that *connection points* have significant influences to Web service composition scheduling.

Composing Concurrent Routing

As shown in Figure 3, three schedulable workflow fragments wf_1, wf_2, and wf_3 are involved in a concurrent routing structure. Theorem 2 defines the relationship between the composed workflow and the workflow fragments in terms of schedulablity.

Theorem 2

Given that workflow fragments wf_1, wf_2, wf_3 are schedulable. If the composition of a concurrent routing of wf_1 and wf_2 (i.e. $\begin{pmatrix} wf_1 \\ wf_2 \end{pmatrix}$) is schedulable, then a new composition consisting of a concurrent routing of wf_1 and wf_2 and another fragment wf_3 in the form of $\begin{pmatrix} wf_1 \\ wf_2 \end{pmatrix} \rightarrow wf_3$ is schedulable if and only if a *connection point* is safe for two *scheduling bridges* over $(wf_1 \rightarrow wf_3)$ and $(wf_2 \rightarrow wf_3)$.

Proof of Theorem 2

It is easy to see the sufficient condition holds for Theorem 2.

For the necessary condition, we need to consider what would be happening in terms of the transactional property as a whole. It is known that a *connection point* is safe over the bridges of $(wf_1 \rightarrow wf_3)$ and $(wf_2 \rightarrow wf_3)$.

1. Backward recovery: Let *connection point* between $(wf_1 \rightarrow wf_3)$ and $(wf_2 \rightarrow wf_3)$ be ck. Because ck is safe for both bridges, it allows the recovery to head for either wf_1 or wf_2 via the bridge. Take another *connection* point in wf_1 for example, the recovery mechanism works well because wf_1 is schedulable. The same is true for a connection point in wf_2.

   Moreover, since $\begin{pmatrix} wf_1 \\ wf_2 \end{pmatrix}$ is schedulable, ck is able to move back to any connection point within $\begin{pmatrix} wf_1 \\ wf_2 \end{pmatrix}$. As each individual fragment is schedulable, the backward recovery will proceed smoothly.

2. Forward recovery: Forward recovery is guaranteed because wf_3 is schedulable.

Therefore, we can conclude that $\begin{pmatrix} wf_1 \\ wf_2 \end{pmatrix} \rightarrow wf_3$ is schedulable.

For concurrent routing structures, the scheduler may choose to execute activities with c property first at run time, because this can guarantee the process to undo the previously executed activities in case of execution failures. Therefore, a path with c transactional property may own a higher priority than others, which results in decaying the concurrent routing into a sequential routing.

Composing Alternative Routing

For an alternative routing appended with another workflow fragment, if the composite workflow is able to execute from the start point to the end point via one of its paths, then the schedulable feature is guaranteed.

Theorem 3

Given that workflow fragments wf_1, wf_2, wf_3 are schedulable, if the composition of an alternative routing of wf_1 and wf_2, i.e., $\begin{pmatrix} wf_1 \\ wf_2 \end{pmatrix}$, is schedulable, the new composition consisting of the alternative routing and wf_3, i.e., $\begin{pmatrix} wf_1 \\ wf_2 \end{pmatrix} \rightarrow wf_3$, is schedulable, if and only if the *connection point* is safe for at least one of *scheduling bridge*s over $(wf_1 \rightarrow wf_3)$ and $(wf_2 \rightarrow wf_3)$.

The proof is omitted here, since it is similar to the proof of Theorem 2.

Composing Iterative Routing

When composing iterative routing $(wf_1)^*$ with another fragment wf_2 in the form $(wf_1)^* \rightarrow wf_2$, the transactional property of the composed workflow is equivalent to that of a sequential composition in the form of $wf_1 \rightarrow wf_1 \rightarrow wf_2$ which we have

discussed in Section "Composing Sequential Routing".

General Workflows

Given that a series of workflow fragments wf_1, ..., wf_n are schedulable, a general workflow is denoted as Θwf_i $(1 \le i \le n)$. Here, Θ stands for a sequence of applications of constructs that belong to $\{\rightarrow, (), \langle \rangle, ()^*\}$. Note that we use wf_{i+1} to indicate an immediate successor of wf_i, while wf_i is an immediate predecessor of wf_{i+1}.

Theorem 4 (Decidable)

A composition of a series of workflow fragments, i.e., Θwf_i, is schedulable or not is decidable.

Proof of Theorem 4

The safety of a *connection point* has very important influence to the transactional property of a composed workflow. First, let a composed workflow wf be in the form of Θwf_i $(1 \le i \le n)$, $wf' = wf \setminus wf_n$. Thus, we have $wf = wf' \theta_{n-1} wf_n$, $\theta_{n-1} \in \{\rightarrow, (), \langle \rangle, ()^*\}$. Since the transactional property of wf_n is decidable, and the safe connection point concept is applicable to analyse the transactional property of the compound of wf' and wf_n, we can look into the transactional property of wf' as a replacement. Similarly, we suppose that there exists workflow fragment wf'' such that $wf'' = wf \setminus (wf_{n-1} \theta_{n-1} wf_n)$, and thereby the transactional property of wf is equivalent to that of wf''. In this way, more workflow fragments can be gradually separated from workflow wf until we reach fragment wf_1. Since the transactional property of wf_1 is decidable, it is clear that the transactional property of wf is decidable.

It is clear that the transactional property of a composed workflow can be derived by applying a;; mentioned theorems. A safe *connection point* works like a safeguard which can enable the transactional properties of a composed workflow to be determined as early as possible. Ultimately, it provides transactional support for scheduling Web services that have different transactional properties.

DISCUSSIONS AND CONCLUSION

Web services transaction management is a driving force behind current Web service standards and recommendations. To catch up with the soaring complexity of composite Web services, more transactional support beyond traditional compensation-based solutions are on demand. In this chapter, we concentrated on deriving the transactional properties of composite Web services. The transactional properties of underlying workflow constructs have been investigated in terms of sequence, splits (AND and OR/XOR), joins (AND and OR/XOR) and iteration. Concept "transactional property connection point" has been introduced to describe the complex relationship of Web services' transactional properties. We have discussed the scheduling issue in a Web service environment where traditional transaction protocols are insufficient to cope with. In addition, attention has also been given to scheduling issues. We attempt to answer whether a workflow is schedulable or not and how to determine its transactional property. This work contributed to the current Web service composition research in the following aspects:

- Classified the transactional properties of single Web services and composite Web services.
- Analysed the influences of Web service composition structures towards transactional properties.
- Established a theoretical framework to specify and derive transactional properties of Web services.

These contributions can help manage Web service applications by pre-analysing the candidate services and scheduling the proper composition scheme from the perspective of transaction management. The proposed theoretical framework can be used to evaluate and refine the Web service composition schemes, and help design the exception handling and compensation processes for Web service composition applications.

ACKNOWLEDGMENT

This work is supported by the Australian Research Council Discovery Project under the grant number DP0557572. It is support in part by Natural Science Foundation Project of CQ under the number CSTC 2010BB2006.

REFERENCES

Andrews, T., Curbera, F., Dholakia, H., Goland, Y., Klein, J., Leymann, F., et al. (2003). *Business Process Execution Language for Web Services (BPEL4WS) 1.1.*

Arkin, A., Askary, S., Fordin, S., Jekeli, W., Kawaguchi, K., Orchard, D., et al. (2002). *Web Service Choreography Interface (WSCI) 1.0.*

Bhiri, S., Godart, C., & Perrin, O. (2005). *Reliable Web Services Composition using a Transactional Approach.* Paper presented at the 2005 IEEE International Conference on e-Technology, e-Commerce, and e-Services (EEE 2005), Hong Kong, China.

Bhiri, S., Perrin, O., & Godart, C. (2005). *Ensuring Required Failure Atomicity of Composite Web Services.* Paper presented at the Proceedings of the 14th international conference on World Wide Web, WWW 2005, Chiba, Japan.

Cabrera, L. F., Copeland, G., Feingold, M., Freund, R. W., Freund, T., & Johnson, J. (2003). *Web Services Coordination*. WS-Coordination.

Cabrera, L. F., Copeland, G., Feingold, M., Freund, R. W., Freund, T., & Johnson, J. (2005). *Web Services Atomic Transaction*. WS-Atomic-Transaction.

Cabrera, L. F., Copeland, G., Feingold, M., Freund, R. W., Freund, T., & Joyce, S. (2005). *Web Services Business Activity Framework*. WS-BusinessActivity.

Choi, S., Kim, H., Jang, H., Kim, J., Kim, S. M., & Song, J. (2008). A framework for ensuring consistency of Web Services Transactions. *Information and Software Technology, 50*(7-8), 684–696. doi:10.1016/j.infsof.2007.07.001

Garcia-Molina, H., & Salem, K. (1987). *Sagas.* Paper presented at the Proceedings of the Association for Computing Machinery Special Interest Group on Management of Data 1987 Annual Conference, San Francisco, California.

Gray, J. (1981). *The Transaction Concept: Virtues and Limitations (Invited Paper).* Paper presented at the Very Large Data Bases, 7th International Conference, Cannes, France, Proceedings.

Gray, J., & Reuter, A. (1993). *Transaction Processing: Concepts and Techniques*. Morgan Kaufmann.

Grefen, P. W. P. J. (2002). *Transactional Workflows or Workflow Transactions?* Paper presented at the DEXA '02: Proceedings of the 13th International Conference on Database and Expert Systems Applications, London, UK.

Guidi, C., Lucchi, R., & Mazzara, M. (2007). A Formal Framework for Web Services Coordination. *Electronic Notes in Theoretical Computer Science, 180*(2), 55–70. doi:10.1016/j.entcs.2006.10.046

Li, L., Liu, C., & Wang, J. (2007). *Deriving Transactional Properties of Composite Web Services.* Paper presented at the IEEE International Conference on Web Services, Salt Lake City, Utah, USA.

Little, M. (2003). Transactions and Web Services. *Communications of the ACM, 46*(10), 49–54. doi:10.1145/944217.944237

Little, M., & Freund, T. (2003). *A Comparison of Web Services Transaction Protocols.*

Liu, C., & Zhao, X. (2008). Towards Flexible Compensation for Business Transactions in Web Service Environment. *Journal on Service Oriented Computing and Applications, 2*(2-3), 79–91. doi:10.1007/s11761-008-0024-5

Mehrotra, S., Rastogi, R., Korth, H. F., & Silberschatz, A. (1992). *A Transaction Model for Multidatabase Systems.* Paper presented at the ICDCS.

Melliar-Smith, P. M., & Moser, L. E. (2007). Achieving Atomicity for Web Services Using Commutativity of Actions. *J. Universal Computer Science, 13*(8), 1094–1109.

OASIS Business Transactions TC. (2004).

OASIS Web Services Composite Application Framework (WS-CAF) TC. *(2004).*

Schmit, B. A., & Dustdar, S. (2005). Model-driven Development of Web service Transactions. *International Journal of Enterprise Modeling and Information Systems Architecure, 1*(1).

Schuldt, H., Alonso, G., Beeri, C., & Schek, H.-J. R. (2002). Atomicity and Isolation for Transactional Processes. *ACM Transactions on Database Systems, 27*(1), 63–116. doi:10.1145/507234.507236

Tentative Hold Protocol Part 1: White Paper. *(2001).*

Tentative Hold Protocol Part 2: Technical Specification. *(2001).*

Vaculin, R., Wiesner, K., & Sycara, K. (2008). *Exception Handling and Recovery of Semantic Web Services.* Paper presented at the ICNS '08: Proceedings of the Fourth International Conference on Networking and Services, Washington, DC, USA.

Web Services Transactions Specifications. *(2005).*

Weihl, W. E. (1988). Commutativity-Based Concurrency Control for Abstract Data Types. *IEEE Transactions on Computers, 37*(12), 1488–1505. doi:10.1109/12.9728

Wu, P., Fekete, A., & Rohm, U. (2008). The Efficacy of Commutativity-Based Semantic Locking in a Real-World Application. *IEEE Transactions on Knowledge and Data Engineering, 20*(3), 427–431. doi:10.1109/TKDE.2007.190728

Zhao, W., Moser, L. E., & Melliar-Smith, P. M. (2008). A Reservation-Based Extended Transaction Protocol. *IEEE Transactions on Parallel and Distributed Systems, 19*(2), 188–203. doi:10.1109/TPDS.2007.70727

KEY TERMS AND DEFINITIONS

Web Service Transaction: A unit of procedures performed within a Web service platform for fulfilling a certain objective, and treated in a coherent and reliable way independent of other transactions. Different from traditional database transactions, Web service transactions use compensations to guarantee the atomicity property.

Workflow Construct: An element in workflow modelling, which can designate the routing of workflows. Common workflow constructs include sequential routing, concurrent routing (And-Split/Join), alternative routing (Or-Split/Join) and iterative routing (Loop)

Workflow Fragment: A part of a workflow, which normally indicates a part with single entry and single exit.

Chapter 3
Demand Driven Web Services

Zhaohao Sun
University of Ballarat, Australia

Dong Dong
Hebei Normal University, China

John Yearwood
University of Ballarat, Australia

ABSTRACT

Web services are playing a pivotal role in e-business, service intelligence, and service science. Demand-driven web services are becoming important for web services and service computing. However, many fundamental issues are still ignored to some extent. For example, what is the demand theory for web services, what is a demand-driven architecture for web services and what is a demand-driven web service lifecycle remain open. This chapter addresses these issues by examining fundamentals for demand analysis in web services, and proposing a demand-driven architecture for web services. It also proposes a demand-driven web service lifecycle for the main players in web services: Service providers, service requestors and service brokers, respectively. It then provides a unified perspective on demand-driven web service lifecycles. The proposed approaches will facilitate research and development of web services, e-services, service intelligence, service science and service computing.

INTRODUCTION

Web services are Internet-based application components published using standard interface description languages and universally available via uniform communication protocols (ICWS, 2009). With the dramatic development of the Internet and the web in the past decade, web services have been flourishing in e-commerce, e-business, artificial intelligence (AI), and service computing. They have also offered a number of strategic advantages such as mobility, flexibility, interactivity and interchangeability in comparison with traditional services (Hoffman, 2003).

The fundamental philosophy of web services is to meet the needs of users precisely and thereby increase market share and revenue (Rust & Kannan, 2003). Web services have helped users reduce the cost of information technology (IT) operations and allow them to closely focus on their own core

DOI: 10.4018/978-1-61520-819-7.ch003

competencies (Hoffman, 2003). At the same time, for business marketers, web services are very useful for improving interorganizational relationships and generating new revenue streams (Sun & Lau, 2007). Furthermore, web services can be considered a further development of e-business (Gottschalk, 2001), because they are service-focused business paradigms that use two-way dialogues to build customized service offerings, based on knowledge and experience about users to build strong customer relationships (Rust & Kannan, 2003). However, one of the intriguing aspects of web services is that any web service cannot avoid similar challenges encountered in traditional services such as how to meet the customer's demands in order to attract more customers.

Service-oriented architecture (SOA) is an important topic for service computing, service science and service intelligence (Singh & Huns, 2005). The special form of SOA in web services is Web service architectures. Web service architectures are the basis for engineering many activities in web services. Therefore, there are many web service architectures proposed in the web service community (Erl, 2006; Alonso, et al, 2004). Papazoglou (2003) proposes a hierarchical service-oriented architecture (SOA) for web services. Burstein, et al. (2005) propose a semantic web services architecture. However, the existing web service architectures are mainly from the perspective of implementation (Benatallah, et al, 2006) rather than from a demand perspective. It seems that demand-driven web service architecture and corresponding web services have not yet received any attention, to our knowledge, although demand is a critical force for developing web services, just as demand is a driving factor for microeconomics.

Demand is a fundamental concept of economics. Demand refers to "the quantities that people are or will be willing to buy at different prices during a given time period provided that other factors affecting these quantities remain the same" (Wilkinson, 2005, p. 75). The demand for a firm's products determines its revenues and also enables

the firm to plan its production (Wilkinson, 2005, p. 71). Then demand is a decisive factor for market. Demand theory is an important part in microeconomics and managerial economics (Wilkinson, 2005, pp. 73-120). Demand theory in managerial economics examines demand curves, demand equations, demand analysis, demand chain, impact factors on demand, demand estimation and so on. Demand analysis is a factor driving e-marketing and e-business strategy objectives (Chaffey, 2007, p. 344). Demand analysis assesses current and projected demand for e-commerce services amongst existing and potential customer segments (Chaffey, 2007, p. 344). Demand chain has drawn attention in the field of supply chain management and customer relationship management since the end of last century (Walters, 2006). The demand chain can be defined as "The complex web of business processes and activities that help firms understand, manage, and ultimately create consumer demand" (Rainbird, 2006). The following problems arise in web services: what is the demand of main service players in web services? what is the demand theory for web services? what is demand analysis? What is a demand chain in web services? what is the mathematical analysis of demand in web services? These problems remain open in web services. This chapter addresses these issues by providing a mathematical analysis for web services taking into account the demand of service players in web services.

The web service lifecycle (WSLC) is a fundamental topic for web services and service computing. The web service lifecycle is also the basis for engineering and managing web services. However, the existing models for web service lifecycles have not paid sufficient attention to the main players in web services and the demand of the main players for web services. If the main players and their demands are ignored in web services, then the healthy development of web services might be problematic, because ignorance of demand in economy and business will lead to economic recession. Therefore, this chapter will address the above mentioned issues by examining fundamentals for demands in web services, and proposing a demand-driven architecture for web services. It also reviews the existing web service lifecycles and proposes a demand-driven web service lifecycle for the main players in web services: Service providers, service requestors and service brokers, respectively. The key ideas behind this chapter are that SOA is fundamental for service intelligence (SI) and service science (SS). Web services are an important application field of SI and SS. Web service architecture is a logical realization of SOA in web services. The demand of main players and their intelligent agents is a central part for web services. Mathematical analysis of demands in web services is a basis for developing demand analysis and demand theory of web services. A WSLC can be considered as a logical implementation of web service architecture. The demand-driven WSLCs are a logical realization of the WSLC. The proposed approach will facilitate the research and development of web services, e-services, service intelligence, service science and service computing.

To this end, the remainder of this chapter is organized as follows. First of all, we review SOA, Web services architecture, web services life cycle and classify main players in web services. Then we analyse demands in web services mathematically, which leads to a new classification for e-commerce. We also examine demand relationships among service providers, brokers and requestors in web services and demand chain in web services. Then we examine web service architectures and provide a demand-driven architecture for web services (DWSOA). We also examine web service lifecycles, propose the demand-driven web service lifecycle for the main players in web services respectively and then discuss the demand-driven web service lifecycles in a unified way. Finally we end the chapter with discussing some future research directions and providing some concluding remarks.

BACKGROUND

Service-oriented architecture (SOA) has been extensively studied in the fields of web services and service-oriented computing (Atkinson, et al, 2004; Singh and Huns, 2005). SOA is a conceptual architecture for implementing e-business, e-services, leaving the networking, transport protocol, and security details to the specific implementation (Gisolfi, 2001). SOA consists of three principal participants: a service provider, a service requestor, and a service broker. These three SOA participants interact using three fundamental operations: publish, find and bind: Service providers *publish* services to one or more service brokers or discovery agencies (Ferris & Farrell, 2003; Burstein, et al, 2005). Service requestors *find* required services via a service broker or a discovery agency and *bind* to them (Gottschalk, et al, 2000; Ferris & Farrell, 2003).

A concrete form of SOA in web services is web service architecture. A web service architecture is a conceptual architecture for implementing web services, which is free of concrete implementation of a web service system owing to its conceptual nature. There are a number of different web service architectures proposed in the web service community. For example, Gottschalk, et al. (2000) propose an IBM web service architecture. This might be the first web service architecture, which is then called a SOA (Gisolfi, 2001). In other words, the web service architecture is the same as SOA in web services. This can be considered as the simplest SOA. Kreger (2001) developed Gottschalk's web service architecture proposed in 2000 by adding artifacts, which mainly consist of service and service description. He uses service registry to replace the service broker in the previous architecture to fulfil the role of discovery agencies (Ferris & Farrell, 2003). Kreger (2001) also provides a business perspective on service provider, requestor and registry. He considers the above-mentioned three fundamental operations: publish, find and bind as the interactions between service provider, service requestor, and service broker. Therefore, Kreger's web service architecture is a further development of web service architectures or SOAs. Talia (2002) explores the open grid services architecture to fully integrate grids and web services, and defines grid as a geographically distributed computation platform composed of a set of heterogeneous machines that users can access via a single interfaces. Burstein, et al. (2005) propose a semantic web services architecture, and consider semantic web services as web services in which semantic web ontologies ascribe meanings to published service descriptions so that software systems representing prospective service clients can interpret and involve them. They also examine the main interactions of web services between service providers and service requestors: service discovery, engagement, and enactment. However, they have not paid much attention to the role of service broker in interactions of web services. They have not focuses on the activities of web services from a viewpoint of web services lifecycle either.

Numerous techniques, approaches, methods have been proposed to facilitate or support the main stages of the entire web service lifecycle (Wu & Chang, 2005). A large number of web service lifecycles have also been proposed to improve web services with their applications. For example, Atkinson, et al. (2004) propose a process model for a typical service, which consists of resources, service logic, and a message-processing layer that deals with message of exchanges. In this model, messages arrive at the service and are acted on by the service logic, utilizing the service's resources as required. This model can be considered as an anatomy of a service in SOA, because it only focuses on the processing of a service rather than the interactions of service providers, requestors and brokers. Kreger (2001) considers web services development lifecycle as the design, deployment, and runtime requirements for each of the players in web services: service registries, providers, and requestors. Each player has specific requirement

for each phase of four phases in the development lifecycle: build, deploy, run and manage. Benatallah, et al. (2006) implement a model-driven framework for web service development lifecycle in a prototype platform, Service Mosaic, to model, analyze, and manage service models including business protocols, and adaptors. This framework at least includes protocol definition, protocol analysis, and protocol data management, which are fundamental issues that affect the web service development lifecycle from an implementation perspective. However, they have focused on neither WSLC nor the interoperations or interactions of service providers, brokers and requestors from a demand perspective. Narendra and Orriens (2006) consider a web service lifecycle consisting of web service composition, execution, midstream adaptation, and re-execution. We will turn to web services life cycle once again later when we propose demand-driven web services lifecycle.

Humans are one of the most important decisive forces for development of web services. From a viewpoint of multiagent systems (Weiss, 1999; Sun and Lau, 2007), various intelligent agents are also a decisive force for developing intelligent web services. However, few studies have paid sufficient attention to the main players in web services, to our knowledge. In the next section we will first examine main players in web services.

MAIN PLAYERS IN WEB SERVICES

This section will look at the players involved in web services and some corresponding architectures.

There are mainly three players related to web services: web service requestors, web service brokers, and web service providers (Sun & Lau, 2007; Singh & Huhns, 2005), as shown in Figure 1.

Web service requestors also denote web service users, buyers, customers, consumers, receivers, clients, and their intelligent agents. Web service brokers denote web service intermediaries,

Figure 1. Main players in web services

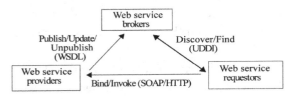

middle agents, registry (Kreger, 2001), discovery agency (Ferris & Farrell, 2003) and their intelligent agents (Burstein, et al, 2005). Web service providers (Kreger, 2001) denote web service owners, sellers, senders and their intelligent agents. Web service requestors, brokers, and providers are the most integral players in web services transactions (Deitel, et al, 2004, p. 52). Gisolfi (2001) mentioned these three players in the simple service oriented architecture (SOA) for web services. In this architecture, web service providers create web services and advertise them to potential web service requestors by registering the web services with web service brokers, or simply offers web services (Dustar & Schreiner, 2005). The web service provider needs to describe the web service in a standard format, and publish it in a central service registry. The service registry or broker contains additional information about the service provider, such as address and contact of the providing company, and technical details about the service. Web service providers may integrate or compose existing services (Limthanmaphon & Zhang, 2003) using intelligent techniques. They may also register descriptions of services they offer, monitor and manage service execution (Dustar & Schreiner, 2005). Web service requestors retrieve the information from the registry and use the service description obtained to bind to and invoke the web service. Web service brokers maintain a registry of published web services and might introduce web service providers to web service requestors. They use universal description discovery integration (UDDI) to find the requested web services, because UDDI specifies a registry or "yellow pages" of services (Singh &

Huhns, 2005, p. 20). They also provide a searchable repository of service descriptions where service providers publish their services, service requestors find services and obtain binding information for these services.

This architecture is simple because it only includes three players (as mentioned above) and three basic operations for web services: publish, find and bind. In fact, some behaviors of web service agents are also fundamentally important in order to make web services successful. These fundamental behaviors at least include communication, interaction, collaboration, cooperation, coordination, negotiation, trust and deception (Singh & Huhns, 2005; Sun & Finnie, 2004; Burstein, et al, 2005).

Papazoglou (2003) proposes an extended service-oriented architecture. The players involved in this architecture are more than that in the simple SOA, because it includes service provider, service aggregator, service client, market maker, and service operator.

A service aggregator is a service provider that consolidates services provided by other service providers into a distinct value-added service (Papazoglou, 2003). Service aggregators develop specifications and/or codes that permit the composite service to perform functions such as coordination, monitoring quality of service (QoS) (Burstein, et al, 2005) and composition. In our view, a service aggregator should be differentiated from a service provider. We can use *web service recommender* or web service composer to replace service aggregator, because recommendation and composition are most important activities in web services.

The main task of web market makers is to establish an efficient service-oriented market in order to facilitate the business activities among service providers to service brokers and service requestors. In the traditional market, the service broker is working in the market, while the market maker makes the market operating.

The web service operator is responsible for performing operation management functions such as operation, assurance and support (Papazoglou, 2003).

From the viewpoint of multiagent systems (Weiss, 1999; Henderson-Sellers & Giorgini, 2005), there are still other players involved in web services, such as web service advisors, web service managers, web service composers, web service recommenders, web service consultants, and so on. Further, an activity of web services usually is implemented by a few intelligent agents within a multiagent web service system (Sun & Finnie, 2004). Therefore, more and more intelligent players or agents will be involved in web services with the development of automating activities of web services. Although some of these will be mentioned in the later sections, we mainly focus on service providers, brokers and requestors in what follows.

MATHEMATICAL ANALYSIS OF DEMAND IN WEB SERVICES

This section will analyze demands in web services from a mathematical perspective and then discuss the demand relationships in web services.

Demand is an important concept in microeconomics. Jackson and McIver (2004, p. 74) defines demand as "a schedule that shows the amounts of a product that consumers are willing and able to purchase at each specific price in a set of possible prices during some specified period of time". The basic law of demand is "All else being constant, as price falls, the corresponding quantity demanded rises". Alternatively, the higher the price is, the less corresponding quantity demanded.

Demand analysis has drawn attention in e-business. Chaffey (2007) defines demand analysis as "assessment of the demand for e-commerce services among existing and potential customer segments" (p. 218). He then analyzes the factors that affect demand for e-commerce services

(Chaffey, 2007, pp. 150-60.) and uses demand analysis to examine current projected customer use of each digital channel with different markets (Chaffey, 2007, p. 344).

Demand, in particular "on-demand" (Dan, et al, 2004), has also drawn some attention in web services. For example, Burstein, et al. (2005) examine functional and architectural demands or requirements for service discovery, engagement and enactment in terms of the semantic web service architecture. However, in the above-mentioned discussion, it seems that the subject of the demand and its objective are ignored to some extent. For example, who demands what from where is usually unclear. It may not be critical for traditional economics and e-commerce. However, it is useful for web services to know who, what and where exactly for web services, which can be seen in the examination of web service lifecycle. Further there has not been a mathematical theory or analysis of demand in e-commerce and web services. In what follows, we examine the mathematical foundation of demand in order to fill this gap and then use it to develop demand-driven web services.

We can analyze "demand" mathematically as follows. A man M demands something S provided by N. In other words, from a mathematical viewpoint, demand is a 3-ary relation that can be denoted as *Demand* (m, n, s). In the context of web services, we can explain *Demand* (m, n, s) as: a player m demands web service s provided by player n. For example, "service requestor r demands web service consultation c provided by service broker b" can be denoted as *Demand* (r, b, c). More generally, demand as a 3-ary relation can be denoted as: Let M, N, and S be a nonempty set respectively, $M = \{m_1, m_2 ... m_1\}$, $N = \{n_1, n_2 ..., n_J\}$, $S = \{s_1, s_2, ... s_K\}$, then any subset D^3 of $M \times N \times S$, $D^3 \subseteq M \times N \times S$, is a demand relation. In web services, N and M can denotes all the service requestors and all the service providers or brokers respectively. S represents all the web services provided on the web.

In business practice, this 3-ary demand relation is usually simplified as a binary relation D^2 or a unary relation D^1: For example, in B2C e-commerce, we only focus on: who demands what, that is, $D^2 \subseteq M \times S$ represents "customers m demands a good s," where M denotes all the service requestors or all the service providers. Further, in B2C e-commerce, we usually do not care about "who demands what" but only care about "what that are demanded", that is, $D^1 \subseteq S$ represents the good that is demanded. Therefore, from a demand's perspective, there are three different types of e-commerce: D^1 e-commerce, D^2 e-commerce and D^3 e-commerce.

- D^1 e-commerce only focuses on the goods that are transacted. Such an e-commerce is usually used for statistical analysis.
- D^2 e-commerce only focuses on the customer and the goods that are purchased by the customer or the seller, and that the goods that are sold. Therefore, D^2 e-commerce corresponds to a B2C e-commerce.
- D^3 e-commerce focuses on all the service providers, requestors, and goods that are transacted. Therefore, D^3 e-commerce is an organization that oversees the activities in web services or e-commerce.

In fact, taking into account the amount and payment associated with demand relation, we introduce demand functions respectively for D^1 e-commerce, D^2 e-commerce and D^3 e-commerce. For example, let A and P be non-empty sets, then any function $d^1 : S \rightarrow A \times P$, $d(s) = a \cdot p$, is a demand function taking into account the amount A of demand and the corresponding price P per a unit demand. For example, in D^1 e-commerce, a customer demands 100 textbooks on e-commerce, and the price is AUD\$100.00 per textbook. Then, the corresponding demand function value is

$$d^1(book) = 100 \cdot 100 = 10000$$

where the customer and provider are technically ignored. This demand function represents the total price for the demanded 100 textbooks.

Similarly, in D^2 e-commerce, $d^2(David, book) = 100 \cdot 100 = 10000$ represents that David demands 100 textbooks on e-commerce with the price of AUD\$10000.00, where the providers are technically ignored.

In D^3 e-commerce, $d^3(David, book) = 100 \cdot 100 = 10000$ represents that David demands 100 books on e-commerce provided by Amazon.com with the price of AUD\$10000.00. This is a complete form for demand in a transactional web service.

From the above discussion, we can see that there is an inclusion relationship among D^1 e-commerce, D^2 e-commerce and D^3 e-commerce, as illustrated in Figure 2.

In demand-driven web services, we need a 3-ary demand relation taking into account the main players in web services (see the previous section). This demand relation can be illustrated in Demand relations in Web services.

In D^3 web services, demand is a 3-ary relation, that is, service requestors demands service brokers or providers to provide certain web services, and vice versa. However, what properties this 3-ary relation has in the context of web services remains open. Some stages in the web lifecycle may be absent since the demand disappears. There are also many situations resulting in demand cancellation.

In Table 1, the first column consists of a service provider, a service requestor, and a service broker.

Figure 2. Interrelationship among D^1, D^2, and D^3 e-commerce

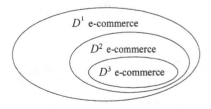

Table 1. Demand relations in web services

WS activities	Provider	Requestor	Broker
Provider	N/A	Binding, discovery, negotiation, invocation, billing, contract	discovery, recommendation, invocation, billing, contract
Requestor	QoS, description, representation, identification, search, match, discovery, negotiation, invocation, contract	N/A	Finding, consultation, personalization, recommendation, adaptation, mediation negotiation,
Broker	Publication, management search, match, Discovery, billing, contract	invocation, billing, contract	N/A

The first row lists a service provider, a service requestor, and a service broker. WS activities in the top left cell denote all the web service activities (or operations) in all the cell (m, n), where m an n denote rows and columns respectively. This implies that cell (m, n) contains the web service activities that are demanded. For example, cell $(1, 2)$ contains web service binding, discovery, negotiation, invocation, billing, contract, all of which are demanded by the web service provider to the web requestor, where cell $(2, 1)$ contains web service QoS, description, representation, identification, search, match, discovery, negotiation, invocation, contract, all of which are demanded by the web service requestor to the web service provider.

Even if the web service requestor demands the web service provider to represent web services (web service representation), the web service provider might not represent web services by himself. Instead, he may demand others to do so. In this way, a web service demand chain is formed

in web services. For example, the web service requestor demands service consultation from a service broker, while the service broker demands web service representation and publication from a service provider. The service provider demands the most powerful web service tools from the ICT developer to realize the web service representation and publication, as shown in Figure 3. The extended form of a web service demand chain is a web service demand network in web services, just as there are supply chain networks in e-commerce (Chaffey, 2007).

It should be noted that supply chain management and demand chain management have been seriously studied in business, marketing and management (Chaffey, 2007, pp. 266-300; Rainbird, 2004; Walters, 2006), whereas demand chain and demand chain management have not drawn significant attention in e-business and e-commerce, to our knowledge. This situation might be changed in web services, because service customers' demands play a vital role in web services.

Figure 3. A demand chain in web services

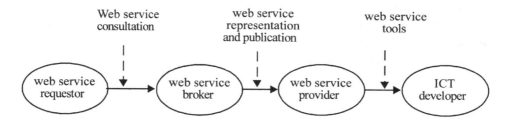

Figure 4. DWSOA: A demand-driven SOA for web services

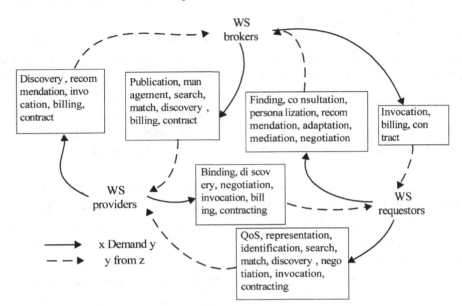

What are the majority of customers' demands as well as their expectation and propensity in web services? and how do demand chain and demand network as well as demand network management impact on web services? How can we integrate demand chain analysis with the proposed mathematical analysis of demand? These problems remain open. We will address them in another article, and will not look at them any more because they are beyond the scope of this chapter.

DWSOA: A DEMAND DRIVEN ARCHITECTURE FOR WEB SERVICES

This section will review a few web service architectures and then provide a demand-driven architecture for web services.

We have briefly mentioned different service-oriented architectures (SOA) for web services in the section "Background". In fact, web service architectures have been a research topic for engineering web services (Alonso, et al, 2004). There have been a large number of web service architectures

proposed in the past years. For example, Wu and Chang (2005) provide a conceptual architecture of web services for service ecosystems. Garcia and de Toledo (2006) propose an extended web service architecture providing QoS management for web services. However, the existing web service architectures are mainly from the perspective of developers rather than from a demand perspective. Based on the above demand analysis for web services, we can propose a demand-driven SOA for web services (DWSOA), as shown in Figure 4. Note that in Figure 4, x and z denote either WS providers, brokers or requestors, y denotes WS activities.

In the DWSOA, WS (web service) providers demand WS discovery, recommendation, invocation, billing, and contract from WS brokers; WS brokers demand WS invocation, billing, contract from WS requestors; WS requestors demand WS finding, consultation, personalization, recommendation, adaptation, mediation, negotiation from WS brokers; and so on. From the viewpoint of previously mentioned demand relation in web services, the above-mentioned demand relations are 3-ary, and corresponds to

1. Demand (WS providers, WS brokers, WS activities) = {WS discovery, recommendation, invocation, billing, and contract};

2. Demand (WS brokers, WS requestors, WS activities) = {WS invocation, billing, contract};

3. Demand (WS requestors, WS brokers, WS activities) = {WS finding, consultation, personalization, recommendation, adaptation, mediation, negotiation};

and so on. It should be noted that there are inter-demands among the WS providers, brokers and requestors in the DWSOA, although the demands among them are not symmetric. In other words, the service requestor demands the service consultation from the service broker, whereas the service broker does not demand service consultation from the service requestor.

We do not believe that all activities in the web services have been covered in the DSWOA. For example, WS engagement, enactment, and management (Burstein, et al, 2005) are not included in the DSWOA. The key idea behind it is that we expose the demand relationship among WS providers, brokers and requestors. This is the basis for demand-driven web service lifecycles, which will be discussed in later sections.

WEB SERVICE LIFECYCLE

This section mainly reviews web service lifecycles and discusses the corresponding issues.

From the perspective of computer science, the notion of lifecycle originated from software engineering (Pressman, 2001). It describes the life of a software product (development) from its conception, to its implementation, delivery, use, and maintenance (Pfleeger & Atlee, 2006). A traditional software development lifecycle mainly consists of seven phases: planning, requirements analysis, systems design, coding, testing, delivery and maintenance. Based on this, a web service

lifecycle consists of the start of a web service, the end of web service and its evolutionary stages that transform the web service from the start to the end.

There have been a large number of attempts to address web service lifecycle in the web service community, as discussed in the section "Background". Further, Glatard, et al. (2008) examine a SOA enabling dynamic service grouping for optimizing distributed workflow execution. Leymann (2003) discusses a lifecycle of a web service based on explicit factory-based approach, in which a client uses a factory to create "an instance" of a particular kind of service. The client can then explicitly manage the destruction of such an instance, or it can be left to the grid environment. Sheth (2003) proposes a semantic web process lifecycle that consists of web service description (annotation), discovery, composition and execution or orchestration. Wu and Chang (2005) consider service discovery, service invocation and service composition as the whole lifecycle of web services. Zhang and Jeckle (2003) propose a lifecycle for web service solutions that consists of web service modeling, development, publishing, discovery, composition, collaboration, monitoring and analytical control from a perspective of web service developers. Kwon (2003) proposes a lifecycle of web services consisting of four fundamental steps: web service identification, creation, use and maintenance. Tsalgatidou and Pilioura (2002) propose a web service lifecycle that consists of two different layers: a basic layer and a value-added layer. The basic layer contains web service creation, description, publishing, discovery, invocation and unpublishing (Gottschalk, et al, 2000), all of these activities are necessary to be supported by every web service environment. The value-added layer contains the value-added activities of composition, security, brokering, reliability, billing, monitoring, transaction handling and contracting. These activities bring value-added functionality and better performance to any web service environment. They acknowledge that some of these activities take place at the web service requestor's site, while others take place at the web service broker's or provider's site. They also explore technical challenges related to each activity in the web service lifecycle. However, they have not classified the proposed activities of stages in their lifecycle based on web service requestors, providers, and brokers in detail. Some organizations also propose their own web service lifecycle. For example, W3C proposes a service lifecycle for web service management, which is expressed as state transition diagrams (W3C, 2004). Sun Microsystems considers the lifecycle of web services consisting of four stages: design/build, test, deploy/execute, and manage (Sun Microsystems, 2003), which can be considered a model for web service developers.

Based on the above analysis, we can find that there are at least the following activities of web services that have been mentioned in the reviewed web service lifecycles, all of these can be classified into two categories: development-oriented web service activities and business-oriented web service activities.

- Development-oriented web service activities: Web service modeling, representation, design/building, test, publishing, unpublishing, deployment, execution, re-execution, orchestration, collaboration, monitoring, analytical control, maintenance, and management,
- Business-oriented web service activities: Web service creation, identification, description (annotation), publishing, finding, discovery, use, invocation and binding (Gottschalk, et al, 2000), adaptation, composition, security, brokering, recommendation, reliability, billing, monitoring, transaction handling and contracting.

This classification does not produce a crisp mathematical partition, because, some activities such as web service representation, management, and creation can be considered in both kinds of web

service activities. However, such a classification reflects the fact that some existing web service lifecycles are proposed from the implementation perspective of the web service developers (Burstein, et al, 2006), whereas other web service lifecycles are proposed from the perspective of business. Generally speaking, web service providers pay more attention to development-demanded web service activities than web service brokers and requestors, whereas web service brokers and requestors pay more attention to Business-demanded web service activities than web service providers.

From a market perspective, web services mainly consist of three kinds of players: Service providers, service requestors and service brokers (Tang, et al, 2007). Different players require different web service lifecycles. Therefore, what is a web service lifecycle from the demand viewpoint of web service providers, brokers and requestors respectively? How many stages does a web service lifecycle consist of? These problems are interesting for examining demand-driven web services.

Further, demand is an important factor for market and economy development (Chaffey, 2007, p. 150). The decrease of demand is an implication for economic recession. Different players generally have different demands for web services, different demands have also different web service lifecycles. Therefore, what is the demand-driven web service lifecycle from the viewpoint of web service providers, brokers and requestors respectively? These issues still remain open in web services. The following sections will address these issues by examining the web service lifecycle from a demand viewpoint.

It should be noted that everybody, whether an application user, developer, financier, businessman, or an e-commerce manager, has enjoyed or will enjoy some tangible benefits from web services (Guruge, 2004) such as searching information using Google and doing business online. At the same time, he or she demands more and more web services with the development of the Internet. Therefore, we do not examine the demand of everybody for web services, but the demand of the main players in web services in what follows, that is, we will look at demand-driven web service lifecycles for web service providers, requestors and brokers respectively.

A PROVIDER'S DEMAND DRIVEN WEB SERVICE LIFECYCLE

In web services, a web service provider usually demands a web service requestor to commit some web service activities and also demands a web service broker to commit some web service activities. Therefore, based on the above demand analysis for web services, a provider's demand-driven web service lifecycle mainly consists of web service finding, identification (Kwon, 2003), description/representation (Burstein, et al, 2005), creation (Kwon, 2003; Tang, et al, 2007), discovery, composition (Limthanmaphon & Zhang, 2003; Tang, et al, 2007; Burstein, et al, 2005), recommendation (Sun & Lau, 2007), negotiation (Hung, et al, 2004; Burstein, et al, 2005), invocation (Burstein, et al, 2005), contracting, use and reuse (Kwon, 2003), execution or orchestration, management and monitoring (Dustar & Schreiner, 2005), maintenance (Kwon, 2003), billing and security (Tang, et al, 2007).

Web service identification aims to identify appropriate services (Ladner, 2008). Web service invocation is to invoke the discovered web service interface. Web services are published to the intranet or the Internet repositories for potential users to locate (Tang, et al, 2007). Web service unpublishing is sometimes no longer available or needed, or it has to be updated to satisfy new requirements (Tang, et al, 2007)

Web service composition primarily concerns requests of web service users that cannot be satisfied by any available web service (Bucchiarone & Gnesi, 2006; Narendra & Orriens, 2006). One form of simple web service composition is to combine a set of available web services to obtain a composite service that might be recommended to the users. In other words, web service composition is a process in which a single web service requested from a service requestor can be satisfied by an aggregation of different services provided by several independent web services providers. More strictly, web service composition refers to the process of creating customized or personalized services from existing services by a process of dynamic discovery, integration and execution of those services in order to satisfy user requirements (Wang, et al, 2008). Web service composition is a key challenge to manage collaboration among web services (Limthanmaphon & Zhang, 2003). It refers to intelligent techniques and efficient mechanisms of composing arbitrarily complex services from relatively simpler services available over the Internet. Service composition can be either performed by composing elementary or composite services. Composite services in turn are recursively defined as an aggregation of elementary and composite services (Dustdar & Schreiner, 2005).

There are many techniques existing for web service composition. For example, Tang, et al (2007) propose an automatic web service composition method taking into account both services' input/output type compatibility and behavioral constraint compatibility. Cheng, et al. (2006) use case-based reasoning (CBR) to support web service composition. Further, Dustdar and Schreiner (2005) discuss the urgent need for service composition and the required technologies to perform service composition as well as present several different composition strategies. Web service composition is becoming an important topic for service computing, because composing web services to meet the requirement of the web service requestor is the most important issue for web service providers and brokers.

REQUESTOR'S DEMAND DRIVEN WEB SERVICE LIFECYCLE

In web services, a web service requestor usually demands a web service provider and a web service broker to commit some web service activities respectively. Therefore, based on the above demand analysis for web services, a requestor's demand-driven web service lifecycle mainly consists of web service consultation, creation (Burstein, et al, 2005), representation, search (Ladner, 2008), matching (Ladner, 2008), finding, discovery (Tang, et al, 2007; Burstein, et al, 2005), identification (Burstein, et al, 2005), composition, mediation (Ladner, 2008; Burstein, et al, 2005), personalization, adaptation, negotiation (Gottschalk, et al, 2000), evaluation (Burstein, et al, 2005) and recommendation, QoS (Burstein, et al, 2005), invocation (Burstein, et al, 2005), contracting (Burstein, et al, 2005).

Web service discovery is a process of finding the most appropriate web service needed by a web service requestor (Singh & Huhns, 2005; Burstein, et al, 2005). It identifies a new web service and detects an update to a previously discovered web service (Ladner, 2008). Services may be searched, matched, and discovered by service requestors by specifying search criteria and then be invoked (Dustdar & Schreiner, 2005; Tang, et al, 2007). Service invocation is restricted to authorized users (Dustdar & Schreiner, 2005). There have been a variety of techniques and approaches developed for web service discovery. For example, OWL-S (an OWL-based Web service ontology of W3C) provides classes that describe what the service does, how to ask for the service, what happens when the service is carried out, and how the service can be accessed (Ladner, 2008).

Web service mediation aims to mediate the request of web service from the web service requestor. Web service negotiation consists of a sequence of proposal exchanges between the two or more parties with the goal of establishing a formal contract to specify agreed terms on the web service (Yao, et al, 2006). Through negotiation, web service requestors can continuously customize their needs, and web service providers can tailor their offers. In particular, multiple web service providers can collaborate and coordinate with each other in order to satisfy a request that they can't process alone.

However, a web service requestor might not need to know how the web services are retrieved, discovered and composed internally. Therefore, search, matching, and composition might be less important for a web service requestor.

A BROKER'S DEMAND DRIVEN WEB SERVICE LIFECYCLE

Brokering is the general act of mediating between requestors and providers in order to match service requestor's needs and providers' offerings. It is a more complicated activity than discovery (Tang, et al, 2007). A broker should enable universal service-to-service interaction, negotiation, bidding and selection of the highest quality of service (QoS) (Singh & Huhns, 2005, pp. 345-346). Brokering is supported by HP web services platform as a HP web intelligent broker (Tsalgatidou & Pilioura, 2002). After discovering web service providers that can respond to a user's service request, HP web services platform negotiates between them to weed out those that offer services outside the criteria of the request.

In web services, a web service broker usually demands a web service provider and a web service requestor to undertake some web service activities respectively. Therefore, based on the above demand analysis for web services, a broker's demand-driven web service lifecycle mainly consists of web service consultation, publication, search, matching (Burstein, et al, 2005), discovery, personalization, adaptation, composition, negotiation, recommendation, management, invocation, contracting and billing.

We propose web service consultation as the start of the broker's demand-driven web service lifecycle, because the web service requestor provides a request for a web service so that the web service broker begins to consultation. In order to provide a service consultation, the web service broker has to conduct web service search, by using a search tool/engine such as google.com and beidu.com. During the web service search, the web service broker uses any techniques of web service matching such as CBR (Sun & Finnie, 2004). After discovering a number of web services, the web service broker can select one of them to recommend it to the web service requestor. If the requestor accepts the recommended web service, then the web service can be considered as a web service use/reuse; that is, the existing web service has been reused by customers.

Web service recommendation aims at helping web service requestors in selecting web services more suitable to their needs. Web service recommendation is a significant challenge for web service industry, in particular for web service brokers. Web service recommendation can be improved through optimization, analysis, forecasting, reasoning and simulation (Kwon, 2003). Recommender systems have been studied and developed in e-commerce, e-business and multiagent systems (Sun & Finnie, 2004). Sun and Lau has examined case based web service recommendation based on the analysis of customer experience and experience-based reasoning (Sun & Lau, 2007). However, how to integrate web service recommendation, composition and discovery in a unified way is still a big issue for web services.

Different web service requestors have different preferences and expectations. Therefore, a web service broker has to personalize web services in order to meet the requirement of the web service requestor satisfactorily. It is necessary to compose web services based on the requirement of requestors in order to personalize the web service. At the same time, web service composition allows web

service brokers to create a composite web service for requestors rapidly (Tang, et al, 2007).

Billing concerns service brokers and service providers (Tang, et al, 2007). Service brokers create and manage taxonomies, register services and offer rapid lookup for services and companies. They might also offer value-added information for services, such as statistical information for the service usage and QoS data.

A UNIFIED PERSPECTIVE ON DEMAND DRIVEN WEB SERVICE LIFECYCLES

Based on the above discussion, the stages involved in the demand-driven web service lifecycle for web service providers, requestors and brokers can be summarized in Figure 5. Some of the detailed activities have not been listed in the table because of space limitations. From Figure 5, we can intuitively find that service requestors and brokers are the dominant force for developing web services, which will be examined in more detail in another paper. In what follows, we discuss the above proposed demand-driven web service lifecycles from a unified perspective.

Some activities in web services are common demands of the main players: service providers, brokers, and requestors. This means that they share some common web service activities. However, different players in web services demand the same activity in a different way. For example, the service provider demands "web services search" also means that s/he asks web services developers or her/his technology agents to provide efficient web services search function for his or her business. On the other hand, the service requestor demands "web services search" means that s/he requires a fast search function from the service provider or broker in order to obtain the most satisfactory web services as soon as possible.

Finding, search and matching are not unique activities or operations related to web services,

Figure 5. Demand driven web service lifecycles: A unified perspective

Players in web services	identification	representation	creation/publishing	search/matching	finding/discovery	consultation	personalization	composition	recommendation	adaptation	mediation	negotiation	invocation	binding	billing	contract	security	maintenance	evaluation/QoS	management
Provider	X	X	X		X			X	X		X	X	X	X	X	X	X	X		X
requestor	X	X	X	X	X	X	X	X	X	X	X	X		X	X	X	X	X	X	
Broker	X		X	X	X	X	X	X	X	X	X	X	X		X	X		X		X

because they are also involved in database and case based reasoning (CBR). For example, Google uses search and matching to provide web services. In fact, search can be considered the most common demand for everyone who accesses the Internet or the web. Adaptation, retrieval, classification (Ladner, 2008), use/reuse (Kwon, 2003), retention or feedback are not unique activities related to web services either, because they are also stages of CBR cycle (Sun & Finnie, 2004). Web service invocation, binding, billing, contract (Tang, et al, 2007) can be considered as the common features for any commercial activities. Therefore, we need not discuss each of them in detail in the context of web services. Based on the above discussion, the most important activities in web services can be web service discovery, composition and recommendation: The service requestors demand the service providers and brokers for web services discovery and recommendation; the service brokers demand the service providers for web services discovery and composition; the service providers demands up-to-date techniques and tools for web services discovery, composition and recommendation. In a more general sense, all the above-mentioned activities of web services can be considered as a demand from web services to all the stakeholders of web services. This demand asks web service developers to provide services with high QoS and advanced tools for all the ac-

tivities of web services. Therefore, these services can be considered as meta-web services and we will examine the hierarchy of demands in web services in future work.

It should be noted that the activities in web services should be classified in a hierarchical way (main services and subservices). For example, identification, finding, search and matching can be subactivities of web service discovery (Burstein, et al, 2005). Dan, et al. (2004) argues that the subactivities of web service contract consist of offering creation, customer order and negotiation, monitoring, billing and reporting. Burstein, et al. (2005) examines the subactivities of web service discovery, engagement, enactment and management. Then we can examine the hierarchical structure of activities or interoperations in web services assuming that publish, find, and bind are the fundamental activities of web services.

FUTURE RESEARCH DIRECTIONS

Understanding the demand of stakeholders of web services is a critical factor for further development of web services. This chapter only focuses on demand-driven web services from a demand perspective of the main players in web services: service providers, brokers, and requestors. In fact, these demands from the web service providers, brokers, and requestors not only require to be met from themselves but also from more stakeholders of web services, in particular, the web service developers with the strong background of information communication technology (ICT). They will provide technological solution for the main activities of web service lifecycle such as web service description and discovery (Garcia & Toledo, 2006), composition (Papazoglou, et al, 2006), billing, contracting. For example, the engineering of web service composition and recommendation are a research direction (Papazoglou, et al, 2006). In future work, we will explore implementation issues for engineering of web service composition and recommendation.

The proposed demand-driven web service lifecycles are still in a linear form. Providing other forms of demand-driven web service lifecycle is also a research direction. In future work, we will develop demand-driven models for web service lifecycle in a spiral and iterative way with corresponding diagrams, as done in software engineering.

Applying intelligent techniques to web services and automating the process stages in the demand-driven web service lifecycle is another research direction (Petrie & Genesereth, 2003). In future work, we will integrate web service discovery, composition and recommendation using soft case based reasoning.

Demand is an important concept in economics. However, there is less attention in web services. In future work, we will investigate the computing basis of demand and then improve the above-mentioned web service lifecycle. For example, we will examine demand as a 4-ary relation (seller, buyer, service, price) from a mathematical and business viewpoint and propose a hierarchical structure for demand-driven e-commerce and demand-driven web services. We will also further analyse the demands between service players, and provide the related instruction/guidance for web service design and development in order to develop demand-driven framework for Web services.

CONCLUSION

This chapter first looked at main players in web services, provided a mathematical analysis of demand in web services. It also examined the demand relationship among service providers, brokers and requestors in web services and the demand chain in web services. Then the chapter reviewed web service architectures and provided a demand-driven architecture for web services (DWSOA). It also reviewed web service lifecycles, proposed the demand-driven web service lifecycle for the main players in web services respectively and then discussed the demand-driven web service lifecycles in a unified way. The proposed approach in this chapter can facilitate the engineering and management of web services, and the research and development of web services, e-services, service intelligence and service science. In the future work, besides above-mentioned future research directions, we will develop demand-driven framework for Web services by extending Table 2 to include as many stages or activities of web services life cycle as possible. We will also use the proposed approaches to study business models further and try to apply them to Web services design.

ACKNOWLEDGMENT

This research is partially supported by the Ministry of Education Hebei, China under a key research Grant No. ZH200815 and other research grants provided by the College of Mathematics and Information Science, Hebei Normal University, China.

REFERENCES

W3C (2004). Web service management: Service life cycle. Retrieved December 26, 2008, from http://www.w3.org/TR/2004/NOTE-web servicelc-20040211/

Alonso, G., Casati, F., Kuno, H., & Machiraju, V. (2004). *Web Services: Concepts, Architectures and Applications*. Berlin: Springer-Verlag.

Atkinson, M., DeRoure, D., Alistair Dunlop, A., et al. (2004). Web service grids: An evolutionary approach. *UK e-Science Technical Report Series*. Retrieved July 6, 2009 from http://www.nesc.ac.uk/technical_papers/ UKeS-2004-05.pdf

Benatallah, B., Reza, H., & Nezhad, M. (2006, July/August). A model-driven framework for web services life-cycle management. *IEEE Internet Computing*, 55–63. doi:10.1109/MIC.2006.87

Bucchiarone, A., & Gnesi, S. (2006). A survey on services composition languages and models. In *Proceedings of the International Workshop on Web Services – Modeling and Testing* (Web service-MaTe 2006), Palermo, Sicily, June 9 (pp.51-63).

Burstien, M. (2005). A semantic Web services architecture. *IEEE Internet Computing*, *9*(5), 72–81. doi:10.1109/MIC.2005.96

Chaffey, D. (2007). *E-Business and E-Commerce Management* (3rd ed.). Harlow, UK: Prentice Hall.

Cheng, R., & Su, S. Yang, F., & Li, Y. (2006). Using case-based reasoning to support web service composition. In V.N. Alexandrov et al. (Eds.), *ICCS 2006, Part IV* (LNCS 3994, pp. pp. 87-94). Berlin, Heidelberg: Springer-Verlag.

Dan, A., Kuebler, D., & Davis, D. (2004). Web services on demand: WSLA-driven automated management. *IBM Systems Journal*, *43*(1), 136–158. doi:10.1147/sj.431.0136

Deitel, H. M., Deitel, P. J., DuWadt, B., & Trees, L. K. (2004). *Web Services: A technical Introduction*. Upper Saddle River, NJ: Prentice Hall.

Dustdar, S., & Schreiner, W. (2005). A survey on web services composition. *International Journal Web and Grid Services*, *1*(1), 1–30. doi:10.1504/IJWGS.2005.007545

Erl, T. (2006). *Service-Oriented Architecture (SOA): Concepts, Technology, and Design*. Upper Saddle River, NJ: Prentice Hall.

Ferris, C., & Farrell, J. (2003). What are web services? *Communications of the ACM*, *46*(6), 31. doi:10.1145/777313.777335

Garcia, D. Z. G., & de Toledo, M. B. F. (2006). A web service architecture providing QoS management. In *Proceedings of the Fourth Latin American Web Congress* (LA-Web '06) (pp. 189-198).

Gisolfi, D. (2001). Web services architect: Part 1: An introduction to dynamic e-business. Retrieved July 8, 2009 from http://www.ibm.com/developerworks/webservices/library/ws-arc1

Glatard, T., Montagnat, J., Emsellem, D., & Lingrand, D. (2008). A service-oriented architecture enabling dynamic service grouping for optimizing distributed workflow execution. *Future Generation Computer Systems*, *24*(7), 720–730. doi:10.1016/j.future.2008.02.011

Gottschalk, K., et al. (2000). Web Services architecture overview. Retrieved July 15, 2009 from http://www.ibm.com/developerworks/webservices/library/w-ovr

Guruge, A. (2004). *Web Services: Theory and Practice*. Amsterdam: Elsevier Inc.

Henderson-Sellers, B., & Giorgini, P. (Eds.). (2005). *Agent-Oriented Methodologies*. Hershey, PA: Idea Group Publishing.

Hoffman, K. D. (2003). Marketing + MIS = E-Services. *Communications of the ACM*, *46*(6), 53–55. doi:10.1145/777313.777340

Hung, P. C. K., Li, H., & Jeng, J. J. (2004). Web service negotiation: An overview of research issues. In *Proc of 37th Hawaii Intl Conf on System Sciences* (pp. 1-10).

ICWS. (2009). http://conferences.computer.org/icws/2009/.

Jackson, J., & McIver, R. (2004). *Microeconomics* (7th ed.). Australia: McGraw-Hill.

Kreger, H. (2001). Web services conceptual architecture (WSCA 1.0), IBM Software Group. Retrieved March 28, 2009, from http://www.cs.uoi.gr/~zarras/mdw-ws/WebServicesConceptualArchitectu2.pdf

Kwon, O. B. (2003). Meta web service: building web-based open decision support system based on web services. *Expert Systems with Applications, 24*, 375–389. doi:10.1016/S0957-4174(02)00187-2

Ladner, R. (2008). Soft computing techniques for web service brokering. *Soft Computing, 12*, 1089–1098. doi:10.1007/s00500-008-0277-0

Leymann, F. (2003). Web Services: Distributed Applications without Limits: An Outline. In *Proceedings Database Systems for Business, Technology and Web BTW*, Leipzig, Germany, Feb 26 – 28, 2003, Springer. Retrieved April 1, 2208, from http://doesen0.informatik.uni-leipzig.de/proceedings/paper/keynote-leymann.pdf

Limthanmaphon, B., & Zhang, Y. (2003). Web service composition with case-based reasoning. In *ACM Intl Conf Proc Series (Vol. 143), Proc. 14th Australasian Database Conf*, Adelaide, Australia (pp. 201-208).

Miller, G. (2005). NET vs. J2EE. *Communications of the ACM, 48*(7), 64–67.

Narendra, N. C., & Orriens, B. (2006). Requirements-driven modeling of the web service execution and adaptation lifecycle. In S. Madria et al. (Eds.), *ICDCIT* (LNCS 4317, pp. 314-324).

Papazoglou, M. P. (2003). Service-Oriented Computing: Concepts, Characteristics and Directions. In *Proceedings of 4th Intl Conf on Web Information Systems Engineering* (WISE2003) (pp. 3-12).

Papazoglou, M.P., Traverso, P, Dustdar, S. & et al. (2006). Service-oriented computing research roadmap. Retrieved April 4, 2009, from http:drops.dagstuhl.de/opus/volltexte/2006/524/

Petrie, C., Genesereth, M., et al. (2003). Adding AI to web services. In L. van Elst, V. Dignum, & A. Abecker (Eds.), *AMKM 2003* (LNAI 2926, pp. 322-338).

Pfleeger, S. L., & Atlee, J. M. (2006). *Software Engineering: Theory and Practice* (3rd ed.). Beijing: Pearson Education, Inc.

Pressman, R. S. (2001). *Software Engineering: A Practitioner's Approach* (5th ed.). Boston: McGraw-Hill.

Rainbird, M. (2004). Demand and supply chains: The value catalyst. *International Journal of Physical Distribution & Logistics Management, 34*(3/4), 230–250. doi:10.1108/09600030410533565

Rust, R. T., & Kannan, P. K. (2003). E-service: A new paradigm for business in the electronic environment. *Communications of the ACM, 46*(6), 37–42. doi:10.1145/777313.777336

Schneider, G. P. (2003). *Electronic Commerce* (4th ed.). Boston, MA: Thomson Course Technology.

Sheth, A. (2003). Semantic web process lifecycle: Role of semantics in annotation, discovery, composition and orchestration. Invited Talk, WWW 2003 Workshop on E-Services and the Semantic Web, Budapest, Hungary, May 20.

Singh, M. P., & Huhns, M. N. (2005). *Service-oriented Computing: Semantics, Processes, and Agents*. Chichester: John Wiley & Sons, Ltd.

Sun, Z., & Finnie, G. (2004). *Intelligent Techniques in E-Commerce: A Case-based Reasoning Perspective*. Berlin, Heidelberg: Springer-Verlag.

Sun, Z., & Finnie, G. (2005). A unified logical model for CBR-based e-commerce systems. *International Journal of Intelligent Systems, 20*(1), 29–46. doi:10.1002/int.20052

Sun, Z., & Lau, S. K. (2007). Customer experience management in e-services. In J. Lu, D. Ruan, & G> Zhang (Eds.), *E-Service Intelligence: Methodologies*, Technologies and Applications (pp. 365-388). Berlin, Heidelberg: Springer-Verlag.

Sun Microsystems. (2003). Web services life cycle: Managing enterprise Web services, White Paper. Retrieved December 18, 2008, from http://www.sun.com/software

Talia, D. (2002). The open grid services architecture: Where the grid meets the web. *IEEE Internet Computing*, *6*(6), 67–71. doi:10.1109/MIC.2002.1067739

Tang, X. F., Jiang, C. J., Ding, Z. J., & Wang, C. (2007). A Petri net-based semantic web services automatic composition method. [in Chinese]. *Journal of Software*, *18*(12), 2991–3000.

Tsalgatidou, A., & Pilioura, T. (2002). An overview of standards and related technology in web services. *Distributed and Parallel Databases*, *12*, 135–162. doi:10.1023/A:1016599017660

Wang, M., Cheung, W. K., Liu, J., Xie, X., & Lou, Z. (2006). E-service/process composition through multi-agent constraint management. In *Intl Conf on Business Process Management* (BPM 2006), Vienna, Austria (LNCS 4102, pp. 274-289).

Wang, M., Liu, J., Wang, H., Cheung, W. K., & Xie, X. (2008). On-demand e-supply chain integration: A multi-agent constraint-based approach. *Expert Systems with Applications*, *34*(4), 2683–2692. doi:10.1016/j.eswa.2007.05.041

Waters, D. (2006). Demand chain effectiveness-supply chain efficiencies: A role for enterprise information management. *Journal of Enterprise Information Management*, *19*(3), 246–261. doi:10.1108/17410390610658441

Weiss, G. (Ed.). (1999). *Multiagent Systems: A modern approach to Distributed Artificial Intelligence*. Cambridge, MA: MIT Press.

Wiki (2009). Retrieved April 2, 2009, from http://en.wikipedia.org/wiki/Demand_(economics).

Wilkinson, N. (2005). *Managerial Economics: A Problem-Solving Approach*. Cambridge: Cambridge University Press.

Wu, C., & Chang, E. (2005). A conceptual architecture of distributed web services for service ecosystems. In S. Dascalu (Ed.), *18th International Conf on Computer Applications in Industry and Engineering* (CAINE 2005) (pp. 209-214).

Yao, Y., Yang, F., & Su, S. (2006). Flexible decision making in web services negotiation. In J. Euzenat & J. Domingue (Eds.), *AIMSA 2006* (LNAI 4183, pp. 108-117).

Zhang, L. J., & Jeckle, M. (2003). The next big thing: Web services composition. In M. Jeckle & L.J. Zhang (Eds.), *ICWS-Europe* (LNCS 2853, pp. 1-10).

ADDITIONAL READING

Bell, M. (2008). *Service-Oriented Modeling (SOA): Service Analysis, Design, and Architecture*. Chichester, UK: John Wiley and Sons Ltd.

Breu, R. Breu1, M., Hafner, M., & Nowak, A. (2005). Web service engineering advancing a new software engineering discipline. In D. Lowe & M. Gaedke (Eds.), *ICWE 2005* (LNCS 3579, pp. 8-18).

Brown, A., Johnston, S., & Kelly, K. (2002). Using Service-Oriented Architecture and Component-based Development to Build Web Services. Retrieved 10 July 2009, from http://www.ibm.com/developerworks/rational/library/510.html#download

Chen, L., & Tao, F. (2008). An intelligent recommender system for web resource discovery and selection. In Ruan, D., Hardeman, F., & van der Meer, K. (Eds.), *Intelligent Decision and Policy Making Support Systems* (pp. 113–140). Berlin, Heidelberg: Springer. doi:10.1007/978-3-540-78308-4_7

Cheng, M.-Y., Tsai, H.-C., & Chiu, Y.-H. (2009). Fuzzy case-based reasoning for coping with construction disputes. *Expert Systems with Applications*, *36*(2), 4106–4113. doi:10.1016/j.eswa.2008.03.025

Cheng, R., & Su, S. Yang, F., & Li, Y. (2006). Using case-based reasoning to support web service composition. In V.N. Alexandrov et al. (eds.), *ICCS 2006, Part IV* (LNCS 3994, pp. 87-94). Berlin Heidelberg: Springer-Verlag.

Chung, J. Y., Lin, K. J., & Mathieu, R. G. (2003). Web services computing: Advancing software interoperability. *Computer*, *36*(10), 35–37. doi:10.1109/MC.2003.1236469

Costantini, S. (2008). Agents and Web Services. Retrieved April 04, 2009, from http://www.cs.nmsu.edu/~epontell/backbone/aug08/content/Articles/sadri2/paper.pdf

Han, W., Xingdong Shi, X., & Chen, R. (2008). Process-context aware matchmaking for web service composition. *Journal of Network and Computer Applications*, *31*(4), 559–576. doi:10.1016/j.jnca.2007.11.008

Jeong, B., Cho, H., & Lee, C. (2009). On the functional quality of service (FQoS) to discover and compose interoperable web services. *Expert Systems with Applications*, *36*(3), 5411–5418. doi:10.1016/j.eswa.2008.06.087

Küster, U., König-Ries, B., Stern, M., & Klein, M. (2007). DIANE: An integrated approach to automated service discovery, matchmaking and composition. In *Intl Conf on World Wide Web* (WWW2007), May 8–12, 2007, Alberta, Canada (pp. 1033-1041).

Lau, R. Y. K. (2007). Towards a web services and intelligent agents-based negotiation system for B2B eCommerce. *Electronic Commerce Research and Applications*, *6*(3), 260–273. doi:10.1016/j.elerap.2006.06.007

Lawler, J. P. (2007). *Service-Oriented Architecture: SOA Strategy, Methodology, and Technology*. Hoboken: Taylor & Francis Ltd. doi:10.1201/9781420045017

Lu, J., Ruan, D., & Zhang, G. (Eds.). (2006). *E-Service Intelligence*. Berlin, Heidelberg: Springer Verlag.

Madhusudan, T., & Uttamsingh, N. (2006). A declarative approach to composing web services in dynamic environments. *Journal of Decision Support Systems*, *41*(2), 325–357. doi:10.1016/j.dss.2004.07.003

Park, C.-S., & Park, S. (2008). Efficient execution of composite Web services exchanging intensional data. *Journal of Information Science*, *178*(2), 317–339. doi:10.1016/j.ins.2007.08.021

Psaila, G., & Wagner, R. R. (Eds.). (2008). *E-Commerce and Web Technologies: 9th International Conference, EC-Web 2008*, Turin, Italy, September 3-4, 2008, Proceedings (LNCS). Berlin Heidelberg: Springer Verlag.

Richter, M. M. (2009). The search for knowledge, contexts, and case-based reasoning. *Engineering Applications of Artificial Intelligence*, *22*(1), 3–9. doi:10.1016/j.engappai.2008.04.021

Rust, R. T., & Kannan, P. K. (Eds.). (2002). *E-Service: New Directions in Theory and Practice*. Armonk, NY: M.E. Sharpe.

Sahai, A., & Graupner, S. (2005). *Web Services in the Enterprise: Concepts, Standards, Solutions, and Management (Network and Systems Management)*. New York: Springer.

Song, R., Korba, L., & Yee, G. (Eds.). (2007). *Trust in E-services: Technologies, Practices and Challenges*. Hershey, PA: IGI Global.

Talukder, A. K., & Yavagal, R. R. (2007). *Mobile Computing: Technology, Applications and Service Creation*. New York: McGraw-Hill Inc.

Tatemura, J., & Hsiung, W. P. (2006). Web service decomposition: Edge computing architecture for cache-friendly e-commerce applications. *Electronic Commerce Research and Applications*, *5*(1), 57–65. doi:10.1016/j.elerap.2005.08.001

Ting, I.-H., & Wu, H. J. (Eds.). (2009). *Web Mining Applications in E-commerce and E-services*. Berlin, Heidelberg: Springer Verlag. doi:10.1007/978-3-540-88081-3

Web Services Activity. (n.d.). Retrieved April 3, 2009, from http://www.w3.org/2002/ws/arch/.

Wooldridge, M. (2002). *An Introduction to Multiagent Systems*. Chichester, UK: John Wiley & Sons Ltd.

Zhao, J. L., & Cheng, H. K. (2005). Web services and process management: a union of convenience or a new area of research? *Journal of Decision Support Systems*, *40*(1), 1–8. doi:10.1016/j.dss.2004.04.002

KEY TERMS AND DEFINITIONS

Web Services: Generally speaking, web services are all the services available on the Web or the Internet from a business perspective. The first web services were information sources (Schneider, 2003). From a technological perspective, web services are Internet-based application components published using standard interface description languages and universally available via uniform communication protocols. This definition is currently used in the web service community.

Web Service Discovery: The process of searching, matching a machine-processable description of a Web service. It aims to find appropriate web services that meet the requirement of the customers.

Web Service Lifecycle (WSLC): It consists of the start of a web service, the end of web service and its evolutionary stages that transform the web service from the start to the end. Many activities are included in a WSLC such as web service discovery, composition, recommendation and management.

Demand Theory: A part of microeconomics. It examines demand curves, demand equations, demand analysis, demand chain, impact factors on demand, demand estimation and so on. Demand analysis assesses current and projected demand for e-commerce services amongst existing and potential customer segments.

Service Computing: A research field about service science, science intelligence, service technology, service engineering, service management, and service applications. It is the most general representation form of studying service in computing discipline. Service computing and service-oriented computing are used interchangeably.

Web Service Architecture: A Web service architecture is a high level description for web services, which is free of concrete implementation of a web service system.

A Web Service Demand Chain: A chain linking players related to web services, similar to supply chain in e-commerce. For example, the web service requestor demands service consultation from service broker, while the service broker demands web service representation and publication from service provider. The service provider demands the most powerful web service tools from the ICT developer to realize the web service representation and publication.

Multiagent Systems: An intelligent system consisting of many intelligent agents. An intelligent agent can be considered as a counterpart of a human agent in intelligent systems.

Intelligent System: A system that can imitate, automate some intelligent behaviors of human being. Expert systems and knowledge based systems are examples of intelligent systems. Currently intelligent systems is a discipline that studies the intelligent behaviors and their implementations as well as impacts on human society.

Section 2
Intelligent Technologies

Chapter 4
Dynamic Maintenance of Service Orchestrations

Manel Fredj
INRIA Paris-Rocquencourt, France

Apostolos Zarras
University of Ioannina, Greece

Nikolaos Georgantas
INRIA Paris-Rocquencourt, France

Valérie Issarny
INRIA Paris-Rocquencourt, France

ABSTRACT

Service-oriented architectures evolved rapidly as the solution to the latest requirements for loosely-coupled distributed computing. Into this broad context several approaches emerged towards the discovery and the systematic composition/orchestration of services. One of the next challenges in this field is the maintenance of service-oriented architectures towards accomplishing the ultimate goal of constructing eternal service-oriented systems out of loosely-coupled basic engineering elements. The particular problem we deal with in this paper is the dynamic maintenance of service orchestrations in the presence of unavailable services. Specifically, we focus on the dynamic substitution of stateful services that become unavailable during the execution of service orchestrations. As an answer to this problem, we propose the SIROCO middleware platform based on ontology which is further detailed along with an experimental evaluation of our first prototype. Our findings show that SIROCO provides the necessary means for achieving dynamic maintenance with a reasonable expense on the execution of service orchestrations.

INTRODUCTION

Service Oriented Architecture (SOA) is an architectural style that emerged recently as the answer to the latest requirements for loosely-coupled distributed computing (Cardoso & Sheth, 2006). Inline with the conventional distributed computing paradigm, a functionality is decomposed into distinct architectural elements, distributed over the network. Nevertheless, in SOA the basic architectural elements (i.e., services) are by

DOI: 10.4018/978-1-61520-819-7.ch004

themselves autonomous systems that have been developed independently from each other. Moreover, services evolve independently. A service may be deployed, or un-deployed at anytime. Its implementation, along with its interface may change without prior notification. Services are typically combined in a loosely-coupled manner by building service orchestrations. Basically, an orchestration is a workflow that consists of a set of activities which exchange data with a set of services. The orchestration incarnates the basic control and dataflow dependencies that govern the execution of these activities.

In the context of SOA, several research efforts grew with the main focus being on the discovery and the systematic composition/orchestration of services, e.g., (Ben Mokhtar *et al.*, 2006; Berardi *et al.*, 2005; Yang & Papazoglou, 2004). One of the next challenges in this field is the maintenance of service orchestrations towards accomplishing the ultimate goal of constructing eternal service-oriented systems out of loosely-coupled basic architectural elements (Fredj *et al.*, 2008). To this end, in this chapter we focus on *the dynamic maintenance of a set of executing orchestrations upon the unavailability of a service that is required for the execution of these orchestrations*. To deal with this problem, we propose an approach that enables the dynamic substitution of the unavailable service with an available one. The proposed approach is aimed at W3C Web services (W3Ca, 2004); we assume that services exchange information with the rest of the world within SOAP messages; service interfaces are specified in SA-WSDL (W3Cb, 2007); finally, service orchestrations are specified in terms of BPEL (IBM, 2002). Dealing with the dynamic substitution of stateless services is more or less straightforward. Thus, we concentrate on the worst case that involves the dynamic substitution of stateful services. According to the standard WS-Resource Framework (OASIS, 2004), we assume that service state descriptions may be provided, along with service interface descriptions.

Several approaches that deal with the unavailability of services, e.g., (Salatge & Fabre, 2007), rely on the construction of fault tolerant service groups out of unreliable services. The formulation of fault-tolerant groups of services as proposed in the state of the art seems difficult to apply when considering that the constituent services may be offered by competitive organizations or businesses. In this realistic scenario no independent business (e.g., a hotel) will accept to register its online service as a passive backup member of a group of services. Similarly, no independent business will accept to register its online service in a group that realizes active replication, while knowing that this will involve devoting precious resources to the group without any actual benefit (many reservations made by the same customer to each of the active replicas, while only one of them will be validated at the end of the protocol that realizes the reservation process through the active replication group). Similarly, in the field of dynamic reconfiguration of conventional distributed systems, several approaches tackled the issue of substituting an entity for another prefabricated backup entity (Kramer & Magee, 1990; Goudarzi & Kramer, 1996; Hauptmann & Wasel, 1996; Minsky *et al.*, 1996; Warren & Sommerville, 1996; Bidan *et al.*, 1998; Blair *et al.*, 2000; Poladian *et al.*, 2004). As previously discussed, the problem of service substitution is far more complex. In SOA, we can assume the possible existence of several semantically compatible services capable of performing the same or similar tasks. However, each one of them constantly serves requests and can not be considered as a passive backup for other services.

Therefore, the service substitution process that we are after consists of (1) discovering candidate substitute services out of a set of semantically compatible services that can be used in place of a service, which becomes unavailable and, (2) trying to identify one amongst these candidates that can be used as an actual substitute; whenever possible the selected substitute service must be such that its current state can be synchronized with the state of the unavailable service. Based on the above, our contribution is SIROCO, a middleware platform that enables the dynamic maintenance of service orchestrations upon the unavailability of services used in these orchestrations.

The rest of this chapter is structured as follows. Section 2 provides the necessary background on dynamic substitution of basic engineering elements in conventional distributed systems and discusses work related to service substitution in particular. Section 3 discusses in detail our approach to the problem of dynamic service substitution in SOA. Section 4 presents an evaluation of our first prototype. Finally, Section 5 provides our conclusions and future research issues.

BACKGROUND & RELATED WORK

Background

To provide a background on the dynamic substitution of basic engineering elements in conventional distributed systems, we rely on a generic reconfiguration cycle, which provides an abstract descriptive view of reconfiguration approaches that have been proposed in the past (the interested reader may refer to (Zarras *et al.*, 2006) for a more detailed survey).

Conceptually, the basic entities involved in the reconfiguration cycle are the *Reconfigurable System (RS)*, its *Context* or *Environment (CE)*, and the *Reconfiguration Management System (RM)*. CE consists of prefabricated passive functional entities that can be used for the reconfiguration of RS. RM provides all the functionalities that are necessary for the reconfiguration of RS. Conventional approaches assume that RS is described at an abstract level in terms of components and connectors. Based on that, they deal with the reconfiguration of RS in terms of adding, removing and substituting components (Kramer & Magee, 1990; Goudarzi & Kramer, 1996; Minsky *et al.*,

1996; Bidan *et al.*, 1998; Kramer & Magee, 1985; Hofmeister & Purtilo, 1993), and connectors (Blair *et al.*, 2000; Kon *et al.*; 2002).

The reconfiguration cycle typically comprises a sequence of phases that take place during the lifetime of RS. These phases support the reconfiguration of RS whenever needed. In Phase 1, RS executes normally, while RM monitors RS. The monitoring tasks typically include checkpointing the state of RS as this state changes. Phase 2 takes place whenever a cause for reconfiguration emerges. RM detects the emerging cause for reconfiguration after having observed current monitoring data and compared it with execution constraints. In Phase 3, RM prepares RS for reconfiguration. This preparation concerns components affected by the intended reconfiguration and may take several forms. For example, request blocking (Kramer & Magee, 1990; Goudarzi & Kramer, 1996; Bidan *et al.*, 1998), request redirection (Minsky *et al.*, 1996) or request queuing may be enforced on components that interact with a component that must be substituted. In Phase 4, RM determines the contribution of CE to the new configuration. In Phase 5, RM adapts RS to the new configuration. In this phase, the substitution of components or connectors further implies transferring the state of the elements used in the current configuration to their substitute elements (Warren & Sommerville, 1996; Blair *et al.*, 2000). Finally, in Phase 6, RM carries out the final reconfiguration actions, which typically comprise producing a new configuration description and putting RS back to normal execution (Phase 1)).

Related Work

Concerning the particular problem of service substitution, there have been few interesting approaches, which we discuss in the remainder of this section. These approaches mainly focus on enabling the substitution of services, while introducing minimum changes in the clients that use these services, i.e. the service orchestrations in our particular system model.

In (Melloul & Fox, 2004) the authors propose a framework that allows defining abstractions, which are called service composition patterns. A composition pattern can be refined into various alternative concrete service compositions. Consequently, an orchestration developed with respect to the composition pattern can exploit these alternatives without any changes. A similar approach that involves abstractions is proposed in (Yang & Papazoglou, 2004).

Moreover, in (Taher *et al.*, 2006) another approach is proposed, which is based on the definition of abstractions, named abstract services. An abstract service represents a set of alternative concrete services that offer the same functionality, via different interfaces. Technically, the abstract service interface can be mapped into the interfaces of the alternative concrete services. Then, a service orchestration that has been built based on the abstract service interface may use, any of the alternative concrete services, without changes in the orchestration. Going one step further, in (Athanasopoulos *et al.*, 2009) we discuss the need for a systematic process that mines service abstractions out of existing services that offer similar functionality via different interfaces.

In the same spirit, (Ponnekanti & Fox, 2004) discusses the issue of substituting a target service with another concrete service, in the particular case where the interfaces of both services are derived from the same popular, or standardized interface. To deal with such substitution scenarios, various types of incompatibilities between the services' interfaces (structural, value, encoding, semantic), are identified and handled in the proposed approach. Moreover, corresponding resolution options are proposed for structural and value incompatibilities. Based on these resolution options an adapter is generated. The adapter provides the interface of the target service, which is implemented based on the functionality that is provided by the interface of the substitute service.

Then, the adapter can be accessed by a service orchestration using the original target interface to access the functionality of the substitute service without any changes in the orchestration. The assumption that the interfaces of the current and the substitute services are derived from the same popular or, standardized interface is taken into account in (Ponnekanti, 2003). In this case, the proposed framework exploits a service repository that manages information about available services and adapters that can be used to map the functionality of a service to other services that offer the same functionality via different interfaces. Based on the service repository, a target service can be replaced by a substitute service as long as the repository contains a corresponding adapter. The development of adapters for pairs of services that may get involved in a substitution scenario is assigned to the corresponding service providers.

Finally, the framework proposed in (Motahari Nezhad *et al.*, 2007) provides mechanisms that aim at detecting both structural and protocol incompatibilities for pairs of services that can be involved in a substitution scenario.

Although all of the aforementioned approaches are valuable towards enabling service substitution, the main issue that still remains open is dealing with the substitution in the particular case of stateful services that become unavailable during the execution of service orchestrations. This issue is the main focus of the SIROCO approach and consequently constitutes the distinctive feature of SIROCO, compared to the state of the art in service substitution.

DYNAMIC SERVICE SUBSTITUTION IN SIROCO

SIROCO offers a *Reconfiguration Manager*, RM (Figure 1), that provides the necessary functionality for maintaining the execution of service orchestrations in the presence of unavailable services. Without loss of generality, we assume that RM is

Figure 1. Overview of SIROCO

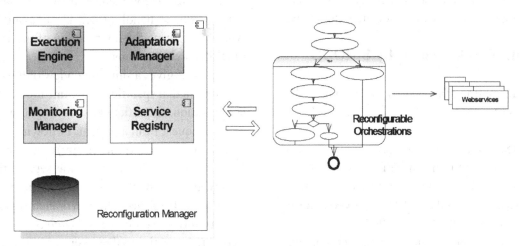

a centralized entity. However, the proposed approach can be extended in a quite straightforward way towards a coordinated set of RMs. The basic constituents of the SIROCO RM are:

- A BPEL *execution-engine* that carries out the execution of service orchestrations that are provided to SIROCO by users. In particular, a user may provide as input to SIROCO a BPEL orchestration description and require its instantiation, or even require the instantiation of an orchestration that is already available through SIROCO (i.e., it has been previously registered to SIROCO possibly by a different user).
- A *service-registry* that manages information concerning Web services that can be used for the execution of service orchestrations registered to SIROCO.
- A *monitoring-manager* that inspects the set of orchestrations that are executing through the SIROCO execution-engine.
- An *adaptation-manager* that dynamically reconfigures the orchestrations when necessary.

Therefore, from the point of view of SIROCO the role of RS is played by a set of orchestrations

that are concurrently executing through the SIROCO execution-engine. The role of CE is played by Web services that have been registered to the SIROCO service-registry. These services have been independently developed and deployed in certain sites. Taking an example, consider that the SIROCO RM has been provided with an orchestration description that offers online medical help to patients. This orchestration may be instantiated multiple times by the SIROCO execution-engine for different patients, doctors and pharmacies. Initially, the orchestration receives from the patient his personal details and symptoms. Following, it forwards the patient's symptoms to an associated doctor. At the same time, the patient's social security record is updated with a new tuple that contains information about the patient's e-visit to the associated doctor; this information is inserted in the database of the national social security service. The orchestration waits for the reception of the doctor's prescription which is sent back to the patient. Depending on its contents, the prescription is further forwarded to an associated pharmacy along with the patient's details. The Web services involved in this orchestration are: the one used to communicate with the patient, the one that allows online interaction with the associated doctor's office, the national social security service and the service offered by the associated pharmacy.

Information Managed by SIROCO

The information managed by the SIROCO RM consists of:

- Descriptions of service orchestrations, specified in terms of BPEL (IBM,2002).
- Descriptions of the Web services that have been registered to SIROCO, given in terms of SA-WSDL (W3Cb, 2007).
- Descriptions of the state that is managed by the Web services that have been registered to SIROCO, specified in terms of *WS-ResourceProperties* documents (OASIS, 2004). Providing state descriptions for the services is not mandatory in SIROCO. Nevertheless, SIROCO takes advantage of this information, if available, towards dealing with dynamic service substitution.

Specifying Service Orchestrations

The specification of service orchestrations in SI-ROCO is standardized and quite straightforward. Briefly, a BPEL (IBM, 2002) orchestration specifies a set of activities, which may be either simple or structured. Simple activities may involve the reception of a message, the invocation of a service operation, or the reply to a message. Structured activities prescribe control flow dependencies for a set of constituent activities (sequential execution, concurrent execution, conditional execution, etc.). A BPEL specification further comprises the definition of variables which serve as placeholders for the data exchanged with the services during the execution of the BPEL activities. Finally, BPEL supports the specification of fault handling and compensation activities. Such application-specific activities, introduced by the authors of a BPEL orchestration, may also serve for handling the unavailability of a service. In general, we see

these facilities as complementary to our approach, which aims at handling service unavailability without requiring the intervention of the authors of BPEL orchestrations.

Figure 2, gives a simplified view of the BPEL description that specifies the online medical help conversation. In particular, a *receive activity* accepts a request from a patient. Following, a *flow activity* (i.e., a concurrent activity) is used towards interacting concurrently with the service that is deployed at the doctor's office and the national social security service. The first branch of the flow activity further comprises a *switch activity* (i.e., a conditional activity) that interacts, if necessary, with the service that is deployed in the pharmacy.

Specifying Service Descriptions

Typically, Web service descriptions are specified using WSDL. Nevertheless, in SIROCO we employ a standard extension of this notation, which allows us to add semantic annotations to standard WSDL descriptions. The purpose of adding semantic annotations to service descriptions is twofold:

- Service interfaces (i.e., PortTypes) are annotated with semantic concepts defined in an OWL ontology offered by SIROCO to enable the classification of services that offer semantically compatible functionality in corresponding semantic categories. The OWL ontology that we assume relies on a well-known thesaurus of concepts, called WordNet (WordNet, 2006).
- Operations offered by a service interface are annotated with either the UpdateState, or the QueryState OWL concept (Figure 3) in order to distinguish between operations that update the state of the service and operations that simply query the state of the service. As explained later, this distinction serves for enriching a BPEL orchestration with activities that allow the SIROCO monitoring-manager to checkpoint (if

Figure 2. The online medical help BPEL orchestration

```
<process name = "OnlineMedicalHelp">
<partnerLinks>
<partnerLink name="patient" partnerLinkType="PatientPT"/>
<partnerLink name="doctor" partnerLinkType="GeneralPractitionerPT"/>
<partnerLink name="social_security" partnerLinkType="SocialSecurityPT"/>
<partnerLink name="pharmacy" partnerLinkType="PharmacyPT"/>
</partnerLinks>
<variables>
----------------------------------------..
</variables>
<sequence>
  <receive partnerLink="patient" portType="PatientPT"
      operation="receiveSymptoms" variable="patientRequest">
  <invoke partnerLink="doctor" portType="GeneralPractitionerPT"
    operation="getCoordinates" outputVariable="doctorCoordinates">
  <assign>................</assign>
<flow>
  <invoke partnerLink="social_security" portType="SocialSecurityPT"
      operation="updatePatientRecord" inputVariable="socialSecurityRequest">
  <sequence>
  <invoke partnerLink="doctor" portType="GeneralPractitionerPT"
    operation="enqueueRequest" inputVariable="doctorRequest">
  <receive partnerLink="doctor" portType="GeneralPractitionerPT"
    operation="getPrescription" variable="doctorReply">
  <assign>.............</assign>
  <reply partnerLink="patient" portType="PatientPT"
    operation="receiveSymptoms" inputVariable="patientReply">
  <switch>
  <case condition= ....>
    <assign>.......................</assign>
  <invoke partnerLink="pharmacy" portType="PharmacyPT"
    operation="issueRequest" inputVariable="pharmacyRequest">
  </case>
  <otherwise>
    <empty>
  </otherwise>
  </sequence>
  </flow>
  </sequence>
  </process>
```

**Check pointing activity
insertion point**

possible) the state of a service before the execution of activities that invoke operations, which change the state of the service. Checkpointing is possible if the description of the service is further associated with a description of the service state.

The semantic annotation of service descriptions is a responsibility of the service providers who should further collaborate with the SIROCO administrator who is in charge of validating the service descriptions and extending the SIROCO

OWL ontology, whenever necessary. Regarding our scenario, Figure 4 gives a simplified (UML-like) view of the interface (i.e., the GeneralPractitionerPT port type) that is offered by a service, which provides access to a doctor's office. The interface is annotated with a reference to the GeneralPractitioner OWL concept (Figure 5). Each operation of the GeneralPractitionerPT interface is annotated with a reference to the UpdateState or the QueryState OWL concepts (Figure 3). The *enqueueRequest()* operation, for instance, is characterized with the UpdateState concept because it

Figure 3. Ontology concepts used for distinguishing SA-WSDL operations with respect to their impact on the service state

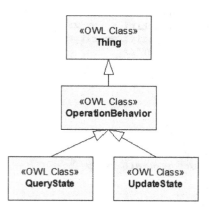

inserts a request from a patient in a waiting queue managed by the service.

Specifying Service State Descriptions

According to the WS-ResourceProperties standard, a service state description defines an XML complex type that consists of one or more state properties. Still according to the standard, the values of each property can be queried or updated by sending standardized SOAP messages towards the service; the service is obliged to provide corresponding functionality that handles these messages. The messages are characterized by the names of the properties involved.

In SIROCO, we require that the properties that constitute a service state description are defined with respect to the SIROCO OWL ontology. Each property corresponds to a SIROCO OWL concept, which is further associated with an XML data type (simple or complex). The XML elements that constitute the property are also defined with respect to the SIROCO OWL ontology. If a property p is defined as a subclass of another property q one of the following conditions must hold for their associated datatypes, $type_p$, $type_q$:

- $type_p$ is equal to $type_q$.

Figure 4. Semantically annotated WSDL description of the GeneralPractitionerPT interface

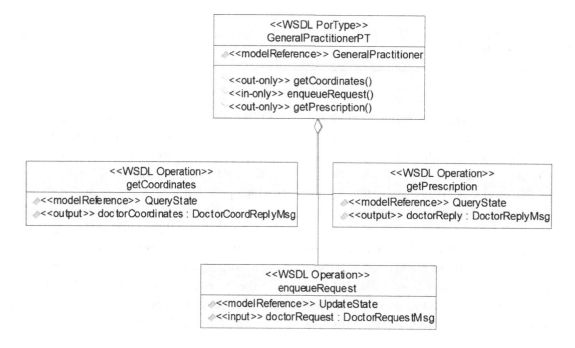

Figure 5. Ontology concepts used for the semantic characterization of medical services

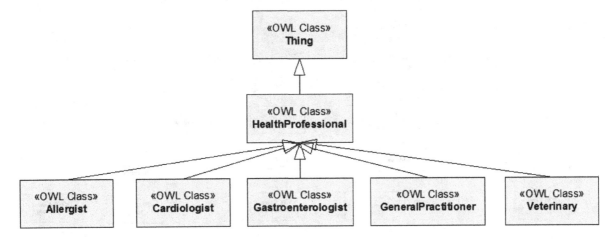

- $type_p$ is derived from $type_q$ by XML restriction (i.e., the values of $type_p$ are a subset of the values of $type_q$).

- $type_p$ is derived from $type_q$ by XML extension (i.e., both $type_p$ and $type_q$ are XML complex types, and $type_p$ inherits the XML elements of $type_q$ and further defines additional XML elements).

Providing service state descriptions is a collaborative task that involves the service providers and the SIROCO administrator who is in charge of validating the state descriptions and possibly extending the SIROCO OWL ontology, if needed.

In our scenario, the state description of a service that provides the GeneralPractitionerPT interface is given in Figure 6. Figure 7, gives part of the SIROCO OWL ontology that includes the concepts involved in the state description of

Figure 6. State description of a service that provides the GeneralPractitionerPT interface

```
<element name = "Patient">
   <complexType>
     <sequence>
     <element name="Name" type = "string" minOccurs = "1" maxOccurs = "1"/>
     <element name="Address" type = "string" minOccurs = "1" maxOccurs = "1"/>
     <element name="PhoneNumber" type = "string" minOccurs = "1" maxOccurs = "1"/>
     <element name="Email" type = "string" minOccurs = "0" maxOccurs = "1"/>
     <element name="Symptoms" type = "string" minOccurs = "1" maxOccurs = "1"/>
     </sequence>
   </complexType>
</element>

<element name="GeneralPractitionerQueue">
   <complexType>
     <sequence>
     <element ref="Patient" minOccurs = 0 maxOccurs = "unBounded"/>
     </sequence>
   </complexType>
</element>
```

Figure 7. Ontology concepts used for defining the state of medical services

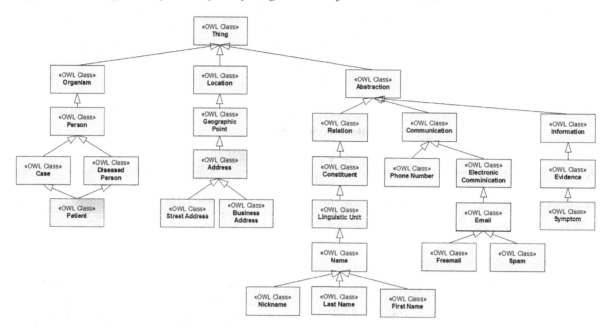

the service. The description models the waiting queue managed by the service, i.e., the state is a complex XML type that consists of zero or more Patient properties; each property further consists of 5 elements corresponding to the Name, Address, Phone Number, Email and Symptoms of a patient; all 5 elements are of the same XML type (i.e., XML string).

Service Substitution Cycle

Phase 1: Normal RS Execution

During this phase, the SIROCO BPEL execution-engine is in charge of the concurrent execution of a set of orchestrations that are instantiated according to users' requests. Specifically, at any time a user may provide as input to the BPEL execution-engine a new orchestration description along with *abstract* descriptions of the services required for the execution of this orchestration (we use the term abstract to refer to SA-WSDL descriptions that do not contain any binding information). Based on this information a number

of preparatory steps are performed before instantiating the new orchestration.

First, the SIROCO service-registry is searched for services that can be used for the execution of the orchestration. The service-registry maintains service catalogs. Each catalog corresponds to a different semantic category of services and therefore it is characterized by an OWL semantic concept such as the ones given in Figure 5. Each service catalog is progressively populated (during the lifetime of RS) with *concrete* SA-WSDL descriptions of services (we use the term concrete to refer to SA-WSDL descriptions that contain binding information) that are registered to the service-registry. Hence, given the semantic concept that characterizes the abstract SA-WSDL description of a service that is required for the execution of the new orchestration, the corresponding service-registry catalog is located. The catalog is then searched for a concrete service description whose WSDL interface syntactically matches the WSDL interface that is specified in the abstract service description. If multiple concrete services are discovered in this step, one of them is randomly selected.

In our scenario, the execution of the online medical help orchestration (Figure 2) amounts to locating a service-registry catalog, annotated with the GeneralPractitioner (Figure 5) semantic concept. Following, the catalog is searched for a concrete service description that specifies an interface that syntactically matches the GeneralPractitionerPT interface, described in Figure 4. The service discovery step is followed by the enrichment of the orchestration description with checkpointing activities. In particular, a concrete service description --resulting from the previous step-- may be associated with a service state description. Moreover, every operation of the interface that is offered by the discovered concrete service is characterized by a semantic annotation (Figure 3) that specifies whether or not the operation changes the state of the service. Based on this information, the BPEL description of the new orchestration is searched for activities that invoke operations which change the state of the service. For every such activity a, a checkpointing activity that precedes a is added in the orchestration. As prescribed by the WS-ResourceProperties standard, the checkpointing activity (1) constructs a standardized message that queries the values of the properties that are specified in the service state description, (2) sends the message towards the service, and (3) waits for the reception of a corresponding reply message that contains the current values of the properties that constitute the state of the service. The state data are enriched with identifiers that characterize the orchestration and the activity a. Finally, the state data are forwarded to the SIROCO monitoring-manager, which stores them persistently.

In our scenario, the orchestration description of Figure 2 must be enriched with checkpointing activities. Such an activity must be added, for instance, before the activity that invokes the *enqueueRequest()* operation on the service that offers the GeneralPractitionerPT interface (highlighted

in Figure 2). The message that queries the contents of the waiting queue managed by the service (i.e., the list of the Patient properties specified in the WS-ResourceProperties document of the service (Figure 6)) is given in Figure 8 (a). An example of a response message that contains the service state data is given in Figure 8 (b).

The preparation for the execution of the enriched orchestration ends by parsing the orchestration description towards the construction of (1) an abstract control-flow dependency graph (CDG) (e.g., Figure 9) and (2) an abstract dataflow dependency graph (DDG) (e.g. Figure 10), which shall serve for the dynamic maintenance of the orchestration. The nodes in both graphs are the basic BPEL activities of the orchestration. Typically, in the control-flow graph, a dependency from an activity a to an activity b specifies that the execution of a precedes the execution of b. In the dataflow graph, a dependency from an activity a to an activity b specifies that the output produced by a as a result of interacting with a service is utilized by b as an input to the same or another service. The CDG and DDG are given as input to the adaptation-manager. Finally, the BPEL execution-engine begins the execution of the enriched orchestration.

Phase 2: A Cause for Dynamic Substitution Occurs

This phase takes place upon the occurrence of a cause for dynamic service substitution. While the BPEL execution-engine of SIROCO executes orchestrations, interaction with the involved Web services may result into an exception which serves as a notification that a service is not available. If such an exception is caught, the execution-engine notifies the SIROCO adaptation-manager. Technically, in our prototype interactions with Web services are realized through the standard JAXRPC mechanism. Therefore, the execution-engine checks for standard JAXRPC exceptions

Figure 8. Checkpointing messages for a service that provides the GeneralPractitionerPT interface; the messages are generated with respect to the state description of Figure 6

Figure 9. CDG for the online medical help scenario

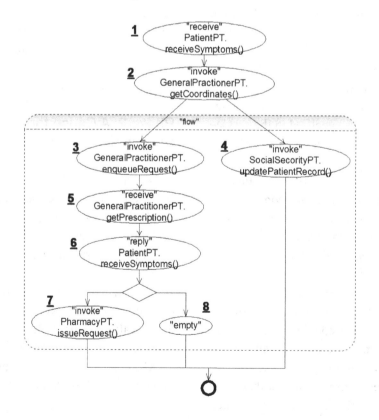

Figure 10. DDG for the online medical help scenario

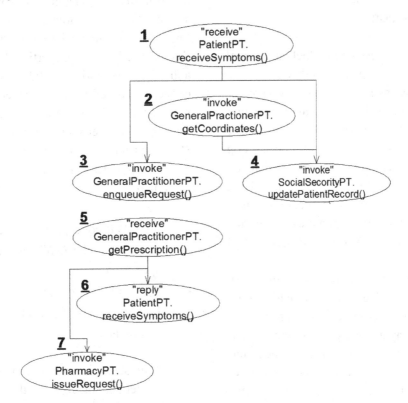

(e.g., RemoteException) that may be thrown while an activity attempts to interact with a Web service.

In our scenario, assume the following failure scenario which shall be used in the remainder of this section: the online medical help orchestration has been instantiated twice for different patients that contact the same doctor; a RemoteException exception is caught by the execution-engine; the exception refers to the first orchestration and specifically it is caught during the execution of the activity that invokes the *getPrescription()* operation on the GeneralPractitionerPT service (i.e., activity 5 in Figure 9); as a result the execution-engine notifies the adaptation-manager about the unavailability of this service.

Phase 3: Preparing the Substitution

This phase begins when the SIROCO adaptation-manager is notified about the occurrence of an exception in the execution of an orchestration. The SIROCO adaptation-manager checks the set of executing orchestrations for other affected orchestrations. The set of affected orchestrations consists of the orchestration that failed to interact with the service and all other executing orchestrations that interact with the unavailable service. The execution of certain of the affected orchestrations may be in points where they have already interacted with the unavailable service, while the execution of certain others may be in points where the first interaction with the unavailable service will take place in the activities that follow. In both cases, the adaptation-manager blocks the execution of the affected orchestrations to prevent the occurrence of further exceptions.

In our example, the set of affected orchestrations includes both of the instantiated online medical help orchestrations.

Phase 4: Planning the Substitution Actions

With the affected orchestrations blocked, the goal of this phase is to discover candidate substitute services that may take the place of the unavailable service. To this end, the adaptation-manager contacts the service-registry. As in Phase 1, the service-registry looks for the service catalog that contains descriptions of services that are semantically compatible with the unavailable service. Technically, this is the catalog that is characterized by the OWL semantic concept that also characterizes the SA-WSDL description of the unavailable service.

In our scenario, for instance, the registry locates the service catalog that is characterized by the GeneralPractitioner concept (Figure 4). The service catalog may include several concrete SA-WSDL descriptions of services that provide different interfaces. The service catalog is searched for services whose interface syntactically matches the interface of the unavailable service. In particular, the GeneralPractitioner catalog is searched for concrete SA-WSDL descriptions of services that provide the GeneralPractitionerPT interface. The search results are divided in two sets. The first set, *StateCompatibleServices*, contains descriptions of services that are associated with service state descriptions (i.e., WS-ResourceProperties documents) which are semantically compatible with the service state description of the unavailable service. The second set, *StateIncompatibleServices*, contains all other descriptions of services with matching interfaces. Obviously, if the unavailable service is not accompanied with a service state description, *StateCompatibleServices* = Ø.

To avoid the extra overhead of checking for state compatibility between service state descriptions at the time when there is a need to substitute an unavailable service, state compatibility relations are established as the SIROCO service-registry is progressively populated with service descriptions. The semantic compatibility of two service state descriptions st, st' is defined according to the following intuition. As discussed in Subsection 3.1, the properties that constitute st and st' correspond to SIROCO OWL ontology concepts. Therefore, we consider that st is compatible with st' if there exists a *one-to-one* and *onto* mapping between the properties of st and st'. According to this mapping every property $p_{st} \in st$ should be mapped to a property $p_{st'} \in st'$ such that:

- the OWL concept that corresponds to p_{st} is equal to the OWL concept that corresponds to $p_{st'}$, or,
- the OWL concept that corresponds to p_{st} is a subclass of the OWL concept that corresponds to $p_{st'}$.

In our scenario, suppose that the General-Practitioner catalog contains the description of a candidate substitute service, which is associated with the state description that is given in Figure 11. As detailed in Figure 12, the state description of the candidate substitute service (Figure 11) is semantically compatible with the state description of the unavailable service (Figure 6). Specifically, Patient is an OWL subclass of Case (Figure 7). Figure 12 further details how the elements that constitute Patient are recursively mapped into the elements that constitute the Case property; Address is an OWL subclass of Location, Symptoms is an OWL subclass of Evidence, etc.

The two state compatibility constraints that we use guarantee that state data that have been obtained by checkpointing the unavailable service can be transformed into state data that can be handled by a candidate substitute service. As explained in Subsection 3.1, every OWL concept is associated with a corresponding XML data type. Therefore, if a property $p_{st} \in st$ is mapped into a property $p_{st'} \in st'$ such that the first of the

Figure 11. State description of a candidate substitute service that provides the GeneralPractitionerPT interface

```
<element name = "Case">
   <complexType>
     <sequence>
     <element name="Name" type = "string" minOccurs = "1" maxOccurs = "1"/>
     <element name="Location" type = "string" minOccurs = "1" maxOccurs = "1"/>
     <element name="PhoneNumber" type = "string" minOccurs = "1" maxOccurs = "1"/>
     <element name="Email" type = "string" minOccurs = "0" maxOccurs = "1"/>
     <element name="Evidence" type = "string" minOccurs = "1" maxOccurs = "1"/>
     </sequence>
   </complexType>
</element>

<element name="GeneralistQueue">
   <complexType>
     <sequence>
     <element ref="Case" minOccurs = 0 maxOccurs = "unBounded"/>
     </sequence>
   </complexType>
</element>
```

compatibility constraints hold, then the data type of p_{st} is equal to the data type of $p_{st'}$. In this case, the values of p_{st} can be directly used as values of $p_{st'}$. On the other hand, if a property p_{st} is mapped into a property $p_{st'}$ such that the second of the compatibility constraints hold, then the data type of p_{st} may be equal to the data type of $p_{st'}$, or it may be derived by the data type of $p_{st'}$ by XML restriction, or by XML extension (Subsection 3.1). In the former case (XML restriction), the values of p_{st} can be directly used as values of $p_{st'}$. In the latter case (XML extension), the values of p_{st} contain more XML elements than required for $p_{st'}$. Hence, the values of p_{st} can be transformed into values of $p_{st'}$ simply by removing the extra XML elements.

Nevertheless, the ability to transform state data does not guarantee that the substitution of the unavailable service with a candidate substitute service that belongs in *StateCompatibleServices* shall be successful. This issue is further discussed in the following subsection.

Phase 5: Adapting the Current Configuration

Given the two sets of candidate substitute services (i.e. the *StateCompatibleServices* and the *StateIncompatibleServices* sets) that resulted from the previous phase, the adaptation-manager tries to select a service out of these sets to actually substitute the unavailable service. First, the adaptation-manager queries the monitoring-manager for the latest state data obtained from the unavailable service.

Following, the adaptation-manager iterates over the *StateCompatibleServices* set. For each candidate substitute service $s \in StateCompatibleServices$, the SIROCO adaptation-manager tries to synchronize the current state of s with the state data of the unavailable service. As discussed in the previous subsection, the synchronization may involve transforming the state data of the unavailable service into state data that can be handled by s, with respect to the semantic mapping between the state descriptions of the services.

Regarding our scenario, assume that the adaptation-manager selects from the *StateCompatibleServices* set the service s that is associated

Figure 12. Semantic state compatibility mapping for the state descriptions of Figures 6 and 11

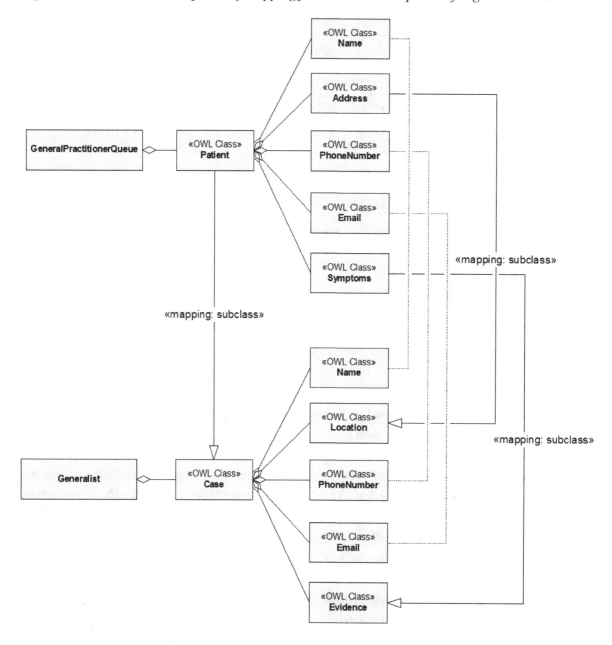

with the state description of Figure 11. The XML data types of the elements that constitute the state property of *s* (Figure 11) are equal to the data types of the elements that constitute the state property of the unavailable service (Figure 6). Therefore, the transformation of state data (Figure 8 (b)) that have been obtained from the unavailable service is

quite simple. According to the semantic mapping of Figure 12, the transformation amounts to simply renaming certain XML tags (e.g., the Patient property should be renamed to Case, the Address element should be renamed to Location, etc.).

Then, the adaptation-manager tries to update the properties that characterize the state of *s*

Figure 13. State synchronization message for the candidate substitute service; the message is generated with respect to (1) the state descriptions of the unavailable and the candidate substitute services (Figures 6, 11) and, (2) the semantic mapping between these state descriptions (Figure 12)

```
<SetResourceProperties>
 <Insert>
  <Case>
   <Name> ... </Name>
   <Location> ... </Location>
   <PhoneNumber> ... </PhoneNumber>
   <Email> ... </Email>
   <Evidence> ... </Evidence>
  </Case>
  <Case>
   <Name> ... </Name>
   <Location> ... </Location>
   <PhoneNumber> ... </PhoneNumber>
   <Email> ... </Email>
   <Evidence> ... </Evidence>
  </Case>
  ...............................................................
 </Insert>
</SetResourceProperties>
```

with respect to the transformed state data of the unavailable service. According to the WS-ResourceProperties standard, this step involves sending to *s* a standardized SetResourceProperties message. In our scenario, the synchronization between the states of the two services involves inserting the contents of the waiting queue of the unavailable service, into the waiting queue of the substitute service by sending the message that is given in Figure 13.

The result of the synchronization may be successful or not. In the latter case, *s* shall respond to the adaption-manager with a standardized fault message and the adaptation-manager shall proceed with another service from the *StateCompatibleServices* set. In our scenario, for instance, the waiting queue of the candidate substitute service may be full. In this case, the SetResourceProperties message shall fail and the next candidate will be examined by the adaptation-manager. If the state synchronization fails for all candidate services that belong to the *StateCompatibleServices*, the SIROCO adaptation-manager randomly se-

lects a service from the *StateIncompatibleServices* set.

Phase 6: Completing the Execution

The goal of this phase is to put the affected orchestrations back to normal execution. This task highly depends on the outcome of the previous phase.

In particular, if the adaptation-manager discovers a service substitute in the *StateCompatibleServices* set, the execution of all the affected orchestrations is resumed from the points where they were stopped (i.e., from the activities that were blocked or failed). In our example, we assumed 2 instances of the online medical help orchestration, affected by the unavailability of the GeneralPractitionerPT service. The execution of the first orchestration failed during activity 5 (Figure 9, 10), while the execution of the second one was blocked right before contacting the GeneralPractitionerPT service for the first time (i.e., before activity 2). Therefore, in this case the first orchestration is resumed from activity 5, while the second one is resumed from activity 2.

One the other hand, if the adaptation-manager discovers a service substitute in the *StateIncompatibleServices* set, the affected orchestrations are rolled-back to a point that precedes the first interaction with the unavailable service. Identifying this point involves using the CDG and the DDG of the affected orchestrations, while further taking into account the checkpointing activities that relate to the rest of the services used in these orchestrations. In our example, the first interaction with the unavailable service was during activity 2. Hence, the execution of both orchestrations is rolled-back to activity 2.

EVALUATION

To evaluate the basic concepts of SIROCO we developed a first prototype and performed a number of experiments. The prototype and all our experiments were based on the AXIS SOAP engine and the Apache Tomcat application server. The SIROCO BPEL engine currently does not support full-featured BPEL orchestrations (e.g., handlers, pick activities, wait activities are not supported).

The main benefit from using SIROCO for the development of service orchestrations is the ability to dynamically maintain them to confront the unavailability of the services involved. On the other hand, the price to pay for this ability is the need for enriching the orchestrations with additional checkpointing activities, which introduce an overhead in the execution of the orchestrations. Hereafter, we use the term enhanced-orchestration to refer to an orchestration enriched with checkpointing activities. Respectively, we use the term original-orchestration to refer to an orchestration that does not include checkpointing activities.

Based on the previous remarks we performed two sets of experiments. In the first set, we compared the execution time of enhanced-orchestrations against the execution time of the original-orchestration in various scenarios of normal execution (i.e., there were no unavailable services during the orchestrations execution). In the second set of experiments, we measured the execution time of enhanced-orchestrations in various failure scenarios that can not be handled by the original-orchestrations.

In both sets of experiments, we used BPEL orchestrations that combine 5 Web services ($WS_1, WS_2, ..., WS_5$), each one of which offered 10 operations. The control flow of the orchestrations was derived from a combination of two well-known work-flow patterns (Sequence and Parallel-Split (Van Der Aalst *et al.*, 2003)). Specifically, each orchestration consists of a flow activity that comprises 5 sequence activities ($SQ_1, SQ_2, ..., SQ_5$) which execute concurrently. Each sequence SQ_i consists of 10 basic activities ($A_{SQ_{i1}}, A_{SQ_{i2}}, ..., A_{SQ_{i10}}$) which invoke the operations of WS_i . The dataflow dependencies between the activities were set according to the following pattern: the output messages of the service operations invoked in activities $A_{SQ_{ij}, i \in \{1,2\}, j \in \{1..9\}}$ have been used for constructing input messages for the service invocations of the activities $A_{SQ_{(i+1)(j+1)}}$, $A_{SQ_{(i+2)(j+1)}}$, $A_{SQ_{(i+3)(j+1)}}$. In both sets of experiments, we used 4 different variants of orchestrations, where we varied the number of operations of each service that change the state of the service as follows: 1, 2, 5 and 10 operations per service. Therefore, we varied the number of checkpointing activities introduced in the orchestrations from 5 to 50. Finally, in both sets of experiments, the SIROCO RM was deployed on an 1.6 GHz Intel Centrino, with 1GB RAM, while the services were deployed on 1.7 Intel Pentium, with 1 GB RAM.

Figure 14 (a) summarizes the results from the 1st set of experiments (average execution times with a 95% confidence interval of 1%). Expectedly, the overhead of the checkpointing

Figure 14. Experimental results

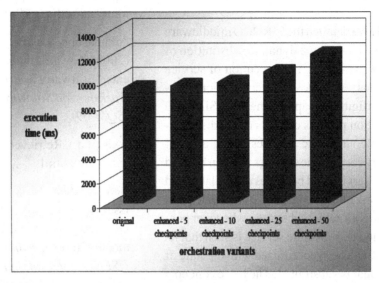

(a) 1st set of experiments.

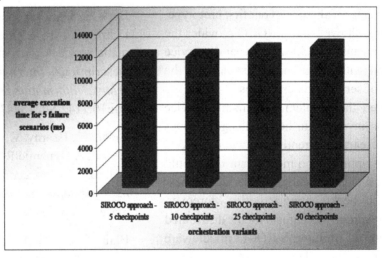

(b) 2nd set of experiments.

activities introduced by SIROCO in the execution of the orchestrations is linear to the number of checkpoints.

In the 2nd set of experiments, we assessed the SIROCO approach in 5 different failure scenarios where WS_1 became unavailable. Specifically, in each scenario i; $i \in \{1..5\}$, we generated an exception during the execution of activity $A_{SQ_{1(5+i)}}$

. We assumed a candidate substitute for WS_1 for which the state synchronization was successful. The results from this set of experiments are summarized in Figure 14 (b) (average execution times for the 5 failure scenarios with a 95% confidence interval of 2%). As we can observe the overall maintenance overhead introduced by SIROCO in the presence of unavailable services is quite reasonable.

CONCLUSION

In this paper we detailed the SIROCO middleware platform that enables the dynamic substitution of stateful services during the execution of service orchestrations. As opposed to conventional dynamic reconfiguration approaches, the SIROCO reconfiguration process consists of (1) discovering candidate substitute services out of a set of semantically compatible services that can be used in place of a service that becomes unavailable and (2) identifying one amongst these candidates that can be used as an actual substitute; whenever possible the selected substitute service is such that its current state can be synchronized with the state of the service that is substituted. The basic concepts of SIROCO were discussed in detail along with an experimental evaluation of our first prototype. Our findings showed that SIROCO provides the necessary means for achieving dynamic service substitution with a reasonable expense on the execution of service orchestrations.

However, the problem of dynamic service substitution involves further challenging issues for future research. Currently, we focus our efforts towards an optimization mechanism that would allow the efficient enrichment of service orchestrations with checkpointing activities. Moreover, we work towards a mechanism for the distributed coordination of multiple SIROCO middleware instances. Finally, we plan to extend our approach to enable the substitution of unavailable services with semantically compatible services that provide different interfaces.

REFERENCES

W3C (2004). Web Services Architecture. Retrieved from http://www.w3c.org/TR/ws-arch.

W3C (2007). Semantic Annotations for WSDL and XML Schema. Retrieved from http://www.w3c.org/TR/sawsdl.

Apache Tomcat. (n.d.). Retrieved from http://tomcat.apache.org/

Athanasopoulos, D., Zarras, A., & Issarny, V. (2009). Towards the Maintenance of Service Oriented Software. In *Proceedings of the 3rd CSMR Workshop on Software Quality and Maintenance (SQM'09)*.

Axis (n.d.). Retrieved from http://ws.apache.org/axis/index.html

Ben Mokhtar, S., Kaul, A., Georgantas, N., & Issarny, V. (2006). Efficient Semantic Service Discovery in Pervasive Computing Environments. In *Proceedings of the 7th ACM/IFIP/USENIX International Middleware Conference (MIDDLEWARE'06)* (LNCS 4290, pp. 240-259).

Berardi, D., Calvanese, D., DeGiacomo, G., Lenzerini, M., & Mecella, M. (2005). Automatic Service Composition Based on Behavioral Descriptions. *International Journal of Cooperative Information Systems*, *14*(4), 333–376. doi:10.1142/S0218843005001201

Bidan, C., Issarny, V., Saridakis, T., & Zarras, A. (1998). A Dynamic Reconfiguration Service for CORBA. In *Proceedings of the 4th IEEE International Conference on Configurable Distributed Systems* (pp. 35-42).

Blair, G. S., Blair, L., Issarny, V., Tuma, P., & Zarras, A. (2000). The Role of Software Architecture in Constraining Adaptation in Component-Based Middleware Platforms. In *Proceedings of the 2nd ACM/IFIP/USENIX International Middleware Conference (MIDDLEWARE'00)* (pp. 164-184).

Cardoso, J., & Sheth, A. (2006). *Semantic Web Services, Processes and Applications*. Springer. doi:10.1007/978-0-387-34685-4

Fredj, M., Georgantas, N., Issarny, V., & Zarras, A. (2008). Dynamic Service Substitution in Service-Oriented Architectures. In *Proceedings of the IEEE International Conference on Services Computing (SCC'08)* (pp. 101-104).

Goudarzi, K. M., & Kramer, J. (1996). Maintaining Node Consistency in the Face of Dynamic Change. In *Proceedings of the 3rd IEEE International Conference on Configurable Distributed Systems* (pp. 62-69).

Hauptmann, S., & Wasel, J. (1996) On-line Maintenance with On-the-y Software Replacement. In *Proceedings of the 3rd IEEE International Conference on Configurable Distributed Systems* (pp. 70-80).

Hofmeister, C., & Purtilo, J. M. (1993). Dynamic Recon_guration in Distributed Systems: Adapting Software Modules for Replacement. In *Proceedings of the 13th IEEE International Conference on Distributed Computing Systems* (pp. 101-110).

IBM. Microsoft Corporation, & BEA (2002). Business Process Execution Language for Web Service (BPEL4WS) v.1.0. Retrieved from http://www.ibm.com/developerworks/webservices/library/ws-bpel/

Kon, F., Cost, F., Blair, G., & Campbell, R. H. (2002). The Case of Reective Middleware. *Communications of the ACM, 45*(6), 33–38. doi:10.1145/508448.508470

Kramer, J., & Magee, J. (1985). Dynamic Configuration for Distributed Systems. *IEEE Transactions on Software Engineering, 11*(4), 424–436. doi:10.1109/TSE.1985.232231

Kramer, J., & Magee, J. (1990). The Evolving Philosophers Problem: Dynamic Change Management. *IEEE Transactions on Software Engineering, 16*(11), 1293–1306. doi:10.1109/32.60317

Melloul, L., & Fox, A. (2004). Reusable Functional Composition Patterns for Web Services. In *Proceedings of the IEEE International Conference on Web Services (ICWS'04)* (pp. 498-506).

Minsky, N., Ungureanu, V., Wang, W., & Zhang, J. (1996). Building Reconfiguration Primitives into the Law of a System. In *Proceedings of the 3rd IEEE International Conference on Configurable Distributed Systems* (pp. 62-69).

Motahari Nezhad, H. R., Benatallah, B., Martens, A., Curbera, F., & Casati, F. (1996). SemiAutomated Adaptation of Service Interactions. In *Proceedings of the International World Wide Web Conference (WWW'07)* (pp. 993-1002).

OASIS. (2004). Web Services Resource Properties (WS-ResourceProperties). Retrieved from http://docs.oasis-open.org/wsrf/2004/06/wsrf-WS-ResourceProperties-1.2-draft-04.pdf

Poladian, V., Sousa, J. P., Garlan, D., & Shaw, M. (2004). Dynamic Configuration of Resource-Aware Services. In *Proceedings of the 26th IEEE-ACM-SIGPLAN International Conference on Software Engineering (ICSE'04)* (pp. 604-613).

Ponnekanti, S. R. (2004) Application-Service Interoperation Without Standardized Service Interfaces. In *Proceedings of the 1st IEEE International Conference on Pervasive Computing and Communications* (pp. 30-37).

Ponnekanti, S. R., & Fox, A. (2004). Interoperability Among Independently Evolving Web Services. In *Proceedings of the 5thACM/IFIP/USENIX International Middleware Conference (MIDDLEWARE'04)* (pp. 331-351).

Salatge, N., & Fabre, J. C. (2007). Fault Tolerance Connectors for Unreliable Web Services. In *Proceedings of the 37th Annual IEEE/IFIP International Conference on Dependable Systems and Networks* (pp. 51-60).

Taher, Y., Benslimane, D., Fauvet, M.-C., & Maamar, Z. (2006). Towards an Approach for Web Services Substitution. In *Proceedings of the 10th International Database Engineering and Applications Symposium* (pp. 166-173).

Van Der Aalst, W., Hofstede, A. T., Kiepuszewski, B., & Barros, A. (2003). Workflow Patterns. *Distributed and Parallel Databases, 14*(3), 5–51. doi:10.1023/A:1022883727209

Warren, I., & Sommerville, I. (1996). A Model for Dynamic Configuration which Preserves Application Integrity. In *Proceedings of the 3rd IEEE International Conference on Configurable Distributed Systems* (pp. 81-88).

WordNet 3.0 (2006). Princeton University. Retrieved from http://wordnet.princeton.edu/

Yang, J., & Papazoglou, M. (2004). Service Components for Managing the Lifecycle of Service Compositions. *Information Systems, 29*(2), 97–125. doi:10.1016/S0306-4379(03)00051-6

Zarras, A., Fredj, M., Georgantas, N., & Issarny, V. (2006). Engineering Reconfigurable Distributed Software Systems: Issues Arising for Pervasive Computing. In *Rigorous Development of Complex Fault-Tolerant Systems* (LNCS 4157, pp. 364-386).

KEY TERMS AND DEFINITIONS

Dependability: The dependability of a computing system is the ability to deliver a service that can justifiably be trusted.

Middleware: The middleware is a software layer that stands between the networked operating system and the application and provides well known reusable solutions to frequently encountered problems like heterogeneity, interoperability, security and dependability.

Service-Oriented Applications: The service-oriented applications are built on top of services which have well defined interfaces, composing them into loosely-coupled structures.

Service Unavailability: A system is considered unavailable when it is not ready to deliver correct service.

Dynamic Service Substitution: A service (a) is a substitute for a service (b) if the service (a) offers a functionality (Fa) that is able to replace at runtime a functionality (Fb) provided by the service (b).

Chapter 5
Modeling and Describing an Ontological Knowledge Framework for Integrated Public Service Delivery

Sietse Overbeek
Delft University of Technology, The Netherlands

Marijn Janssen
Delft University of Technology, The Netherlands

Patrick van Bommel
Radboud University Nijmegen, The Netherlands

ABSTRACT

Public organizations are moving away from their practice to supply common, non-electronic services by becoming more demand-driven and orientating on e-service delivery. The services that can be offered by such organizations are fragmented due to constitutional, legal, and jurisdictional limitations. Integrated service delivery can facilitate the process to let public organizations offer a collective bundle of electronic services to meet complex client demands. The main concepts for integrated service delivery are studied in this chapter and relationships, relational constraints, and interdependencies between the main concepts for integrated service delivery have been determined. This has been done by developing an ontology for integrated service delivery that is based on studying public domain knowledge from different viewpoints. The ontology can enable support for organizations that wish to participate in integrated service delivery processes and monitor the execution of services.

INTRODUCTION

Contemporary governments are experiencing a shift from supplying common, non-electronic services towards more demand-driven and personalized electronic service delivery (see e.g. Chen, 2003). The evolution of information technology and new requests of service from the modern society compelled the evolutions of new solutions for the interaction between citizens and

DOI: 10.4018/978-1-61520-819-7.ch005

their governments (Sabucedo, Rifón, Pérez, & Gago, 2009). As a result, governments are focusing more on their client's needs and less on their own functionalities, organizational structures, and boundaries. Initially, public organizations focused on recurring client needs instead of on irregular needs. As such, assessing needs and reacting to needs do not provide the flexibility to react to new needs or even changes in laws and regulations. Public services are fragmented due to constitutional, legal, and jurisdictional limitations. As a consequence, governments are often acting in silo structures, but nowadays are forced to cooperate with other government agencies and even partners in the private sector. Integrated Service Delivery (ISD) can provide an opportunity for public organizations to collectively offer a coordinated bundle of services that match variable client needs (Kraaijenbrink, 2002). This should diminish fragmentation of service delivery. Furthermore, ISD improves information sharing and collaborative work between government systems and their clients (Zhu, Li, Shi, Xu, & Shen, 2009).

The focus of the research reported in this chapter is to determine relationships, relational constraints, and interdependencies between the main concepts for ISD. Insights in relationships among functionalities, constraints that apply for such relationships, and services provided by organizations are required. For example, if a citizen requests a driver's license at the municipality he also needs to be registered in the citizens' registry and he must be eligible to drive a motorized vehicle. These insights are needed because ISD requires that public organizations collaborate with each other. This understanding contributes to distinguish the key concepts and relations that form the basis for coordinating the activities necessary for ISD. This is realized by the development of an ontological knowledge framework for integrated public service delivery, which aligns and abstracts knowledge of the public domain from several viewpoints. By studying the public domain from organization-, actor-, service-,

resource-, and event-centric viewpoints in, we attempt to develop a rich ontology for ISD that is well-balanced between several perspectives.

Ontologies are becoming increasingly essential for organizations, because they are looking towards them as vital machine-processable semantic resources for many application areas (Jarrar & Meersman, 2008). An ontology is an agreed understanding of a certain domain, formally represented as logical theory in the form of a computer-based resource. Complex software applications such as e-services for the public domain can meaningfully communicate to exchange data and thus make such data transactions interoperate independently of their internal technologies by sharing an ontology. Relating the notion of ontology to the research described in this chapter, it can be noticed that organizations sharing an ontology which includes semantics related to the public domain create a starting point for realizing ISD. Because an ontology that is shared by public organizations is an agreed understanding of the public domain and as such enables to identify essential concepts and relations between concepts in such processes it enables interoperability. Ultimately, the ontology should help to exchange information and monitor the execution of services. A graphical model of the ontological knowledge framework is presented in this chapter, which includes a language to determine requirements for ISD based on the ontology. This is followed by a textual description of the model before this chapter is concluded.

VIEWPOINTS ON INTEGRATED PUBLIC SERVICE DELIVERY

We adopt an approach to study the public domain from several viewpoints so that a rich ontological knowledge framework for ISD can be developed based on knowledge that is aligned and abstracted from the public domain. In this case, a viewpoint prescribes from which perspective concepts for ISD in the public domain should be studied. Key concepts and relations between those concepts in the public domain can be studied from several viewpoints, such as organization-, actor-, service-, resource-, and event-centric viewpoints (Dang, Hedayati, Hampel, & Toklu, 2008; ARIS EPC, 2009; Yuan & Lu, 2009). From an organization-centric view, domain knowledge is acquired by applying a bottom-up approach which consists of meticulously studying organizational processes that include information on the supply of public services during process fulfillment. Several process models have been created as a result of this study.

Besides studying existing organizational processes in the public domain, we have analyzed from an actor-centric view how actors participating in such processes would fulfill their part of a process in a public organization. For ISD the tasks of several types of actors need to be coordinated, as for complex services multiple actors are involved in delivering a service. In this case, an actor can be defined as an entity that is able to perform a task, such as a human or a computer. An example of an actor in the public domain is a citizen. The service-centric view describes concrete services offered by organizations that are required by actors for successful process fulfillment. An example of an e-service is the possibility to open a bank account on the Web. The resource-centric view describes resources belonging to an organization and which processes consume which resources. An actor can be a resource of an organization, but computers and office furniture are also considered as resources. Finally, the event-centric view describes events that are transmitted between a set of integrated and interacting services. Such events are consumed or produced by actors in organizations. An example of an event in the public domain can be the event 'residence permit form received' when a citizen receives his residence permit from the government.

The aforementioned viewpoints are now used to align and abstract public domain knowledge from the so-called *expat* case in the public domain, which is part of the is the long-term 'B-dossier'

research project (see: http://www.b-dossier.nl). Results of this project are specifically aimed at providing computer-based support for government agencies to realize a more integrated service delivery. Expats are, in this case, persons who live in another country and want to come over to The Netherlands for their work. For this purpose they will at least need a (temporary) residence permit, a registration in the citizens' registry, a bank account, a job, a health insurance, and housing. Organizational process models have been developed for each of these scenarios that can be studied to abstract public domain knowledge for the ontological knowledge framework.

ALIGNING AND ABSTRACTING PUBLIC DOMAIN KNOWLEDGE

The expat case contains typical problems of ISD and involves public organizations that need to collaborate together. An example of a problem related to ISD is to bridge the digital divide among citizens (Ke & Wei, 2004). Citizens lacking Internet access at home should still be able to use e-services by other means, such as community self-service terminals. Another example of a problem that will be addressed in this research, is the overcoming for successful ISD (as already mentioned in the first section), namely the observation that governments are often acting in silos. Nowadays they are forced to cooperate with other government agencies as well as partners in the private sector.

Public domain knowledge as part of the expat case is aligned and abstracted by studying the case using the different viewpoints. Eventually, this abstract knowledge is used as the basis for the creation of an ontological knowledge framework for ISD in the public domain. Figure 1 visualizes that public domain knowledge is gathered from several viewpoints and that this knowledge is input for ontology creation. Subsequently, the ontology can be used as a basis to provide support for ISD in the public domain.

Figure 1. Aligning and abstracting public domain knowledge for ontology creation

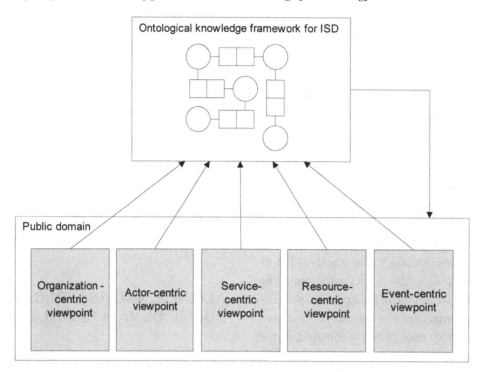

From an organization-centric viewpoint, organizational processes have been studied that are part of the expat case. This has resulted in the creation of several process models. From an actor-centric view, eleven interviews have been conducted with expats to understand how they participated in process fulfillment during their attempts to acquire a residence permit, a registration in the citizens' registry, and so on. From a service-centric viewpoint, it is studied which services are required to let an expat successfully acquire a residence permit, to register in the citizens' registry, etc. From a resource-centric viewpoint, it is determined which organizational resources are utilized when an expat participates in an organizational process. Finally, an event-centric viewpoint embraces events that appear as part of process fulfillment. The event 'request for health insurance received' is an example of an event that occurs if an expat sends a request for a health insurance to an insurance company. Next,

organizational processes are studied resulting in the creation of several process models.

Process Models from the Expat Case

A high-level process model containing composite processes that are required to fulfill when requesting a residence permit for expats has been developed during our research and is shown in Figure 2.

This model is created using the Business Process Modeling Notation (BPMN) (OMG, 2006), which is an industry standard graphical notation for representing organizational processes and it is used by the Dutch government. The model is based on information concerning the processes related to the acquisition of a residence permit provided by the Dutch Immigration and Naturalization Service (INS). Figure 2 shows that there are three composite processes involved when obtaining a residence permit. First, a temporary residence permit has to be requested by an expat followed by the request of a permanent residence

Figure 2. High-level process model for requesting and receiving a residence permit

permit before registering at the municipality. To comprehend what the composite processes exist of, detailed process models for the composite processes shown in figure 2 have been developed. For example, a low-level process model for requesting a residence permit is shown in figure 3. It can be noticed that several parties are involved in the process to let an expat obtain a temporary residence permit. The process starts by the expat requesting to obtain a residence permit from the INS. The remaining process steps can then be fulfilled until the expat collects the residence permit from the INS. Note that the process for requesting a residence permit can be represented in various ways and that the representation shown in Figure 3 is but one of the possible ways.

Studying public processes in which multiple parties interact is but one of the ways to achieve a better understanding of ISD. This organization-centric viewpoint on ISD identifies how public processes are arranged by public organizations such as the INS, municipalities, and embassies. Next, we concentrate on how public processes are fulfilled by actors in the expat case and which knowledge related to ISD can be gathered from an actor-centric viewpoint.

Process Fulfillment by Actors in the Expat Case

From an actor-centric viewpoint, eleven interviews have been conducted with expats to understand how they participated in process fulfillment during their attempts to acquire a residence permit, a registration in the citizens' registry, and so on. Lessons learned from this actor-centric view can-

not only be used to improve current governmental processes and public service delivery, but they are for the purpose of this chapter also used to understand ISD from an actor's point of view (Pihlanto, 1994). In the case of the interviews the intended actors can be equated to the interviewed expats.

Central issues related to the residence permit process that were experienced by the interviewed expats are concerned with: Information that is presented in Dutch only, governmental Web sites that are not functioning properly, contradictory information presented by multiple public organizations, and serious human mistakes during service delivery. The latter is related with loss of documents and failing / forgetting to inform other parties in the process. These issues obviously appeal to improve ISD, of which the ontological framework can act as a step in the right direction. Our research contributes to at least partly resolve the aforementioned issues as follows. The issue of presenting contradictory information can be resolved by letting public organizations share an ontology such as is presented in the next section, so that an agreed understanding is realized concerning the public domain. Different semantics are avoided if information regarding the public domain is exchanged between organizations that share the same ontology of the public domain. Based on the ontology, integrated public e-services can communicate to exchange data and thus make such data transactions interoperate independently of technology. This can at least partly resolve the issue of malfunctioning government Web sites. Serious human mistakes during service delivery can be diminished when more insight is provided how services can be offered and integrated for

Figure 3. Low-level process model for requesting a residence permit

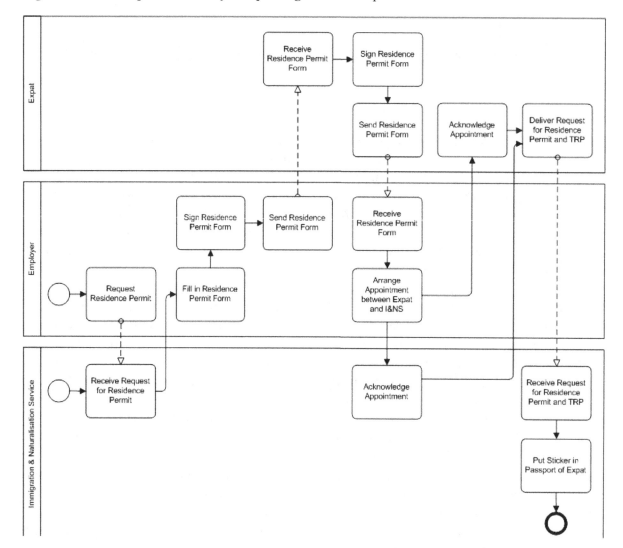

repeatable service requests. Next, it is studied which services are involved in the expat case from a service-centric viewpoint.

Service Delivery in the Expat Case

Insight is provided which services are involved when studying the low-level process for requesting a residence permit depicted in figure 3. As can be noticed in figure 3, an expat's employer first requests a residence permit. This request is then received by the INS. This involves an e-

service materialized by a Web page on which the employer can request the permit. This service is provided by the INS. The employer can print the request form and then it can be sent to the expat who requires to sign and return it to the employer. After this step in the process, an appointment is made between the expat and the INS organization by the employer. This can be regarded as a non-electronic service offered by the employer to the expat. Subsequently, the expat delivers his request for a residence permit and his temporary residence permit at the INS. Finally, the INS puts a sticker in the expat's passport so that he can legally register himself at the municipality. The latter can also be considered as a non-electronic service that is provided by the INS.

Several recommendations to improve service delivery during the process to request a residence permit can be made. First, the form to request a residence permit has to be signed by the expat's employer and the expat. This step can be automated by providing the possibility to sign the form digitally instead of by using pen and paper. This requires that such an e-service is accessible for the INS, the employer, and the expat. Administrative burden can be diminished even more if an expat is not required to bring the form for requesting a residence permit as well as his temporary residence permit to the INS by sending these pieces of evidence electronically to the INS up front. Of course, a sticker should still be provided the old-fashioned way by bringing the passport to the INS, simply because passports are still paper-based. Consequently, studying processes as part of the expat case from a service-centric viewpoint reveals recommendations for further improvement of existing services (Zhu et al., 2009). In the next section it is discussed which resources are consumed by organizations during process fulfillment in the expat case.

Resource Consumption in the Expat Case

The low-level process model shown in figure 3 can be studied to understand which types of resources are consumed during fulfillment of an organizational process in the expat case. Resources are all entities required for the operation of organizations (Zacarias, Pinto, Magalhães, & Tribolet, in press). A human resource employee is an actor that can be considered as a resource belonging to the organization that is going to employ the expat. The expat can also be considered as a resource of his employer. The human resource employee

prepares the form for the request of a residence permit. During the procedure to prepare this form, the employee utilizes a computer and a printing device as resources. As a resource of the INS, a clerical worker makes sure that the expat receives a sticker in his passport once the expat shows up at the INS to deliver the form to request a residence permit and his temporary residence permit. This clerical worker also utilizes a computer to process the expat's request.

The extent to which resources are consumed can be diminished by improving existing services such as is mentioned in the previous section. By decreasing the amount of paperwork the human resource employee, the clerical worker, and the expat will be unburdened a bit. Printing devices will also be less required, but transforming non-electronic acts to electronic acts will demand more from computer devices as a resource. Studying the expat case from a resource-centric viewpoint reveals recommendations which resources are consumed by public organizations and how resource consumption can possibly be diminished. By studying the expat case from an event-centric viewpoint, such as is shown in the next section, it is clarified how services depend on each other and which actors require which services.

Event Generation in the Expat Case

Events arise during process fulfillment and are transmitted between integrated and interacting services (Yuan & Lu, 2009). An event can be defined as a significant change in state. Such events are consumed or produced by actors in organizations. Several events can be distinguished in the residence permit process shown in figure 3, such as the event 'residence permit form received'. A subsequent event that is produced by the receiving expat is the 'residence permit signed' event. Another example is the event 'sticker placed in passport' in the final stage of the residence permit process. Getting to grips with organizational events is important to realize successful ISD, because coordinating and orchestrating events between services provides insight in how services depend on each other and which actors require which services.

In this context, the notion of an Event-Driven Service-Oriented Architecture (EDSOA) needs to be introduced. This EDSOA, or simply *architecture*, defines a methodology for designing and implementing computer-based applications and systems in which events are transmitted between a set of integrated and interacting services (Yuan & Lu, 2009). An actor that consumes an event can subscribe to an architecture that manages such events, and an actor that produces an event publishes to this architecture. When an event is broadcasted by an actor, the architecture facilitates that this event is forwarded to a demanding actor. If a demanding actor is unavailable, the architecture can facilitate the storage of the event and try to forward it later. This architecture-based coordination of events can be dubbed as *event coordination* (Sheng, Benatallah, & Maamar, 2008; Malone & Crowston, 1994). Building applications and systems based on an EDSOA allows these applications and systems to be more responsive, since such systems are more oriented to unpredictable and asynchronous environments. Eventually, implementation of an EDSOA that is based on the ontological knowledge framework discussed in the remainder of this chapter can enable ISD and orchestration of events between services in practice. This will not be dealt with in this chapter but is part of a future research effort.

Now that we have gathered insights on processes in the public domain from several viewpoints with respect to a case in which typical problems for ISD are illustrated, it is possible to develop an ontology that contributes to distinguish the key concepts and relations that form the basis for coordinating the activities necessary for ISD.

ORM MODEL OF THE ONTOLOGY FOR ISD

Figure 4 shows an Object-Role Modeling (ORM) model of the proposed ontological framework for integrated public service delivery. ORM is a conceptual data modeling technique, which can not only be used for the conceptual modeling of database models, but for a variety of modeling purposes such as the modeling of ontologies.

In an ORM model, ovals represent object types (which are counterparts of classes), whereas boxes represent relations between object types. These relations are dubbed as fact types. For more details on Object-Role Modeling, see e.g. Halpin (2001), Hofstede and Weide (1993), and Overbeek, Bommel and Proper (2007).

There are eight central concepts that are part of the ontology and result from knowledge gained from the expat case previously discussed. These are the concepts of role, actor, service, process, resource, organization, event, and an Event-Driven Service-Oriented Architecture (EDSOA) concept. The description of a public process from an organization-centric view, such as shown in figure 3, forms the basis of introducing the 'organization' concept in the ontology. The concepts of service, resource, and event are part of the corresponding viewpoints discussed in the previous section and can also be (partly) distinguished in the ARIS EPC model. The role concept is introduced in the ontology to be able to denote a specification of an actor enactment. An actor is a resource of an organization that enacts a role during process performance or, on a more granular level, task performance. An employee enacting the role of registrar at a municipality is an example of such an actor at a public organization. A citizen is also an example of an actor in the public domain. Finally, the concepts of event and event-driven service-oriented architecture have been introduced.

Figure 4. An ontological framework for integrated public service delivery

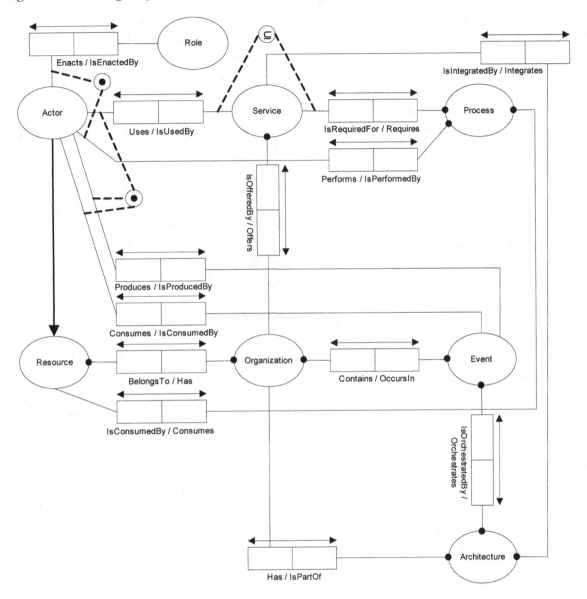

Regarding the ORM model of the ontological knowledge framework for ISD shown in figure 4, it can be noticed that three different constraints can be distinguished. These are the *mandatory*, *uniqueness*, and *subset* constraints. These constraints are discussed in the following section to understand the relations between concepts in the ontology.

Constraints in the ORM Model

The mandatory constraint is sometimes referred to as the *total role* constraint. It expresses that each instance of an object type has to play the role to which the total role constraint is related. For example, figure 4 shows that every *process* is performed by an *actor*. The population of elements in an ORM model, such as instances of object types, fact types (i.e. relations between object types), and roles (one of the two parts that constitute a relation between object types) can be found by applying the population function as introduced by Bommel, Hofstede and Weide (1991). By means of the population function it is possible to reason about the constraints in an ORM model in a precise way. This function can be referred to as **Pop** and can be modeled as follows:

Pop: OT $\rightarrow \wp(\Omega)$

The set OT contains object types. Note that roles and fact types are subsets of object types. The set Ω can be referred to as the *Universe of Instances*, abbreviated to UoI. The Universe of Instances contains all possible instances of types found in an ORM model. Mandatory or total role constraints found in the ORM model of the ontological knowledge framework for ISD can now be expressed by applying the population function. For example, the total role constraint connected to the role 'OccursIn' can be expressed as follows:

Pop(*Event* **)** = **Pop(** *OccursIn* **)**

It is now trivial to express each total role constraint that spans one role by using the population function such as above. However, two total role constraints spanning multiple roles can be identified in the ORM model of the ontological framework. First, note that if an actor uses a service, that actor also produces and consumes an event. This is expressed by the total role constraint spanning over the roles 'Uses', 'Produces', and 'Consumes'. Formally, this can be expressed as follows:

Pop(*Actor* **)** = **Pop(** *Uses* **)** $\cup$ **Pop(** *Produces* **)** $\cup$ **Pop(** *Consumes* **)**

Another complex total role constraint that can be found in the ORM model spans the roles 'Enacts' and 'Performs'. This is to make sure that an actor enacting a role should also perform a process and vice versa.

Uniqueness constraints are used to express that instances of object types may play a certain combination of roles at most once (Bommel, Hofstede, & Weide, 1991). This restriction can be generalized as follows: if a certain combination of object type instances occurs in a set RO of roles, then this combination should occur at least *n* and at most *m* times in this set.

Note that RO $\subseteq$ OT. The uniqueness constraint can be expressed by using the following *frequency* function:

Frequency: RO $\times$ N $\times$ N $\rightarrow \wp(\Omega)$

Related to figure 4, the expression **Frequency** ($\{Has, IsPartOf\}, 0, 1$) shows that a combination of instances in the set of roles 'Has' and 'IsPartOf' should occur at least 0 and at most 1 times in this set. Instances of the object type 'Organization' play the role of 'Has' and instances of the object type 'Architecture' play the role of 'IsPartOf'. A combination of an architecture instance playing the role of 'IsPartOf' and an organization instance playing the role of 'Has' cannot occur more than once.

Subset constraints can be used to indicate that instances of an object type that play a certain role are also part of a set of instances that play another role. In figure 4, a subset constraint is used to indicate that each service that is used by an actor should be required for some process. Formally, this can be described as follows:

Pop(*IsUsedBy* **)** $\subseteq$ **Pop(** *IsRequiredFor* **)**

A graphical representation of the three types of constraints that are used in the ORM model of

Figure 5. A meta ORM model of the mandatory, uniqueness, and subset constraints

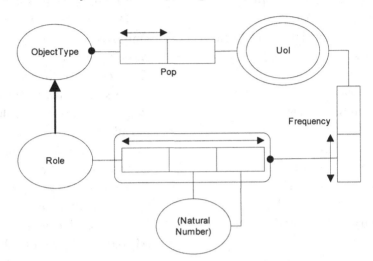

the ontological knowledge framework for ISD is shown in figure 5.

Next, we will extend the ORM model with a language which will function as a query and constraint language. This language is used to specify requirements for participants and concepts as part of the ISD process such as actors, organizations, and architectures.

Language for Integrated Public Service Delivery

A conceptual language that is directly associated with the conceptual modeling language ORM is LISA-D (Hofstede, Proper, & Weide, 1993; Gils, 2006). This modeling language provides the opportunity to describe properties of the underlying domain in terms of the domain language, and yet has the full power of logical languages such as first-order predicate calculus. The names of the roles that instances of object types can play are shown in figure 4. These verbalizations enable to navigate over the conceptual schema. By adding these names we have essentially created a LISA-D language that is suitable to specify requirements for ISD based on the ontology. Figure 4 is, therefore, the basis for our language. We will now present

the verbalizations as shown in the figure. Observe that we have chosen to display only the query-form of the verbalizations. The asserting form can easily be derived from it. We give an example at the end of this section.

First, requirements can be specified for actors in public organizations that wish to supply and integrate their services by adapting the ontological knowledge framework of figure 4. To show how LISA-D works, a very simple query can be derived from the ORM model as follows:

- **Actor ... Uses Service ...**

Such sentences can be combined to form queries that result in specific requirements for participants in ISD or fundamental notions, such as the architecture concept, to realize ISD. For an actor, the following simple queries can be modeled in LISA-D:

- **Actor ... Enacts Role ...**
- **Actor ... Performs Process ...**
- **Actor ... Produces Event ...**
- **Actor ... Consumes Event ...**
- **Actor ... BelongsTo Organization ...**
- **Actor ... IsConsumedBy Process ...**

More complex sentences can be formed by using the logical operators AND, OR, and NOT. A more complex sentence related to figure 4 can be composed as follows:

* **Actor ... Uses Service ... AND Consumes Event ... AND Produces Event ...**

Such queries can also be used in a set-theoretical context to indicate that a whole set of instances play a role. For instance, the following example query can be used to make explicit which events are produced by actors and also consumed by actors.

* **Event ... IsProducedBy Actor AND Event ... IsConsumedBy Actor**

Now that example query-form verbalizations have been discussed, it is possible to introduce an assertion by using LISA-D and the ontological knowledge framework. Recall from the process model of figure 3 that an expat called 'John Doe' may sign a residence permit form. Once he has signed such a form, an event 'residence permit form signed' is generated to indicate that the status of this form has changed. Next, this form is send to John's employer who receives it. Assume that the contact person of John's employer is called 'Jane Doe'. John and Jane both work at 'Acme' company. If the form is successfully send and received the events 'residence permit form sent' and 'residence permit form received' are generated. These example facts can be easily derived from the ontological model by using the following queries to gather events produced by actors and consumed by actors. Several examples can be verbalized, such as:

* **Actor 'John Doe' BelongsTo Organization 'Acme' AND Actor 'Jane Doe' BelongsTo Organization 'Acme'**

* **Actor 'John Doe' Enacts Role 'Expat' AND Actor 'Jane Doe' Enacts Role 'HR employee'**
* **Actor 'John Doe' Performs Process 'Request Residence Permit' AND Process 'Request Residence Permit' Requires Service 'Deliver Residence Permit'**
* **Event 'residence permit form signed' IsProducedBy Actor 'John Doe' AND Event 'residence permit form signed' IsConsumedBy Actor 'Jane Doe'**
* **Event 'residence permit form sent' IsProducedBy Actor 'John Doe' AND Event 'residence permit form sent' IsConsumedBy Actor 'Jane Doe'**
* **Event 'residence permit form received' IsProducedBy Actor 'Jane Doe' AND Event 'residence permit form received' IsConsumedBy Actor 'John Doe'**

These example facts derived from an ontological knowledge base can surface the relations between object instances and the actual population of the ontological model in a practical situation.

To increase usability for public organizations that wish to adopt the ontological framework shown in figure 4, the ontology might be specified in multiple specification languages, such as XML, RDF, RDF-S, OWL, etc. (Jarrar & Meersman, 2008). These languages are specifically designed for use by computer-based applications that need to process the content of information instead of just presenting information to human actors. However, the Web Ontology Language OWL facilitates greater machine interpretability of Web content than that supported by e.g. XML, RDF, and RDF Schema (RDF-S) by providing additional vocabulary along with a formal semantics (Jarrar & Meersman, 2008). To increase successful adaptation and machine interpretability of our ontological framework, an OWL specification of

Figure 6. A partial OWL representation of the ontological framework for integrated public service delivery

```
<owl:Class rdf:ID = "Resource" />
<owl:Class rdf:ID = "Actor">
  <rdfs:subClassOf rdf:resource = "#Resource" />
</owl:Class>
<owl:Class rdf:ID = "Role" />
<owl:Class rdf:ID = "Service" />
<owl:Class rdf:ID = "Process" />
<owl:Class rdf:ID = "Organization" />
<owl:Class rdf:ID = "Event" />
<owl:Class rdf:ID = "Architecture" />
<owl:ObjectProperty rdf:ID = "Enacts">
  <owl:inverseOf rdf:resource= "IsEnactedBy" />
  <rdfs:domain rdf:resource = "#Actor" />
  <rdfs:range rdf:resource = "#Role" />
</owl:ObjectProperty>
<owl:ObjectProperty rdf:ID = "Uses">
  <owl:inverseOf rdf:resource= "IsUsedBy" />
  <rdfs:domain rdf:resource = "#Actor" />
  <rdfs:range rdf:resource = "#Service" />
</owl:ObjectProperty>
<owl:ObjectProperty rdf:ID = "Produces">
  <owl:inverseOf rdf:resource= "IsProducedBy" />
  <rdfs:domain rdf:resource = "#Actor" />
  <rdfs:range rdf:resource = "#Event" />
</owl:ObjectProperty>
....
<owl:Restriction>
  <owl:onProperty rdf:resource="#Orchestrates.Event" />
  <owl:minCardinality rdf:datatype=
  "&xsd;nonNegativeInteger">1</owl:minCardinality>
</owl:Restriction>
```

the ontological framework that has been visualized in ORM so far is presented in the next section.

OWL DESCRIPTION OF THE ONTOLOGY FOR ISD

A partial OWL representation of the ontological framework for integrated public service delivery is shown in figure 6. This representation verbalizes the concepts, relations, and constraints of the ORM model shown in figure 4.

Representing the ontological concepts and relations between those concepts by means of OWL yields differences compared to modeling it

in ORM. However, both languages intend to express the same meaning. For example, the ORM uniqueness constraint that spans over 'Enacts / IsEnactedBy' cannot be expressed in OWL, as it is implied by definition (Jarrar & Meersman, 2008). I.e., the formalization of ObjectProperties in OWL does not allow the same tuple to appear twice in the same set, such as Enacts = {<actor1 ,role1>,<actor1,role1>}. The other uniqueness and mandatory constraints are all expressed as a cardinality restriction in OWL. For instance, the mandatory constraint on 'Orchestrates' is expressed in OWL by the constraint 'owl:minCardinality'. An 'owl:minCardinality' constraint of one or more means that all instances of the class must have a value for the property.

The differences in modeling the ontology as described above illustrate different ways of characterizing the ontology. The contrast in formalizations and constructs of both languages causes such differences. The choice of which language is more suitable for specifying an ontology depends on the application scenario and perspectives of the ontology (Jarrar & Meersman, 2008). For example, ORM and EER are suitable for database and XML-based application scenarios since they are extensive in their treatments of data set integrity. Description logic based languages such as OWL seem to be more applicable for deductive and reasoning-based application scenarios, as they focus on the expressiveness and the decidability of axioms.

As a next step in this research, an event-driven service-oriented architecture will be developed that adopts the proposed ontological framework for integrated service delivery as the knowledge base. The ontological framework provides a foundation for describing actor context, public processes, resources, etc. Therefore, the ontology helps the architecture to dynamically compose a personalized process flow and automate the execution of the process flow.

CONCLUSION

Contemporary governments are focusing on their client's needs and less on their own functionalities, organizational structures, and boundaries. Integrated Service Delivery (ISD) can provide an opportunity for public organizations to collectively offer a coordinated bundle of services that match variable client needs. This should also diminish fragmentation of service delivery. The focus of the research reported in this chapter is to determine relationships, relational constraints, and interdependencies between the main concepts for ISD. Insights in relationships among functionalities and constraints that apply for such relationships have been provided by means of an ontological knowledge framework for ISD. This framework is based on studying public domain knowledge as part of a case in which expats come over to The Netherlands to work. Knowledge from this case is aligned and abstracted by applying several viewpoints so that a rich ontological knowledge framework for ISD can be developed. An ontological knowledge framework is created based on the abstracted domain knowledge. Ontological concepts, relationships between concepts, and ontological constraints are modeled by means of an ORM model. Verbalizations of the modeled constructs are realized by describing a language for ISD using the conceptual language LISA-D. Finally, the ontology is made machine-readable by providing an OWL-based translation.

Future work consists of the development of an EDSOA that is based on the ontological framework for ISD. Such an architecture defines a methodology for designing and implementing computer-based applications and systems in which events are transmitted between a set of integrated and interacting services (Yuan & Lu, 2009). Implementation of an architecture based on the ontological framework can enable ISD and orchestration of events between services in practice.

REFERENCES

ARIS EPC. (n.d.). Retrieved February 10, 2009, from the ARIS EPC Wiki: http://en.wikipedia.org/wiki/Event-driven_process_chain.

Chen, H. (2003). Digital government: technologies and practices. *Decision Support Systems*, *34*(3), 223–227. doi:10.1016/S0167-9236(02)00118-5

Dang, J., Hedayati, A., Hampel, K., & Toklu, C. (2008). An ontological framework for adaptive medical workflow. *Journal of Biomedical Informatics*, *41*(5), 829–836. doi:10.1016/j.jbi.2008.05.012

Halpin, T. (2001). *Information modeling and relational databases, from conceptual analysis to logical design*. California: Morgan Kaufmann.

Jarrar, M., & Meersman, R. (2008). Ontology engineering - the Dogma approach . In Dillon, T., Chang, E., Meersman, R., & Sycara, K. (Eds.), *Advances in Web Semantics I* (pp. 7–34). Berlin, Germany: Springer.

Ke, W., & Wei, K. K. (2004). Successful e-government in Singapore. *Communications of the ACM*, *47*(6), 95–99. doi:10.1145/990680.990687

Kraaijenbrink, J. (2002). Centralization revisited? Problems on implementing integrated service delivery in The Netherlands. In R. Traunmüller, & K. Lenk (Eds.), *Electronic Government, 1st International Conference, EGOV 2002, Aix-en-Provence, France, September 2 - September 5, 2002, Proceedings* (pp. 10-17). Berlin, Germany: Springer.

Malone, T. W., & Crowston, K. (1994). The interdisciplinary study of coordination. *ACM Computing Surveys*, *26*(1), 87–119. doi:10.1145/174666.174668

OMG. (2006). *Business Process Modeling Notation (BPMN) Version 1.0 (OMG Final Adopted Specification)*. Needham, MA: Object Management Group.

Overbeek, S. J., van Bommel, P., & Proper, H. A. (2007). Visualizing formalisms with ORM models . In Meersman, R., Tari, Z., & Herrero, P. (Eds.), *On the Move to Meaningful Internet Systems 2007: OTM 2007 Workshops, Vilamoura, Portugal, November 25 - 30, 2007, Proceedings, Part I* (pp. 709–718). Berlin, Germany: Springer. doi:10.1007/978-3-540-76888-3_93

Pihlanto, P. (1994). The action-oriented approach and case study method in management studies. *Scandinavian Journal of Management, 10*(4), 369–382. doi:10.1016/0956-5221(94)90024-8

Sabucedo, L. M. A., Rifón, L. E. A., Pérez, R. M., & Gago, J. M. S. (2009). Providing standard-oriented data models and interfaces to eGovernment services: A semantic-driven approach. *Computer Standards & Interfaces, 31*(5), 1014–1027. doi:10.1016/j.csi.2008.09.042

Sheng, Q. Z., Benatallah, B., & Maamar, Z. (2008). User-centric services provisioning in wireless environments. *Communications of the ACM, 51*(11), 130–135. doi:10.1145/1400214.1400241

ter Hofstede, A. H. M., Proper, H. A., & van der Weide, Th. P. (1993). Formal definition of a conceptual language for the description and manipulation of information models. *Information Systems, 18*(7), 489–523. doi:10.1016/0306-4379(93)90004-K

ter Hofstede, A. H. M., & van der Weide, Th. P. (1993). Expressiveness in conceptual data modelling. *Data & Knowledge Engineering, 10*(1), 65–100. doi:10.1016/0169-023X(93)90020-P

van Bommel, P., ter Hofstede, A. H. M., & van der Weide, Th. P. (1991). Semantics and verification of object-role models. *Information Systems, 16*(5), 471–495. doi:10.1016/0306-4379(91)90037-A

van Gils, B. (2006). *Aptness on the Web*. Ph.D. thesis, Radboud University, Nijmegen, The Netherlands.

Yuan, S.-T., & Lu, M.-R. (2009). An value-centric event driven model and architecture: a case study of adaptive complement of SOA for distributed care service delivery. *Expert Systems with Applications, 36*(2), 3671–3694. doi:10.1016/j.eswa.2008.02.024

Zacarias, M., Pinto, H. S., Magalhães, R., & Tribolet, J. (in press). A 'context-aware' and agent-centric perspective for the alignment between individuals and organizations. *Information Systems*.

Zhu, D., Li, Y., Shi, J., Xu, Y., & Shen, W. (2009). A service-oriented city portal framework and collaborative development platform. *Information Sciences, 179*(15), 2606–2617. doi:10.1016/j.ins.2009.01.038

KEY TERMS AND DEFINITIONS

Coordination: Coordination is managing dependencies between activities.

Expat: An expat is a person temporarily or permanently residing in a country and culture other than that of the person's upbringing or legal residence.

Integrated Service Delivery: Integrated Service Delivery (ISD) can provide an opportunity for public organizations to collectively offer a coordinated bundle of services that match variable client needs.

Language for Information Structure and Access Descriptions (LISA-D): LISA-D is a modeling language that provides the opportunity to describe properties of the underlying domain in terms of the domain language, and yet has the full power of logical languages such as first-order predicate calculus.

Object-Role Modeling (ORM): ORM is an information modeling language which has a well-defined formal semantics and sufficient expressive power to describe the Universe of Discourse.

Ontology: An ontology is an agreed understanding of a certain domain, formally represented as logical theory in the form of a computer-based resource.

Web Ontology Language (OWL): OWL is an ontology language designed for use by applications that need to process the content of information instead of just presenting information to humans. OWL facilitates greater machine interpretability of Web content than that supported by XML, RDF, and RDF Schema (RDF-S) by providing additional vocabulary along with a formal semantics.

Chapter 6

An Ontological Structure for Semantic Retrieval Based on Description Logics

Hongwei Wang
Tongji University, China

James N. K. Liu
The Hong Kong Polytechnic University, China

Wei Wang
Fudan University, China

ABSTRACT

Current information retrieval either relies on encoding process to describe given item or perform a full-text analysis to search for user-specified words. However, these syntax-based methods only reflect part of the content, so they can hardly ensure content matching. Ontology is an explicit specification of conceptualizations, which can explicitly and formally express the semantic of the concepts and their relationships. Therefore the domain ontology is better for information retrieval at semantic level. The ontological structure is determined by its specific applications. Although there are already several views on ontological structures in different contexts, the word association derived from reasoning the semantic relations between terms, the key point for semantic retrieval, has not been solved properly yet. This chapter proposes a six-element based ontological structure for semantic retrieval, and use description logic to semantically describe the atomic term, complex terms, instances, instances description, attribute assignment and axioms. Then, the new structure is evaluated by the Gruber's criteria including explicitness and objectivity, consistency, extensibility, minimal encoding bias and minimal ontological commitment. Based on the new structure, we propose two reasoning mechanisms, i.e., terms-oriented and instances-oriented, for semantic retrieval application. Meanwhile, conversion mechanisms and determining algorithms are also proposed, which enable the reasoning for various relations in a specific area according to the rules made by domain experts. Finally, we put forward four kinds of rules for information retrieval, and analyze the applications of the new structure in semantic retrieval.

DOI: 10.4018/978-1-61520-819-7.ch006

INTRODUCTION

The contents on the Internet are changing every day. We are witnessing today an exponential growth of data accumulated within organizations and systems. Autonomous data repositories storing different types of data are becoming available for us. This makes it impossible for users to be aware of the locations, structure, query languages and semantics of the data in various repositories. Without the efficient retrieval tools, users have no way to position the exact location where their needed information is. So users have to blindly search every possible server. Obviously, it may be time consuming. Current retrieval methods are mainly based on man-made subject directories or keywords matching. These syntax-based methods with limitations to reveal semantic information only reflect part of the content, so they can hardly ensure content matching (Zghal, Aufaure, & Mustapha, 2007; Köhler, Philippi, Specht, & Rüegg, 2006).

Figure1 shows the general process of the Chinese information retrieval, including segmentation, word association, searching in database and information integration, among which, segmentation, searching in database and information integration have already been studied in-depth (Foo & Li, 2004; Zhang, Lu, & Zou, 2004; Feng, Hu, Zhao, & Yi, 2006; Fu, Kit, & Webster, 2008;

Wang & Du, 2003; Shah, Finin, Joshi, Cost, & Matfield, 2002). In recent years, research efforts focus on word association relating keyword T_i to term set $\{t_{i1}, t_{i2}, ..., t_{im}\}$. In this process, most search engines use the syntactic matching method. That is, to set up a data dictionary, then to search by strictly matching and combinations. This method, however, often gets blunt feedback due to the lack of semantic understanding. For example, if searching for "computer", the feedback may contain "computer mall", "portable computer" and so on, but does not or rarely refer to "laptop". If the word association is available semantically, the efficiency of information retrieval would be promoted (Gruber, 1993a; Guarino, Masolo, Vetere, & Council, 1999; Freitas & Bittencourt, 2000; Finin, Ding, Pan, Joshi, & Kolari, 2005).

Ontology is a useful tool to support the process of word association. In the context of computer and information sciences, an ontological model defines a set of representational primitives with which to model a domain of knowledge or discourse. The representational primitives are typically classes (or sets), attributes (or properties), and relationships (or relations among class members). The definitions of the representational primitives include information about their meaning and constraints on their logically consistent application. In the context of database systems, ontology can be viewed as a level of abstraction

Figure 1. The general process of information retrieval

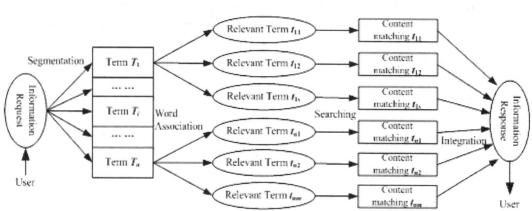

Figure 2. The process of domain ontology creation

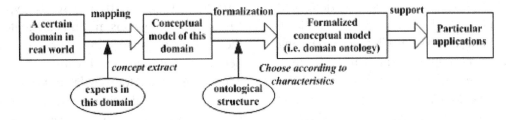

of data models, analogous to hierarchical and relational models, but intended for modeling knowledge about individuals, their attributes, and their relationships to other individuals. Ontologies are typically specified in languages that allow abstraction away from data structures and implementation strategies; in practice, the languages of ontologies are closer in expressive power to first-order logic than languages used to model databases. For this reason, ontologies are said to be at the semantic level, whereas database schema are models of data at the syntactical or physical level. Due to their independence from lower level data models, ontologies are used for integrating heterogeneous databases, enabling interoperability among disparate systems, and specifying interfaces to independent, knowledge-based services.

The ontological structure varies on the background of applications, because different applications may emphasize some different elements of ontology as required. Wang, Jiang, and Hou (2005) presented the process of ontology development, as shown in Figure 2. The first step is the conceptualization, extracting concepts from a certain domain with the participation of field experts. Thus, the domain in real world is mapped into the conceptual model. Then, choose an ontological structure according to the requirement of applications, and formalize the conceptual model in the form of the selected structure using some logic-based language. The formalized conceptual model is the domain ontology. Finally, apply this domain ontology in the particular applications.

To meet requirements of semantic retrieval, the ontological structure needs the ability regarded to not only describing and formalizing the domain conceptual model in real word, but also reasoning for word association. Up to now, several ontological structures have been presented, each focusing on some certain applications. However, there is not yet a widely-approved ontological structure for the applications of semantic retrieval. So it is essential to develop the proper ontological structure for this application field.

LITERATURE REVIEW

Ontology Based Semantic Retrieval Systems

For semantic retrieval, the ontology model is mainly used for word sense disambiguation (WSD) and document annotation.

WSD is to identify which sense of a word is used in any given sentence, when the word has a number of distinct senses. Based on WSD, the users' intentions for what they really want can be better understood meaningfully. Navigli and Velardi (2003) show that query expansion with synonyms or hyperonyms has a limited effect on web information retrieval performance, while other types of semantic information derivable from an ontology are much more effective at improving search results. Some efforts are made on using the relations including synonyms, hyponymy, troponymy, meronymy and entailment from WordNet to disambiguate word senses (Kruse, Naujoks, and Kunze, 2005; Albanese, Capasso, Picariello, and Rinaldi, 2005; Moldovan and Mihalcea, 2000). Zhang and Ma (2009) study Chinese WSD using HowNet for the improvement of the efficiency of Chinese semantic retrieval. Gracia, Trillo, Espinoza, and Mena (2006) propose a method which processes a set of related keywords in order to discover and extract their implicit semantics, obtaining their most suitable senses according to their context. The possible senses are extracted from the knowledge represented by a pool of ontologies available in the Web. This method applies an iterative disambiguation algorithm that uses the measure of semantic relatedness based on Google frequencies. In addition, some domain-specific ontologies are built for information retrieval. Guha, McCool, and Miller (2003) construct an ontology model about person, place, event and organization for WSD. With the ontology, the initial retrieval result is given, coupled with a series of hyperlinks. And the system will understand the users' intentions according to their clicking to hyperlinks.

Metadata is used to describe document contents to make them machine-understandable. Metadata can be expressed in a wide variety of vocabularies and languages. Ontology based annotation refers to the process of creating metadata using ontologies as their vocabularies for improving information retrieval at semantic level. Vallet, Fernández, and Castells (2005) propose a model for the exploitation of ontology-based KBs to improve search over large document repositories. This approach includes an ontology-based scheme for the semi-automatic annotation of documents, and a retrieval system. The retrieval model is based on an adaptation of the classic vector-space model, including an annotation weighting algorithm, and a ranking algorithm. Semantic search is combined with keyword-based search to achieve tolerance to KB incompleteness. Nagypál and Motik (2003) present fuzzy interval-based temporal model capable of representing imprecise temporal knowledge.

This approach naturally subsumes existing crisp temporal models. Furthermore, Nagypál and Motik discuss how this model is integrated with the ontology model to allow annotating ontology definitions with time specifications. A semantic annotation method for web database query result is proposed by adopting the deep annotation procedure in semantic web (Yuan, Li, & Chen, 2008). As a global schema web database should be followed, domain ontology is introduced to the annotation procedure for a completed and consistent annotation result. The query interface and the query result features are analyzed in detail, the strategy of query condition reconfigured is adopted, and then the semantic markups of query result are determined. By collecting web database from different domains, the experiments indicate that the approach proposed can annotate the web database query result properly under the support of domain ontology.

With the introduction of ontology to semantic retrieval, attempts have been made on building ontology based semantic retrieval systems. At present, there already exist a couple of such systems as OntoSeek, Swoogle.

OntoSeek, specifically targeted to online yellow pages and product catalogs, adopts a language of limited expressiveness for content representation, and exploits a large linguistic ontology based on WordNet for content matching. In general, with respect to standard word-matching systems, expressing the content structure by means of a simple representation language increases the precision of the retrieval, while adopting a hierarchy of keywords increases both recall and precision. In OntoSeek, the use of a linguistic ontology results in two further advantages: a decoupling between the user vocabulary and the encoding terminology, and an additional increase of recall and precision due to synonymy handling and sense disambiguation (Guarino, Masolo, Vetere, & Council, 1999).

Swoogle is an implemented system that discovers, analyzes and indexes knowledge encoded in semantic web documents on the Web. Swoogle reasons about these documents and their constituent parts and records meaningful metadata about them. Swoogle provides web-scale semantic web data access service, which helps human users and software systems to find relevant documents, terms and triples, via its search and navigation services. Swoogle also provides a customizable algorithm inspired by Google's PageRank algorithm but adapted to the semantics and use patterns found in semantic web documents (Finin, Ding, Pan, Joshi, & Kolari, 2005).

Compared with the traditional mechanism of information retrievals, OntoSeek and Swoogle can process words and phrases of certain domains rather broadly, and understand natural language to a certain degree. However, there are still some things to do, in particular, to improve the structure of ontology model.

Representative Ontological Structures

A couple of representative ontological structures are listed below:

Naing, Lim, and Goh (2002), Shah, Finin, Joshi, Cost, and Matfield (2002) hold the view that: $O=\{C, A^C, R, A^R, H, X\}$. Where, $C=\{c_1, c_2, ...\}$ represents a set of concepts; $A^C=\{A^C(c_1), A^C(c_2), ...\}$ represents a collection of attribute sets, one for each concept; $R=\{r_1(c_1, c_2), r_2(c_2, c_3), ...\}$ represents a set of relations; $A^R=\{A^R(r_1), A^R(r_2), ...\}$ represents a collection of attribute sets, one for each relation; $H=\{(c_1, c_2), (c_2, c_3), ...\}$ represents a concept hierarchy and it is a set of parent-child relations between concepts in C; $X=\{x_1, x_2, ...\}$ represents a set of axioms and each axiom in X is a constraint on the concept's and relation's attribute values or the relations between concept objects. This structure has a powerful ability to express concepts, and also gives the description set of the axiom, enabling the following ontology reasoning.

Gruber (1993b) defines ontology as: an explicit specification on conceptualization of terms in a domain, which gives the abstract description of the concepts and their relations in the domain. The following 5-tuple based structure is given: $O=(C, R, H, rel, A)$, where, C is the concept set, R is the relation set, H stands for hierarchy in concepts, *rel* stands for relations among concepts, and A is the axiom set. The concepts in a real domain are mapped as the concept set in O, the relations mapped as the relation set, the classifications of concepts mapped as the hierarchy set, and the principles mapped as the axiom set, respectively. This structure can achieve an integral mapping of a specific domain of real world into a domain ontology.

Gómez-Pérez (1998) describes the ontology as: concept, relation, function, axiom and instance based on the principles of classification. Where, the instance refers to a single object of concepts; the relation refers to mutual effect between concepts, formally defined as a subset of n-dimensional Cartesian product of concept sets, denoted as $C_1 \times C_2 \times \cdots \times C_n$; the function is regarded as a special relation denoted as $F: C_1 \times C_2 \times \cdots \times C_{n-1} \to C_n$. This structure has got wide acceptance, and there also exist some applications based on this structure.

Xu (2007) presents a 3-tuple based ontology structure, denoted as $O=(C, P, R)$, where C is the concept set, and P is the property set. $R=\{same-as, kind-of, part-of, contains, associates\}$ is the set of semantic relations between concepts. Where, *associates* refer to all other relations not belonging to the four kinds of relations above. This structure is simple, but seizes the two important points: the concepts and their relations. And it can be used in some particular applications.

Liu (2005) proposes an ontology structure with 6-tuples: $O=(N, F, A, B, R, S)$. Where, N is the name of concept; F is the father ontology of N; A is the property set; B is the object set; R is a network, which contains element relations for B; S is the method set attached to the ontology. This structure highlights the relations among instances of concepts. In addition, this model includes F to emphasize the inheritance relation between concepts in ontology. And this can be used in some particular applications in the field emphasizing these parts.

Generally, each ontological structure above has its own advantages for some specific applications, there are still some problems: (1) lack of the research on the ontological structure for semantic retrieval, especially on the description of relations between the elements and axioms. The ontological structure is application oriented, which means the structure should vary on the actual characteristics of applications. However, the current efforts weigh general-purpose ontological structure to specific purposed structure, and the latter is really needed by information retrieval; (2) lack of research on the consistency checking for domain ontology. As a result, there are semantic conflicts and concept incompletion in domain ontology, thus affecting the accuracy of semantic retrieval; (3) the promotion of ontology development methodology does not correspond to that of ontology designing criteria. The Gruber's principles are the popular criteria for ontology development, but the current efforts take little consideration on how to improve the ontology development methodology for meeting the Gruber's principles.

A NEW ONTOLOGICAL STRUCTURE BASED ON DESCRIPTION LOGICS

Ontological Structure and its Interpretation

Def.1 (ontological structure): Ontological structure can be described as a 6-tuples: $O=<A_T, C_T, X, X_D, A_A, A_X>$.

Where, A_T is an atomic term set, C_T is a complex term set, X is an instance set, X_D is an instance description set, A_A is an attribute assignment set, and A_X is an axiom set.

Def.2 (ontological interpretation): Given $O=<A_T, C_T, X, X_D, A_A, A_X>$, an ontological interpretation is a 2-tuples: $I=<\Delta^I, \cdot^I>$.

Where, $\Delta^I \neq \varnothing$ is the interpretation, and $\cdot^I$ is an interpretation function, which assigns to every atomic class C in A_T a set $C^I \subseteq \Delta^I$, and to every atomic property P in A_T a binary relation $P^I \subseteq \Delta^I \times \Delta^I$, and to every individual e in X an element $e^I \in \Delta^I$.

Def.3 (term relation): Given $O=<A_T, C_T, X, X_D, A_A, A_X>$, D and E are two class terms or property terms. I is any interpretation,

1. If $D^I \subseteq E^I$, we say "E subsumes D", written as $D \sqsubseteq E$;
2. If $D \sqsubseteq E$ and $E \sqsubseteq D$, we say "D is equivalent to E", written as $D \equiv E$;
3. If $D \sqsubseteq \neg E$ and $E \sqsubseteq \neg D$, we say "D does not intersect E, written as $D \sqcap E$; Otherwise, "D intersects E", written as $D \uplus E$.

The relations in Def.3, including subsumption, equivalence, intersection, and non-intersection, are collectively called term relation expression.

Description logics (DL) are a family of knowledge representation languages which can be used to represent the concept definitions of an application domain in a structured and formally well-understood way. The name description logic refers, on the one hand, to concept descriptions used to describe a domain and, on the other hand, to the logic-based semantics which can be given by a translation into first-order predicate logic. Atomic terms can only express limited logics and simple contents, because they are just the basic element with less expressive power. So here the term constructors from Description Logics are adopted to build term formulas, thus, expressing more complex contents (Baader, Calvanese, McGuinness, Nardi, & Patel-Schneider, 2003).

Term formula can be classified into class term formula and property term formula. For instance, in Table 2, **Man ⊓ ∃HasChild.Person** is class term formula, while **HasWife×HasParent** is property term formula.

Below, Table 2 gives ontological interpretations to 15 term constructors. Where, C and D are

Table 2. Term constructors of ontology model and interpretations

Constructor Name	Ontological Interpretation
universal class: $\top$	$\top^I = \Delta^I$
empty class: $\bot$	$\bot^I = \varnothing$
class negation: $\neg C$	$(\neg C)^I = \Delta^I - C^I$
property negation: $\neg P$	$(\neg P)^I = \Delta^I \times \Delta^I \setminus P^I$
intersection: $C \sqcap D, P \sqcap R$	$(C \sqcap D)^I = C^I \cap D^I, (P \sqcap R)^I = P^I \cap R^I$
union: $C \sqcup D, P \sqcup R$	$(C \sqcup D)^I = C^I \cup D^I, (P \sqcup R)^I = P^I \cup R^I$
property multiply: $P \times R$	$(P \times R)^I = \{(a, c) \in \Delta^I \times \Delta^I | \exists b.\ (a, b) \in P^I \wedge (b, c) \in R^I\}$
property inverse: P^-	$(P^-)^I = \{(b, a) \in \Delta^I \times \Delta^I | (a, b) \in P^I\}$
property transitive closure: P^+	$(P^+)^I = \cup_{i \geq 1}(P^i)^I$
property value restriction: $\forall P.C$	$(\forall P.C)^I = \{a \in \Delta^I | \forall b.\ (a, b) \in P^I \rightarrow b \in C^I\}$
property value restriction: $\forall P.\{z\}$	$(\forall P.\{z\})^I = \{a \in \Delta^I | \forall b.\ (a, b) \in P^I \rightarrow b = z^I\}$
limited existential quantification: $\exists P.C$	$(\exists P.C)^I = \{a \in \Delta^I | \exists b.\ (a, b) \in P^I \wedge b \in C^I\}$
limited existential quantification: $\exists P.\{z\}$	$(\exists P.\{z\})^I = \{a \in \Delta^I | \exists b.\ (a, b) \in P^I \wedge b = z^I\}$
at-least number of restriction: $\geq n, P$	$(\geq n, P)^I = \{a \in \Delta^I | |\{b\ |\ (a, b) \in P^I\ \}| \geq n\}$
at-most number of restriction: $\leq n, P$	$(\leq n, P)^I = \{a \in \Delta^I | |\{b\ |\ (a, b) \in P^I\ \}| \leq n\}$

class terms, P and R are property terms, and z is an instance.

Def.4 (term definition item): A term definition item is an equivalence relation, written as $C \equiv D$. Where C is a term, called definiendum, and D is a term formula, called definiens. For instance, **Mother≡Woman ⊓ ∃HasChild.Person** in Table 1.

Def.5 (term expansion): Given ontology $O = \langle A_T, C_T, X, X_D, A_A, A_X \rangle$ and term definition item $C \equiv D$, we can expand term definition item by replacing each occurrence of a complex term in the definiens with the atomic terms it stands for. We end up with a term definition item $C \equiv D'$, where D' contains only atomic terms and no complex terms. We say that D' is the expansion

Table 1. A partial ontology of the family domain following the structure of Def.1

$O = \langle$ { **Person, Woman, Man, Mother, Father, Parent, Child, Son, Daughter, Wife, Husband, Son-in-law, Daughter-in-law, Sex, Grandmother, MotherWithoutSon, HasSex, HasChild, HasMother, HasFather, HasParent, HasSon, HasDaughter, HasHusband, HasWife, HasOffspring, Age, Name, AssociateWith, HasAttribute }, { Woman≡Person ⊓ ∃HasSex.{Female}, Man≡Person ⊓ ∃HasSex.{Male}, Mother≡Woman ⊓ ∃HasChild.Person, Father≡Man ⊓ ∃HasChild.Person, Parent≡Father ⊔** Mother, **Grandmother≡Mother ⊓ ∃HasChild.Mother, Son≡Man ⊓ Child, Daughter≡Woman ⊓ Child, Wife≡Woman ⊓ ∃HasHusband.Man, Husband≡Man ⊓ ∃HasWife. Woman, Son-in-law≡Man ⊓ ∃(HasWife×HasParent).Person, MotherWithoutSon≡Mother ⊓ ∀HasSon.⊥, Daughter-in-law≡Woman ⊓ ∃(HasHusband×HasParent).Person, HasChild≡HasSon ⊔** HasDaughter, **HasParent≡HasFather ⊔** HasMother, **HasHusband≡HasWife⁻, HasParent≡HasChild⁻, HasOffspring≡ HasChild⁺** }, { Female, Male }, { Sex(Female), Sex(Male) }, { **Person ⊑ ∃HasAttribute.Age ⊓ ∃HasAttribute.Name, Age ⊑ ∃HasValue.xsd:Integer, Name ⊑ ∃HasValue.xsd:String}, { Child ⊑ Person, ∃HasSex.{Male} ⊓ ∃HasSex.{Female}, HasSex ⊑ AssociateWith,** hasChild **⊑ AssociateWith, HasMother ⊑ AssociateWith, HasFather ⊑ AssociateWith, HasParent ⊑ AssociateWith, HasSon ⊑ AssociateWith, HasDaughter ⊑ AssociateWith,** hasHusband **⊑ AssociateWith, HasWife ⊑ AssociateWith, HasOffspring ⊑ AssociateWith** } $\rangle$

Note: Terms are written in bold fond with initials in capital letters, similarly hereinafter.

Table 3. Explanation of property term in ontology model

Property Type	Explanation		Symbol	Reverse Symbol
numerical property	inner nature property		**HasAttribute**	**IsAttributeOf**
relational property	special association	part-entirety	**HasPart**	**IsPartOf**
		inherit	**HasKind**	**IsKindOf**
		instantiation	**HasInstance**	**IsInstanceOf**
	user-defined association		**AssociateWith**	**BeAssociatedWith**

of D with respect to O, written as $\Gamma_e(D)$, where Γ_e is called expansion function.

For instance, for **Father≡Man ⊓ ∃HasChild. Person** in Table1, Γ_e(**Father**)≡**Person ⊓ ∃Has-Sex.{Male} ⊓ ∃HasChild.Person**.

Atomic term set A_T contains atomic class terms and atomic property terms. The property is classified as two types: *inner property* and *relational property*. The former expresses the inner natural property of a class, whose data-type is numerical in general. While the latter describes the outer relations between classes, and its data-type still belongs to the class.

Complex term set C_T consists of term definition items subjected to the following restrictions: (i) For any i, j ($i{\neq}j, 1{\leq}i{\leq}n, 1{\leq}j{\leq}n$), $C_i {\neq} C_j$. (ii) If there exist $C_1{'}{\equiv}D_1{'}$, $C_2{'}{\equiv}D_2{'},..., C_m{'}{\equiv}D_m{'}$ in C_T, and $C_i{'}$ occurs in $D_{i-1}{'}$ ($1{<}i{\leq}m, m{\leq}n$), then $C_1{'}$ must not occur in $D_m{'}$. C_T is written as $C_T = \{C_1{\equiv}D_1, C_2{\equiv}D_2,..., C_n{\equiv}D_n\}$, where, $C_i{\in}C_T$, D_i is a term formula, and every term in D_i is from A_T.

Instance set X contains the instances of domain terms, which is classified into class instances and property instances.

Instance description set X_D contains statements for class instances and property instances.

i. The statement for a class instance, written as $C(a)$, means instance a belongs to class C.

ii. The statement for a property instance, written as $P(a, b)$, means there exists relation P between instance a and b.

Attribute assignment set A_A intends for assigning attributes to class terms. A_A can be written as: $\{C_1 {\sqsubseteq} {\exists}$**HasAttribute**$.D_{11} {\sqcap} {\exists}$**HasAttribute**$.D_{12} {\sqcap} ... {\sqcap} {\exists}$**HasAttribute**$.D_{1m_1},...,C_n {\sqsubseteq} {\exists}$**HasAttribute**$.D_{n1} {\sqcap} {\exists}$**HasAttribute**$.D_{n2} {\sqcap} ... {\sqcap} {\exists}$**HasAttribute**$.D_{nm_n}\}$, where, $C_i{\in}A_T{\cup}C_T$ is a class term and $D_i{\in}A_T{\cup}C_T$ is an inner property term.

Axiom set A_X contains the domain principles and restrictions, which is expressed in the form of term relation expression. And usually, intersection relation does not explicitly exist in A_X.

A_T and C_T are both related to property terms including numerical property and relational property. In addition, the relational property can be classified into special association and user-defined association.

HasAttribute/IsAttributeOf is used to assign numerical property to class term. It can be listed explicitly in A_A or be gained by reasoning. For instance, if we have **Man** ⊑ Person and **Person** ⊑ ∃**HasAttribute.Age**∈A_A, then **Man** ⊑ ∃**HasAttribute.Age** can be gained, which means class **Man** has property **Age**.

The relational property contains special association and user-defined association. The special association includes *part-entirety* relation, *inherit* relation and *instantiation* relation. The user-defined association (**AssociateWith/BeAssociatedWith**) has sub-class and instance. For example, **AssociateWith(HasHusband)** or **HasHusband** ⊑ AssociateWith. The special association can be regarded as sub-classes of **AssociateWith/BeAssociatedWith** (i.e. **HasPart**

$\sqsubseteq$ AssociateWith, **HasKind** $\sqsubseteq$ AssociateWith, **HasInstance** $\sqsubseteq$ AssociateWith, **IsPartOf** $\sqsubseteq$ BeAssociatedWith, **IsKindOf** $\sqsubseteq$ BeAssociatedWith, **IsInstanceOf** $\sqsubseteq$ BeAssociatedWith).

HasPart/IsPartOf means *containing* relation, denoted as $C \sqsubseteq \exists$**HasPart**.D or $D \sqsubseteq \exists$**IsPartOf**.C. *Containing* can be classified into *combination* and *aggregation*, so **HasPart**$\equiv$**HasCombination** $\sqcup$HasAggregation, **IsPartOf**$\equiv$**IsCombinationOf** $\sqcup$IsAggregationOf. The *aggregation* can not be gained by reasoning. It has to be listed in A_A. The *combination* can not only be listed in A_A, but also be gained by reasoning. For example, if there exists $A \sqsubseteq \exists$**HasCombinationOf**.B and $B \sqsubseteq$ $\exists$**HasCombinationOf**.C in A_A, then we have $A \sqsubseteq \exists$**HasCombinationOf**.C.

HasKind/IsKindOf means inheritance relation, written as $C \sqsubseteq D$. It can not only be listed in A_X, but also be gained by reasoning. For example, if there exists **Man**$\equiv$**Person** $\sqcap \exists$**Age**.{**male**} in C_T, then **Man** $\sqsubseteq$ Person holds.

HasInstance/IsInstanceOf is to express the instantiation relation. It can not only be listed in X_D in the form of $C(X)$, but also be gained by reasoning. For example, if there exists **Man(Tom)** in X_D and **Man** $\sqsubseteq$ Person holds, then we have **Person(Tom)**.

Ontology Reasoning Based on Description Logics

Def.6 (valid interpretation): Given $O=<A_T, C_T,$ $X, X_D, A_A, A_X>$, if there exists an interpretation I, for every complex term $C \in C_T$, $C^I \neq \emptyset$ holds, and for every instance statement $\alpha \in X_D$, α holds, and for every term relation equation $r \in A_X$, r holds, then we say I is a valid interpretation.

Def.7 (term satisfaction checking): Given $O=<A_T, C_T, X, X_D, A_A, A_X>$, C is a class term or property term to be added into O. If there exists a valid interpretation I making $C^I \neq \emptyset$ holds, we say C is satisfied with respect to O, written as

$O \models C \uparrow$. Otherwise, we say C is not satisfied with respect to O, written as $O \models C \downarrow$.

Def.8 (term subsumption checking): Given $O=<A_T, C_T, X, X_D, A_A, A_X>$, C and D are two class terms or property terms, and $C \sqsubseteq D$ is not in O. If $C^I \subseteq D^I$ always holds for every valid interpretation I, we say D contains C with respect to O, written as $O \models C \sqsubseteq D$.

Def.9 (term equivalence checking): Given $O=<A_T, C_T, X, X_D, A_A, A_X>$, C and D are two class terms or property terms, and $C \equiv D$ is not in O. If $C^I = D^I$ always holds for every valid interpretation I, we say C is equivalent to D with respect to O, written as $O \models C \equiv D$.

Def.10 (term non-intersection checking): Given $O=<A_T, C_T, X, X_D, A_A, A_X>$, C and D are two class terms or property terms, and $C \between D$ is not in O. If $C^I \cap D^I = \emptyset$ always holds for every valid interpretation I, we say C does not intersect D with respect to O, written as $O \models C \between D$. Otherwise, we say C intersect D with respect to O, written as $O \models C \uplus D$.

Def.11 (implication checking for instance statement): Given $O=<A_T, C_T, X, X_D, A_A, A_X>$, and α is an instance statement. If α holds for every valid interpretation I, we say O implies α, written as $O \models \alpha$.

Def.12 (consistency checking for instance statement): Given $O=<A_T, C_T, X, X_D, A_A, A_X>$, and α is an instance statement. If there exists a valid interpretation I making α hold, we say α is consistent with respect to O, written as $O \models \alpha \uparrow$.

Based on the ontological structure in Def.1, we generalize the ontology reasoning into two types: term-oriented reasoning and instance-oriented reasoning.

1. Term-Oriented Reasoning and Conversion

Reasoning on class terms and property terms includes: term equivalence checking, term non-intersection checking, term intersection checking, term subsumption checking, and term satisfaction checking. The following conclusions have been proved in [20-22].

1. Term equivalence checking can be transformed into term satisfaction checking or term subsumption checking. (i.e. $O \models C \equiv D$ $\leftrightarrow O \models C \sqsubseteq D, O \models D \sqsubseteq C$; $O \models C \equiv D \leftrightarrow O \models (C \sqcap \neg D)\downarrow, O \models (\neg C \sqcap D)\downarrow)$

2. Term non-intersection checking can be transformed into term satisfaction checking or term subsumption checking. (i.e. $O \models C \text{ ⊕ } D \leftrightarrow O \models C \sqsubseteq \neg D$, $O \models D \sqsubseteq \neg C$; $O \models C \text{ ⊕ } D \leftrightarrow O \models (C \sqcap D)\downarrow)$

3. Term satisfaction checking and term subsumption checking can be transformed into each other. (i.e. $O \models C \sqsubseteq D \leftrightarrow O \models (C \sqcap \neg D)\downarrow$; $O \models C\downarrow \leftrightarrow O \models C \sqsubseteq \perp)$

4. Term satisfaction checking can be transformed into term expansion satisfaction checking. (i.e. $O \models C\uparrow \leftrightarrow O \models \Gamma_e(C)\uparrow)$

2. Instance-Oriented Reasoning and Conversion

Reasoning on instances statement includes: implication checking for instance statement and consistency checking for instance statement. The following conclusions have been proved in [16-18]

1. Implication checking for instance statement can be converted into consistency check-

ing for instance statement. (i.e. $O \models \alpha \leftrightarrow O \models (X_D \cup \{\neg\alpha\})\downarrow)$

2. Consistency checking for instance statement can be converted into consistency checking for instance statement expansion. (i.e. $O \models X_D\uparrow \leftrightarrow O \models \Gamma_e(X_D)\uparrow)$

Figure 3 shows the relation and conversion between the types of **ontology reasoning**. We have proved: term (expansion) satisfaction checking can be converted into consistency checking for instance statement (expansion). (i.e. $O \models C\uparrow \leftrightarrow \exists\alpha$ making $O \models (X_D \cup \{\alpha\})\uparrow$ holds; $O \models \Gamma_e(C)\uparrow \leftrightarrow \exists\alpha$ making $O \models \Gamma_e(X_D \cup \{\alpha\})\uparrow$ holds). Therefore, we have the conclusions that the two types of ontology reasoning are related to each other (Wang, Jiang and Hou, 2006; Wang, 2004; Yu, Wang and Luo, 2006).

In term-oriented reasoning, the five types of checking can be transmitted on term subsumption checking. Here, we can determine term subsumption checking by comparing the structure of the term formula. According to the algorithm (Baader, Calvanese, McGuinness, Nardi, & Patel-Schneider, 2003), term subsumption can be checked by the following steps: expand the term formula; standardize the term formula; simplify the term formula; compare the structure of the term formula.

In instance-oriented reasoning, the two types of checking can be transmitted to consistency checking for instance statement (expansion). Wang (2004) presents the rules for consistency checking

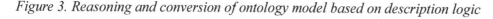

Figure 3. Reasoning and conversion of ontology model based on description logic

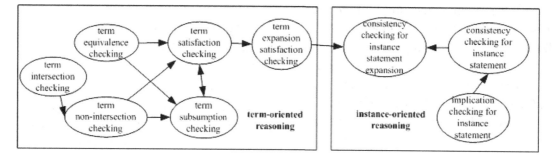

for instance statement (expansion) based on Tableau algorithm in description logic, considering the ontological structure of Def.1.

Ontological Structure Evaluation

The Gruber's criteria are widely accepted for the evaluation of ontological structure, due to its explicitness and objectivity, consistency, extensibility, minimal encoding bias, minimal ontological commitment (Gruber, 1993a). Suppose that $O=<A_T, C_T, X, X_D, A_A, A_X>$ is the original ontological structure, and $O'=<A_T', C_T', X', X_D', A_A', A_X'>$ is derived from O after being added some elements. Evaluation to the new ontological structure in Def.1 is as follows:

1. Explicitness and Objectivity. It requires the domain ontology to explain every term as objectively and explicitly as possible. The ontological structure of Def.1 consists of six elements with the formalization using description logic. This structure enables the clear and logical description to atomic term, complex terms, instances, instances description, attribute assignment and axioms.

2. Consistency. It requires the meanings of ontology itself to be compatible. For the ontological structure of Def.1, we should ensure $O' \models C\uparrow$ holds when adding a new term C to either A_T or C_T. Keep $O' \models \alpha\uparrow$ holding when a new instance α goes into X_D. And ensure $O' \models C\uparrow$, $O' \models X_D\uparrow$ and $O' \models (C\sqcap\neg D)\uparrow$ are all satisfied, when a term subsumption relation $C\sqsubseteq D$ is added to A_X. Otherwise, the new element can not be added into O. The process is done in a similar way in the case of adding a new term equivalence relation or term non-intersection relation.

3. Minimal ontological commitment. It requires that the domain ontology should be in the state of less redundancy. Moreover, all elements in domain ontology should be context-independent. That is, the initial domain ontology established just needs to meet knowledge-sharing in this field and should avoid too much description about specific things. For the ontological structure of Def.1, we should guarantee: (a) Add a new instance statement α in X_D, only if $O \models \alpha$ does not hold; (b) Add $C\sqsubseteq \exists\textbf{HasAttribute}.D$ to A_A, only if $O \models (C\sqsubseteq \exists\textbf{HasAttribute}.D)$ does not hold; (c)Add a new subsumption relation $C\sqsubseteq D$ to A_X, only if $O \models C\sqsubseteq D$ does not hold. Moreover, when we add a new equivalence or non-intersection relation, the processes are similar.

4. Extensibility. It requires that the already existing contents be kept steady when new elements are added. For the ontological structure of Def.1, a new term C can be added to A_T and C_T, only if $O' \models C\uparrow$ holds. Any new instance can be added to X without limitations. A new instance statement can go to X_D only if $O' \models X_D'\uparrow$ holds. We can add elements into A_X only when satisfaction checking of terms in C_T is fulfilled and all kinds of term relations in A_X are satisfied.

5. Minimal encoding bias. It is in semantic level rather than at syntactic level that ontology describes the domain knowledge. It means the domain ontology is coding independent. Description logic is a language, regarded as a sub-language of predicate logic, for describing concepts and their relations, and the reasoning in description logic can be determined. Thereby, description logic can be more applicable to ontology checking. In addition, the description logic can be expressed in RDF/XML format, which is favorable to ontology deployment in web environment. In this study, we use description logic to formalize the ontological structure. However, it should be noted that the new structure can also be described in other knowledge representation languages.

Figure 4. The pre-expansion based use mode of domain ontology

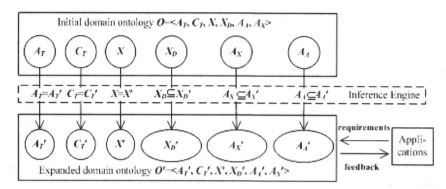

Two Types of Use Modes of Domain Ontology

1. Pre-Expansion Based Use Mode

As mentioned above, an initial domain ontology is required to meet the Gruber's principles, which means the domain ontology should keep as little redundancy as possible when established initially according to the principle of minimal ontological commitment. However, under the pre-expansion based use mode, the domain ontology should be expanded with all possible relations expressed explicitly by ontology reasoning from the initial one. Thus the expanded domain ontology will be concluded in this way with full redundancy for the future use by applications.

Suppose that $O=<A_T, C_T, X, X_D, A_A, A_X>$ is the initial domain ontology, and $O'=<A_T', C_T', X', X_D', A_A', A_X'>$ is the expanded one. The process is shown in Figure 1.

1. $A_T=A_T'$. Atomic terms, including class term and property term, remain unchanged.
2. $C_T=C_T'$. Complex terms also remain unchanged.
3. $X=X'$. Instances remain unchanged.
4. $X_D \subseteq X_D'$. Based on term relations in C_T and A_A, more instance statements can hold by inference, like $C(a)$.
5. $A_X \subseteq A_X'$. We can add more relations in A_X' like $C \sqsubseteq \exists \textbf{HasAttribute}.D$ from term relations in C_T and A_A.
6. $A_A \subseteq A_A'$. Based on term relations in C_T and A_A, we can replenish in A_X' more relations like $A \sqsubseteq B$, $A \equiv B$, $A \bigcap B$.

2. Application Driven Use Mode

Unlike pre-expansion based use mode, some possible relations need not be expressed explicitly at initial time in the application driven use mode until they are used by a certain application. And, the domain ontology will be expanded at run time using ontology inference engine for gaining some necessary relations to meet the certain requirement of the application. In addition, the expanded relations will be deleted once the application is complete. In this mode, the domain ontology will keep the state without redundancy before any application, and return to this state after being used. The process is shown in Figure 5.

APPLICATION OF ONTOLOGICAL STRUCTURE IN SEMANTIC RETRIEVAL

Information Request and Information Response

Def.13 (relational dataset): In order to facilitate discussion, information resource is simplified as a relational dataset with the form of $R(i_d, k_w, a_1, a_2, ..., a_n)$. Where, $i_d \in I_D$ is the ID of information re-

Figure 5. The application driven use mode of domain ontology

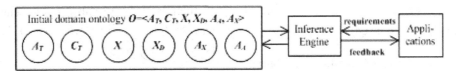

source and I_D is the ID set of information resource, k_w is the subject of information resource, $a_1, a_2, ...,$ a_n are the properties of information resource. $f(i_d,$ $x)$ means the value of information resource i_d on the property x ($x \in \{k_w, a_1, a_2, ..., a_n\}$).

The process of information retrieval can be generalized in two phases: information requesting and information responding. According to Figure1, the information request from users (especially for Chinese) will be processed by the segmentation algorithm, which will generate a series of terms. This is described in Def. 14.

Def.14 (information request): Given a system $I_S = <R, O>$, where, R is the relational dataset of the information resource, and O is domain ontology. ω is the information request submitted to I_S. Information request can be described as:

$$\omega ::= t \mid \omega \wedge \omega' \mid \omega \vee \omega' \mid \omega \wedge \neg \omega' \mid (\omega) \mid \varepsilon \qquad (1)$$

where, t is the term submitted by users and ε is an empty request. Apparently, information request ω is recursively formed from logical calculation between several keywords, which reflects user's expectation.

Def.15 (information response): Given a system $I_S = <R, O>$, and ω is the information request, information response $Q(\omega)$ is the retrieval result from I_S according to ω.

Property 1: Given information request ω and information response Q, the following equations hold:

i. $Q(\omega \wedge \omega') = Q(\omega) \cap Q(\omega')$

ii. $Q(\omega \vee \omega') = Q(\omega) \cup Q(\omega')$

iii. $Q(\omega \wedge \neg \omega') = Q(\omega) \backslash Q(\omega')$

iv. $Q(\varepsilon) = \varnothing$

Semantic Retrieval Rules Based on the New Ontological Structure

We adopt the application driven use mode described in Figure5. When the system gets the keyword t from information request, the reasoning engine will start, and the semantic retrieval rules below are followed for getting results. Given a system $I_S = <R, O>$, and $r(t) = \{i_d \mid f(i_d, k_w) = t, i_d \in I_D\}$ is an ID set of information resource with its subject t.

1. If $t \in A_T \cup C_T$, and t belongs to class term, then the following rules can be chosen according to the semantic level users want:

S_{11}: Start "term equivalence checking" for term set $T_1 = \{l \mid l \equiv t, \ l \in A_T \cup C_T\}$, and the feedback is $Q(t) = \bigcup_{t_i \in T_1} r(t_i)$.

S_{12}: Search C_T for term set $T_2 = \{l_i \mid l \equiv l_1 \sqcup l_2 \sqcup ... \sqcup l_n, \ l \in T_1, \ l_i \in A_T \cup C_T\}$, and the feedback is $Q(t) = \bigcup_{t_i \in T_2} r(t_i)$.

S_{13}: Search C_T for term set $T_3 = \{l_i \mid l \equiv l_1 \sqcap l_2 \sqcap ... \sqcap l_n, \ l \in T_1, \ l_i \in A_T \cup C_T\}$, and the feedback is $Q(t) = \bigcap_{t_i \in T_3} r(t_i)$.

S_{14}: Start "term subsumption checking" for term set $T_4 = \{l' \mid l' \sqsubseteq 1, \ l \in T_1, \ l' \in A_T \cup C_T\}$, and the feedback is $Q(t) = \bigcup_{t_i \in T_4} r(t_i)$.

S_{15}: Start "term subsumption checking" for term set $T_5 = \{l' \mid l \sqsubseteq l', \ l \in T_1, \ l' \in A_T \cup C_T\}$, and the feedback is $Q(t) = \bigcap_{t_i \in T_5} r(t_i)$.

S_{16}: Start "implication checking for instance statement" for instance set $T_6=\{l'|l\ (l'),\ l\in T_1,\ l'\in X\}$, and the feedback is $Q(t) = \bigcup_{t_i\in T_6} r(t_i)$.

S_{17}: Remind users to input relational property P, then start "term subsumption checking" for term set $T_7=\{l'|l'\sqsubseteq \forall P.l或l\sqsubseteq \forall P.l',\ l\in T_1,\ l'\in A_T\cup C_T\}$ and instance set $T_7'=\{l'|l\sqsubseteq \forall P.\{l'\},\ l\in T_1,\ l'\in X\}$. The feedback is $Q(t) = \bigcup_{t_i\in T_7\cup T_7'} r(t_i)$.

S_{18}: Remind users to input relational property P, then start "term subsumption checking" for term set $T_8=\{l'|l'\sqsubseteq \exists P.l或l\sqsubseteq \exists P.l',\ l\in T_1,\ l'\in A_T\cup C_T\}$ and instance set $T_8'=\{l'|l\sqsubseteq \exists P.\{l'\},\ l\in T_1,\ l'\in X\}$. The feedback is $Q(t) = \bigcup_{t_i\in T_8\cup T_8'} r(t_i)$.

We can prove that $S_{11}\subseteq S_{12}\subseteq S_{14}$, $S_{11}\subseteq S_{13}\subseteq S_{15}$, $S_{11}\subseteq S_{16}$. S_{11} achieves high precision for it's equivalence relations-based. S_{14}, S_{15} and S_{16} achieve high recall by being based on subsumption and instantiation relations respectively. S_{17} and S_{18} are used to return some information with relations to the concepts submitted by users, and these relations are chosen and specified by users online.

2. If $t\in X$, then the following rules can be chosen according to the semantic level users want:

S_{21}: Start "consistency checking for instance statement" for the term set $T_1=\{l|l\ (t),\ l\in A_T\cup C_T\}$, and the feedback is $Q(t) = \bigcup_{t_i\in T_1} r(t_i)$.

S_{22}: For every term of T_1 from S_{21}, start one of the rules in (1) above to get the results.

S_{23}: Remind users to input relational property P, then search X_D for instance set $T_2=\{l|P(l,\ t)$ or $P(t,\ l),\ l\in X\}$. The feedback is $Q(t) = \bigcup_{t_i\in T_2} r(t_i)$.

S_{24}: Remind users to input relational property P, then start "term subsumption checking" to get term set $T_3=\{l|l\sqsubseteq \forall P.\{t\},\ l\in A_T\cup C_T\}$. The feedback is $Q(t) = \bigcup_{t_i\in T_3} r(t_i)$.

S_{25}: Remind users to input relational property P, then start "term subsumption checking" for term set $T_4=\{l|l\sqsubseteq \exists P.\{t\},\ l\in A_T\cup C_T\}$. The feedback is $Q(t) = \bigcup_{t_i\in T_4} r(t_i)$.

Among the rules above, S_{21} achieves high precision by searching the classes of the instance terms submitted by users. S_{22} achieves high recall by using the rules in (1) to start a semantic retrieval of the classes of instances. S_{23}, S_{24} and S_{25} return the information that is related to the instances submitted by users, and these relations are chosen and specified by users online.

3. If $t\in A_T\cup C_T$ and t belongs to numerical property term, then the following rules can be chosen according to the semantic level users want:

S_{31}: Start "term equivalence checking" for term set $T_1=\{l|l\equiv t,\ l\in A_T\cup C_T\}$. Then start "term subsumption checking" for term set $T_2=\{l'|l'\sqsubseteq \exists \textbf{HasAllribule}.l,\ l'\in A_T\cup C_T, l\in T_1\}$. The feedback is

$$Q(t) = \bigcup_{t_i\in T_2} r(t_i)\cap\{i_d\ |\ f(i_d,t)\neq\varnothing, i_d\in I_D, t\in T_1\}$$

S_{32}: Search C_T for term set $T_3=\{l_i|l\equiv l_1\sqcup l_2\sqcup \ldots\sqcup l_n,\ l\in T_1,\ l_i\in A_T\cup C_T\}$. If $T_3\neq\varnothing$, start "term subsumption checking" for term set $T_4=\{l'|l'\sqsubseteq \exists \textbf{HasAllribule}.l,\ l'\in A_T\cup C_T,\ l\in T_3\}$. The feedback is

$$Q(t) = \bigcup_{t_i\in T_4} r(t_i)\cap\{i_d\ |\ f(i_d,t)\neq\varnothing, i_d\in I_D, t\in T_3\}$$

S_{33}: Search C_T for term set $T_5=\{l_i|l\equiv l_1\sqcap l_2\sqcap \ldots\sqcap l_n,\ l\in T_1,\ l_i\in A_T\cup C_T\}$. If $T_5\neq\varnothing$, start "term subsumption checking" for term $T_6=\{l'|l'\sqsubseteq \exists \textbf{HasAllribule}.l,\ l'\in A_T\cup C_T,\ l\in T_5\}$. The feedback is

$$Q(t) = \bigcup_{t_i\in T_6} r(t_i)\cap\{i_d\ |\ f(i_d,t)\neq\varnothing, i_d\in I_D, t\in T_5\}$$

S_{34}: Start "term subsumption checking" for term set $T_7=\{l'|l'\sqsubseteq l,\ l'\in A_T\cup C_T,\ l\in T_1\}$. If $T_7\neq\varnothing$, start "term subsumption checking" for term set $T_8=\{l'|l'\sqsubseteq \exists \textbf{HasAllribule}.l,\ l'\in A_T\cup C_T,\ l\in T_7\}$. The feedback is

$$Q(t) = \bigcup_{t_i \in T_8} r(t_i) \cap \{i_d \mid f(i_d, t) \neq \varnothing, i_d \in I_D, t \in T_7\}$$

S_{35}: Start "term subsumption checking" for term set $T_9 = \{l' \mid l \sqsubseteq l', l' \in A_T \cup C_T, l \in T_1\}$. If $T_9 \neq \varnothing$, start "term subsumption checking" for term set $T_{10} = \{l' \mid l' \sqsubseteq \exists \textbf{HasAllribute}.l, l' \in A_T \cup C_T, l \in T_9\}$. The feedback is

$$Q(t) = \bigcup_{t_i \in T_{10}} r(t_i) \cap \{i_d \mid f(i_d, t) \neq \varnothing, i_d \in I_D, t \in T_9\}$$

We can prove that $S_{31} \subseteq S_{32} \subseteq S_{34}$ and $S_{31} \subseteq S_{33} \subseteq S_{35}$. S_{31} achieves high precision by being based on equivalence relation search, S_{34} and S_{35} achieve high recall by being based on inclusion relation search, while S_{32} and S_{33} are in between them.

4. If $t \in A_T \cup C_T$ and t belongs to relational property term, then the following rules can be chosen according to the semantic level users want:

S_{41}: Start "term equivalence checking" for term set $T_1 = \{l \mid l \equiv t$ or $l \equiv t, l \in A_T \cup C_T\}$ and remind users to input a term c. If c is a class team, start "term subsumption checking" for a mixed set of term and instance $T_2 = \{c' \mid c' \sqsubseteq \forall l.c$ or $c \sqsubseteq \forall l.c', c' \in A_T \cup C_T, l \in T_1\} \cup \{c' \mid c \sqsubseteq \forall l.\{c'\}, c' \in X, l \in T_1\}$. If c is a instance, search X_D and start "term subsumption checking" for a mixed set of term and instance $T_2 = \{c' \mid l(c, c')$ or $l(c', c), c' \in X, l \in T_1\} \cup \{c' \mid c' \sqsubseteq \forall l.\{c\}, c' \in A_T \cup C_T, l \in T_1\}$. The final result is $Q(t) = \bigcup_{t_i \in T_2} r(t_i)$.

S_{42}: Start "term equivalence checking" for term set $T_1 = \{l \mid l \equiv t$ or $l \equiv t$, $l \in A_T \cup C_T\}$ and remind users to input a term c. If c is a class term, start "term subsumption checking" for a mixed set of term and instance $T_3 = \{c' \mid c' \sqsubseteq \exists l.c$ or $c \sqsubseteq \exists l.c', c' \in A_T \cup C_T, l \in T_1\} \cup \{c' \mid c \sqsubseteq \exists l.\{c'\}, c' \in X, l \in T_1\}$. If c is an instance, search X_D and start "term subsumption checking" for a mixed set of term and instance $T_3 = \{c' \mid l(c, c')$ or $l(c', c), c' \in X, l \in T_1\} \cup \{c' \mid c' \sqsubseteq \exists l.\{c\}, c' \in A_T \cup C_T, l \in T_1\}$. The final result is $Q(t) = \bigcup_{t_i \in T_3} r(t_i)$.

S_{43}: Search C_T for term set $T_4 = \{l_i \mid l \equiv l_1 \sqcup l_2 \sqcup \ldots \sqcup l_n, l \in T_1, l_i \in A_T \cup C_T\}$. If $T_4 \neq \varnothing$, remind users to input a term c. If c is a class term, start "term subsumption checking" for a mixed set of term and instance $T_5 = \{c' \mid c' \sqsubseteq \exists l.c$ or $c \sqsubseteq \exists l.c'$ or $c' \sqsubseteq \forall l.c$ or $c \sqsubseteq \forall l.c', c' \in A_T \cup C_T, l \in T_4\} \cup \{c' \mid c \sqsubseteq \exists l.\{c'\}$ or $c \sqsubseteq \forall l.\{c'\}, c' \in X, l \in T_4\}$. If c is a instance, search X_D and start "term subsumption checking" for a mixed set of term and instance $T_5 = \{c' \mid l(c, c')$ or $l(c', c), c' \in X, l \in T_4\} \cup \{c' \mid c' \sqsubseteq \exists l.\{c\}$ or $c' \mid c' \sqsubseteq \forall l.\{c\}, c' \in A_T \cup C_T, l \in T_4\}$. The final result is $Q(t) = \bigcup_{t_i \in T_5} r(t_i)$.

S_{44}: Search C_T for term set $T_6 = \{l_i \mid l \equiv l_1 \sqcap l_2 \sqcap \ldots \sqcap l_n, l \in T_1, l_i \in A_T \cup C_T\}$. If $T_4 \neq \varnothing$, remind users to input a term c. If c is a class term, start "term subsumption checking" for a mixed set of term and instance $T_7 = \{c' \mid c' \sqsubseteq \exists l.c$ or $c \sqsubseteq \exists l.c'$ or $c' \sqsubseteq \forall l.c$ or $c \sqsubseteq \forall l.c', c' \in A_T \cup C_T, l \in T_6\} \cup \{c' \mid c \sqsubseteq \exists l.\{c'\}$ or $c \sqsubseteq \forall l.\{c'\}, c' \in X, l \in T_6\}$. If c is a instance, search X_D and start "term subsumption checking" for a mixed set of term and instance $T_7 = \{c' \mid l(c, c')$ or $l(c', c), c' \in X, l \in T_6\} \cup \{c' \mid c' \sqsubseteq \exists l.\{c\}$ or $c' \mid c' \sqsubseteq \forall l.\{c\}, c' \in A_T \cup C_T, l \in T_6\}$. The final result is $Q(t) = \bigcap_{t_i \in T_7} r(t_i)$.

S_{45}: Start "term subsumption checking" for term set $T_8 = \{l' \mid l' \sqsubseteq l, l' \in A_T \cup C_T, l \in T_1\}$. If $T_8 \neq \varnothing$, remind users to input a term c. If c is a class term, start "term subsumption checking" for a mixed set of term and instance $T_9 = \{c' \mid c' \sqsubseteq \forall l.c$ or $c \sqsubseteq \forall l.c'$ or $c' \sqsubseteq \forall l.c$ or $c \sqsubseteq \forall l.c', c' \in A_T \cup C_T, l \in T_8\} \cup \{c' \mid c \sqsubseteq \exists l.\{c'\}$ or $c \sqsubseteq \forall l.\{c'\}, c' \in X, l \in T_8\}$. If c is a instance, search X_D and start "term subsumption checking" for a mixed set of term and instance $T_9 = \{c' \mid l(c, c')$ or $l(c', c), c' \in X, l \in T_8\} \cup \{c' \mid c' \sqsubseteq \exists l.\{c\}$ or $c' \mid c' \sqsubseteq \forall l.\{c\}, c' \in A_T \cup C_T, l \in T_8\}$. The final result is $Q(t) = \bigcup_{t_i \in T_9} r(t_i)$.

S_{46}: Start "term subsumption checking" for term set $T_{10} = \{l' \mid l \sqsubseteq l', l' \in A_T \cup C_T, l \in T_1\}$. If $T_{10} \neq \varnothing$, remind users to input a term c. If c is a class term, start "term subsumption checking" for a mixed set of term and instance $T_{11}=\{\ c'|c'\sqsubseteq\forall l.c$ or $c\sqsubseteq\forall l.c'$ or $c'\sqsubseteq\forall l.c$ or $c\sqsubseteq\forall l.c'$, $c'\in A_T\cup C_T$, $l\in T_{10}\}\cup$ $\{c'|c\sqsubseteq\exists l.\{c'\}$ or $c\sqsubseteq\forall l.\{c'\}$, $c'\in X$, $l\in T_{10}\}$. If c is an instance, search X_D and start "term subsumption checking" for a mixed set of term and instance $T_9=\{c'|l(c,c')$ or $l(c',c)$, $c'\in X$, $l\in T_{10}\}\cup\{c'|c'\sqsubseteq\exists l.\{c\}$ or $c'|c'\sqsubseteq\forall l.\{c\}$, $c'\in A_T\cup C_T$, $l\in T_{10}\}$. The final result is $Q(t)=\bigcap_{t_i\in T_{11}}r(t_i)$.

When the information request contains relational property terms, it is necessary for users to submit concepts online related to the relational property terms. Only by obtaining related concepts which have the above mentioned relation (i.e. relational property terms) can the precision be increased. Among the rules above, S_{41} and S_{42} realize high precision, S_{45} and S_{46} realize high recall, while the others are in between them.

CONCLUSION AND FUTURE RESEARCH

The word association at semantic level using domain ontology is a hot spot in the area of information retrieval. This paper firstly puts forward an ontological structure, consisting of atomic term, complex terms, instances, instances description, attribute assignment and axioms, with new structure expressed in description logic language. Then the ontological structure is evaluated using five criteria given by Gruber. Based on the structure, we propose two reasoning mechanisms (terms-oriented and instances-oriented) for semantic retrieval application, as well as the conversion mechanisms and determining algorithms. All these enable the reasoning for various relations in a specific area according to the rules made by domain experts. Finally, we put forward four kinds of rules for word association using the ontology reasoning mechanisms to improve the semantic understanding ability of information retrieval systems.

We are now cooperating with Hong Kong Polytechnic University and the library of Tongji

University on the construction of an OWL formatted domain ontology of Chinese minority, containing 782 terms of atomic classes and properties, 325 instances with their statements, 235 complex terms, and 42 axioms. At present, the development of a semantic retrieval prototyping system for library collections of Chinese minority literatures is still in progress. The system will adopt Pellet, a reasoning engine that support Tableau algorithm for describing logics, to implement the searching rules proposed in this paper. There will be a human-computer interacting system, and the executions of some searching rules will be driven by users' preferences. The system will show clues derived from ontology reasoning during the searching process, then further understand users' intention according to the online responses, and offer the corresponding searching results.

The future work will focus on the following: (1) efficient algorithm of ontology reasoning based on description logic; (2) engineering methodology of domain ontology; (3) development of the term constructors in description logic form.

ACKNOWLEDGMENT

This work is partially supported by the National Natural Science Foundation of China under Grants No.70501024,70971099, Shanghai Leading Academic Discipline Project (B310), RGC Grant polyU5237/08E and CRG Grants 1-ZV41, G-U756. We also get helps from Ministry of Education (MOE) of China by the Humanity & Social Science Research (05JC870013).

REFERENCES

Albanese, M., Capasso, P., Picariello, A., & Rinaldi, A. M. (2005). Information Retrieval from the Web: An Interactive Paradigm. In *Advances in Multimedia Information Systems* (LNCS 3665, pp. 17-32). Heidelberg: Springer.

Baader, F., Calvanese, D., McGuinness, D. L., Nardi, D., & Patel-Schneider, P. (2003). *The description logic handbook: theory, implementation and applications.* Cambridge: Cambridge University Press.

Feng, B., Hu, G., Zhao, K., & Yi, J. (2006). Research and realization on self-feeding back Chinese words segmentation system. [in Chinese]. *Computer Technology and Development, 16*(5), 7–9.

Finin, T., Ding, L., Pan, R., Joshi, A., Kolari, P., Java, A., & Peng, Y. (2005). Swoogle: searching for knowledge on the semantic web. In *Proc. of the 20th National Conference on Artificial Intelligence and the 17th Innovative Applications of Artificial Intelligence Conference, Pittsburgh, Pennsylvania,*1682-1683. Retrieved March 10, 2007, from https://www.aaai.org/Papers/AAAI/2005/ISD05-007.pdf

Foo, S., & Li, H. (2004). Chinese word segmentation and its effect on information retrieval. *Information Processing & Management, 40*(1), 161–190. doi:10.1016/S0306-4573(02)00079-1

Freitas, F. L. G., & Bittencourt, G. (2000). Cognitive multi-agent systems for integrated information retrieval and extraction over the Web. In *Advances in Artificial Intelligence* (LNCS 1952, pp. 310-319). Heidelberg: Springer.

Fu, G., Kit, C., & Webster, J. J. (2008). Chinese word segmentation as morpheme-based lexical chunking. *Information Sciences, 178*(9), 2282–2296.

Gómez-Pérez, A. (1998). Knowledge sharing and reuse . In Liebowitz, J. (Ed.), *The Handbook on Expert systems.* CRC Press.

Gracia, J., Trillo, R., Espinoza, M., & Mena, E. (2006). Querying the web: a multiontology disambiguation method. In *Proc. of the 6th Int'l Conf. on Web Engineering* (pp. 241-248). Palo Alto, California: ACM.

Gruber, T. R. (1993a). *Toward principles for the design of ontologies used for knowledge sharing.* Paper presented at the International Workshop on Formal Ontology, Padova, Italy.

Gruber, T. R. (1993b). A translation approach to portable ontology specification. *Knowledge Acquisition, 5*(2), 199–220. doi:10.1006/knac.1993.1008

Guarino, N., Masolo, C., Vetere, G., & Council, N. R. (1999). OntoSeek: content-based access to the web. *IEEE Intelligent Systems, 14*(3), 70–80. doi:10.1109/5254.769887

Guha, R., McCool, R., & Miller, E. (2003). Semantic search. In *Proc. of the 12th Int'l Conf. on World Wide Web* (pp. 700-709). Hungary: Budapest: ACM.

Köhler, J., Philippi, S., Specht, M., & Rüegg, A. (2006). Ontology based text indexing and querying for the semantic web. *Knowledge-Based Systems, 19*(8), 744–754. doi:10.1016/j.knosys.2006.04.015

Kruse, P. M., Naujoks, A., Röesner, D., & Kunze, M. (2005). Clever search: a wordnet based wrapper for internet search engines. In *Proc. of the 2nd GermaNet Workshop: Applications of GermaNet II.* Bonn, Germany: Arxiv preprint.

Liu, S. (2005). *A model-theoretic semantics for XML and its applications.* Unpublished doctoral dissertation (in Chinese), Beijing University, Beijing, China.

Moldovan, D. I., & Mihalcea, R. (2000). Using WordNet and lexical operators to improve internet searches. *IEEE Internet Computing, 4*(1), 34–43. doi:10.1109/4236.815847

Nagypál, G., & Motik, B. (2003). A fuzzy model for representing uncertain, subjective and vague temporal knowledge in ontologies. In *On The Move to Meaningful Internet Systems 2003: CoopIS, DOA, and ODBASE* (LNCS 2888, pp. 906-923). Heidelberg: Springer.

Naing, M. M., Lim, E. P., & Goh, D. H. L. (2002). Ontology-based web annotation framework for hyperLink structures. In *Proc. of the Int'l Workshop on Data Semantics in Web Information Systems (DASWIS'02)* (pp. 184-193). Singapore.

Navigli, R., & Velardi, P. (2003). *An analysis of ontology-based query expansion strategies.* Paper presented at the International Workshop on Adaptive Text Extraction and Mining, Cavtat-Dubrovnik, Croatia.

Shah, U., Finin, T., Joshi, A., Cost, R. S., & Matfield, J. (2002). Information retrieval on the semantic web. In *Proc. of the 11th Int'l Conf. on Information and Knowledge Management* (pp. 461-468). New York: ACM.

Song, W., & Zhang, M. (2004). *Semantic Network.* Beijing: High Education Press. (in Chinese)

Vallet, D., Fernández, M., & Castells, P. (2005). An ontology-based information retrieval model. In *The Semantic Web: Research and Applications* (LNCS 3532, pp. 455-470). Heidelberg: Springer.

Wang, H. (2004). *Research on the construction of metadata models based on ontology.* Unpublished doctoral dissertation (in Chinese), Shanghai Jiaotong University, Shanghai, China.

Wang, H., Jiang, F., & Hou, L. W. (2005). Study on development process of semantic-oriented metadata model. [in Chinese]. *Information Science, 23*(1), 95–101.

Wang, H., Jiang, F., & Hou, L. W. (2006). Checking problems of ontology-based metadata extended models. [in Chinese]. *Systems Engineering-theory & Practice, 26*(10), 57–66.

Wang, X., & Du, L. (2003). Automatic segmentation of Chinese using overlaying ambiguity examining method and statistics language model. [in Chinese]. *Journal of Electronics and Information Technology, 25*(9), 1168–1173.

Xu, C. (2007). *Web service match based on ontology reasoning.* Unpublished doctoral dissertation (in Chinese), Ocean University of China, Qingdao, China.

Yu, C., Wang, H., & Luo, Y. (2006). Extended ontology model and ontology checking based on description logics. In Wang et al. (Eds.), *Fuzzy Systems and Knowledge Discovery: Vol. 4223. Artificial Intelligence* (pp. 607-610). Heidelberg: Springer.

Yuan, L., Li, Z., & Chen, S. (2008). Ontology-Based Annotation for Deep Web Data. [in Chinese]. *Journal of Software, 19*(2), 237–245. doi:10.3724/SP.J.1001.2008.00237

Zghal, H. B., Aufaure, M. A., & Mustapha, N. B. (2007). A model-driven approach of ontological components for on-line semantic web information retrieval. *Journal of Web Engineering, 6*(4), 309–336.

Zhang, M., Lu, Z., & Zou, C. (2004). A Chinese word segmentation based on language situation in processing ambiguous words. *Information Sciences, 162*(3-4), 275–285. doi:10.1016/j.ins.2003.09.010

Zhang, M., & Ma, J. (2009). An approach to Chinese word sense disambiguation based on HowNet. *Computer Technology and Development (in Chinese), 19*(2), 9-11, 15.

KEY TERMS AND DEFINITIONS

Ontology: An ontology is an explicit formal specifications of the terms in the domain and relations among them. An ontology defines a common vocabulary for researchers who need to share information in a domain. It includes machine-interpretable definitions of basic concepts in the domain and relations among them. The reasons for developing an ontology are: (1) To share common understanding of the structure of information among people or software agents; (2) To enable reuse of domain knowledge; (3) To make domain assumptions explicit; (4) To separate domain knowledge from the operational knowledge; (5) To analyze domain knowledge

Semantic Retrieval: Semantic retrieval is a process used to improve online searching by using data from semantic networks to disambiguate queries and web text in order to generate more relevant results. The user provides the search engine with a phrase which is intended to denote an object about which the user is trying to gather information. There is no particular document which the user knows about that s/he is trying to get to. Rather, the user is trying to locate a number of documents which together will give him/her the information s/he is trying to find. Semantic retrieval lends itself well here. Rather than use ranking algorithms such as Google's PageRank to predict relevancy, semantic retrieval uses semantics, or the science of meaning in language to produce highly relevant search results. In most cases, the goal is to deliver the information queried by a user rather than have a user sort through a list of loosely related keyword results.

Ontology Reasoning: Ontology reasoning based on Description Logics can be classified into two types: (1) term-oriented reasoning, which is the reasoning on class terms and property terms including term equivalence checking, term non-intersection checking, term intersection checking, term subsumption checking, and term satisfaction checking; (2) instance-oriented reasoning, which is the reasoning on instances statement including implication checking for instance statement and consistency checking for instance statement. The two types of ontology reasoning are related, and can be converted to each other. With the ontology reasoning, the automatic word association will be enabled at semantic level for information retrieval.

Description Logic: Description logics (DL) are a family of knowledge representation languages which can be used to represent the concept definitions of an application domain in a structured and formally well-understood way. The name description logic refers, on the one hand, to concept descriptions used to describe a domain and, on the other hand, to the logic-based semantics which can be given by a translation into first-order predicate logic. Description logic was designed as an extension to frames and semantic networks, which were not equipped with formal logic-based semantics. They form a middle ground solution: including some more expressive operations than propositional logic and having decidable or more efficient decision problems than first order predicate logic. Description logic was given its current name in the 1980s. Previous to this it was called terminological systems, and concept languages. Today description logic has become a cornerstone of the Semantic Web for its use in the design of ontologies. The OWL-DL and OWL-Lite sublanguages of the W3C-endorsed Web Ontology Language (OWL) are based on description logic.

Gruber's Criteria: Gruber discusses ontologies as design artifacts, and outlines a set of design criteria to guide ontology development. These criteria are: (1) Clarity: Definitions should be objective, free of social or computational context, and documented with natural language; (2) Coherence: The defining axioms should be logically consistent and sanction inferences consistent with the definitions. (3) Extendibility: The ontology should anticipate new used of the shared vocabulary. (4) Minimal encoding bias: Encoding bias occurs when a choice of representation is made simply for the convenience of notation. The conceptualization should be specified at the knowledge level without depending on a particular symbol-level encoding. (5) Minimal ontological commitment: An agent is said to commit to an ontology when its actions are consistent with the ontology's definitions. An ontology should make a minimal number of claims about the world being modeled.

Chapter 7
A Framework on Data Mining on Uncertain Data with Related Research Issues in Service Industry

Edward Hung

Hong Kong Polytechnic University, Hong Kong

ABSTRACT

There has been a large amount of research work done on mining on relational databases that store data in exact values. However, in many real-life applications such as those commonly used in service industry, the raw data are usually uncertain when they are collected or produced. Sources of uncertain data include readings from sensors (such as RFID tagged in products in retail stores), classification results (e.g., identities of products or customers) of image processing using statistical classifiers, results from predictive programs used for stock market or targeted marketing as well as predictive churn model in customer relationship management. However, since traditional databases only store exact values, uncertain data are usually transformed into exact data by, for example, taking the mean value (for quantitative attributes) or by taking the value with the highest frequency or possibility. The shortcomings are obvious: (1) by approximating the uncertain source data values, the results from the mining tasks will also be approximate and may be wrong; (2) useful probabilistic information may be omitted from the results. Research on probabilistic databases began in 1980s. While there has been a great deal of work on supporting uncertainty in databases, there is increasing work on mining on such uncertain data. By classifying uncertain data into different categories, a framework is proposed to develop different probabilistic data mining techniques that can be applied directly on uncertain data in order to produce results that preserve the accuracy. In this chapter, we introduce the framework with a scheme to categorize uncertain data with different properties. We also propose a variety of definitions and approaches for different mining tasks on uncertain data with different properties. The advances in data mining application in this aspect are expected to improve the quality of services provided in various service industries.

DOI: 10.4018/978-1-61520-819-7.ch007

INTRODUCTION

Data mining has been widely used as an important process to improve the quality of services in service industry, e.g., targeted marketing and churn reduction using classification, store-layout design and promotion design using association rule mining, and customer segmentation using clustering. In fact, nowadays, service systems (such as customer service systems) depend heavily on data mining (business intelligence) to analyze collected user data in order to learn from them and improve the next interactions or services provided to the users again.

There has been a large amount of research work done on mining on relational databases, which are often used in service industry. Commercial vendors such as IBM, Microsoft, Oracle, SPSS Inc., DBMiner Technology Inc. as well as research institutions have been producing commercial products or research prototypes to accomplish these mining tasks. Classical sub-areas of data mining include association rules (patterns that associate features in data to discover, for example, interesting spending patterns among customers), clustering (grouping of similar data such as customers records) and classification (assigning data into predefined classes, e.g., identifying profitable customers that are likely to churn).

These works were done on databases that store data in exact values. However, in many real-life applications such as those commonly used in service industry, the raw data are usually uncertain when they are collected or produced. Sources of uncertain data include readings from sensors (such as RFID tagged in products in retail stores), information extracted using probabilistic parsing of input sources, classification results (e.g., identities of products or customers) of image processing using statistical classifiers, results from predictive programs used for stock market or targeted marketing as well as predictive churn model in customer relationship management. These uncertain data may be in the form of an exact value with margins of error, sometimes with or without a probability distribution (or density) function. The result may also be represented as an interval or a set of values, one of which may be the real value.

In this chapter, we will mainly use an example of a banking system for illustration purpose. Readers are reminded that similar techniques could be applied to other application systems in other application domains. Consider a bank receives a loan application. It may consider the applicant's credit worthiness, assets, and liabilities. The credit worthiness may be uncertain because different agencies may collect different credit histories (possibly with errors) and generate different credit scores. Assets and liabilities are in fact uncertain values due to ever-changing stock prices and interest rates, hard-to-evaluate intangible assets (e.g., patents, copyrights), and the rapid trading in global market. Clustering of past applications into different clusters (groups of similar applications) may provide the manager or decision maker a clear picture of possible main categories of applications. By comparing the new loan application with those clusters (main categories of similar applications) may help the user to make a decision of approving or rejecting the application. Careful examination of some clusters of customers may also reveal valuable customers who could be sold high-value products through up-selling or cross-selling, which is an important element of customer relationship management.

However, since traditional databases only store exact values, uncertain data are usually transformed into exact data by, for example, taking the mean value (for quantitative attributes) or by taking the value with the highest frequency or possibility. This makes the storage, query and mining much simpler by using existing commercial database systems and mining techniques, but the shortcomings are obvious:

1. By approximating the uncertain source data values, the results from the mining tasks

will also be approximate and may be wrong. For example, the locations of centroids of clusters become deviated from the real ones, or some data may be assigned to the wrong clusters. As a result, in the above example, the new loan application may be assigned to a wrong cluster (category of similar applications) and a wrong decision of approval or rejection may be made.

2. *Useful probabilistic information may be omitted from the results.* For example, there is a region of locations where an uncertain data object X may be located, with a particular probability for each location. It is found that X has a probability 0.8 to be located closer to the centroid of cluster A rather than the centroid of cluster B. However, by storing the weighted average location of X in the database, the original probabilistic result may be completely simplified to "X is located closest to cluster A and is assigned to cluster A" only. For example, the probabilistic information that "the new loan application has a probability of 60% to be similar to a particular cluster" may be simplified as "the new loan application is similar to a particular cluster", where the information of "60% probability" is now lost which may be originally an important information for the manager to make a correct decision.

Research on probabilistic databases began in 1980s. Recently, the proliferation of other areas such as sensor networks and image processing gains the attention of researchers to work on how to support various kinds of interesting queries that can be asked on these uncertain data. While there has been a great deal of work on supporting uncertainty in databases, there is increasing work on mining on such uncertain data. Therefore our objective is to propose a framework where:

1. uncertain data are classified into different categories,

2. different *probabilistic data mining* techniques are applied directly on these uncertain data,

3. results are produced to preserve the accuracy and the possible interesting knowledge mined from the original uncertain data.

While considering uncertain data, there are many common concerns across different data mining tasks, such as the probabilistic distances/similarity measures. Thus in studying this research area, we need to address the following issues:

1. **Categorization of uncertain data:** define categories and properties of uncertain data under different dimensions, and identify the unique characteristics and problems within a category as well as common ones across different subsets of categories;

2. **Theoretical analyses:** modify the existing common definitions used in data mining tasks such as distance measures to incorporate probabilistic information; introduce new definitions or modify existing definitions such as support and confidence of association rules if necessary; ascertain the theoretical correctness; determine the criteria where data mining by approximating uncertain data will produce wrong results or results that are worse than the results produced by directly processing on uncertain data;

3. Algorithm design for association rule mining, clustering and classification:
   ○ develop *probabilistic algorithms* by (i) modifying the existing non-probabilistic algorithms and (ii) proposing new algorithms that run on uncertain data directly and produce correct results;
   ○ propose approximate probabilistic algorithms which are intermediate between the two categories of (i) existing non-probabilistic algorithms working on certain data, and (ii) the

above probabilistic algorithms; the approximate probabilistic algorithms produce results that are intermediate between the above two categories in terms of accuracy and running time; derive the approximation ratios.

4. **Implementation and experiments:** implement and empirically evaluate the above algorithms on uncertain data to compare (in terms of accuracy and running time) with the approach of using existing algorithms on exact data transformed from uncertain data; analyze the results and provide suggestions on the criteria where each kind of algorithms is the best suitable.

This chapter would like to introduce to the readers the applications and problems of incorporating uncertainty into service systems and applications. First, it describes some previous related work, followed by different categories of uncertain data. Next, a framework for the researchers to investigate into the issues of uncertain data mining is introduced. The framework provides a research methodology for researchers to compare different possible approaches. Then, modified probabilistic distance measure is described. Examples of issues encountered in uncertain data mining such as association rule mining and clustering are given. Researchers are more interested in the above two data mining tasks, and so research on classification on uncertain data is still in an early development stage. Finally, a high-level example is given to illustrate how uncertain data mining may help service industry before concluding this chapter.

PREVIOUS WORK

Researchers began working on *probabilistic databases* (uncertain data are stored in probabilistic data models) in late 1980s. An earlier attempt was done to incorporate probabilities on disjoint events (tuples) (Cavallo & Pittarelli, 1987) or attributes

(Barbara, Garcia-Molina & Porter, 1992) into the relational data model. Barbara, Garcia-Molina & Porter (1992)'s algebra and independence assumption among attributes were extended respectively by Dey & Sarkar (1996) with new operations and by Lakshmanan, Leone, Ross & Subrahmanian (1997) with different probabilistic strategies and interval probabilities. Aggregate operations were then considered in Ross, Subrahmanian & Grant (2005). The research on uncertain data management was further extended to other kinds of databases such as temporal databases (Dekhtyar, Ross & Subrahmanian, 2001) and object databases (Eiter, Lu, Lukasiewicz & Subrahmanian, 2001). The semistructured (XML) databases were also extended with independence assumption (Nierman & Jagadish, 2002), arbitrary probabilistic distributions among children with a formal theory and algebra (Hung, Getoor & Subrahmanian, 2003b) as well as interval probabilities (Hung, Getoor & Subrahmanian, 2003b; Hung, Getoor & Subrahmanian, 2007) and aggregate operations (Hung, 2005). Details can be found in a survey paper (Hung, 2009).

In this chapter, we will consider probabilistic relational databases. The data mining on other probabilistic data models will be a possible extension. As mentioned above, there are several probabilistic relational models, but there has never been any formal categorization of these models. We will show our categorization in the next section. The categorization is important because some uncertain data models may share some common characteristics which may indicate common issues we need to address across different data mining tasks. The categorization also simplifies the analysis of the requirements of different algorithms.

Data mining has been well studied under the following three main categories: association rule mining, clustering and classification. These works were done on traditional relational databases where data are stored in exact values.

Association rules show relationships among attributes. An association rule is in the form $X \rightarrow Y$

where itemsets X and Y are disjoint subsets of a set of items I. The support of a rule is defined as the percentage of transactions that contain $X \cup Y$. A rule's confidence is defined as the ratio of the number of transactions that contains $X \cup Y$ to that contains X. The rule mining problem is to identify all rules with supports and confidences over some thresholds. Rules can be generated from large (frequent) itemsets. The apriori algorithm was proposed in Agrawal & Srikant (1994). Using hash tables to improve efficiency was proposed in Park, Chen & Yu (1995). An FP-tree was proposed in Han, Pei & Yin (2000) to generate frequent patterns without candidate generation. Uncertain data may mean imprecise observations of some attributes (items) or even the whole event (object/transaction). For example, in a medical diagnosis, the doctor may not be certain for the symptoms of fever and rash when they are not obvious, which produces uncertainty in the attribute level. If more than one doctor gives a diagnosis to one patient, we have more than one observation to one object (event), with each diagnosis having its relative likeliness (i.e., probability), which induces uncertainty in the object level. We will see later how the original apriori algorithm can be modified to work on uncertain data. We also examine the applicability of some existing techniques including hashing and FP-tree. In addition to binary association rules, we will also consider quantitative association rules, i.e., some attributes are quantitative, where the classical case (on exact data) was studied in Srikant & Agrawal (1996), Miller & Yang (1997). Research has also been done on outsourcing of association rules mining (Wong, Cheung, Hung, Kao & Mamoulis, 2007; Wong, Cheung, Hung & Liu, 2008; Wong, Cheung, Hung, Kao & Mamoulis, 2009). In this chapter, we will also examine the original definition of association rules to see whether it is needs modification for the uncertain data.

Clustering groups similar data into clusters. Jain, Murty & Flynn (1999) give a very good survey of clustering. Examples of uncertain data include imprecise locations of objects in sensor networks where immediate updates are impractical. There are many clustering methods. We will first consider the possibilities of extensions of a few representative ones in the prototype-based (k-means), density-based (DBSCAN (Ester, Kriegel, Sander & Xu, 1996)), and grid-based clustering (Hinneburg & Keim, 1999). Other kinds of clustering algorithms will be considered in the future. K-means algorithm assigns each object to a cluster with the closest centroid (prototype). Various distance measures between uncertain objects need to be defined for this purpose. Just like there are different definitions of clusters on exact data, we will also provide a few definitions of k-means clusters on uncertain data according to the definition of centroid (certain or uncertain) and the cluster membership (exact or fuzzy). In fact, the fuzzy-membership version of k-means (called fuzzy c-means) was proposed in Bezdek (1974) on exact data. The membership is fuzzy because it is divided among the clusters with weights corresponding to how "good" the clusters are. We will generalize it for uncertain objects later. Possible modifications on density-based and grid-based algorithms will also be discussed there. We notice that this research area has been increasingly attracting several researchers' attention, e.g., Kriegel and Pfeifle have modified DBSCAN and OPTICS (Kriegel & Pfeifle, 2005b) for density-based clustering on uncertain data without fuzzy membership. Recently researchers are also interested in clustering of web search results to help users to look for relevant web pages more easily (Xiao & Hung, 2008).

Classification assigns objects to predefined classes. Well known methods include decision tree induction (Murthy, 1998) and naive Bayesian classifier (Langley, Iba & Thompson, 1992). Both of them are used on exact data. Towards the end of this chapter, we describes briefly the possible modifications. Clustering algorithms such as w-k-means have also been incorporated into classification algorithm to produce decision cluster classifiers (Li, Hung, Chung & Huang, 2008). Other methods to improve classification accuracy include removing outliers detected by efficient outlier detection algorithms (Hung & Cheung, 2002; Szeto, & Hung, 2009).

CATEGORIZATION OF UNCERTAIN DATA

In this chapter, we will describe our categorization of uncertain data and propose several enhanced algorithms for association rule mining, clustering and classification. In this section, we will first introduce categorization of different uncertain data.

Here we consider relational data where every attribute only contains one value. The uncertainty of data can appear in two levels: the attribute level and/or the object (or tuple/transaction) level. In the attribute level, due to the uncertain nature or actual system limitation in the data collection phase, the imperfect data quality leads to uncertain attribute values. In principle, an uncertain attribute value may extend over the whole attribute domain. To be more practical and computationally efficient, we will only consider, for an attribute of an object, discrete values or range values whose probabilities are greater than zero or some given threshold. The set of these values are called the *attribute interpretation domain* of that attribute of a given object, where each value is an *attribute interpretation*. In the other words, an attribute interpretation is a value that the particular attribute of a specified object may actually contain. The union of these values is called the *attribute uncertainty domain*. Note that the uncertainty domain is a set of single values for "discrete value" case and a set of one or more ranges for "range of value" case. The set of ranges may not be identical to the union of the ranges because of possible overlappings.

A *probability distribution function* (PDF, for discrete values) can be defined to describe the probability distribution of interpretations. Essentially, a PDF can be defined over the attribute domain so that the values outside the uncertainty domain have zero probability. For example, consider a car park monitoring service system. The value of the "color" attribute of a car, obtained from an image processing system taking pictures of cars parked in a car park, may be uncertain due to the dim lighting. Using a discrete attribute, the system may conclude that the car may be "dark red", "light red", or "pink" with a PDF *Pcolor* where the probabilities of these possible values are given as: *Pcolor* ("*DarkRed*") = 0.6, *Pcolor* ("*LightRed*")=0.3, *Pcolor* ("*Pink*")=0.1, *Pcolor* returns zero for other values. In the continuous counterpart of the above discrete attribute example, the system may store uncertain RGB values as ranges of values, with a *probability density function* (pdf, for continuous values) to describe the probability density of the interpretations.

Usually, we use an object to represent one event (or an operation, an observation, a transaction, etc). However, when an event is uncertain and has one or more possible cases, we may like to represent each case by a "possible object" separately, which we call an *object interpretation* to distinguish it from an ordinary object used to represent a certain event. In other words, an object may consist of a set of one or more object interpretations. For example, an economy analysis service system may use two different predictive programs to predict "the GDP growth rate, inflation rate, unemployment rate" of 2006. An uncertain result may be obtained with the following object interpretations: (2006, 3±0.2, 2.5±0.15, 4.3±0.26), (2006, 2.9±0.2, 2.4±0.13, 4.5±0.29). This set of object interpretations is called the *object interpretation domain* of the uncertain object. Note that the *object uncertainty domain* (the union of the object interpretations) is identical to the object interpretation domain. Similarly we can define a PDF to define the probability distribution of the object interpretations.

We can categorize uncertain data under the following six dimensions divided in two levels:

1. *Attribute Level* (for each object/tuple/ transaction)
   a. *Attribute Discreteness*: Attribute values are discrete (single values) or continuous (ranges of values)?
   b. *Attribute Uncertainty Cardinality*: The maximum size of the attribute uncertainty domain. Note: The cardinality for the "continuous" case is the sum of the size of the ranges in the uncertainty domain.
   c. *Attribute Probabilistic Completeness*: The PDF or pdf is complete (sum or integral equals 1)?
2. *Object (or Tuple/Transaction) Level*
   a. *Object Uncertainty Cardinality*: The maximum size of the object uncertainty domain.
   b. *Object Probabilistic Completeness*: The PDF of object interpretations is complete (sum or integral equals 1)?
   c. *Attribute Probabilistic Relationship*: The probabilistic relationship among attributes (e.g., probabilistic independence?)

Using the above dimensions, traditional certain or exact data are: (i) attribute and object uncertainty cardinalities equal to 1; (ii) attribute and object probabilistically complete. Note that it is possible to transform the uncertainty domain and PDFs of the attribute level to those of the object level under certain assumptions and vice versa.

This transformation is useful in our algorithm design illustrated later.

This categorization is important because, as shown later, it allows us to incrementally modify the existing algorithms or add features in our novel algorithms to accommodate the different characteristics of the uncertain data in a systematic manner.

Towards the end of this chapter, we will describe how we can incrementally modify the existing algorithms when the data are uncertain in different dimensions. We will consider the spectrum of data uncertainty by *different combinations of the following properties*: (I) object probabilistic incomplete, (II) object uncertainty cardinality > 1, (III) some attribute is probabilistic incomplete, (IV) some attribute's uncertainty cardinality > 1, (V) a probability distribution function (i.e., a joint probability table) or a probability density function is given over the product of all attributes' uncertainty domains. In cases (III) and (IV), the probabilistic independence assumption among attributes is made, unless specified otherwise. Uncertain data have at least one of the above properties. Table 1 shows the properties of some probabilistic relational data models described in the previous section.

Table 1. Properties of some probabilistic relational data models

Properties	Model references			
	[A]	**[B]**	**[C]**	**[D]**
(I) object probabilistic incomplete	no	no	yes	no
(II) object uncertainty cardinality > 1	yes	no	yes	yes
(III) attribute probabilistic incomplete	no	yes	no	no
(IV) attribute uncertainty cardinality > 1	no	yes	no	yes
(V) PDF/pdf given over product of attributes	no	no	no	no

Note: The models denoted by [A], [B], [C] and [D] are Cavallo & Pittarelli (1987), Barbara, Garcia-Molina & Porter (1992), Dey & Sarkar (1996), and Lakshmanan, Leone, Ross & Subrahmanian (1997) respectively. In [A] model, 1 tuple per relation. In [D], interval probabilities are used; original representation is in attribute level while annotated representation is in object level.

FRAMEWORK

A suggested framework of data mining on uncertain data involves the development of analytic solutions (e.g., for probabilistic distance measures) and data structures (e.g., index structures for nearest neighbors, frequent itemsets), algorithm design (modifying existing algorithms and developing new probabilistic and approximate algorithms), theoretical analysis of algorithms, and implementation of a probabilistic data mining system. Experiments should be conducted to compare the performance of the following approaches:

1. transform uncertain data to exact data and apply existing data mining algorithms on them (output as *Result 4* in Figure 1)
2. use the original uncertain data, develop and apply the following algorithms on them:
    a. algorithms modified from the existing data mining algorithms (*Result 2*)
    b. novel probabilistic algorithms (*Result 1*)
    c. develop and apply approximate algorithms that (i) may not make the full use of the uncertainty information of uncertain data, (ii) may use approximate definitions and/or techniques, and (iii) may have running time and result quality intermediate between those of (1) and (2). (*Result 3*)

Under this framework, the results should be analyzed and verified whether the resulting quality and running time are decreasing from Result 1/2, 3, to 4. *One of the goals is to develop novel probabilistic algorithms to produce results (Result 1) of a higher quality in shorter running time compared with the results (Result 2) produced by modified algorithms while the overheads compared with producing Result 4 are small.* It is also important to find the criteria where each approach is the best suitable.

Figure 1. A framework of data mining on uncertain data

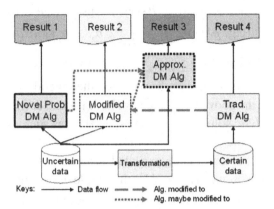

PROBABILISTIC DISTANCE MEASURES

As uncertain data are considered, changes are required on some original definitions. One important definition is the distance measure, which will be described below. Furthermore, we may also need to modify the original definition of association rules or propose new measures in addition to the support and confidence. Moreover, modifications of other definitions including density, reachability and entropy may also be considered.

We call a *probabilistic object* (or PO) an object with its uncertainty domain and its PDF/pdf. Consider two POs X, Y whose pdfs are $p_X(x), p_Y(y)$, where x and y are locations of X and Y, $UD(X)$ and $UD(Y)$ are the uncertainty domains of X and Y, $d(x, y)$ is the distance between x and y. The following give the expected distance and the pdf of the distance between X and Y.

Expected distance between X and Y =
$$\int_{UD(x)} \int_{UD)y)} d(x,y) p_X(x) p_Y(y) dx dy$$

We can define a pdf $d_{X,Y}$ which returns the probability that the distance between X and Y equals k as follows:

$$d_{X,Y}(k) = \int_{UD(x)} \int_{UD)y)} F(x,y) p_X(x) p_Y(y) dx dy$$

where k is a real number ≥ 0; $F(x, y) = 1$ if $d(x, y) = k$; $F(x, y) = 0$ otherwise.

When PDFs (e.g. $PX(x)$) are used instead of pdfs (e.g. $pX(x)$), $\int_{UD(x)} \int_{UD(y)} p_X(x) p_Y(y) dx dy$ is changed to $\sum_{UD(X)} \sum_{UD(Y)} p_X(x) p_Y(y)$.

Because it is very hard to solve the general case like the above in practice, we have tried to derive analytic solutions for some special cases such as when the pdfs are uniform distributions. Moreover, instead of the expected distance between two POs, we also consider the simpler cases such as the expected distance between a point and a PO. Note that a point has the minimum expected squared distance from a PO if and only if it has the minimum expected distance from that PO. Thus, one way to simplify the derivation is to consider expected squared distances which are easier to derive than expected distances. Below give some examples of our results. Consider the uniform distribution. As shown in Figure 2, the expected squared distance between a point and a PO whose uncertainty domain is (i) a line is $c2 + (a2 - ab + b2)/3$; (ii) a circle is $c2 + r2/2$; (iii) a sphere is $c2 + 3r2/5$.

In Xiao & Hung (2007), several methods are proposed to calculate the expected distance, among which Approximation by Single Gaussian (ASG) can obtain results of very high accuracy in a very short execution time. In Xiao & Hung (2007), a theorem states that the expected distance obtained by ASG is equivalent to the result of computing the average of distances between all random samples.

Existing approaches involve distance computations between samples of two objects, which is very computationally intensive. On one hand, it is expensive to calculate and store the actual distribution of the possible distance values between two uncertain objects. On the other hand, the expected distance (the weighted average of the pairwise distances among samples of two uncertain objects) provides very limited information

Figure 2. Two simplified cases for derivation of analytic solutions of probabilistic distance

and also restricts the definitions and usefulness of queries and mining tasks. In Hung & Xiao (2008) and Xiao, Hung & Hung (in press), we propose several approaches to calculate the mean of the actual distance distribution and approximate its variance. Based on these, we suggest that the actual distance distribution could be approximated using a standard distribution like Gaussian or Gamma distribution. Experiments on real data and synthetic data show that our approach produces an approximation in a very short time with acceptable accuracy (about 90%). We suggest that it is practical for the research communities to define and develop more powerful queries and data mining tasks based on the distance distribution instead of the expected distance.

MODIFICATION OF EXISTING DATA MINING ALGORITHMS

Association Rule Mining

Binary Association Rules

Our first basic approach is based on the apriori algorithm (Agrawal & Srikant, 1994). The simplest case is property (I), i.e., data are certain except each transaction (object) has a probability which may not be one. We can add a weight (the probability) to each transaction. The original algorithm can be modified by adding the weight to the itemsets' counts. For property (II), we can simply treat each object interpretation as a separate object weighted by its probability obtained from the object's PDF. If the data has property (III), the weights (probabilities) of different itemsets from the same object are the products of the probability of the object multiplied by the probabilities of the existence or non-existence of the items (with the independence assumption). Any probabilistic strategy to calculate the joint probability will be used instead if it is specified. Otherwise, the independence assumption will be used. For property (V), a PDF is specified on the set of possible itemsets, so the probability given by the PDF for an itemset is multiplied by the object probability to produce the final weight of this itemset. For the above four properties, the approach of hash tables (Park, Chen & Yu, 1995) can be modified by adding the counts with the weight of an itemset rather than 1 as in the original case. The approach of FP-trees (Han, Pei & Yin, 2000) can be similarly modified for property (I), (II) and (V) but not (III) because when an object is read, it updates the count in the nodes on the path in the FP-tree (where the path indicates the set of items in the object). However, now different combinations of items in an object may have different weights, which cannot be maintained. Unless we transform the uncertainty domains and PDFs of the attribute level to those of the object level, then the uncertain data has the property (V).

Because the attributes are binary, so the probability p of the existence of an item also derives the probability $(1 - p)$ of its non-existence, so the property (IV) is absorbed in (III). In Chui, Kao & Hung (2007), we study the problem of mining frequent itemsets from uncertain data under a probabilistic framework. We consider transactions whose items are associated with existential probabilities and give a formal definition of frequent patterns under such an uncertain data model. We show that traditional algorithms for mining frequent itemsets are either inapplicable or computationally inefficient under such a model. A data trimming framework is proposed to improve mining efficiency. Through extensive experiments, we show that the data trimming technique

can achieve significant savings in both CPU cost and I/O cost.

Quantitative Association Rules

Quantitative association rules (Srikant & Agrawal, 1996; Miller & Yang, 1997) can be categorized as (1) (static or dynamic) discretization of quantitative attributes, and (2) distanced-based. For (1), property (IV) means that an attribute has more than one possible value with a PDF. One approach is to try all combinations using the possible values and compute their probabilities. Pruning techniques should be considered for this potentially exponential computation cost. For (2), we can use our probabilistic distance measure. This research topic is one of those that should be addressed.

Clustering

Generalized Fuzzy Membership of Uncertain Data

As briefly mentioned before, we have a few options to represent the cluster membership: exact (complete) or fuzzy (partial). Consider the following (the fuzzy membership in Bezdek (1974) corresponds to item 1(b) below):

1. When we consider a point and some clusters, (a) the point has an exact (complete) membership to the cluster which is the "best" (where the definition of "best" can be based on the distance from the cluster's centroid, or the density within a region and the connectivity to the cluster, etc), or (b) the membership is fuzzy and divided among the clusters with weights corresponding to how "good" the clusters are.

2. When we consider a set of points or a region (which is the object uncertainty domain of a particular PO), their exact/fuzzy memberships are transformed to the PO's (a) exact membership, or (b) fuzzy membership. The

transformation of (a) can be the weighted mode while that of (b) can be the weighted average.

Therefore, uncertain data that have only properties (I) and/or (III) only have one point in each object's uncertainty domain, i.e., the cluster membership can be either 1(a) or 1(b). For others, a cluster membership can be one of the following combinations (in the order of possibly increasing uncertain information): (A):1(a)+2(a), (B):1(a)+2(b), (C):1(b)+2(a), and (D):1(b)+2(b).

K-Means

The centroid of a cluster can be defined as an exact data point or a PO in the order of increasing complexity and (possibly) correctness as follows (note: we are working on the correctness of saying that the following have the increasing correctness):

1. If the data PO's uncertainty cardinality equal 1 (only properties (I) and/or (III)), the cluster's centroid as a point is computed as the (weighted) mean of the objects that belongs to this cluster. The weight is the object's probability multiplied by its degree of membership to this cluster.
2. Otherwise, (a) each data PO is represented by a point (weighted average) and then a point centroid is computed as above (note: the memberships are weighted average); or (b) a point centroid is computed by weighted average over the uncertainty domains of the data POs (note: weighted over the probabilities and memberships); (c) a PO centroid is computed which has a PDF/pdf showing the probabilities of places that the centroid is located (note: this computation over the uncertainty domains is very expensive).

The probabilistic distance measures introduced previously are necessary tools as we need to determine the distance between a PO and a cluster and

the PO's cluster membership. Recent work such as Ngai, Kao, Cheng, Chau, Yip & Chui (2006) considers Case 2(b) above.

DBSCAN and Grid-Based Clustering

DBSCAN (Ester, Kriegel, Sander & Xu, 1996) finds for a cluster a set of core points that are dense and reachable and a set of border points that are reachable to those core points. When a point is replaced by a PO, the corresponding definitions like neighbourhood and density need modifications. Exact membership is used in Kriegel & Pfeifle (2005a) and Kriegel & Pfeifle (2005b). Grid-based clustering (Hinneburg, & Keim, 1999), which divides the space into grid cells and forms clusters from dense cells, may require only slight modifications such as the process of computing the density. There are many other clustering methods, which should be also considered.

Classification.

In building the decision tree (Murthy, 1998), the split of the training objects leads to the option of exact/fuzzy memberships again. The measures (such as entropy, gini and classification error) used to determine the best way to split the objects also require the corresponding modifications. In the naive Bayesian classifier (Langley, Iba & Thompson, 1992), the computation of conditional probabilities and prior probabilities should be weighted by the probabilities in the objects as well as the attributes. Other classifiers will also be considered.

OTHER RESEARCH ISSUES TO ADDRESS AND AN EXAMPLE APPLICATION ON SERVICE INDUSTRY

Because the original designs of existing algorithms do not take the uncertainty and probabilities into consideration, the above approach of modifying them may have a high penalty in performance due to the high complexity of problem and data themselves. Therefore, the next step is to design and develop novel algorithms tailor-made for different kinds of uncertain data which may be more efficient. On the other hand, it may be a good idea to sacrifice a little accuracy or quality of the results if we can obtain the results in much shorter running time. This leads to the idea of approximate algorithms, which may not take all the probabilistic information into consideration. In fact, some of the options mentioned above (such as exact membership, point centroids) reduce the running time and give approximate results. We will examine how these categories of algorithms perform on the uncertain data.

It is also important to implement and empirically evaluate the above approaches, analyze the results and provide suggestions on the criteria where each kind of algorithms is the best suitable.

Finally, before concluding this chapter, we would like to suggest two simple example of the above uncertain data mining problems in some service industries. The first example is the motivating example at the beginning of this chapter: a bank receives a loan application and an uncertain clustering application may help the manager to decide whether to approve or reject the loan application. We consider that the applicant's credit worthiness, assets, and liabilities are represented in uncertain values (a range interval of possible values), and hence, the loan application is represented as a probabilistic object. First, we cluster previous loan applications (represented as probabilistic objects) using an enhanced version of K-means algorithm which works on uncertain data. Clusters are represented by their uncertain centroids (again, probabilistic objects). Different uncertain clustering algorithms may produce cluster centroids in different forms. For example, if the approach in Ngai, Kao, Cheng, Chau, Yip & Chui (2006) is used, then the cluster centroids will be points rather than probabilistic objects.

Expected distance can be calculated between the new loan application and clusters' centroids in order to derive the degree of similarities between the new loan application and each cluster. Fuzzy cluster memberships of the new loan application can then suggest the manager how likely the new loan application is similar to a particular cluster of other previous loan applications. Finally the manager can make an educated decision based on the above findings.

Frequent itemset mining on uncertain data may also be helpful in customer service systems. For example, customer information may be collected via interactions with customers. These information may contain uncertainty (e.g., their interests, assets, which are usually told by customers in some vague terms). Similar interesting patterns (frequent itemsets) can be mined across different customers in order to discover useful knowledge that may help improve customer relationship through targeted marketing as well as customer retention program.

CONCLUSION

We have shown the significance of developing data mining techniques on uncertain data as well as presented a research framework. We have introduced a categorization scheme to classify uncertain data into different categories with different properties. We have introduced a framework which provides a research methodology to develop a variety of mining algorithms for different kinds of uncertain data. Our future works include implementing and evaluating the details of the above algorithms as well as proposing other novel and approximate algorithms.

ACKNOWLEDGMENT

This work has been partially supported by grant PolyU 5174/07E, 5191/09E from Hong Kong

RGC, grants A-PA5S, A-PH10, A-PH40, A-SA14, G-U524 and 1-ZV5P from PolyU.

REFERENCES

Agrawal, R., & Srikant, R. (1994). Fast algorithms for mining association rules in large databases. In *Proc. of International Very Large Databases Conference* (pp. 589–598).

Barbara, D., Garcia-Molina, H., & Porter, D. (1992). The management of probabilistic data. *IEEE Transactions on Knowledge and Data Engineering, 4*(5), 487–50. doi:10.1109/69.166990

Bezdek, J. (1974). Cluster validity with fuzzy sets. *Journal of Cybernetics, 3*(3), 58–73. doi:10.1080/01969727308546047

Cavallo, R., & Pittarelli, M. (1987). The theory of probabilistic databases. In *Proceedings of the 13th International Conference on Very Large Data Bases* (pp. 71-81).

Chui, C. K., Kao, B., & Hung, E. (2007). Mining frequent itemsets from uncertain data. In *Proc. of the 11th Pacific-Asia Conference on Knowledge Discovery and Data Mining (PAKDD-2007)*.

Dekhtyar, A., Ross, R., & Subrahmanian, V. (2001). Probabilistic temporal databases, I. [TODS]. *ACM Transactions on Database Systems, 26*(1). doi:10.1145/383734.383736

Dey, D., & Sarkar, S. (1996). A probabilistic relational model and algebra. [TODS]. *ACM Transactions on Database Systems, 21*(3), 339–369. doi:10.1145/232753.232796

Eiter, T., Lu, J., Lukasiewicz, T., & Subrahmanian, V. (2001). Probabilistic object bases. *ACM Transactions on Database Systems, 26*(3), 264–312. doi:10.1145/502030.502031

Ester, M., Kriegel, H., Sander, J., & Xu, X. (1996). A density-based algorithm for discovering clusters in large spatial databases with noise. In *Proc. of 2nd Int'l Conf. on Knowledge Discovery and Data Mining*, (pp. 226-231).

Han, J., Pei, J., & Yin, Y. (2000). Mining frequent patterns without candidate generation. In *Proc. of ACM SIGMOD* (pp. 1–12).

Hinneburg, A., & Keim, D. (1999). Optimal grid-clustering: towards breaking the curse of dimensionality in high-dimensional clustering. In *Proc. of the 25th VLDB Conf.*, (pp. 506-517).

Hung, E. (2005). *Managing Uncertainty and Ontologies in Databases*. Unpublished doctoral dissertation, University of Maryland, College Park.

Hung, E. (2009). Probabilistic XML. In Aggarwal, C. C. (Ed.), *Managing and Mining Uncertain Data*. Springer. doi:10.1007/978-0-387-09690-2_12

Hung, E., & Cheung, D. (2002). Parallel mining of outliers in large database. [DAPD]. *Distributed and Parallel Databases, 12*, 5–26. doi:10.1023/A:1015608814486

Hung, E., Getoor, L., & Subrahmanian, V. (2003a). Probabilistic Interval XML. In *Proc. of International Conference on Database Theory (ICDT)*, Siena, Italy.

Hung, E., Getoor, L., & Subrahmanian, V. (2003b). PXML: A Probabilistic Semistructured Data Model and Algebra. In *Proceedings of the 19th International Conference on Data Engineering (ICDE)* (pp. 467-478).

Hung, E., Getoor, L., & Subrahmanian, V. (2007). Probabilistic Interval XML. [TOCL]. *ACM Transactions on Computational Logic, 8*(4), 1–38. doi:10.1145/1276920.1276926

Hung, E., & Xiao, L. (2008). An efficient representation model of distance distribution between two uncertain objects. In *Proc. of IEEE First Pacific-Asia Workshop on Web Mining and Web-based Application 2008 (WMWA'08), in conjunction with the 12th Pacific-Asia Conference on Knowledge Discovery and Data Mining (PAKDD-2008)*, Osaka, Japan.

Jain, A., Murty, M., & Flynn, P. (1999). Data clustering: A review. *ACM Computing Surveys*, *31*(3), 264–323. doi:10.1145/331499.331504

Kriegel, H., & Pfeifle, M. (2005a). Density-based clustering of uncertain data. In *Proc. 11th Int. Conf. on Knowledge Discovery and Data Mining (KDD'05)* (pp. 672-677).

Kriegel, H., & Pfeifle, M. (2005b). Hierarchical density-based clustering of uncertain data. In *Proc. 5th IEEE Int. Conf. on Data Mining (ICDM'05)*.

Lakshmanan, V., Leone, N., Ross, R., & Subrahmanian, V. (1997). Probview: A flexible probabilistic database system. *ACM Transactions on Database Systems*, *22*(3), 419–469. doi:10.1145/261124.261131

Langley, P., Iba, W., & Thompson, K. (1992). An analysis of bayesian classifiers. In *Proc. of the 10th National Conf. on Artificial Intelligence* (pp. 223-228).

Li, Y., Hung, E., Chung, K., & Huang, J. (2008). Building a decision cluster classification model for high dimensional data by a variable weighting k-means method. In *Proc. of the Twenty-First Australasian Joint Conference on Artificial Intelligence*, Auckland.

Miller, R., & Yang, Y. (1997). Association rules over interval data. In *Proc. 1997 ACM-SIGMOD'97*.

Murthy, S. (1998). Automatic construction of decision trees from data: a multidisciplinary survey. *Data Mining and Knowledge Discovery*, *2*(4), 345–389. doi:10.1023/A:1009744630224

Ngai, J., Kao, B., Cheng, R., Chau, M., Yip, K., & Chui, C. K. (2006). Efficient Clustering of Uncertain Data, in *Proc. of The 2006 IEEE International Conference on Data Mining* (pp. 436-445), Hong Kong.

Nierman, A., & Jagadish, H. (2002). ProTDB: Probabilistic data in xml. In *Proc. of the 28th VLDB Conference*, Hong Kong, China.

Park, J., Chen, M., & Yu, P. (1995). An effective hash-based algorithm for mining association rules. In *Proc. of ACM SIGMOD* (pp. 175-186).

Ross, R., Subrahmanian, V., & Grant, J. (2005). Aggregate operators in probabilistic databases. *Journal of the ACM*, *52*, 54–101. doi:10.1145/1044731.1044734

Srikant, R., & Agrawal, R. (1996). Mining quantitative association rules in large relational tables. In *Proc. of ACM SIGMOD* (pp. 1-12).

Szeto, C. C., & Hung, E. (2009). Mining outliers with faster cutoff update and space utilization. In *Proc. of the 13th Pacific-Asia Conference on Knowledge Discovery and Data Mining (PAKDD-2009)*, Bangkok, Thailand.

Wong, W. K., Cheung, D. W., Hung, E., Kao, B., & Mamoulis, N. (2007). Security in outsourcing of association rule mining. In *Proc. of the 33rd International Conference on Very Large Data Bases (VLDB)*, University of Vienna, Austria.

Wong, W. K., Cheung, D. W., Hung, E., Kao, B., & Mamoulis, N. (2009). An audit environment for outsourcing of frequent itemset mining. In *Proceedings of the VLDB Endowment (PVLDB)*, 2.

Wong, W. K., Cheung, D. W., Hung, E., & Liu, H. (2008). Protecting privacy in incremental maintenance for distributed association rule mining. In *Proc. of the 12th Pacific-Asia Conference on Knowledge Discovery and Data Mining (PAKDD2008)*, Osaka, Japan.

Xiao, L., & Hung, E. (2007). An efficient distance calculation method for uncertain objects. In *Proc. of 2007 IEEE Symposium on Computational Intelligence and Data Mining (CIDM)*, Honolulu, Hawaii, USA.

Xiao, L., & Hung, E. (2008). Clustering web-search results using transduction-based relevance model. In *Proc. of IEEE First Pacific-Asia Workshop on Web Mining and Web-based Application 2008 (WMWA'08), in conjunction with the 12th Pacific-Asia Conference on Knowledge Discovery and Data Mining (PAKDD2008)*, Osaka, Japan.

Xiao, L., Hung, E., & Hung, R. Y. S. (in press). An Efficient Representation Model of Distance Distribution Between Uncertain Objects. *Computational Intelligence*.

Section 3
Applications and Case Studies

Chapter 8
Business Transformation Workbench:
A Practitioner's Tool for Business Transformation

Juhnyoung Lee
IBM T. J. Watson Research Center, USA

Rama Akkiraju
IBM T. J. Watson Research Center, USA

Chun Hua Tian
IBM China Research Laboratory, China

Shun Jiang
IBM China Research Laboratory, China

Rong Zeng Cao
IBM China Research Laboratory, China

Siva Danturthy
IBM Global Services India

Ponn Sundhararajan
IBM Global Services India

Rakesh Mohan
IBM T. J. Watson Research Center, USA

Wei Ding
IBM China Research Laboratory, China

Carl Nordman
IBM Global Business Services, USA

ABSTRACT

Business transformation is a key management initiative that attempts to align people, process and technology of an enterprise more closely with its business strategy and vision (Lee, 2005). Business transformation is an essential part of the competitive business cycle. Existing consulting methods and tools do not address issues such as scalability of methodology, data and knowledge management, method enforcement, asset reuse and governance, consolidated views of upstream and downstream analyses well, to name a few. This paper presents Business Transformation Workbench which is a practitioner's tool for business transformation addressing these problems. It implements a methodical approach that was devised to analyze business transformation opportunities and make business cases for transformation initiatives and thereby provides decision-support to the consultants. The Business Transformation Workbench builds on a component-based model of a business and offers a consolidated view into clients' operations, organization, staffing, processes and IT. It provides an intuitive way to evaluate and

DOI: 10.4018/978-1-61520-819-7.ch008

understand various opportunities in staff and IT consolidation and process standardization. It embodies structured analytical models, both qualitative and quantitative, to enhance the consultants' practices. The Business Transformation Workbench has been instantiated with data from finance management domain and applied to address a client situation as a case study. An alpha testing of the tool was conducted with about dozen practitioners. The feedback has been encouraging. 90% of the consultants who tested the BT Workbench tool felt that the tool would help them do a better job during a client engagement. The tool is currently being piloted with customer engagements in a large IT consulting organization.

INTRODUCTION

Business transformation is a key management initiative that attempts to align people, process and technology of an enterprise closely with its business strategy and vision. Business transformation is often achieved by taking a holistic look at various dimensions of an enterprise such as business models, management practices, business processes, organizational structure and technology and optimizing them with best-practice or differentiated methods to reach a strategic end state. For example, business transformation in the enterprise finance area would, among others, optimize financial processes such as accounts receivables, eliminate non-value-added tasks, improve efficiency and productivity of people, and reduce errors by using technologies. Business transformation is considered an essential part of the competitive business cycle.

Consulting service companies in the business transformation area brand technology and consulting as their core product and service offerings. These offerings include models, methods and tools devised for facilitating business transformation. While the state-of-the-art business transformation consulting models and methods are useful, there are a number of general problems that need to be addressed to make them more effective. First, the current approaches are often limited in scalability because they demand subject matter experts to work with a variety of disconnected data, tools, templates and other assets. It is often cumbersome and difficult to streamline the data gathering and management manually. Data and documents often reside in multiple folders distributed among several machines. Consistency checking across data can only be done manually, and the process requires experts. Additionally, it is hard to capture a structured thinking process without a tool which enforces the process or method. Furthermore, it is difficult to disseminate and reuse knowledge effectively, if it is not captured systematically. In addition, assets such as knowledge, models and methods are not necessarily managed. For example, more often than not, there is no version control in place, and updating the assets is hard to do consistently across the board. Also, it is difficult to visualize multiple views with scattered documents of a process view, a metrics view, a component view, a resource view, etc., which, in turn, makes it hard to link up upstream and downstream analyses.

This paper presents a practitioner's tool for business transformation addressing these problems. Business Transformation Workbench is a productivity tool for business consultants. It is a tool to analyze business performance, to identify transformation opportunities and to assess the business value of specific transformation initiatives. The tool helps visualize the linkages of various enterprise models such as the business component model (CBM), the business process model, the value driver model, the organization model, the IT application model, and the solution model. It captures the direct linkages between these models and infers and presents the indirect linkages, thereby, providing valuable insight on how changing one aspect of an enterprise impacts the others qualitatively.

Using this tool, consultants can examine which business functions and components are underperforming in comparison to industry benchmark measures and why. By investigating the organizational responsibilities and IT application portfolio in conjunction with business components, shortfalls such as duplications, over-extensions, gaps and deficiencies can be identified and reasoned. Specific solutions can be discovered to address the identified shortfalls. Financial benefits of implementing specific solutions can be analyzed further via conducting a business case analysis. The Business Transformation Workbench embodies a method for conducting the above mentioned analyses in a structured manner to provide useful insights and various reports to consultants. The tool is populated with generic Finance & Accounting data and can be customized for specific clients' need. It embodies best practices and methodologies in a tool, which also helps address scalability, data management, and governance, linkages to upstream and downstream activities, analyses around benchmarking, component business model-based analysis, and business case preparation.

The rest of this paper is structured as follows: In Section 2, we provide a motivating example of business transformation and explain how it is performed. In Section 3, we describe functionalities of the BT Workbench, including the consolidated views linking various models in enterprises, both qualitative and quantitative financial analytics of business transformation initiatives, and reporting. Section 4 discusses the technical aspects for the system design and implementation. In Section 5, we present how the presented tool can be used by practitioners for a real-world case by revisiting the motivating example presented in Section 2. Section 6 presents results from an evaluation of the BT Workbench tool by a group of practitioners and discusses the implications. Section 7 summarizes previous work in the area of business transformation and the practitioner's tools, and discusses how the presented approach fits in the landscape. Finally, in Section 8, conclusions are drawn and future work is outlined.

TERM DEFINITION

Before we proceed with next sections, we define a few terms that will be used throughout the rest of the paper:

- *Business process*: A business process is a flow of one or more business activities (Curtis, 1992; APQC 2010). A business process when executed accomplishes a specific business objective. For example, 'Process accounts payable and expense reimbursements' is a typical business process in the finance management domain.
- *Business activity*: A business activity is the lowest level task in a business process (Curtis, 1992; APQC 2010). For example 'Accounts Payable' business process contains activities such as: 'Approve Payments', 'Process taxes', 'Retain records,' etc.
- *Business component*: A business component is an abstract business element. It is a collection of similar and related business activities from various business processes (IBM, 2005). From this point of view, business processes can be thought of as flows of activities between and within components. A component is defined by a set of people, processes and technology needed by its business function. For example, 'Accounts Payable Processing' is a business component, and the 'Process accounts payable and expense reimbursements' may contain activities involved in the 'Accounts Payable Processing' component. A business component enables business processes.
- *Component Business Model (CBM)*: Component business model is a method developed by IBM to help analyze clients' business from multiple perspectives such as people, process and technology (IBM, 2005). The intersection of these views of-

Figure 1. A sample component business map

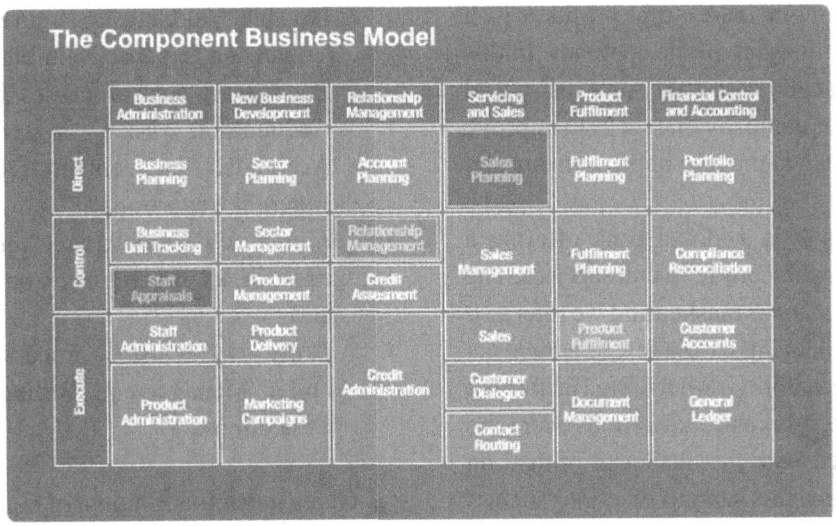

fers is claimed to improve insights for decision-making. A CBM is, in essence, a component view of a business where all the similar business activities of a given company's business processes are grouped into components. A sample component business map of a fictitious company is shown in Figure 1. It is represented as a two dimensional matrix: The columns are created after analyzing a business's functions, competencies, and value chain. The rows are defined by actions and their accountability levels. The top row, "direct," represents all those components in the business that set the overall strategy and direction for the organization. The middle row, "control," represents all the components that translate those plans into actions, in addition to managing the day-to-day operation of those activities. The bottom row, "execute," contains the business components that actually execute the detailed activities and plans of an organization. The "Component Business Map" shows activities across lines of business, without the constrictions of geographies, internal silos or business units. The component business map for a company is typically represented on a single page. Maps of companies in an industry sector may be similar, but those of different industries may be drastically different.

MOTIVATING SCENARIO

Business transformation initiatives are typically focused on two aspects of any given company's performance: increasing revenues and/or reducing costs – two main contributors to the business's profit. The initiatives that focus on revenue improvement include reducing the revenue leakage, and increasing or creating new sources of revenue, or both. While reducing revenue leakage deals with efficiency improvements, creating new sources of revenue or increasing revenue potential deals with managing innovation. The initiatives that focus on cost reductions, on the other hand, are concerned with operational efficiency and effectiveness. The specific objectives of business transformation initiatives vary, depending on the type of transformation (e.g., cost reductions vs.

revenue enhancements), but the overall goal remains the same; it is to increase the profits as well as the future profitability of the company. In this section, we present a case study of a real-world financial services company that seeks to improve its profit margins via process improvements and cost reductions.

BigThrift Bank is a global bank offering a multitude of financial products and services. The name of the company is masked and we refer to it as BigThrift Bank in this case study. Its annual net revenue is thirteen billion dollars. BigThrift Bank has grown via mergers and acquisitions over time and is now faced with the challenge of dealing with duplicate business support functions such as human resources and finance management that have come to be part of the company via mergers and acquisitions. Here are the specifics of the inefficiency problems the bank faces currently:

- BigThrift Bank has identified almost 400 disparate finance-related applications and systems; many were inherited from businesses it acquired.
- Few finance functions or processes are standardized and optimized across the company world-wide.
- 10% of the workforce world-wide is engaged in finance and accounting related activities, which are a support function.
- The overall cost of finance is about 3% of the yearly revenue.

Realizing that if left unaddressed such inefficiencies result in unrealized merger and acquisition potentials, the company has decided to embark upon business transformation projects. The objective of these projects is to optimize financial processes, eliminate non-value-added tasks, improve efficiency and productivity of people, and reduce errors by using technologies. The specific finance functions that were considered include:

- *Procure to Pay*: processes such as Accounts Payable, Purchasing (indirect & direct), Travel and Expense Reimbursement,
- *Record to Report*: processes such as General Accounting, Fixed Assets, Financial Accounts, Management Accounting, and External Reporting,
- *Financial Planning and Analysis*: processes such as Budgeting, Capital Planning, and
- *Order to Cash*: processes such as Order Management, Billing, Credit and Collections.

Given the limited amount of funds available to implement the transformation projects, BigThrift Bank needs to decide how to spend its investment money so as to maximize the potential benefits from the transformation projects. It has commissioned an IT consulting firm to investigate the opportunities for its finance process improvements and help evaluate the opportunities. The job of the consulting firm is to evaluate the business performance of BigThrift Bank, identify specific opportunities for improvement, propose recommendations and a roadmap for achieving the transformation, and provide a business case for the recommendations.

We present techniques and methodologies used by consultants in the past in the related work section and then introduce our methods and models implemented in the BT Workbench in Sections 3 and 4. We present the results of the analysis of BigThrift Bank by using the BT Workbench in Section 5.

BUSINESS TRANSFORMATION WORKBENCH

When embarking upon business transformation initiatives clients need to understand when and where their business is underperforming, how to address the shortfalls, and the impact of the transformation initiatives on their business. For example, what is the impact of a specific process redesign on my current organization? What technology implementations, consolidations and upgrades does the process redesign prescribe? What is the impact of these technological changes on the organization? Should I consolidate the duplicate organizations to form a shared services center internally? Or should I outsource this particular business function altogether? What is the business case for each of these scenarios? Clients need answers to these kinds of questions. The consultants that prescribe changes need to answer these questions for clients. In this effort, we are concerned with developing a tool and a method that would help consultants to help analyze the clients' business from various perspectives, identify opportunities for improvement, suggest solutions to address those opportunities and help provide the business case for implementing those solutions.

Business Transformation Workbench provides an integrated view of various business models and data, including component business models, a business process model such as APQC (American Product Quality Council) Process Classification Framework (PCF) (APQC, 2010) and SAP Business Process Hierarchy (BPH), a value driver model, an IT infrastructure map, an organization structure map, and a solution catalog, with the models linked each other, as shown in Figure 2. It automates traditional component business model-based analyses in the form of visual queries and inference. For example, one can ask questions such as which metrics help measure the performance of a given business component? What are the IT systems that support the business functions represented by a business component? Which organizations implement the business functions represented by a business component? Which transformation solutions can address a given shortfall? These questions are answered in the tool via the explicit and the inferred linkages made among different models such as the component model, IT system model, organizational model,

metrics model etc. This is sometimes referred to as daisy chain analysis in the tool. The tool automates the component performance analysis by comparing the metrics that help measure the performance of a component with benchmark data. This is referred to as 'heat map' analysis in the tool. The underperforming components can be marked as shortfalls based on whether it is caused by a misaligned IT system or by an organization. This identification and marking of shortfalls is referred to as 'shortfall assessment' in the tool. Finally, the tool provides business benefit analyses in terms of value drivers and standard financial metrics for business case analysis such as NPV (Net Present value), IRR (Internal Return Rate), ROI (Return on Investment), and payback time. The BT Workbench provides normative and constructive business performance analysis models, so it can be easily configured for different types of clients, initiatives, and projects.

BT Workbench provides views of enterprise CBM maps, value drivers, and business activities and provides intuitive navigation through all of them, for practitioners that have been trained in the concepts and the tool. It enables analysts to navigate the views and identify dependencies and causal relationships among value drivers and business activities and components. It also enables analysts to pinpoint business activities and value drivers supported and improved by solutions and services. It provides detailed value driver reports with charting generated by advanced value modeling. Also, it provides detailed financial analysis reports with charting generated by advanced value modeling. BT Workbench is comprised of three components at the highest level:

- *Model Template*, which is an Excel file providing a template for data preparation and storage for analyses,
- *Transformation Analyzer*, which is a Windows application where you can explore various model views, conduct CBM-

Figure 2. Overview of the business transformation workbench

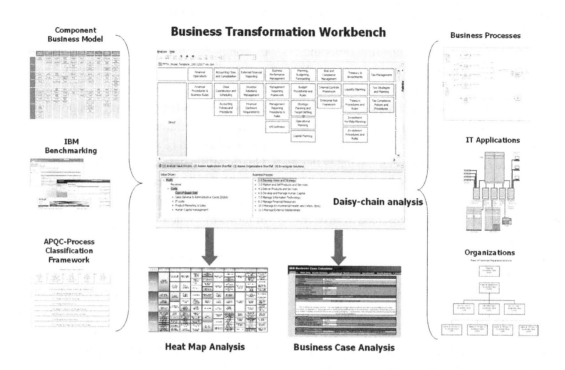

based analyses, and identify transformation initiatives for proposal, and

- *Business Case Calculator*, which is an Excel-based tool where you can perform business case analysis for the initiatives identified in the Transformation Workbench.

These three components are seamlessly connected to each, and so the user can move back and forth among the components in a straightforward manner. In the following sections, we will describe in detail various functionalities of the BT Workbench one by one.

MODEL TEMPLATE

To run business transformation analyses in the system, a certain set of models and content are prepared following a certain set of rules. The content preparation can be done by using the provided Model Template, which is an MS Excel file with formatting for the content. There are two parts in the content preparation. One is to prepare the 6 base models, which include models for Business Component, Business Process, Value Drivers, Applications, Organizations, and Solutions. The other is to link these base models, which is explained in the next section.

It is required to provide content for all 6 base models in 6 separate worksheets in the Model Template: one model in each worksheet – Business Component, Business Process, Value Drivers, Applications, Organizations, and Solutions. With the installation of the BT Workbench, the Model Template comes with a set of sample content for each of the base models derived from available benchmark data, such as APQC, IBM Benchmarking data, and solution and service offering catalogs. Certain data entries such as metric may have a set of attributes which may be used in

Figure 3. Value driver tree in model template

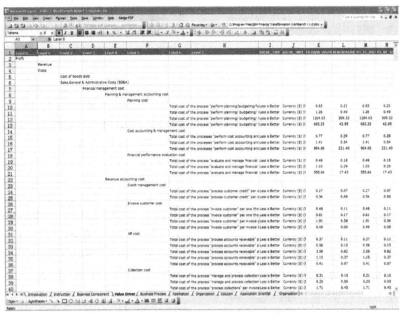

various analyses. Figure 3 shows an example of the value driver tree in the Model Template with a few metrics attributes such as value type, value unit, benchmark value, median value, as-is value and to-be value.

The model content is generically in a tree form. As long as the structure is maintained, the user can add, delete and modify instances in the tree. A model worksheet is named after the model that will be in it.

MODEL MAPPING

In BT Workbench, models are mapped to each other. This linking enables the capability to answer various queries. As mentioned, we call this linking of models and the ability to query them "Daisy-Chain analysis." With simple binary mapping of models, the system infers correlations across multiple models, which provides qualitative understanding on how models are related. For example, with the daisy-chain analysis, the user can see all the business processes and activities

that are associated with a business component. In turn, the user can see all the metrics (along with their values) and value drivers of the selected business processes, and so s/he can qualitatively see the overall performance of the component.

For the 6 base models, the user can provide initial model mapping to Business Processes in the Model Template file – 5 kinds of links, i.e., Comp2BizProc, VD2BizProc, App2BizProc, Org2BizProc, and Sol2BizProc. We use a hub-and-spoke approach to linking of models, i.e., all models are linked to the business process model instead of each model linking to each other model as shown in Figure 4. Each model mapping is stored in a separate mapping worksheet bearing the mapping name. The Model Template file provides a set of sample model mapping in the mapping worksheets. The user can add, delete, modify instances in the mapping worksheets by changing entries in the source cell and target cell columns. If the user does not want to create model mapping information at this stage, the user should remove the provided sample data in the mapping worksheets (or worksheets themselves). This

Figure 4. Daisy-chain of models

model mapping information in this file is optional, and not required to run the tool for analyses.

The BT Workbench additionally provides a user interface, i.e., Model Mapping Editor, for creating more complicated model mappings. Additional model mapping created with the editor will also be added to the Model Template file, when saved in BT Workbench. Figure 5 shows the GUI editor for model mapping. It allows the user to select a source model and a target model. On the source side we only allow mappings to be made from the leaf nodes. We gray out all other

nodes of the tree. The target model is for now always the business process model. The model mapping editor also provides tree views of the selected source and target models. In the tree view, the user can map entries in the source and the target models by using check-boxes and buttons.

We allow mappings to be made to all levels of the business process tree. Mappings are allowed to be made to all levels of the business process tree mainly to deal with mappings between metrics and business processes. There could be metrics for all levels of business process. For example, IBM Industry Benchmarking Wizard has measures and metrics at process level, at process group level. One can imagine metrics even at the process category level. The Model Mapping Editor allows the user to capture such mappings. However, it does not want to allow for the same kind of possibility from the source side because opening up the entire tree on both sides could open up possibilities for redundant mappings and sometimes even conflicting mappings. To avoid any confusion and redundancy in mappings, the source side opens for mapping only at the leaf

Figure 5. Model mapping editor

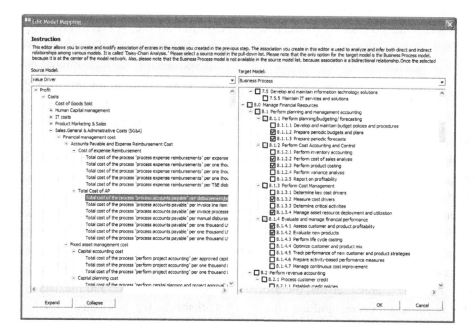

node level whereas on the target side we allow mappings to be made to all levels. Another important note is that associations made to children get propagated up to the parent but not vice versa. If a component is mapped to a process, we do not assume that the component implements all activities in that process. For this reason, we do not propagate process level mappings down to activities.

MODEL VALIDATION

The prepared content in the Model Template Excel file is first parsed and validated by the system, before being imported to the BT Workbench. The instruction for formatting content for analyses in BT Workbench was briefly described in previous sections. If the content does not follow the required format set by the rules, the BT Workbench data validating program, generates error messages to help the user repair the format of content. Appendix A summarizes the error messages from the data validating program.

TRANSFORMATION ANALYZER

The second component of the BT Workbench, Transformation Analyzer, provides the following analysis capabilities, which we will go over one by one in the following sections:

- Daisy-Chain Analysis
- Business Component Performance Analysis (also known as Heat Map Analysis)
- Shortfall Assessment for both IT application and organization
- Solution Analysis
- Business Report Generation in MS Excel and PowerPoint

Before we explain these capabilities of the tool, we refresh readers' memory on the Component Business Model.

COMPONENT BUSINESS MODELING

Component Business Modeling is a novel business modeling technique from IBM which the consulting industry increasingly utilizes to understand and transform businesses (IBM, 2005). A component business model represents the entire business in a simple framework that fits on a single page. It is an evolution of traditional views of a business, such as ones through business units, functions, geography, processes or workflow. The component business model methodology helps identify basic building blocks of business, where each building block includes the people, processes and technology needed by this component to act as a standalone entity and deliver value to the organization.

After a comprehensive analysis of the composition of each business, a consultant can map these individual building blocks, or components, onto a single page. Each component business map is unique to each company. The columns are created after thorough analysis of a business's functions and value chain. The rows are defined by actions. The top row, "direct," shows all of those components in the business that set the overall strategy and direction for the organization. The middle row, "control," represents all of the components in the enterprise which translate those plans into actions, in addition to managing the day-to-day running of those activities. The bottom row, "execute," contains the business components that actually execute the detailed activities and plans of an organization. The component business map shows activities across lines of business, without the constrictions of geographies, internal silos or business units. Figure 7 shows an example of a Component Business Model map rendered in the BT Workbench.

Figure 6. Component business model rendered in the BT workbench

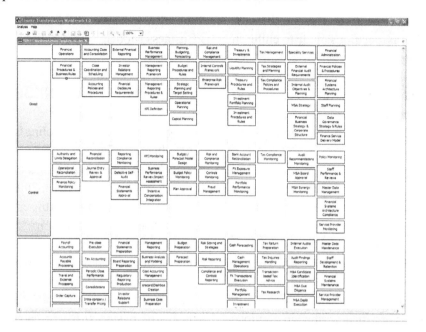

This single page perspective provides a view of the business which is not constricted by barriers that could potentially hamper the ability to make meaningful business transformation. The component business model facilitates to identify which components of the business create differentiation and value. It also helps identify where the business has capability gaps that need to be addressed, as well as opportunities to improve efficiency and lower costs across the entire enterprise.

DAISY-CHAIN ANALYSIS

The "Daisy-Chain Analysis" is a visual query that allows the user to explore the business maps and understand the correlations and dependencies among business entities. The results of the query is shown in the views of the models in the BT Workbench highlighting entries in the models directly and indirectly associated. For examples, this capability can interactively identify one or more business components associated with a

particular value driver. Conversely, it can find one or more value drivers that are affected by the performance of a particular business component. The associations between value drivers and business components are discovered through their relationships with business processes and activities set by using the Model Mapping Editor. Similarly, BT Workbench can identify and show dependencies between business activities and IT applications, and also between business activities and solutions and initiatives, both IT and business-driven.

It is important to note that the relationships are transitive, and so it is possible to infer indirect associations between value drivers and IT applications/solutions, also between components and IT applications/solutions, and so on, through their direct linkages with entries in the business process model. Also, transitivity is used in inferring indirect relationship to ancestor entries when there is a direct relationship set for a child in a tree structured model. Figure 6 shows an example of a Daisy-Chain Analysis when a business component, "Financial Procedures & Business Rules" is clicked. The system highlights all the business

Figure 7. Daisy-Chain Analysis

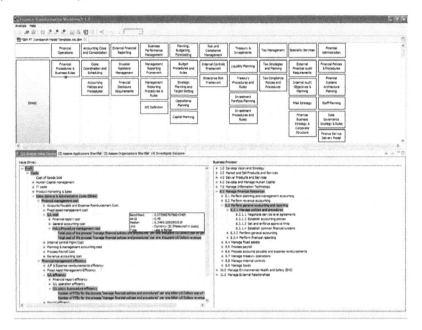

processes directly linked to the component, and also highlights all the metrics and value drivers indirectly linked to the component through those highlighted business processes. The user can see attribute values such as the as-is value and benchmark value by a mouse-over operation.

To support the Daisy-Chain Analysis, the BT Workbench system captures the basic relationship information in the Model Template file and also linkages set up with Model Mapping Editor, as explained in earlier sections.

BUSINESS COMPONENT PERFORMANCE ANALYSIS

The Business Component Performance Analysis is an essential capability of CBM where the user discovers one or more "hot" components that are associated with one or more business strategies and/or pain points. In the traditional CBM analysis, this step was conducted manually by the business consultants relying on his/her knowledge and expertise in the business domain. The BT

Workbench automates the capability as visual queries, by taking metrics values into account with the analysis. First, the system allows the user to explore the value driver tree to identify one or more value drivers that may be associated with a certain business strategy/pain point. The discovery of "hot" components that affect the business strategy can be accomplished. Then the system colors the identified hot components differently to distinguish ones that affect positively or negatively to the strategy. The BT Workbench system compares the industry benchmark and the as-is value of the operational metrics and performance indicators associated with the components to decide on their color. Figure 8 shows an example of a CBM map showing the result of a Business Component Performance Analysis.

An algorithm for coloring business component in the Business Component Performance Analysis is as follows: The BT Workbench system compares the three values – as-is (from client), benchmark, and median values (from IBM Benchmarking Wizard) of each every metric associated with each business component. The business

Figure 8. CBM map after a business component performance analysis

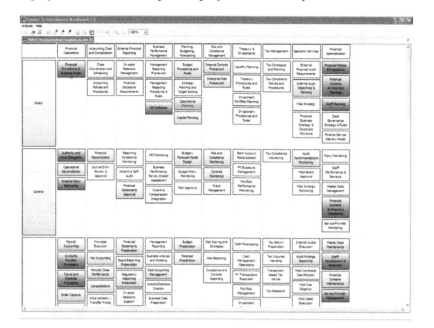

component is colored green, if the as-is value of each and every metric associated with this component is better than the corresponding benchmark value. The business component is colored yellow, if it has at least one metric whose as-is value is better the median value but worse then the benchmark value, and all the other metrics have as-is value which is better than the benchmark value. Finally, the business component is colored red, if it has at least one metric whose as-is value is worse then the median value. Please note that the notion of "being better" compares differently for different metric value types: For the "Less is Better" type: A is better, if A < B. However, for the "More is Better" type: A is better, if A > B.

Depending on analysis needs, there may be many variants of the component color coding algorithms for the Business Component Performance Analysis. Here is a quick description of a few algorithms for consideration:

- **AT LEAST ONE**: the current algorithm. The Business Component Performance Analysis engine identifies all the business components associated with the current value driver, and discovers ones at least one of whose associated metrics has the as-is value worse than the benchmark value; the engine colors the components red, while coloring the other components green. This algorithm is most aggressive in identifying "hot" components.

- **ALL**: This algorithm locates at the other end of the spectrum of Business Component Performance Analysis algorithms. It is most generous in identifying "hot" components. The Business Component Performance Analysis engine discovers business components all of whose associated metrics have the as-is value worse than the benchmark value; the engine colors the components red, while coloring the other components green.

- **MAJORITY without weights**: This algorithm locates in the middle of the spectrum. The Business Component Performance Analysis engine discovers business components more than half of whose associated metrics have the as-is value worse than the benchmark value; the engine colors the components red, while coloring the other components green.

- **MAJORITY with weights**: This algorithm assumes some weight value assigned to each metric (which we do NOT have in our current system/requirement). Also, it assumes some threshold value which will be compared to a component's "heat" value. The heat value of a component is computed by applying the difference of as-is values and benchmark values of associated metrics and their weights. Depending on how we formulate the equation, this algorithm can provide various results. In some sense, this is a generic algorithm for the three special cases above.

Another twist we can consider is the spectrum of colors. We can add more colors (in addition to red and green) to represent the "heat" degree ("temperature") of components. One example is the use of yellow in Figure 8 to indicate the mediocre performance between red and green. We will not go into the details of this aspect in this paper.

SHORTFALL ASSESSMENT OF AS-IS IT AND ORGANIZATION

The Shortfall Assessment allows the user to map the existing IT infrastructure or organization structure against the "hot" components identified in the Business Component Performance Analysis. It helps understand how the current IT infrastructure or organization structure, such as applications, network capabilities or certain departments, supports the business, especially, for those hot components. The analysis requires collecting the information on the current IT infrastructure or organization structure. Then the mapping of IT applications or organization structure to the

components becomes, again, an execution of a simple data query to the basic model mapping.

BT Workbench visualizes the mapping on the CBM map by overlaying IT applications and/or organization structure on components. Then, the user can visually classify possible IT shortfalls into several types. Typically, four types of opportunities tend to arise. First, a gap indicates that a hot component does not have any IT/organizational support. The enterprise may want to consider an IT/organizational investment to improve the component's performance and support the intended business transformation. Second, a duplication indicates that a component is supported by multiple IT applications or multiple departments, possibly, deployed over time. The business may want to consolidate the applications to improve performance and reduce cost in communication and maintenance overhead. Third, a deficiency indicates that the current application lacks key functionality, or is poorly designed, and so incurs a project opportunity. Finally, an over-extension indicates that a system designed to support one business component is extended beyond its core capability to support others. Different definitions for the shortfall types may apply.

Figure 9 shows a BT Workbench view after a shortfall assessment. Colored triangles overlaid on hot components represent IT applications of the business under analysis, while colored squares represent organizations. The overlay helps the consultants visually categorize and label shortfalls. As the user labels the identified shortfalls to components, the labels also visually remain on the hot components. Additionally, the business components labeled having some sort of shortfalls are added to the shortfall tree which is shown at the lower right-hand corner of the screen.

SOLUTION ANALYSIS

Once IT/organizational shortfalls are identified and classified, one or more solution catalogs are

Figure 9. Shortfall assessment

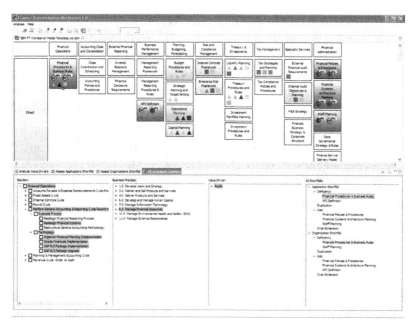

used to identify IT transformation initiatives to address the shortfalls and support the intended business transformation. BT Workbench allows the user to explore the solution space to identify one or more solutions that may address one or more shortfalls of interest. The discovery of solutions for supporting components associated with a shortfall can be automatically conducted by executing the "Daisy-Chain" queries that correlate solutions and components by using their relationships to business processes. In addition, BT Workbench allows the user to manually correlate them, if desired.

For example, the shortfall tree (and the CBM view) shown in Figure 9 indicates that the "Financial Procedures & Business Rules" component has deficiencies in IT applications and organizations supporting it. A click on the component in the shortfall tree highlights all the possible solutions for the component from the solution catalog shown in the lower left-hand corner of the screen. It is important to note that the inference of solutions and initiatives for a business component is an example of the daisy-chain analysis (Lee, 2005; Lee 2006). By using the model mapping captured in the daisy-chain of models described in earlier sections, the system identifies solutions indirectly linked to a component through their direct relationships to business processes.

BUSINESS REPORTS

BT Workbench generates a number of business intelligence reports for an executive summary of the analyses, including sophisticated interactive charts. It allows saving the shortfall assessment results in the Model Template Excel file, so that the analysis results and annotations can be viewed again in later BT Workbench sessions. It generates a simple Analysis Report in an Excel file, which shows the analysis results from the Business Component Performance Analysis, the Shortfall Analysis, and the Solution Investigation Analysis. The user can perform further Excel based analyses using the data exported from the BT Workbench. In addition, the user can add/delete/edit annotations on the analysis results in this report file.

Figure 10. Heat map exported to an MS PowerPoint file

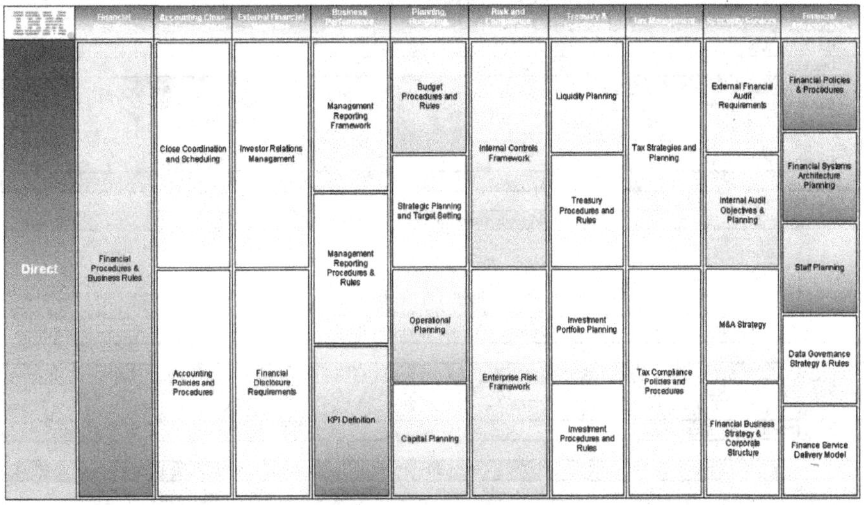

Furthermore, the user can export CBM-based analysis results, i.e., various heat maps, to a MS PowerPoint file for viewing, annotation, and presentation. Figure 10 shows an example of a heat map (only the "Direct" part) exported to a PowerPoint file. It exports the identified solution and the associated business processes to the Business Case Calculator 2.0 tool for further business case analysis, as described in the next section.

BUSINESS CASE CALCULATOR

Until now, using the BT Workbench, we have described how a consultant can identify opportunities for business transformation. The next step is to evaluate recommended solutions to build business cases for them. The evaluation has to accurately model the potential benefits that can be achieved by implementing the recommended solutions while, at the same time, considering the costs and investments involved. BT Workbench provides a Business Case Calculator tool.

The Business Case Calculator (BCC) is an MS Excel-based tool, with a pre-built template for conducting financial analysis of investments. The pre-built tool has templates for capturing two main aspects of financial analysis: costs and benefits. The financial models include Discounted Cash Flow (DCF) and real-options analysis. If the benefits outweigh the costs in present day's terms, then the project is expected to be profitable. The BCC tool also provides templates for conducting sensitivity analysis to estimate the variance of expected profits. It also calculates the standard financials such as Return on Investment (ROI), Net Present Value (NPV) and Internal Rate of Return (IRR) of the project, and break even period. The advanced analytics provide a real-options model to analyze the value of staging decisions in a project. In this section, we describe the details of our Business Case Calculator module embodied in the BT Workbench.

BCC hosts the APQC processes and their metrics for Finance & Accounting domain from IBM's Benchmarking Wizard. It provides a method for automatically adding new benefits on the fly to the analysis. When a new benefit is created, it provides in-built linkages to other parts of the analysis for it to be automatically included (if user so chooses) in the overall analysis. It links up the Business Case Calculator with other qualitative analysis and the CBM-based analysis of business transformation opportunities.

Figure 11. A snapshot of the Business Case Calculator

Client Data	
Company	Big Thrift Bank
Geography	Americas
Industry	Financial Services
Project timeframe and projection	
Expected start - year	2008
Forecast selection	Year
Expected start - quarter	1st
Number of periods	6
Project description	
Solution area	
Brief description of project and scope	

This is a financial services company. They have grown via mergers and acquisitions and have acquired inefficiencies in their processes via duplications. This project aims to address those inefficiencies by recommending consolidation of duplicate systems and creation of shared services for finance and accounting processes. This business case computes the potential financial benefits of such recommendations.

Project Financial Information	
Yearly Discount Rate	18.00%
Consider Terminal Value?	Yes
Growth Rate for TV calculation	2.00%

Benefit Calculation Configuration	
Tool mode	Complete Version - benefit specific scenario/realization parameters
Each benefit will have its own realization and scenario variables in the next tab	

The BCC tool standardizes the key input and output of a typical business case, and yet, allows enough flexibility for users, to modify and add benefits and reports, making it easier to customize the application for the needs of a particular project. For example, users can change the period of analysis (quarterly, yearly, etc.), forecast duration (the number of years), discount rate and benefits realization options (standard vs. custom), as shown in Figure 11.

When a particular business transformation initiative is implemented, it impacts the metrics of the process – hopefully, in a positive way. Given a specific solution, the processes that will get impacted and their corresponding metrics that will be improved are automatically loaded into BCC from the BT Workbench. In addition, the industry benchmark values for these metrics and the as-is values of the clients' performance metrics are also loaded from the Model Template file which stores the data prepared at the beginning of analysis. Assuming that, as a result of implementing best-practice solution implementation, the client's metrics improve from the as-is values to the industry median or even the best in the pack, we can automatically compute the potential ben-

efits attainable. This calculation serves as a baseline for the consultants to work with. In addition, BCC provides flexibility in the benefit calculation, so that the users can fine-tune the benefit calculation, and/or add additional variables or additional benefits altogether. Figure 12 shows an example of the benefit calculation worksheet which shows the calculation of benefits from improvement in Accounts Payable process. In this worksheet, the users can select the period of analysis (quarterly, yearly, etc.), forecast duration (the number of years), discount rate and benefits realization options. In addition, the BCC tool can accommodate several benefits, group them into categories, and link those categories to the high level KPIs (Key Performance Indicators), resembling the value trees. This capability makes it easy to find out how benefits are distributed across various user specified categories.

Once benefits are computed per year, they are amortized over the period of financial analysis automatically by the BCC tool as shown in figure 13.

Once the costs and other client specific data are provided as input to the BCC tool, it automatically computes the key financials and presents

Figure 12. A snapshot of the Benefit Calculation worksheet

Description of variables	Variable Type	AS IS case	Industry Median	Industry Benchmark	Improvement factor	TO BE case
Benefit description	Improve Fixed Asset Accounting Process					
Process Name	8.4.3 Perform Fixed Asset Accounting					
Description of variables	Variable Type	AS IS case	Industry Median	Industry Benchmark	Improvement factor	TO BE case
Cost Measures						
Total cost of the process "perform fixed asset accounting" per one thousand US Dollars revenue	Value Driver	$0.10	$0.19	$0.07		$0.07
Total cost of the process "perform fixed asset accounting" per one thousand US Dollars cost of continuing operations	Value Driver	$0.20	$0.33	$0.09		$0.09
Total cost of the process "perform fixed asset accounting" per fixed asset transaction	Value Driver	$6.00	$8.62	$2.34		$2.34
Total cost of the process "perform fixed asset accounting" per fixed asset journal entry line item processed	Value Driver	$2.00	$2.63	$1.09		$1.09
Total cost of repair and maintenance per one thousand US Dollars gross value of fixed assets	Value Driver	$15.00	$24.74	$13.11		$13.11
Total cost of depreciation expense per one thousand US Dollars revenue	Value Driver	$21.57	$29.48	$12.55		$12.55
Personnel cost (including benefits) of the process "perform fixed asset accounting" per one thousand US Dollars revenue	Value Driver	$0.05	$0.09	$0.04		$0.04
Personnel cost (including benefits) of the process "perform fixed asset accounting" per one thousand US Dollars cost of continuing operations	Value Driver	$0.10	$0.16	$0.07		$0.07
Personnel cost (including benefits) of the process "perform fixed asset accounting" per fixed asset transaction	Value Driver	2.50	$4.61	$0.74		$0.74
Personnel cost (including benefits) of the process "perform fixed asset accounting" per fixed asset journal entry line item processed	Value Driver	$1.50	$2.24	$0.58		$0.58
Systems cost of the process "perform fixed asset accounting" per one hundred thousand US Dollars revenue	Value Driver	$1.00	$2.10	$0.35		$0.36
Systems cost of the process "perform fixed asset accounting" per one hundred thousand US Dollars cost of continuing operations	Value Driver	$2.00	$2.20	$0.37		$0.37
Total cost of the processes "perform fixed asset accounting" per year	Computed	$130,000.00				$95,604.80
Personnel cost of the processes "perform fixed asset accounting" per year	Computed	$65,000.00				$48,025.24
Systems cost of the process "perform fixed asset accounting" per year	Computed	$13,000.00				$4,504.52
Cycle Time Measures						
Cycle time in days to capitalize a fixed asset purchase	Value Driver	21.00	24.00	2.00		2.00
Efficiency and Quality Measures						
Number of FTEs for the process "perform fixed asset accounting" per one billion US Dollars revenue	Value Driver	1.00	1.56	0.59		0.59
Number of FTEs for the process "perform fixed asset accounting" per one billion US Dollars cost of continuing operations	Value Driver	1.00	2.64	0.98		0.98
Number of fixed asset transactions per "perform fixed asset accounting" FTE	Value Driver	30,000.00	10,120.10	55,555.56		55,555.56
Number of fixed asset journal entry line items per "perform fixed asset accounting" FTE	Value Driver	20,000.00	22,599.06	98,980.20		98,980.20
Average return on fixed assets	Value Driver	0.40	0.20	0.41		0.41
Indicate formula for total value on AS IS and TO BE CASE - same		$130,000.00				$95,604.80
Total Cash Flow impact of the benefit per period after 100% realized						$34,395.20
Description of the rationale behind te benefit, available benchmarks, sources of information and approach to quantification						

an executive summary with charts. Figure 14 shows the financial analysis result. Among the financial measures reported in the financial analysis, *Net present value* (NPV) is a standard method for the financial appraisal of long-term projects (Bodie, 2004). It measures the excess or shortfall of cash flows, in present value (PV) terms, once financing charges are met. NPV is formally defined as present value of net cash flows when each cash inflow/outflow is discounted back to its PV:

$$\mathrm{NPV} = \sum_{t=0}^{n} \frac{C_t}{(1+r)^t}$$

Where t is the time of the cash flow, n is the total time of the project, r is the discount rate, and C_t is the net cash flow (the amount of cash) at time t. NPV is an indicator of how much value an investment or project adds to the value of the company. With a particular project, if C_t is a positive value, the project is in the status of discounted cash inflow in the time of t. If C_t is a negative value, the project is in the status of discounted cash outflow in the time of t. Generally speaking, companies will accept appropriately risked projects with a positive NPV.

Internal Rate of Return (IRR) is a finance metric used by businesses to decide whether

Figure 13. A snapshot of benefits realization schedule

Benefit 15			2008	2009	2010	2011	2012	2013	Total Expected
8.4.3 Perform Fixed Asset Accounting									
Total benefit Value at 100% per YEAR		$34,395.20							
Benefit value and realization schedule - base case			40%	60%	100%	100%	100%	100%	
Benefit value and realization schedule - base case			13,758.1	20,637.1	34,395.2	34,395.2	34,395.2	34,395.2	171,976.0
Benefit estimated value range	Conservative scenario	75.00%	10,318.6	15,477.8	25,796.4	25,796.4	25,796.4	25,796.4	128,982.0
	Aggressive scenario	125.00%	17,197.6	25,796.4	42,994.0	42,994.0	42,994.0	42,994.0	214,970.0
Benefit realization per period - base case			0.0	0.0	0.0	0.0	0.0	0.0	0.0
Benefit estimated value range	Conservative scenario	75.00%	0.0	0.0	0.0	0.0	0.0	0.0	0.0
	Aggressive scenario	125.00%	0.0	0.0	0.0	0.0	0.0	0.0	0.0
Benefit Category	8.4.3 Perform Fixed Asset Accounting		Comments on the benefit:						

Benefit 19			2008	2009	2010	2011	2012	2013	Total Expected
8.6.1 Process accounts payable (AP)									
Total benefit Value at 100% per YEAR		$520,000.00							
Benefit value and realization schedule - base case			0%	60%	100%	100%	100%	100%	
Benefit value and realization schedule - base case			0.0	312,000.0	520,000.0	520,000.0	520,000.0	520,000.0	2,392,000.0
Benefit estimated value range	Conservative scenario	75.00%	0.0	234,000.0	390,000.0	390,000.0	390,000.0	390,000.0	1,794,000.0
	Aggressive scenario	125.00%	0.0	390,000.0	650,000.0	650,000.0	650,000.0	650,000.0	2,990,000.0
Benefit realization per period - base case			0.0	0.0	0.0	0.0	0.0	0.0	0.0
Benefit estimated value range	Conservative scenario	75.00%	0.0	0.0	0.0	0.0	0.0	0.0	0.0
	Aggressive scenario	125.00%	0.0	0.0	0.0	0.0	0.0	0.0	0.0
Benefit Category	8.6.1 Accounts Payable		Comments on the benefit:						

Benefit 20			2008	2009	2010	2011	2012	2013	Total Expected
8.6.2 Process expense reimbursements									
Total benefit Value at 100% per YEAR		$213,822.12							
Benefit value and realization schedule - base case			40%	60%	100%	100%	100%	100%	
Benefit value and realization schedule - base case			85,528.8	128,293.3	213,822.1	213,822.1	213,822.1	213,822.1	1,069,110.6
Benefit estimated value range	Conservative scenario	75.00%	64,146.6	96,220.0	160,366.6	160,366.6	160,366.6	160,366.6	801,833.0
	Aggressive scenario	125.00%	106,911.1	160,366.6	267,277.7	267,277.7	267,277.7	267,277.7	1,336,388.3
Benefit realization per period - base case			0.0	0.0	0.0	0.0	0.0	0.0	0.0
Benefit estimated value range	Conservative scenario	75.00%	0.0	0.0	0.0	0.0	0.0	0.0	0.0
	Aggressive scenario	125.00%	0.0	0.0	0.0	0.0	0.0	0.0	0.0
Benefit Category	8.6.2 Process expense reimbursements		Comments on the benefit:						

Figure 14. Financial analysis result

Project Forecasted Cash Flow							
Description	2008	2009	2010	2011	2012	2013	Total
Benefit Details							
8.4.3 Perform Fixed Asset Accounting	13,758.1	20,637.1	34,395.2	34,395.2	34,395.2	34,395.2	171,976.0
8.6.1 Process accounts payable (AP)	0.0	312,000.0	520,000.0	520,000.0	520,000.0	520,000.0	2,392,000.0
8.6.2 Process expense reimbursements	85,528.8	128,293.3	213,822.1	213,822.1	213,822.1	213,822.1	1,069,110.6
Spend Management Improvement	0.0	15,000,000.0	25,000,000.0	0.0	0.0	0.0	40,000,000.0
Total Benefits	99,286.9	15,460,930.4	25,768,217.3	768,217.3	768,217.3	768,217.3	43,633,086.6
Cost Details							
Ongoing Costs of Service Provider	4,000,000.0	4,000,000.0	4,000,000.0	0.0	0.0	0.0	12,000,000.0
Migration Costs	4,500,000.0	0.0	0.0	0.0	0.0	0.0	4,500,000.0
Retain internal governance of P2P process	50,000.0	55,000.0	60,000.0	0.0	0.0	0.0	165,000.0
Total Project Costs	(8,550,000.0)	(4,055,000.0)	(4,060,000.0)	0.0	0.0	0.0	(16,665,000.0)
CF Totals							
Net projected cash flow from the project	(8,450,713.1)	11,405,930.4	21,708,217.3	768,217.3	768,217.3	768,217.3	26,968,086.6
Terminal value						4897385.409	4,897,385.4
Project final cash flows	(8,450,713.1)	11,405,930.4	21,708,217.3	768,217.3	768,217.3	5,665,602.7	31,865,472.0
Metrics							
Net present Value without terminal value - NPV	15,258,836						
Net present value considering terminal value - NPV (1)	17,072,982						
Internal Rate of Return - IRR	143.08%						
Return on Investment - ROI	161.82%						

they should make investments (Bodie, 2004). It is an indicator of the efficiency of an investment (as opposed to NPV, which indicates value or magnitude). IRR is the annualized effective compounded return rate which can be earned on the invested capital, i.e., the yield on the investment. A project is a good investment proposition if its IRR is greater than the rate of return that could be earned by alternative investments (investing in other projects, buying bonds, even putting the money in a bank account). Thus, IRR should be compared to an alternative cost of capital including an appropriate risk premium. In general, if IRR is greater than the project's cost of capital, or hurdle rate, the project will add value for the company.

Return On Investment (ROI) or *Rate Of Return* (ROR) is the ratio of money gained or lost on an investment relative to the amount of money invested (Bodie, 2004). ROI is usually given as a percent rather than decimal value. ROI does not indicate how long an investment is held. However, ROI is most often stated as an annual or annualized rate of return, and it is most often stated for a calendar or fiscal year.

Payback period refers to the period of time required for the return on an investment to repay the sum of the original investment (Bodie, 2004). It is intuitively the measure that describes how long something takes to pay for itself: shorter payback periods are obviously preferable to longer payback periods (all else being equal). Payback period is widely used due to its ease of use.

SYSTEM IMPLEMENTATION

In the development of BT Workbench, while the emphasis was made on the design of the business analysis architecture, the technical design and implementation of the system was as much challenging as its business counterpart. In this section, we discuss some of the technical challenges we encountered during system implementation, starting with the system architecture design of the BT Workbench. There were a few architectural alternatives we considered for the implementation of the Workbench. They include a pure MS Excel-based application, a Web browser-based application, and a pure Eclipse Rich Client Platform (RCP) application.

MS Excel is an extensively used platform in the business practice. It is not only a data container, but also a powerful tool providing various capabilities for numerical analysis. It is also extensible via VBA (Visual Basic for Application) programming for customizing Excel behavior. Also, MS Excel uses MS COM technology which enables a component-level access to Excel files. By using the component API of Excel and VBA programming, the users can respond to Excel events and manipulate Excel file content easily. Recent Excel releases support MS .Net technology which provides a programming environment to support Office extensions. The .Net technology provides a rich set of user interface components and an object-oriented programming environment.

However, the users must have a license of the Professional Edition of MS Office to run applications built on .Net, which is often a constraint in a business environment. Without .Net support, VBA programming in Excel does not support object-orientation and provides relatively poor routine function library support, which is a less appealing environment for building complex, modern business applications such as BT Workbench.

Another alternative considered for BT Workbench was a Web browser-based application, which is popular among modern business applications. The most obvious advantage is that the users do not have to install any software to access the application. The only thing required for the users is a Web browser. On the other hand, due to the nature of Web applications, it would require users to have a network connection while running the application. An additional disadvantage is that, because of the relatively limited capability of HTML, it is less efficient and effective to provide complicated user interfaces in Web applications compared to native desktop applications, even while modern Web scripting technologies have significantly improved UI and other complicated aspects of programming for Web applications.

Yet another choice for the BT Workbench implementation was Eclipse RCP, which is relatively new. It is based on the Java technology, and provides a mature framework where plug-ins can be added to build complex, modern native desktop applications with by structurally stacking up programming building blocks or plug-ins. Developers can easily leverage third party products or rich sets of solutions from open source communities. Its plug-in architecture provides a powerful extension mechanism to extend and reuse previous efforts.

Along with the advantages and disadvantages of the alternative approaches, various requirements and constraints, both technical and business, were factors in deciding the system architecture for the BT Workbench. We summarize them here.

The technical requirement of the Workbench dictates that it should provide the ability for users to enter and customize model content for business analyses, the ability to model links between business models, the ability to visualize CBM maps and other business models, the ability to show the daisy-chain relationships between business models by following the model links, the ability to generate various business intelligence reports, and the ability to extend further calculation for business case analyses. Additionally, we had a requirement of reusing some of the assets we have already built in our previous efforts in this domain, especially, an editor and viewer of CBM maps in Eclipse, and a daisy-chain analysis prototype, again, built in Eclipse.

On the other hand, we were asked to meet a few constraints originated from the perspective of targeted users, i.e., consultants who work in the field of business transformation for their clients. One constraint is the use of MS Office as the front-end tool. Most consultants will are trained for using MS Office suite. It is often unrealistic to introduce applications in different platforms, because of its implications on training and budget. A related consideration for MS Office suite as the front-end tool is that consultants often have only the Standard Edition of Office suite on their computer. This fact implies that the adoption of .Net technology for Office programming (which requires users to have the Professional Edition) is not an option at this point. Another constraint was about the availability of network connection for the users. It turns out that consultants often prefer native desktop applications for their client work, because they often need to use applications while traveling or on clients' site. In such situations, network access is not always guaranteed.

For this last constraint and the limited capability in user interface development, we decided to drop the Web-based option. Instead, we came up with an architecture which combines Excel for the front-end user interface and quantitative analysis and Eclipse for other areas, especially for supporting various model views and performing CBM-based qualitative analyses. Excel is further used for business model input and data storage. Figure 15 shows the system architecture of the BT Workbench, which is comprised of four components: (A) business models and mappings in Excel, (B) model visualization and qualitative analyses in Eclipse RCP, (C) quantitative business case analysis in Excel, and (D) reports generated in Excel and PowerPoint. We use Apache POI (Apache, 2009) to interface the Eclipse RCP application with the Excel files. While POI provides a useful set of APIs to integrate MS Office programs and Java-based programs such as Eclipse RCP applications, its support for data persistence in Excel files is somewhat unstable. Sometimes, it crashes the Excel file, if certain advanced features are included in the Excel file. To ensure data exports to Excel worksheets and start the Excel file correctly, we came up with a mechanism that utilizes a temporary file for data export and starts the Excel application. By using the workbook open event handler in VBA, we load data from the temporary file to the destination Excel file. The existence of the temporary file is invisible to the user, and the operation is seamless.

CASE STUDY: BIGTHRIFT BANK

We now revisit the BigThrift Bank scenario, which was introduced in Section 2. The readers may recall that BigThrift Bank hired an IT consulting company to help evaluate its business performance in the area of finance management and to suggest business transformation opportunities to help address those areas that are underperforming. The IT consulting company has adopted the methodology and the BT Workbench that we have developed and described above. In this section, we describe how the IT consulting company applies the methodology systematically to identify opportunities for improvement and to evaluate the potential transformation projects.

As noted earlier, before conducting the analysis using the BT Workbench, certain data preparation is required. The first step is to prepare various models of BigThrift Bank's finance functions. These models include a component business model of its business, the process model, the organizational model, a list or hierarchy of IT applications that help implement the business processes under investigation, and a list or hierarchy of metrics that help measure the processes and the activities under them. In the second step, all of these models are linked with one another by the IT consultants (by using the Model Mapping Editor in BT Workbench). For example, the organization that is responsible for implementing some or all aspects of a business process or activities is linked with the corresponding business processes or activities. Similarly, an IT application is linked

Figure 15. System architecture of the BT Workbench

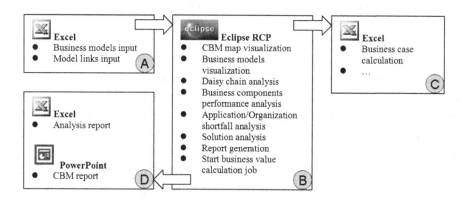

Figure 16. Business component performance analysis result for BigThrift Bank

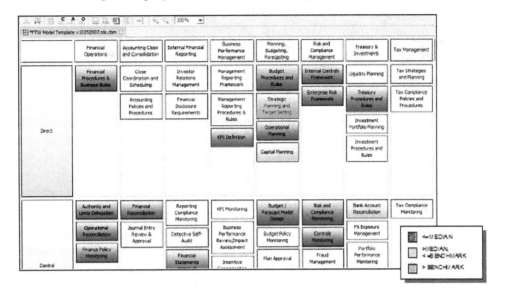

with a business process that it implements. As explained earlier, we use a hub-and-spoke approach to linking of models, i.e., all models are linked to the business process model instead of each model linking to each other model. This approach eliminates the need to specify elaborate linkages that can be cumbersome to specify and hard to maintain (due to the potential conflicts that a user might introduce inadvertently). Once all the linkages are specified, the next step is to gather the clients' data for the operational metrics. This data is required to compare the performance of BigThrift Bank with its' peers in the industry. At this point, a consultant is ready to conduct the analysis on BigThrift Bank's finance functions.

BUSINESS COMPONENT PERFORMANCE ANALYSIS

The first step in the analysis is to identify areas of finance function at BigThrift Bank that are underperforming. For this step, the operational metrics associated with the finance business processes are compared with the benchmark metrics (or client-set target levels) obtained by

surveying other companies in similar industries. This collection of benchmark data is conducted outside of the scope of this project and the data is available for use in any IT consulting project for the IT consulting company. The components whose metrics underperform in comparison to the industry benchmark values are highlighted in yellow. The components whose metrics underperform in comparison to the industry average values are highlighted in red. The components whose metrics perform above the industry benchmark values are highlighted in green. The heat map that is generated for BigThrift Bank is shown below in Figure 16. This business performance analysis indicated that the metrics associated with procure-to-pay function of BigThrift Bank underperform by 30% in comparison with the industry's best and by 15% in comparison with industry's median.

APPLICATION SHORTFALL ASSESSMENT

Then, in the second step, the IT systems that implement the business processes associated with the underperforming business functional areas are

Figure 17. Landscape of IT applications overlaid on component business map

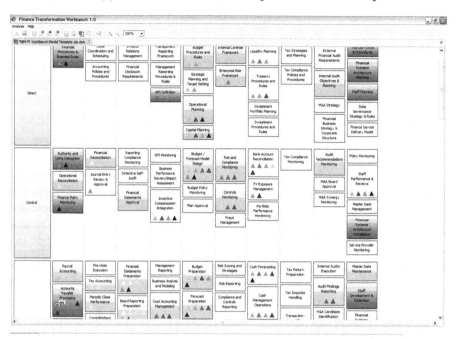

examined in detail. This analysis is facilitated by an innovative visual overlay of information on business components. Figure 17 shows such an IT application overlay. It shows which IT applications implement the business functions of which business components. The triangles represent the IT applications. A mouse-over operation on each triangle in the Workbench provides details about the IT application. We can notice that three IT applications are supporting the 'Accounts Payable Processing' business component in BigThrift Bank. (Accounts Payable Process business component can be seen at the bottom left most part of Figure 17.) The three IT applications are: Oracle-AP, SAP-FI-AP, and TCS-Tally. The existence of multiple IT applications is possibly due to the duplicate systems accrued via mergers and acquisitions. This fact highlights an opportunity for consolidation. The first step is to mark the Accounts Payable Processing component as containing 'duplicate' IT applications. This is one of the types of 'shortfalls' for this component. In the BT Workbench, this component is marked as

a candidate for 'duplicate' shortfall. The noted shortfall is shown as 'D^{app}' to denote application shortfall on the Accounts Payable Processing component.

ORGANIZATION SHORTFALL ANALYSIS

The next step is to investigate the organizations that implement the business components and processes under investigation. Figure 18 shows which organizations implement the business functions of which business components. The squares represent the organizations. A mouse-over operation on each square in the Workbench provides details about the organization. We can notice that two organizations are involved in 'Accounts Payable Processing' component: Accounts and Regional Audit. Although this finding by itself does not mean that two organizations cannot perform the business functions associated with 'Accounts Payable Processing', it certainly raises a flag.

Figure 18. Landscape of organizations overlaid on the component business map

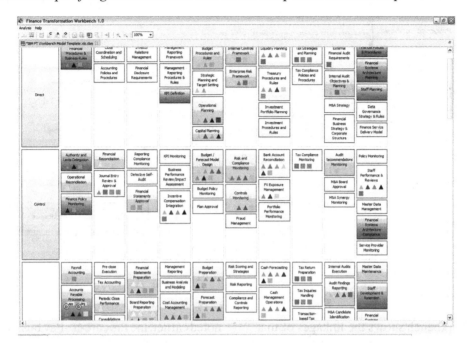

Perhaps there is a better way where a single organization is responsible for managing the accounts payables. If the consultant so chooses, s/he could add a note to herself/himself to investigate this finding further by marking the 'Accounts Payable Processing' component as a potential candidate for organization duplication shortfall. You can notice that the organization duplication shortfall is noted as 'D^{org}' in Figure 18.

In summary, the following things are noted about BigThrift Bank's business performance after conducting the qualitative analysis:

- Business component performance analysis indicated that the metrics associated with procure-to-pay function of BigThrift Bank underperform by 30% in comparison with the industry's best and by 15% in comparison with industry's median.
- IT application analysis indicated that three different IT systems are used to perform the 'Accounts Payable' function.

- Organizational analysis indicated that two different organizations across the company perform the 'Accounts Payable' function

SOLUTION ANALYSIS

Keeping these findings in mind, the IT consulting company now has to propose a solution to BigThrift Bank. Choice of solutions depends on a number of factors: breadth of the pain points, the benefits offered by a solution, client's budget constraints, duration within which improved results are expected, etc. In our case, the 'Redesign Procure-to-Pay Process' solution addresses the application as well as organizational shortfalls. Therefore, the IT consulting company has chosen the 'Redesign Procure2Pay Process' solution as a potential candidate solution for improving the procure-to-pay process of BigThrift Bank.

Figure 19 shows the model linkages which lead to the selection of the solution. Selecting a proposed solution or a set of proposed solutions

Figure 19. Solution analysis result

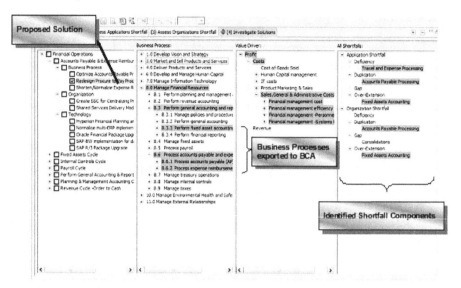

in the BT Workbench shows the linkages of that solution with process, metrics and shortfalls. These linkages help us understand (a) which processes the selected solution impacts (hopefully, positively), (b) which metrics can be used to measure the impact of process improvements to be achievable by implementing the chosen solution, and (c) which of the marked shortfalls the chosen solution address.

The solution analysis indicated helps the consultants get a quick idea at a qualitative level about which solutions can help address clients' shortfalls. The next step is to analyze the potential benefits the client can get by implementing the chosen solution(s) quantitatively. This business case analysis is done by clicking the 'Compute Business Value' button in the BT Workbench.

BUSINESS CASE ANALYSIS

The Business Case Calculator of the BT Workbench was already introduced in Section 3. In this section, we present the computation of financial benefits of implementing the 'Redesign Procure-to-Pay' business solution at BigThrift Bank. As

noted earlier, the Procure-to-Pay business consists of three business processes: accounts payable processing, fixed asset accounting, and travel and expense reimbursements processing. These processes are passed down to BCC for benefit computations. The BCC tool automatically configures itself to capture the preliminary benefits for these processes. As noted earlier, this configuration is done by making a simple assumption that, if the clients' performance metrics are below the benchmark, then implementing the industry best-practice solution for the client would improve the metrics to the benchmark values. Therefore, the difference between the as-is values for the client metrics for each of these processes and the benchmark values gives the expected cost savings. In the case of BigThrift Bank, they chose to represent additional cost savings they would obtain by outsourcing the procure-to-pay function via better spend management. Spend management means that the client is able to make use of the discounts offered by its customers when the bills are paid on or before time. This additional benefit is also taken into the overall cost reductions. The costs that would be incurred by BigThrift Bank

Figure 20. A cost model for the improved procure-to-pay function

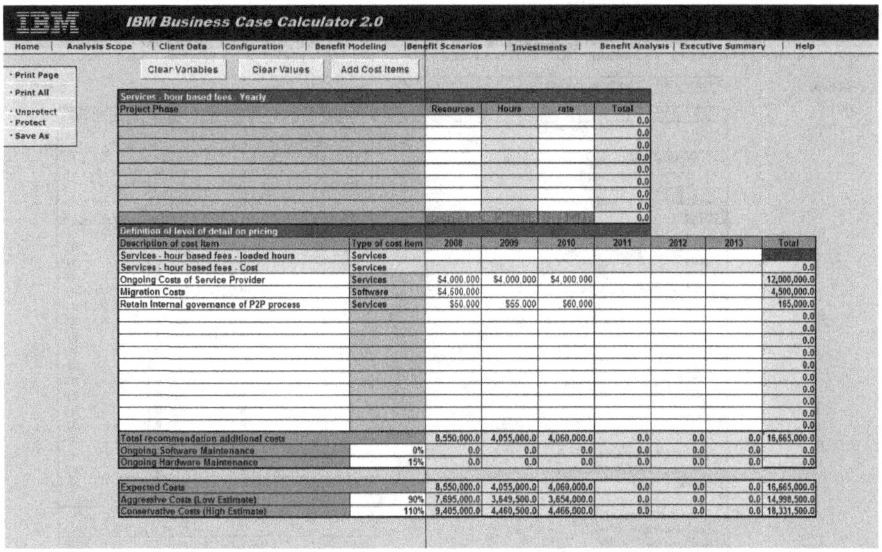

to implement this solution are also modeled. A view of the cost modeling is shown in Figure 20.

The result of the Net Present Value (NPV) analysis is shown below in Figure 21. The results indicate that the project will yield significant cost reductions. The return on investment (ROI) is projected as over 200%.

EVALUATION AND DISCUSSION

In this section, we describe the evaluation that we have conducted on the BT Workbench. The objective of the survey was to assess the usefulness and quality of the BT Workbench for practitioners. More specifically, through this survey, we were interested in obtaining the following information from the alpha testing community of Finance Management practitioners:

- Is there a pain point around value assessment for consultants today? In terms of time it takes to prepare for an analysis?
- Are the consultants satisfied with the current level of tool support they have for con-

ducting value assessment in their projects for clients?
- Do they think the BT Workbench will help them improve their productivity in their value assessment projects?
- How can the tool be further improved?
- If this tool is made available more generally, would the consultants use it in their clients' projects on a regular basis?
- Would the consultants recommend it to other practitioners in the field that are not aware of the tool?

The system was opened up for an alpha test and evaluation for a total of 12 consulting practitioners in the Finance Management area. The alpha testing was conducted over a period of month. Training materials such as instruction to install the tool and get familiarized with the tool's features, user manuals, answers to frequently asked questions, a training video and presentations were made available on a wiki site. Also, a document with additional exercises was prepared for those testers who wanted to test the tool beyond the specified scenarios in the training materials. A feedback area was created on the wiki page where

Figure 21. Cash flow forecast and NPV analysis of the procure-to-pay function

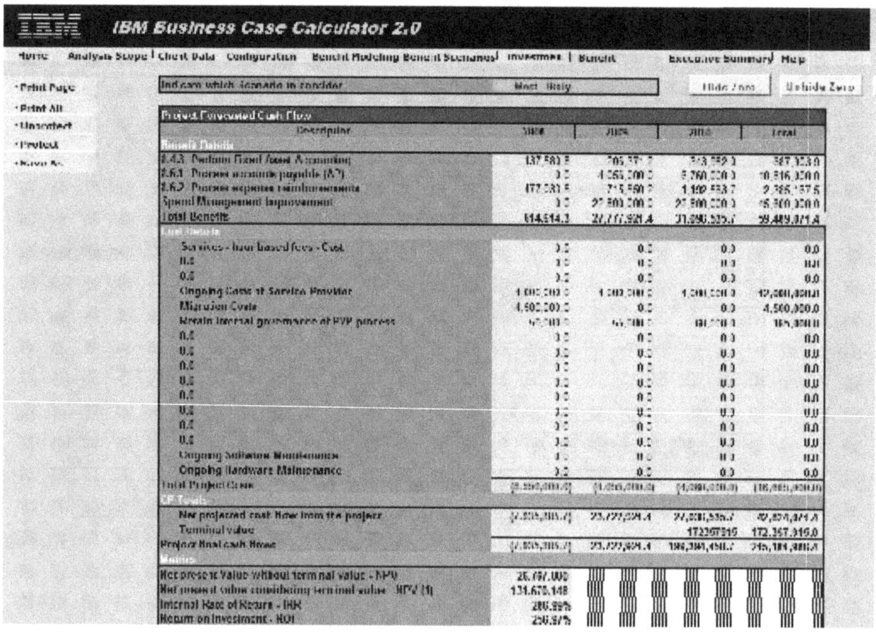

practitioners and testers can provide technical feedback on the working of the BT Workbench. The feedback categories included: bugs, feature requests, clarification, and performance-related ones. The practitioners were provided access to the wiki page and were given an overview of the BT Workbench via conference calls. The set of 12 practitioners participated from across the globe (including North America, Europe, Australia, and South America regions). The development team actively stayed engaged throughout the alpha testing process fixing any critical bugs that prevented the testers from testing the tool features and providing quick fixes and enhancements where applicable with a quick turnaround. The development team also responded to the feedback issues raised on the wiki by the testers promptly. In addition, several conference calls were scheduled at different times to accommodate testers in different time zones to gather feedback verbally during and after the testing process. All the comments made by the testers during the conference calls were duly recorded and meeting minutes sent.

A checklist was prepared to ensure that alpha testers tested all the major features of the tool. The checklist is presented in Appendix B. At the end of the alpha testing feedback period, a survey consisting of 15 questions was conducted on-line and the responses noted. The survey questionnaire administered to the testers is available in Appendix C. We have organized our questionnaire into four sections:

- *Alpha testing process*: We sought feedback on the alpha testing process. This section includes questions such as: How was the testing process? Did it go well?
- *Documentation/Help/Training*: We sought feedback on documentation and training materials. How much time did the tester spend in getting familiarized with the tool? Whether the information provided was sufficient to understand the tool. What additional information would s/he like to see, in what form, to help her understand the tool better. Which documentation helped a tester the most?

- *Feedback on the tool*: We sought feedback on the technical functionality offered by the tool and the usefulness of it for usage in client engagements. When does the tester think the tool would offer most value: pre-sales value assessment or post-sales value assessment?

- *About the Alpha tester*: Does the tester perform value assessments often in her daily job? How does s/he prepare a value assessment today (using a tool or do it manually)? How qualified does s/he feel to judge the tool?

The results of the survey were encouraging and are presented in Appendix D. 60% of the alpha testers felt that they would either definitely or probably use the BT Workbench in their next client engagement for identifying business transformation opportunities and performing business case analysis for their recommendations. All the respondents felt that they would use the tool both in pre-sales and post-sales scenarios. During pre-sales, the tool could be used to make a quick estimation of the benefits that the client would get by implementing the recommendations suggested by the IT consulting company. After sales, the consulting company would be able to gather input for the model from the client and the tool could help estimate the benefits more accurately. 90% of the consultants who tested the BT Workbench tool felt that the tool would help them do a better job during a client engagement. Finally, 90% of the testers said they would definitely or probably recommend the tool to their colleagues. This response is an extremely positive feedback from alpha testers of the BT Workbench tool. We have received about 80 feedback items on the wiki, some of which have already been implemented and incorporated into the latest release of BT Workbench. Some are noted as future features to be implemented. Overall, the alpha testers have tested all the aspects of the tool thoroughly and provided valuable feedback to improve the tool.

Encouraged by the overwhelmingly positive feedback, we are currently preparing a plan to pilot the BT Workbench tool among a select set of visionary practitioners in the Finance Management area to apply it in the field in the context of real-world customer engagements.

RELATED WORK

Business transformation is related to earlier efforts and studies in Business Process Reengineering, Business Process Redesign, Business Process Change Management, Business Process Management, and Enterprise Architecture. *Business process reengineering* (BPR) is a management approach aiming at improvements by means of elevating efficiency and effectiveness of the processes that exist within and across organizations. The key to BPR is for organizations to look at their business processes from an unbiased perspective and determine how they can best construct these processes to improve how they conduct business. The idea came from Michael Hammer in his article in the Harvard Business Review in 1990 (Hammer, 1990; Hammer & Champy 1993). A similar idea was advocated by Thomas H. Davenport and J. Short in a paper published in the Sloan Management Review the same year as Hammer published his paper (Davenport & Short, 1990; Davenport 1993). Process reengineering was adopted at an accelerating pace in the 1990s (Johansson, 1993; Malhotra, 1998; Ponzi & Koenig, 2002). This trend was fueled by the fast adoption of BPR by the consulting industry. The early BPR methodologies were rooted in IT-centric BPR solutions, and share many of the same basic principles and elements. One such model, Process Reengineering Life Cycle approach outlines an iterative application of the following steps: (1) envision new processes, (2) initiating change, (3) process diagnosis, (4) process redesign, (5) reconstruction, and (6) process monitoring. While useful in specific cases, the methodologies did not address important issue of scalable applications from the practitioner's viewpoint. Therefore, there are few tools or information technology that comprehensively facilitates the BPR methodology, and consultants are left with primitive means for practicing the methodology with their clients.

Business Process Management (BPM) is an emerging field of knowledge and research at the intersection between management and information technology, encompassing methods, techniques and tools to design, enact, control, and analyze operational business processes involving humans, organizations, applications, documents and other sources of information (Aalst, 2003; Burlton, 2001; Chang, 2005; Curtis, 1992; Gillot, 2008; Jeston & Nelis, 2006; Ould, 2005; Smith & Fingar, 2003; Spanyi 2003). BPM differs from BPR in that it does not aim at one-off revolutionary changes to business processes, but at their continuous evolution. In addition, BPM usually combines management methods with information technology to make business transformation activities faster and cheaper. BPM systems monitor the execution of the business processes so that managers can analyze and change processes in response to data, rather than just a hunch. BPM allows the organizations to manage their processes as any other assets and improve and manage them over the period of time. The activities which constitute BPM lifecycle can be grouped into five categories: Process Design, Process Modeling, Process Execution, Process Monitoring, and Process Optimization. BT Workbench presented in this paper is viewed the latest effort in improving BPM systems and methodologies with more capabilities and an extended modeling mechanism of CBM, especially in the areas of process diagnosis, process analytics, and solution identification.

Another related concept is *Enterprise Architecture*, which is the description of the current and future structure and behavior of an organization's processes, information systems, personnel and organizational sub-units, aligned with the organization's core goals and strategic direction

(Dietz, 2008; Hybertson, 2009; Ross, 2006). Although often associated strictly with information technology, it relates more broadly to the practice of business optimization in that it addresses business architecture, performance management, organizational structure and process architecture as well. The primary purpose of creating enterprise architecture is to ensure that business strategy and IT investments are aligned. As such, enterprise architecture allows traceability from the business strategy down to the underlying technology. The practice of enterprise architecture involves developing an architecture framework to describe a series of "current", "intermediate" and "target" reference architectures and applying them to align change within the enterprise. These frameworks detail all relevant structure within the organization including business, applications, technology and data. Each framework will provide a rigorous taxonomy and ontology that clearly identifies what processes a business performs and detailed information about how those processes are executed. While enterprise architecture is a key component of the information technology governance process at any organization of significant size, it also ideally relates broadly to the practice of business process management and optimization, because it addresses business architecture, performance management and process architecture as well. BPM systems such as BT Workbench can benefit from enterprise architecture work.

While BT Workbench provides views, models and analysis tools for upstream at an enterprise concerning business transformation and changes, *service-oriented architecture* (SOA) provides a set of principles for the downstream. SOA governs the transformational changes while taking them through to realization phases of systems development and integration (Bell, 2008; Bennett, 2000; Bieberstein, 2005; Cheng, 2007; Erl, 2005; Newcomer & Lomow, 2005). It helps package functionality specified by the transformational changes as interoperable services, and allows different applications to exchange data with one another, traditionally done by EAI (Enterprise Application Integration) frameworks. Service-orientation aims at a loose coupling of services with operating systems, programming languages and other technologies that underlie applications. SOA separates functions into distinct units or services which developers access over a network so that users can combine and reuse them in the production of applications. These services communicate with each other by passing data from one service to another, or by coordinating an activity between two or more services. SOA can be seen in a continuum, from older concepts of distributed computing and modular programming, through to current practices of SaaS (Software as a Service) (Bennett, 2000), and Cloud Computing (Vaquero, 2009).

CONCLUSION AND FUTURE WORK

In this paper, we introduce Business Transformation Workbench, a consulting practitioner's tool for identifying and analyzing business transformation opportunities. It embodies structured analytical models (both qualitative and quantitative) to enhance the consultants' practices. The tool helps visualize the linkages of various enterprise models such as the business component model (CBM), the business process model, the value driver model, the organization model, the IT application model, and the solution model. Using this tool, consultants can examine which business functions and components are underperforming in comparison to industry benchmark measures and why. By investigating the organizational responsibilities and IT application portfolio in conjunction with business components, shortfalls such as duplications, over-extensions, gaps and deficiencies can be identified and reasoned. Specific solutions can be discovered to address the identified shortfalls. Financial benefits of implementing specific solutions can be analyzed further via conducting a business case analysis.

The Business Transformation Workbench has been instantiated with data from finance management domain and applied to address a client situation as a case study. An alpha testing of the tool was conducted with about dozen practitioners. The feedback has been very encouraging. 90% of the consultants who tested the BT Workbench tool felt that the tool would help them do a better job during a client engagement. The tool is currently being piloted with customer engagements in a large IT consulting organization.

The BT Workbench methodology and its software solution is part of an ongoing research initiative on business design and transformation at IBM Research and Global Business Service Divisions. With a methodology and a research prototype in place, we work with practitioners to validate them with real-world business transformation initiatives. In addition to the tool and methodology, in practice, the availability of useful and accurate content and information of business components, value drivers, processes and solutions is critical to meaningful analyses. Further validation results from practices will be reported in the future.

ACKNOWLEDGMENT

The authors thank Abhaykumar Milapchand, Andrew Haskell, Ankur Chandra, David Hawkins, Derek Chu, Henry Chan, Ignacio Terrizzano, John Vergo, Jorge Sanz, Kelly Lyman, Kristen Harrington, Lisa Knight, Marino Fremis, Natalie Jones, Richard Goodwin, Robert Morris, Roger Rachuba, Thomas Li, and Ying Chen for their help with the project and constructive discussion.

REFERENCES

Apache. (2009). Java API to Access Microsoft Format Files. Retrieved from http://poi.apache.org/

APQC (American Productivity & Quality Center). (2010). Process Classification Framework. Retrieved from http://www.apqc.org

Bell, M. (2008). *Introduction to Service-Oriented Modeling. Service-Oriented Modeling: Service Analysis, Design, and Architecture.* Wiley & Sons.

Bennett, K., et al. (2000). Service-Based Software: the Future for Flexible Software. In *Proceedings of the Seventh Asia-Pacific Software Engineering Conference.* IEEE Press.

Bieberstein, N. (2005). *Service-Oriented Architecture (SOA) Compass: Business Value, Planning, and Enterprise Roadmap.* IBM Press.

Bodie, Z. (2004). *Essentials of Investments* (5th ed.). New York: McGraw-Hill/Irwin.

Burlton, R. (2001). *Business Process Management: Profiting From Process.* Sams.

Chang, J. F. (2005). *Business Process Management Systems: Strategy and Implementation.* Auerbach Publications. doi:10.1201/9781420031362

Curtis, B. (1992). Process Modeling. [ACM Press.]. *Communications of the ACM, 35,* 75–90. doi:10.1145/130994.130998

Davenport, T. (1993). *Process Innovation: Reengineering Work Through Information Technology.* Boston: Harvard Business School Press.

Davenport, T., & Short, J. (1990). The New Industrial Engineering: Information Technology and Business Process Redesign. *MIT Sloan Management Review, Summer 1990,* 11-27. MIT Press.

Dietz, J. L. G. (2008). Advances in Enterprise Engineering. In *Proceedings of the 4th International Workshop CIAO! and the 4th International Workshop EOMAS,* held at CAiSE 2008, June 16-17, 2008. Montpellier, France.

Erl, T. (2005). *Service-Oriented Architecture: Concepts, Technology, and Design.* Upper Saddle River: Prentice Hall PTR.

Gillot, J.-N. (2008). *The Complete Guide to Business Process Management.* BookSurge Publishing.

Hammer, M. (1990). Reengineering Work: Don't Automate, Obliterate. *Harvard Business Review,* (July/August): 104–112.

Hammer, M., & Champy, J. (1993). *Reengineering the Corporation: A Manifesto for Business Revolution.* Harper Business.

Hybertson, D. W. (2009). *Model-Oriented Systems Engineering Science: a Unifying Framework for Traditional and Complex Systems.* Auerbach Publications.

IBM. (2005). *Component Business Modeling.* Retrieved from http://www-1.ibm.com/services/us/bcs/html/bcs_componentmodeling.html

Jeston, J., & Nelis, J. (2006). *Business Process Management: Practical Guidelines to Successful Implementations.* Butterworth-Heinemann.

Johansson, H. J. (1993). *Business Process Reengineering: BreakPoint Strategies for Market Dominance.* John Wiley & Sons.

Lee, J. (2005). Model-Driven Business Transformation and Semantic Web. *Communications of the ACM, 48*(12). doi:10.1145/1101779.1101813

Lee, J. (2006). Ontology Management for Large-Scale Enterprise Systems. *Journal of Electronic Commerce Research and Applications, 5*(3).

Malhotra, Y. (1998). Business Process Redesign: An Overview. *IEEE Engineering Management Review, 26*(3).

Newcomer, E., & Lomow, G. (2005). *Understanding SOA with Web Services.* Addison Wesley.

Ould, M. (2005). *Business Process Management: A Rigorous Approach.* Meghan-Kiffer Press.

Ponzi, L., & Koenig, M. (2002). Knowledge Management: Another Management Fad? *Information Research, 8*(1).

Ross, J. W. (2006). *Enterprise Architecture as Strategy: Creating a Foundation for Business Execution*. Harvard Business Review Press.

Smith, H. & Fingar, P. (2004). Business Process Management: The Third Wave. *Journal of Information Systems*. American Accounting Association (AAA).

Spanyi, A. (2003). *Business Process Management Is a Team Sport: Play It to Win!*Anclote Press Imprint of Meghan-Kiffer Press.

van der Aalst, W. M. P., et al. (2003). Business Process Management: A Survey. *Business Process Management, Proceedings of the First International Conference*. Springer Verlag.

Vaquero, L. M. (2009). A Break in the Clouds: Toward a Cloud Definition. *ACM SIGCOMM Computer Communication Review, 39*(1), 50–55. doi:10.1145/1496091.1496100

KEY TERMS AND DEFINITIONS

Business Transformation: A key management initiative that attempts to align people, process and technology of an enterprise closely with its business strategy and vision. Business transformation is often achieved by taking a holistic look at various dimensions of an enterprise such as business models, management practices, business processes, organizational structure and technology and optimizing them with best-practice or differentiated methods to reach a strategic end state.

Business Process: A business process is a flow of one or more business activities. A business process when executed accomplishes a specific business objective. For example, 'Process accounts payable and expense reimbursements' is a typical business process in the finance management domain.

Business Activity: A business activity is the lowest level task in a business process. For example 'Accounts Payable' business process contains activities such as: 'Approve Payments', 'Process taxes', 'Retain records,' etc.

Business Component: A business component is an abstract business element. It is a collection of similar and related business activities from various business processes. From this point of view, business processes can be thought of as flows of activities between and within components. A component is defined by a set of people, processes and technology needed by its business function.

Component Business Model (CBM): A method developed by IBM to help analyze clients' business from multiple perspectives such as people, process and technology. The intersection of these views offers is claimed to improve insights for decision-making. A CBM is, in essence, a component view of a business where all the similar business activities of a given company's business processes are grouped into components.

Daisy Chain Analysis: A visual query that allows the user to explore the business maps and understand the correlations and dependencies among business entities. The results of the query is shown in the views of the models in the BT Workbench highlighting entries in the models directly and indirectly associated.

Heat Map Analysis: An essential capability of CBM where the user discovers one or more "hot" components that are associated with one or more business strategies and/or pain points.

Shortfall Assessment: It allows the user to map the existing IT infrastructure or organization structure against the "hot" components identified in the Business Component Performance Analysis. It helps understand how the current IT infrastructure or organization structure, such as applications, network capabilities or certain departments, supports the business, especially, for those hot components.

Net Present Value: A standard method for the financial appraisal of long-term projects. It measures the excess or shortfall of cash flows, in present value (PV) terms, once financing charges are met.

Internal Rate Of Return: A finance metric used by businesses to decide whether they should make investments. It is an indicator of the efficiency of an investment (as opposed to NPV, which indicates value or magnitude). IRR is the annualized effective compounded return rate which can be earned on the invested capital, i.e., the yield on the investment.

Return on Investment: The ratio of money gained or lost on an investment relative to the amount of money invested. ROI is usually given as a percent rather than decimal value.

Payback Period: The period of time required for the return on an investment to repay the sum of the original investment. It is intuitively the measure that describes how long something takes to pay for itself: shorter payback periods are obviously preferable to longer payback periods (all else being equal).

APPENDIX A: TYPES OF ERRORS CAUGHT DURING THE MODEL VALIDATING STAGE WHEN LOADING THE MODEL TEMPLATE DATA INTO BT WORKBENCH

Error Id	Purpose	Level	Error Message	Sample Message
1	Check if all 6 base models are in the content file	Error	Model sheet is missing	The model/sheet 'Business Component' is expected in the Model Template file.
2	Check if the base models are in a tree structure			
2.1	Check if table headers exist in the base models	Error	Header column expected	The 'Business Component' sheet of import the Model Template file should contain at least one row as header column.
2.2	Check if a table header is not an empty cell	Error	Header column content expected	The 'Business Component' sheet of import the Model Template file should not contain empty cell ('Business Component'!A1) as header column.
2.3	Check if a tree node is missing (Rule: a property cell is the first non-empty cell of one row)	Error	Miss tree node cell	The first non-empty cell ('Business Component'!I11) is in a property column, miss a cell before it as a tree node in sheet 'Business Component'.
3	Check if all mapping sheets are in the file	Warning	Link sheet is missing	The link/sheet 'VD2BizProc' is not found in the Model Template file.
4	Check if the default mappings in the correct format			
4.1	Check if table headers exist in the default mapping	Error	Header column content expected	The 'VD2BizProc' sheet of import the Model Template file should contain at least one row as header column.
4.2	Check if a table header is not an empty cell	Error	Header column expected	The 'VD2BizProc' sheet of import the Model Template file should not contain empty cell ('Business Component'!A1) as header column.
4.4	Check if link source is a formula	Error	Source cell must be a formula	The mapping sheet 'VD2BizProc' of import the Model Template file should has a formula at source cell ('VD2BizProc'!A3).
4.5	Check if link target is a formula	Error	Target cell must be a formula	The mapping sheet 'VD2BizProc' of import the Model Template file should has a formula at target cell ('VD2BizProc'!B3).
4.6	Check if link source is empty	Error	Source cell must not be empty	The mapping sheet 'VD2BizProc' of import the Model Template file contains empty source cell ('VD2BizProc'!A3).
4.7	Check if link target is empty	Error	Target cell must not be empty	The mapping sheet 'VD2BizProc' of import the Model Template file contains empty target cell ('VD2BizProc'!B3).

APPENDIX B: BUSINESS TRANSFORMATION WORKBENCH CHECK LIST

Content Check List

- Loading the tool with content provided with installation package
- Adding/changing the content provided and seeing the changes reflected in the tool
- Adding new linkages between models via Model Mapping Editor

Model View Check List

- Component Business Map (CBM) View
- Value Driver View
- Business Process View
- IT Application View
- Organizational View
- Solution View
- Shortfall View

Business Performance Analysis Check List

- Daisy-Chain Analysis
- Component Performance Analysis
- Application Shortfall Analysis
- Organizational Shortfall Analysis
- Solution Analysis
- Generating Reports from the Business performance analysis module
- Generating Power points from the business performance analysis module
- Invoking the Business Case Calculator 2.0 via the 'Compute Business value' button

Business Case Analysis Check List

- Conducting Business Case Analysis in Business Case Calculator 2.0
- Adding new benefits dynamically and including them in the analysis

APPENDIX C: BUSINESS TRANSFORMATION WORKBENCH SURVEY QUESTIONNAIRE

1. Overall, do you feel that the alpha testing of the IBM Financial Transformation Workbench was successful?
    - ☐ Strongly Agree
    - ☐ Agree
    - ☐ Neutral
    - ☐ Disagree
    - ☐ Strongly Disagree

2. Were the instructions, documentation, and training materials provided on the Wiki site sufficient to help you understand the tool and its capabilities in order to perform the alpha-testing?
    - ☐ Strongly Agree
    - ☐ Agree
    - ☐ Neutral
    - ☐ Disagree
    - ☐ Strongly Disagree

3. Overall, how much time did you spend familiarizing yourself with the tool?
    - ☐ 0-2 hours
    - ☐ 2-4 hours
    - ☐ 4-6 hours
    - ☐ 6-8 hours
    - ☐ Longer

4. Which of the following features of the tool were you able to test? Please check all that apply.
    - ◦ FM Content Check List
        - ☐ Loading the tool with content provided with installation package
        - ☐ Adding/changing the content provided and seeing the changes reflected in the tool
        - ☐ Adding new linkages between models via Model Mapping Editor
    - ◦ Model View Check List
        - ☐ Component Business Map (CBM) View
        - ☐ Value Driver View
        - ☐ Business Process View
        - ☐ IT Application View
        - ☐ Organizational View
        - ☐ Solution View
        - ☐ Shortfall View
    - ◦ Business Performance Analysis Check List
        - ☐ Daisy-Chain Analysis
        - ☐ Component Performance Analysis
        - ☐ Application Shortfall Analysis
        - ☐ Organizational Shortfall Analysis
        - ☐ Solution Analysis
        - ☐ Generating Reports from the Business performance analysis module
        - ☐ Generating Powerpoint slides from the business performance analysis module

      ☐ Invoking the Business Case Calculator 2.0 via the 'Compute Business value' button

   ○   Business Case Analysis Check List

      ☐ Conducting Business Case Analysis in Business Case Calculator 2.0

      ☐ Adding new benefits dynamically and including them in the analysis

5.   With the familiarity you have gained via alpha testing, would you use the IBM BT Workbench tool in your client engagements for identifying business transformation opportunities and performing analysis?

      ☐ Definitely

      ☐ Probably

      ☐ Not Sure

      ☐ Probably Not

      ☐ Definitely Not

6.   With the familiarity you have gained via alpha testing, would you use the IBM BT Workbench tool in your client engagements for preparing a business case for the recommended business transformation initiatives?

      ☐ Definitely

      ☐ Probably

      ☐ Not Sure

      ☐ Probably Not

      ☐ Definitely Not

7.   At what stage in the project would you find the IBM BT Workbench tool most useful?

      ☐ Pre-Sales

      ☐ Post-Sales

      ☐ Both

      ☐ None

      ☐ Other. Please Specify _____

8.   Which of the following features of the tool do you find most valuable and insightful for usage in a client engagement? Please check all that apply.

      ☐ Component Business Map (CBM) for FM domain

      ☐ Various views of an enterprise and the linkages between these views (Value Driver, Business Process, IT application, organizational and solution offering views)

      ☐ Component performance analysis (where components in a CBM map are highlighted in red, green and yellow to show opportunities for improvement)

      ☐ Shortfall analysis (Identification of specific issues for improvement namely IT application shortfalls, and Organizational shortfalls)

      ☐ Generating reports from the business performance analysis module

      ☐ Generating Pwerpoint slides from the business performance analysis module

      ☐ Preparing a business case by using the Business Case Calculator 2.0 provided

9.   Overall, would you say that the IBM BT Workbench tool will help you do your job better during a client engagement?

      ☐ Strongly Agree

      ☐ Agree

      ☐ Neutral

      ☐ Disagree

☐ Strongly Disagree

10. Would you recommend the tool to other IBM GBS FM consultants?
    ☐ Definitely
    ☐ Probably
    ☐ Not Sure
    ☐ Probably Not
    ☐ Definitely Not

11. Would you like to offer any suggestions for improving the IBM Financial Transformation Workbench tool?

----

12. Would you like to give your name in case we want to follow up with you for further feedback?

Name: -------------------------------------

APPENDIX D: DETAILED RESULTS OF THE SURVEY

1. Overall, do you feel that the alpha testing of the IBM Financial Transformation Workbench was successful?				
Strongly Agree		4		40%
Agree		4		40%
Neutral		0		0%
Disagree		2		20%
Strongly Disagree		0		0%
TOTAL RESPONDENTS		10		

2. Were the instructions, documentation, and training materials provided on the Wiki site sufficient to help you understand the tool and its capabilities in order to perform the alpha testing?				
Strongly Agree		1		11%
Agree		6		67%
Neutral		1		11%
Disagree		0		0%
Strongly Disagree		1		11%
TOTAL RESPONDENTS		9		

3. Overall, how much time did you spend familiarizing yourself with the tool?				
0-2 hours		0		0%
2-4 hours		1		10%
4-6 hours		5		50%
6-8 hours		1		10%
More than 8 hours		3		30%
TOTAL RESPONDENTS		10		

4. Which of the following FM Content features of the tool were you able to test? Please check all that apply.				
Loading the tool with content provided with installation package		10		100%
Adding/changing the content provided and seeing the changes reflected in the tool		10		100%
Adding new linkages between models via Model Mapping Editor		5		50%

5. Which of the following Model View features of the tool were you able to test? Please check all that apply.				
Component Business Map (CBM) View		10		100%
Value Driver View		10		100%
Business Process View		9		90%
IT Application View		9		90%

Organizational View		10		100%	
Solution View		10		100%	
Shortfall View		9		90%	

6. Which of the following Business Performance Analysis features of the tool were you able to test? Please check all that apply.

Daisy-Chain Analysis		9		90%	
Component Performance Analysis		9		90%	
Application Shortfall Analysis		9		90%	
Organizational Shortfall Analysis		9		90%	
Solution Analysis		8		80%	
Generating Reports from the Business performance analysis module		9		90%	
Generating Powerpoint slides from the business performance analysis module		9		90%	
Invoking the Business Case Calculator 2.0 via the 'Compute Business value' button		6		60%	

7. Which of the following Business Case Analysis features of the tool were you able to test? Please check all that apply.

Conducting Business Case Analysis in Business Case Calculator 2.0		7		70%	
Adding new benefits dynamically and including them in the analysis		5		50%	

8. With the familiarity you have gained via alpha testing, would you use the IBM BT Workbench tool in your client engagements for identifying business transformation opportunities and performing analysis?

Definitely		4		40%	
Probably		2		20%	
Not Sure		3		30%	
Probably Not		1		10%	
Definitely Not		0		0%	
TOTAL RESPONDENTS		10			

9. With the familiarity you have gained via alpha testing, would you use the IBM BT Workbench tool in your client engagements for preparing a business case for the recommended business transformation initiatives?

Definitely		3		30%	
Probably		2		20%	
Not Sure		3		30%	
Probably Not		2		20%	
Definitely Not		0		0%	
TOTAL RESPONDENTS		10			

10. At what stage in the project would you find the IBM BT Workbench tool most useful?					
Pre-sales		1		10%	
Post-sales		1		10%	
Both		8		80%	
Neither		0		0%	
Other (Specify in write-in area of Question #14)		0		0%	
TOTAL RESPONDENTS		10			
11. Which of the following features of the tool do you find most valuable and insightful for usage in a client engagement? Please check all that apply.					
Component Business Map (CBM) for FM domain		6		60%	
Various views of an enterprise and the linkages between these views (Value Driver, Business Process, IT application, organizational and solution offering views)		9		90%	
Component performance analysis (where components in a CBM map are highlighted in red, green and yellow to show opportunities for improvement)		8		80%	
Shortfall analysis (Identification of specific issues for improvement namely IT application shortfalls, and Organizational shortfalls)		2		20%	
Generating reports from the business performance analysis module		4		40%	
Generating Powerpoint slides from the business performance analysis module		5		50%	
Preparing a business case by using the Business Case Calculator 2.0 provided		6		60%	
12. Overall, would you say that the IBM BT Workbench tool will help you do your job better during a client engagement?					
Strongly Agree		2		20%	
Agree		7		70%	
Neutral		1		10%	
Disagree		0		0%	
Strongly Disagree		0		0%	
TOTAL RESPONDENTS		10			
13. Would you recommend the tool to other IBM GBS FM consultants?					
Definitely		7		70%	
Probably		3		30%	

Not Sure		0		0%	
Probably Not		0		0%	
Definitely Not		0		0%	
TOTAL RESPONDENTS		10			

Chapter 9
Specification of Context for Management of Service-Oriented Systems with WS-Policy4MASC

Vladimir Tosic
NICTA, Australia & The University of Western Ontario, Canada & The University of New South Wales, Australia

Rasangi Pumudu Karunaratne
The University of New South Wales, Australia

Qinghua Lu
NICTA, Australia & The University of New South Wales, Australia

ABSTRACT

Specification of monitored context properties and their influence on operation of service-oriented systems and on management activities is a prerequisite for context-sensitive operation. We researched context specification for a management system performing various management activities and potentially used by mobile service-oriented systems. Due to the similarities between processing and use of context properties and processing and use of quality of service (QoS) metrics, we decided to model context properties analogously to QoS metrics. We built our solutions for specification of context properties and related management activities into two languages: the Web Service Offerings Language (WSOL) and WS-Policy4MASC, the latter of which is the focus of this book chapter. WS-Policy4MASC is a powerful extension of the industrial standard Web Services Policy Framework (WS-Policy) with constructs for specification of information necessary for run-time policy-driven management. The presented constructs related to context increase usefulness of WS-Policy4MASC for management of mobile service-oriented systems.

DOI: 10.4018/978-1-61520-819-7.ch009

INTRODUCTION

IT system management is the process of monitoring and control to ensure regular operation, maximize quality of service (QoS), discover and fix problems, accommodate change, account consumed resources, bill consumers, enforce security, and minimize operational costs. It is necessary to achieve dependable IT systems. Monitoring determines the state of a system, e.g., by measuring or calculating various QoS metrics, determining presence of faults, evaluating satisfaction of requirements and guarantees, and calculating monetary amounts to be paid. Here, QoS is a group of measures of how well (e.g., how quickly, how reliably) a system performs its operations. A QoS metric is a particular measure of QoS. Some examples of QoS metrics are response time, throughput, and availability. On the other hand, control puts the system into the desired state, by performing run-time adaptation (e.g., re-configuration) of a system to ensure its regular operation, in spite of external changes or internal run-time problems (e.g., faults, performance degradations). For example, control of a service-oriented system includes its re-configuration, re-negotiation of contracts between the composed services and between the system and other parties, and re-composition of services. Formal and precise specification of management information is necessary for successful management activities.

One frequent-approach to IT system management is based on policies. A policy formally specifies a collection of high-level, implementation-independent, operation and management goals and/or rules in a human-readable form. Policies are enacted during runtime by middleware that measures or calculates monitored information and executes control actions. A service level agreement (SLA) is another format for specification of this information. It is a special type of contract (a binding and enforceable formal agreement between two or more parties) that specifies QoS (and often price/penalty) information. It can be used as an alternative or a complement to policies. A class of service (a.k.a. service offering) is a predefined SLA that can be used by multiple consumers (i.e., it is not custom-made). While information specified in policies and SLAs is similar in content, SLAs require two or more parties (while policies can be specified for one party only) and, traditionally, architecture of management middleware is different.

Another issue relevant for our research is that the use of mobile service-oriented systems is rapidly increasing. In such systems, services and/or consumers execute in mobile devices, e.g., laptops, personal digital assistants (PDAs), or mobile/cell phones. While at first the term "mobile Web service" was used to denote systems where only consumers were mobile and provider services stationary, the number of mobile provider services is growing. Mobile service-oriented systems support ad hoc integration of diverse software running in mobile devices with other software running on the Internet, primarily through the use of Web service industrial standards. Example application areas are mobile business, fleet management (e.g., truck tracking), and disaster relief.

Management of mobile service-oriented systems has to deal with issues that are not very prominent in management of non-mobile systems. These specific management issues include:

i. context-sensitive operation and management;
ii. relatively frequent disturbances and changes of communication-level QoS;
iii. possibility of relatively frequent disconnection during execution; and
iv. limited resources (e.g., scarce run-time memory, relatively low processing power, limited battery lifetime, and slow wireless links).

In this book chapter, we explore the management issues related to context-sensitivity (i.e., the influence of context on operation and management) of service-oriented systems. There are very different definitions of the term "context" in the literature and we will discuss this in the following section. For now, it suffices to say that we define context as information about external run-time circumstances (e.g., geographic location, events that come from outside, preferences of system's consumers) that characterize the situation of the managed system and influence its operation, but are outside its direct control. Changes in external context (e.g., geographic location of mobile systems) significantly influence not only systems' operation, but management activities. For example, when a truck with a truck-tracking mobile Web service enters USA from Canada, dynamic (run-time) adaptation should be automatically initiated to reconfigure the Web service to use the wireless network for the USA instead of the wireless network for Canada and to reconfigure the Web service operation returning speed of the truck so that results are provided in miles/hour (units used in the USA) instead of in kilometers/hour (units used in Canada).

To enable context-sensitive behavior of a mobile service-oriented system, a management system should support specifying, publishing, monitoring, storing, processing, analyzing, communicating, updating, and using context information. It should also enable using context for monitoring and control activities. All this requires specification of context management information that addresses at least the following four sets of questions:

1. How to formally specify monitored context properties (attributes) in a way useful for management activities?
2. How to formally specify when, where, how, for which parties (e.g., provider, consumer) and by which parties (e.g., provider, consumer, some independent/third party) the context monitoring is performed, as well as when and how values of context properties are transferred between various parties?

3. How to specify various ways in which context properties influence operation of service-oriented systems (particularly provider services), monitoring of service-oriented systems, and dynamic adaptation of service compositions?
4. How can specification of context properties be used for discovery and selection of appropriate service-oriented systems and their QoS?

The past solutions for management of service-oriented systems and for context-sensitivity of mobile service-oriented systems did not fully address these issues. Therefore, in this book chapter, we discuss how appropriate specification of context management information can be added to the existing languages used in management of service-oriented systems and their compositions. We present our conceptual solutions for modeling context and its impact on management activities in a general, language-independent way. These conceptual solutions can be added to different languages for management of service-oriented systems. We implemented an early version of these conceptual solutions as extensions to the Web Service Offerings Language (WSOL) and the corresponding Web Services Offerings Infrastructure (WSOI) management middleware. These implementations were summarized in (Tosic, Lutfiyya, & Tang, 2006a; Tosic, Lutfiyya, & Tang, 2006b). WSOL is based on classes of service and has a limited support for dynamic (run-time) adaptation. On the other hand, our new language WS-Policy4MASC (Tosic, Erradi, & Maheshwari, 2007; Tosic, 2010) is based on policies. As elaborated in (Tosic, Erradi, & Maheshwari, 2007; Tosic, 2010), the crucial advantage of WS-Policy4MASC is much stronger support for dynamic adaptation of service compositions, so there is a broader possible impact of context in WS-Policy4MASC. For a recent WS-Policy4MASC version 0.9 (Karunaratne, 2008), we adapted, extended and improved our conceptual solutions for modeling context and related management activities. In this book chapter we will focus on explaining and illustrating our recent implementations in WS-Policy4MASC and not on our (preliminary) solutions in WSOL.

This book chapter is organized as follows. In the "Background" section, we discuss different definitions of the term "context" and survey the main related work. Then, in the section "Overview of the WS-Policy4MASC Policy Language", we present the main concepts and characteristics of our WS-Policy4MASC language. In the section "Our Approach to Modeling Context", we present and illustrate in the implementation-independent way the main concepts in our solution for modeling context for management of diverse service-oriented systems. The following section "WS-Policy4MASC Implementation of Context Modeling and Its Evaluation" discusses how we implemented the previously presented implementation-independent context modeling solutions in the WS-Policy4MASC language. The examples presented in this section are specific to WS-Policy4MASC. At the end of this section, we discuss how we evaluated (validated) our solutions. In the section "Future Trends" we outline possibilities for further research in this area, while in the section "Conclusion" we summarize the main contributions of our work. After the "References" section, we repeat the key definitions in the section "Key Terms and Definitions".

BACKGROUND

In the mobile computing literature, there are several different definitions of the term "context". One of the most often cited definitions states "Context is any information that can be used to characterize the situation of an entity." (Dey, 2001, p. 5) Similarly, Chen and Kotz (2000, p. 3) provide the definition that "context is the set of environmental states and settings that either determines an application's behavior or in which

an application event occurs and is interesting to the user." They identify four categories of context: computing context (e.g., network connectivity, nearby resources), user context (e.g., user's profile), physical context (e.g., temperature), and time context. They also note the importance of context history. Furthermore, they differentiate between active context that determines behavior of the system and passive context that is relevant but not critical to the system. A somewhat narrower definition from Spanoudakis, Mahbub, and Zisman (2007, pp. 235) states that context is "any type of information regarding an SBS [service-based system] that can change dynamically". The authors discuss that apart from information such as clock time, geographic location, physical environment, and presence of other processes that run on the same platform, this definition also includes information about SLAs that can change dynamically (i.e., during run-time). Moving more towards the SLA-type of information, Herssens, Faulkner, and Jureta (2008, p. 363) state that context is "any information about the interaction between users and a web service, for which an SLA is specified". They identify five categories of context: user, provider, resource, environment, and Web service. From the session/transaction coordination viewpoint, Little (2007, pp. 441) explains context through the sentence "In order to correlate the work of multiple Web Services within the same activity, it is necessary to propagate additional information called the context to each participating service." From the viewpoint of Web service composition, (Rong, Liu, & Liang, 2008) defines context as a collection of collaborating/partner (e.g., provider or consumer) Web services.

While such broad and diverging definitions of context are common, we believe that they are not completely appropriate and useful for the practice of IT system management. In the broadest definitions of context, such as (Dey, 2001), virtually any and every information that is relevant for IT system management can be viewed as context (e.g., because it can be used to characterize a situation of the managed system). With such broad definitions, it is also almost impossible to answer the question: What is not context, but is still relevant for system's operation or management? In the IT systems management literature, the broad term "management information" is already used to denote information that is relevant for IT system management. If all management information is context, then there is no benefit of introducing the new term "context".

We studied many of the existing literature definitions and informal interpretations of the term "context" and concluded that they cover several groups of concepts that have considerably different nature and that must be differentiated for successful system management activities:

i.   Situational circumstances that are external to the managed system and over which the managed system does not have direct control and, thus, is not responsible for. Some examples are: time/weekday/date, geographic location (if the managed system is carried and does not control its movement), competitors' offerings (e.g., whether a competitor offers a similar service at lower prices), external collaborating/partner (e.g., provider, consumer) services, properties and preferences of these partners (although the managed system might choose which partners to accept and limit their preferences to some options, it cannot directly modify these preferences), on-line presence of the partners.

ii. Historical circumstances in execution of the managed system over which the managed system had some control in the past and, thus, is at least partially responsible for. Some examples are: the current state of the managed system (it is a consequence of past actions by the managed system), session states that the managed system has with individual partners, and past values of QoS metrics that the managed system was responsible for.

iii. Current and future circumstances over which the managed system has some control and, thus, is at least partially responsible for. Some examples are: future values of QoS metrics for which the managed system is responsible, functional and QoS guarantees that the managed system promises (e.g., in SLAs or policies), prices that the managed system sets for its use, on-line presence of the managed system.

The facts whether (or not) the managed system is responsible for some circumstances and whether (or not) it can do anything about them in the future are crucial from the management viewpoint and directly determine the managed system's behavior related to these circumstances. Also note that information about the concepts from the second and third group is already maintained in many management systems. Contrary, information about only a few concepts from the first group (e.g., about date/time) is used in the traditional management systems, while the rest is rarely maintained. Importance of some of the concepts from the first group (e.g., geographic location) is significantly higher in mobile systems compared to non-mobile systems.

Therefore, we decided to provide two definitions of the term "context" – one with a broad meaning and the other with a narrow meaning. In the definition with the broad meaning, context is (any and every) information that characterizes situation of the (managed) system. This definition is consistent with the broadest definitions, e.g., Dey (2001), that we found in the literature. On the other hand, our definition with the narrow meaning states that context is information about external run-time circumstances that characterize situation of the (managed) system and influence its operation (i.e., execution, behavior), but are outside its direct control. It includes only the first group of concepts from the above classification. This definition is consistent with the definition of context in linguistics: "the words before and

Table 1. The meaning of the term "context" in various papers

Paper	External Situational Circumstances outside Direct Control				Past Circumstances under Some Control	Current & Future Circumstances under Some Control	
	time	location	external partners	user intention	session state	QoS metrics	SLA
(Dey, 2001)	Yes	Yes					
(Herssens et al, 2008)	Yes	Yes	Yes			Yes	Yes
(Little, 2007)					Yes		
(Amundsen & Eliassen, 2008)	Yes	Yes				Yes	
(Spanoudakis et al., 2007)						Yes	Yes
(Chen et al., 2006)			Yes				
(Rong et al., 2008)				Yes			
Our narrow definition	Yes	Yes	Yes	Yes			

after a word or passage in a piece of writing that contribute to its meaning" (Farlex, 2009). Using this narrow definition, context of a service-oriented system does not include a description of the system's implementation, input values provided by a consumer, changes to its state caused by execution, or values of QoS metrics. For example, current clock time and country of location are context for a mobile banking Web service, but account balance is not (it is part of Web service's state). Similarly, response time of code that implements a Web service is not context (it is determined by internal processes), but network delay time for Web service messages over the Internet is context (it is external and not under direct control). On-line presence of external collaborators/partners is context, while on-line presence of the managed system is not context (the managed system can change it at least in some situations; if the managed system cannot change its on-line presence, then the underlying cause, such as lack of network connectivity, is context). In this book chapter, we will use the narrow definition of context and will explicitly note when we refer to the broad definition. We also define the term "context property" as an attribute (aspect) of context. In the above examples, current clock time, country of loca-

tion, network delay time, presence of external collaborators/partners, and network connectivity are five different context properties.

Many recent research projects and papers are related to context modeling, processing, and/or management in mobile computing. They explored the concept of context in various circumstances and from various viewpoints. These related works (see Table 1) used various definitions of context, oftentimes with a different meaning compared to our narrow definition (but within our broad definition). We will review here only several past works that can be viewed as most closely related to our topic of context modeling for management of service-oriented systems or our narrow definition of the term "context".

Probably the closest related work to our research is (Herssens, Faulkner, & Jureta, 2008). This paper presents an SLA management approach to ensure that after a change of context, SLAs are adapted automatically and with minimal human intervention (i.e., autonomically). These authors are aware of (and reference) some of our past publications on WSOL and WSOI. An issue with their approach is that SLA adaptation cannot be done at will, because there are many potential consistency issues. Although their approach tries to capture dependencies among various management information items (including context properties and QoS metrics), it seems that they have treated these complicated dependencies in a somewhat simplistic manner. Furthermore, their definition of context is significantly different from our definition with the narrow meaning, although there are some overlaps. Our improved context modeling solutions in WS-Policy4MASC provides support for adaptation that is not present in related work, including (Herssens, Faulkner, & Jureta, 2008).

Several specialized formats for specification of context were developed (e.g., see Strang & Linnhoff-Popien, 2004; Chen, Yang, & Zhang, 2006; Baldauf, Dustdar, & Rosenberg, 2007; Bolchini, Curino, Quintarelli, Schreiber, & Tanca, 2007), but they are different from the developed models for specification of other management information (e.g., QoS) and cannot be viewed as directly applicable in management systems for various management activities and various types of service-oriented systems. For example, context models and representations developed by the Semantic Web community, such as (Forstadius, Lassila, & Seppanen, 2005), are not directly useful for management because they do not describe in detail management activities to be performed and are not accompanied by appropriate management infrastructures. Another example is (Sheng & Benatallah, 2005), which describes ContextUML – a UML extension (profile) for modeling context-aware Web services. Their model includes modeling of context properties (attributes), their retrieval from context sources, binding of context to context-aware objects, and triggering of adaptation after context changes. Thus, their model addresses many (albeit not all) aspects relevant for use of context in management systems. The problem is that this modeling is done in a way that is not similar to the modeling of other management information, so its integration into general management systems would be very difficult. In the section "Our Approach to Modeling Context",

we will explain that it is important to have a context model that is consistent with the models for specification of other management information.

(Amundsen & Eliassen, 2008) presents a model that combines resource QoS metrics and context properties, developed for the dynamic mobile middleware called QuAMobile. This model does not consider specifics of service-oriented systems and does not address all issues in context management. However, note the authors' claim that design of self-managed mobile computing systems has to consider both context information and QoS metrics. This viewpoint agrees with our approach, which was first published in (Tosic, Lutfiyya, & Tang, 2006a). Our work deals with the specifics of management of service-oriented systems (e.g., adaptation of Web service compositions).

A somewhat different type of related work is (Wibisono, Zaslavsky, & Ling, 2008), which presents a context service framework to facilitate context management in mobile environments. Their work focuses on dealing with quality of context (the topic that our work does not address), but does not address the issues we focus on. We see compatibilities and possible integrations between our work and their work.

Little (2007) presents the Web Service Context (WS-Context) as a specification defining a shared context structure, which relates to activities between Web services. The title of this work makes it sound like a crucial related work to our research. However, their definition of context actually means "session/transaction history" and is, thus, substantially different from our definition of context with the narrow meaning. The author claims that WS-Context is the only Web service specification that describes a generic context (i.e., session/transaction) management mechanism. In fact, many other Web service technologies with session management were published previously, such as the early version of the WSOI management middleware described in (Tosic, Pagurek, Patel, Esfandiari, & Ma, 2005).

Note that the main languages in management of service-oriented systems do not contain context-related concepts. Notable examples of these languages are the Web Service Level Agreement (WSLA) language (Keller & Ludwig, 2003), WS-Agreement (Ludwig, Dan, & Kearney), and the Web Services Policy Framework – WS-Policy (W3C Web Services Policy Working Group, 2007). As argued in (Tosic, Pagurek, Patel, Esfandiari, & Ma, 2005), WSLA has higher run-time overhead than WSOL. Since run-time overhead is an important issue in mobile (and, particularly, embedded) systems, we have not proceeded with extension of WSLA. (Another argument against WSLA extension is that WSLA is no longer supported.) Since WS-Agreement is only a general framework for specification of contracts, without direct support for detailed specification of QoS-related information, we decided that its extension would be too complicated. As will be explained in the next section, our WS-Policy4MASC is an extension of WS-Policy (a general framework for specification of policies), which makes it attractive to the large number of current and potential future users of WS-Policy.

The general conclusion of our literature survey is that these past projects and papers did not completely explore context specification and management for mobile service-oriented systems from the viewpoint of a management system for various management activities and various types of service-oriented systems (including non-mobile). Similarly, a model and format for specifying context properties through extensions of existing management information models and formats for service-oriented systems would be beneficial, but was not developed prior to our research project.

OVERVIEW OF THE WS-POLICY4MASC LANGUAGE

WS-Policy4MASC (Tosic, Erradi, & Maheshwari, 2007) is a powerful language for formal specifica-

tion of management policies for service-oriented systems. It has been used in the Manageable and Adaptable Service Compositions (MASC) middleware for management of service-oriented systems (particularly service compositions), as described in (Erradi, Tosic, & Maheshwari, 2007). The design and prototype implementation of the MASC middleware were based on the Microsoft. NET 3.5 platform. However, WS-Policy4MASC is a general-purpose language for description of management information and its use is not limited to the MASC middleware or the Microsoft.NET platform or even the orchestration type of Web service compositions. WS-Policy4MASC extends the Web Services Policy Framework – WS-Policy (W3C Web Services Policy Working Group, 2007), an industrial specification standardized by the World Wide Web Consortium (W3C).

WS-Policy is a general framework for specifying various Web service properties in a way that complements the widely-used industrial standards the Web Services Description Language (WSDL) and the Web Services Business Process Execution Language (WSBPEL). It defines an extensible container to hold domain-specific policy assertions. In the WS-Policy model, a policy is defined as a collection of policy alternatives, each of which is a collection of policy assertions. WS-PolicyAttachment defines a generic mechanism that associates a policy with subjects to which the policy applies, such as WSDL or WSBPEL constructs. Various policy subjects are possible, such as process, flow, links, service, endpoint, operation, message, or message part. A policy scope is a set of policy subjects to which a policy may apply. WS-Policy has many good features, such as simplicity, extensibility, and flexibility (e.g., policies can be specified inside and outside WSDL and WSBPEL files). Nevertheless, it must be noted that WS-Policy is only a general framework, while the details of the specification of particular categories of policies will be defined in specialized languages – domain-dependent extensions of WS-Policy. Currently, only standard extensions for security, reliable messaging, and a few other management areas that were not the focus of our project had been published. It is not clear whether and when some standard specialized languages for the specification of QoS, context properties, business value metrics (at least prices and penalties), and other management information will be developed. Some unification and standardization of common elements (e.g., expressions) of various WS-Policy languages would reduce the overhead of supporting this framework. Further, WS-Policy does not detail where, when, and how policies are monitored and evaluated. Since many policies have to be monitored and controlled during run-time, WS-Policy needs better support for management applications, including explicit specification of such management information. Consequently, we had to develop a new domain-independent WS-Policy extension, which we named WS-Policy4MASC.

WS-Policy4MASC extends WS-Policy by defining new types of WS-Policy policy assertions. These are not domain-specific policy assertions because they can be used for representing functional constraints, QoS requirements and guarantees, adaptation (control) actions, security capabilities, business value metrics (e.g., prices), and other information. Compared to an a posteori combination of several single-domain policy solutions, a true integration of different domains (as done in WS-Policy4MASC and a few older works, e.g., WSOL) leads to better specification of inter-domain dependencies, increased interoperability between domains, and lower total run-time overhead (Tosic, Pagurek, Patel, Esfandiari, & Ma, 2005). WS-Policy4MASC mandates no changes to WS-Policy constructs, so they can be used with WS-Policy4MASC in the same way as for other WS-Policy policy assertions. Using standard WS-PolicyAttachment mechanisms, WS-Policy4MASC policy assertions can be attached to WSDL constructs describing individual Web services or their parts (e.g., service, endpoint, operation, message constructs) and/or WSBPEL

or Microsoft's Extensible Application Markup Language (XAML) constructs describing Web service compositions or their parts (e.g., process, sub-process, activity). Analogously to WS-Policy, the syntax of WS-Policy4MASC is based on the Extensible Markup Language (XML) and defined using XML Schema.

Figure 1 shows the main concepts and relationships in WS-Policy4MASC version 0.9 (Karunaratne, 2008). The main difference from WS-Policy4MASC version 0.8 (Tosic, Erradi, & Maheshwari, 2007) is the addition of probability policy assertions (and the support for specification of context, which is not shown in Figure 1, but is discussed later in this book chapter). WS-Policy4MASC constructs can be classified into "real" policy assertions and auxiliary constructs. The "real" policy assertions describe the operation and management goals and/or rules, while the auxiliary constructs specify additional details necessary for use of the "real" policy assertions (for technical reasons, the auxiliary constructs are specified as WS-Policy policy assertions, but cannot be used in management without the "real" policy assertions).

In WS-Policy4MASC version 0.9 there are 5 types of "real" policy assertions (all inheriting from the abstract construct "MASCPolicyAssertion") relevant for run-time management (particularly, dynamic adaptation) of service-oriented systems:

1. Goal policy assertions specify requirements (e.g., 128 bit security must be used) and guarantees (e.g., response time of a particular activity has to be less than 1 second) to be met in desired normal operation. In the MASC middleware, they guide monitoring activities, primarily evaluation of various monitored conditions. Specification of Web service requirements/guarantees for monitoring activities was addressed by a number of past languages, such as WSLA (Keller & Ludwig, 2003) and WSOL.

Figure 1. The main concepts and relationships in WS-Policy4MASC (Version 0.9)

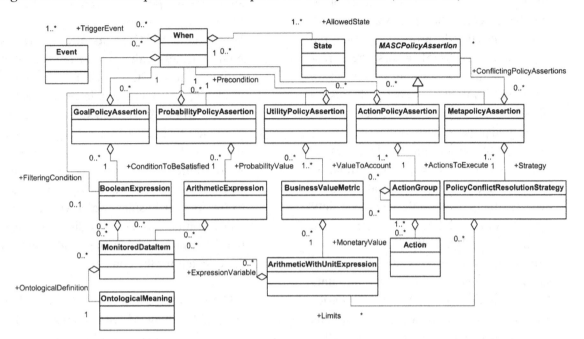

While such a concept was necessary in WS-Policy4MASC to support monitoring activities, WS-Policy4MASC solutions in this area offer only minor advantages, summarized in (Tosic, Erradi, & Maheshwari, 2007).

2. Action policy assertions specify diverse actions to be taken if certain conditions are met (e.g., some goal policy assertions were not satisfied). For example, these actions can be removal, addition, replacement, skipping, or retrying of a sub-process (or individual activity) or process termination. In MASC, they guide adaptation and other control actions (and a few aspects of monitoring, such as monitored data transfer). One of the distinctive characteristics of WS-Policy4MASC, compared to the related work, is built-in support for a diverse range of common service composition and business process adaptation actions, presented in (Tosic, Erradi, & Maheshwari, 2007). These supported actions address various frequent adaptation needs, including (but not limited to) customization (e.g., versioning), corrective adaptation for fault management, and optimization for QoS (performance) and business value management. For example, assume that there is a known type of system faults that is relatively easy to detect with functional pre- or post-conditions and for which there is a known set of corrective actions (execution of these actions is the system's dynamic adaptation). To address such situations with WS-Policy4MASC, these pre-/post-conditions are specified in a goal policy assertion and the corrective actions are specified in an action policy assertion. The triggering event for the action policy assertion is non-satisfaction of the goal policy assertion and the action policy assertion can specify additional filtering conditions that narrow possible causes to the target system fault. That is, when the pre-/post-conditions in the goal policy assertion are not met, an event is raised. The

raising of this event leads to evaluation of the filtering conditions. If they are satisfied, this indicates that the probable reason is the system fault we want to handle, so the corrective actions in the action policy assertion are executed. Simple performance problems are addressed in an analogous manner (in such cases, goal policy assertions describe limits of acceptable performance). More complicated situations (e.g., requiring correlation of events and/or complex causal chains of events and actions, possibly with uncertainty whether some situations will occur) can also be specified in WS-Policy4MASC.

3. Utility policy assertions specify expressions for calculating monetary amounts quantifying diverse business value metrics assigned to particular run-time situations (e.g., non-satisfaction of some goal policy assertion, execution of some action, another event). They can be used by MASC for accounting/billing and, indirectly, for selection between alternative action policy assertions. Specification of diverse (both financial and non-financial) business value metric types in utility policy assertions is one of the most important contributions of WS-Policy4MASC and is discussed in detail in (Tosic, 2010) and, to a lesser degree, in (Tosic, Erradi, & Maheshwari, 2007).

4. Probability policy assertions specify probabilities that particular situations will occur. As explained in (Tosic, 2010), they can be used for specification of risks and trust in various parties.

5. Meta-policy assertions specify which action policy assertions are mutually conflicting (i.e., their conditions are satisfied at the same time, but their actions must not be executed together) and which business value driven conflict resolution strategies should be used to decide which action policy assertion to execute. Meta-policy assertion specification of diverse business value maximization

strategies for policy conflict resolution is another significant original contribution of WS-Policy4MASC. Meta-policy assertions guide business value driven management activities in MASC, which are elaborated in (Tosic, 2010) and, to a lesser degree, in (Tosic, Erradi, & Maheshwari, 2007). For example, (Tosic, 2010) presents an algorithm that calculates which of the conflicting action policy assertions (representing different dynamic adaptation options) leads to the highest business value (taking into consideration company's business strategy that determines which business value metrics are relevant for the company).

In addition to these 5 new types of "real" policy assertions, WS-Policy4MASC enables specification of additional detailed information that is necessary for run-time policy-driven management (particularly, adaptation) of service-oriented systems and overcomes some other limitations of WS-Policy (e.g., imprecise semantics of policy assertions' effects on policy subjects). Some of this information (e.g., which party performs evaluation/execution of a policy assertion, which party is responsible for meeting a goal) is specified in attributes of the above-mentioned "real" policy assertions. Much more information is specified in additional auxiliary WS-Policy4MASC constructs, specifying ontological meaning, monitored data items (e.g., monitored QoS metrics), states, state transitions, schedules, events, scopes, and various types of expression (Boolean, arithmetic, arithmetic-with-unit, string, time/date/duration). Many of these auxiliary constructs are not shown in Figure 1, to prevent overcrowding.

The most important among the auxiliary constructs is the "When" construct that specifies when something (e.g., evaluation of a goal policy assertion, execution of actions in an action policy assertion, or calculation and billing of monetary amounts specified in utility policy assertions) should happen in the MASC middleware. It contains information about one or more states in which this occurs, one or more events (e.g., Web service operation executed) that can each independently trigger this occurrence, and an optional filtering Boolean condition to be satisfied. WS-Policy4MASC has built-in constructs for specification of a wide range of events (and, as mentioned above, adaptation actions) common in management of service-oriented systems and business processes they implement. Further, the language is extensible, so new types of events (and actions) can be defined easily.

The auxiliary construct "OntologicalMeaning" provides some support for specification of semantics of monitored data items. The actual definitions of ontological concepts are in external (reusable and extensible) ontologies. Thus, the construct "OntologicalMeaning" specifies the namespace of the used ontology and the name of the ontological concept within this ontology (e.g., "measurementOntology:Availability" or "currencyOntology:USDollar"), as well as identification of the language in which this ontology is defined. These external ontologies can be specified in any of the currently used ontology languages, such the Web Ontology Language (OWL), but we provided a very simple ontology schema that is the default ontology language. If a management party does not understand the used ontology language, it can still perform simple syntax matching of namespaces and names.

While the MASC middleware (Erradi, Tosic, & Maheshwari, 2007) is based on the orchestration type of Web service compositions (where there is a central entity directing invocation of all other services), WS-Policy4MASC can also be used in choreographies (where there is no such central entity). A distinction should be made between private policies of individual choreography participants (or groups of orchestrated participants) and mutually agreed public policies that form a contract (SLA) between choreographed parties. Private policies for an independent participant are stored in the policy repositories of that participant, who then processes them internally. Private policies for a group of orchestrated participants are usually stored in the policy repository of their orchestrator (but more distributed arrangements are also possible). Contractual public policies between choreographed parties are stored in policy repositories of all relevant parties (and only those parties). This relevance is determined by the content of several attributes (such as "Management-Party", "ResponsibleParty", "BeneficiaryParty", "PayingParty", and several others) describing roles of particular parties. Events specified in contractual public policies have to be exchanged between all relevant parties in the contract. This can all be specified (explicitly or implicitly) with the current version of WS-Policy4MASC. Further, it is possible to specify control actions common in Web service choreographies (e.g., contract re-negotiation), because some of these actions (relevant also for orchestrations) are already built into the WS-Policy4MASC language grammar (schema) and because WS-Policy4MASC is extensible. However, because such WS-Policy4MASC extensions can be specified in different ways, interoperability would be improved if the most common missing actions are also standardized in the WS-Policy4MASC grammar. This is an item for future work.

It is important to note that WS-Policy4MASC addresses context in the broader sense of this term with a number of constructs. Out of the three categories of context identified earlier in this book chapter, WS-Policy4MASC has very strong support of the last two. Most importantly, many WS-Policy4MASC constructs specify current and future circumstances over which the managed system has control (i.e., the third group of context concepts from our classification). For example, definition of QoS metrics is done in the "MonitoredDataItem" construct, functional and QoS guarantees are specified in goal policy assertions, while prices are specified in utility policy assertions. Related to this, there are special actions ("MonitoredDataCollection" and "MonitoredDataTransfer") specifying monitoring and transfer of QoS metrics and special events (e.g., "MonitoredDataItemUpdated" for notification when values of QoS metrics change, "GoalPolicyAssertionSatisfied" for notification when the guarantees are met or not met). Furthermore, the historical circumstances in execution of the managed system (i.e., the second group of context concepts from our classification) can also be specified. In particular, the current state is specified in the "State" construct, while the filtering Boolean expression in the "When" construct can be used for description of how past values of QoS metrics influence which WS-Policy4MASC policy assertions are relevant in particular circumstances. Some of the support for this group of context concepts is in the MASC middleware, instead of the WS-Policy4MASC language. Notably, process instance identification (ID) is used in MASC for session/transaction management. Contrary to the last two groups of context constructs from our classification, there was not enough support in WS-Policy4MASC version 0.8 for the first group of concepts, i.e., the situational circumstances that are external to the managed system. This is the group of concepts that belongs to our narrow definition of context. The strongest WS-Policy4MASC version 0.8 support here is for time/date/duration expressions. While it is syntactically possible to specify specific external context properties (such as location) in "MonitoredDataItem" constructs, the semantics of this is not completely appropriate (as will be discussed later in this book chapter). Therefore, we decided to build into WS-Policy4MASC version 0.9 (Karunaratne, 2008) comprehensive support for context monitoring and context-sensitive service-oriented system management, which we will explain in the remainder of this book chapter.

OUR APPROACH TO MODELING CONTEXT

We have noted in the "Introduction" section that to enable context-sensitive operation and management, at least four sets of questions about specification of context information should be answered. We will discuss our approach to modeling context through answers to these questions.

1. How to formally specify monitored context properties in a way useful for management activities? Our approach to this question has four key aspects, discussed in the following paragraphs:
    a. support for well-defined, detailed, and precise specifications,
    b. modeling of context properties analogously to QoS metrics,
    c. extension of existing management information formats for Web services and corresponding management middleware, and
    d. outsourcing of definitions of context property types into external ontologies.

First, it is crucial to understand that to perform management activities with minimal human intervention, the information about these activities must be unambiguous, detailed, precise, and in a well-defined format that can be interpreted by software. Without this, management cannot succeed in the long-run. For example, if the information is not detailed and precise (e.g., there is no information where monitoring is done), the management system might rely on some implicit assumptions and conventions (e.g., that all monitoring is done on provider side), but after a change of circumstances (e.g., there is a new need for some consumer-side monitoring), which happens very frequently in modern IT systems, the management system is no longer appropriate. The saying: "You cannot control what you cannot monitor and you cannot monitor what you cannot describe" is popular in the IT system management community. Therefore, our research always aims at such details and precision that enable flexible management (but are not incurring too high overhead).

Second, during our study of various formats for specification of context information in the past published literature and also our examination of how context impacts management activities, we noticed significant similarities in both semantics and syntax of context properties and other management information, particularly QoS metrics. Both QoS metrics and context properties are groups of diverse attributes monitored during run-time that have to be described in detail for successful management activities. Further, both context properties and QoS metrics are measured/calculated, aggregated, transferred, processed, stored, and accounted in a similar manner. Additionally, context properties often have the data type containing numerical value and associated measurement unit, which is the most common format for QoS metrics and other management information. Using different formats to describe similar information can lead to problems in interoperability and increases run-time overhead, which is an important issue in mobile devices. Therefore, we decided to model context properties analogously to QoS metrics. However, it is important to note that there are also differences between QoS metrics and context properties, which justify the need for separate specification of context properties. Most importantly, the managed system is responsible for values of QoS metrics, while this is not the case for context properties. These differences can affect specification and calculation of prices and monetary penalties. Also, whenever value of a context property changes, there is a need to reevaluate which context-dependent management activities are relevant in the new context, while a change in value of a QoS metric usually has a less immediate effect. Thus, specification of

context properties is similar, but not identical to the specification of QoS metrics.

Third (but closely related to the previous point), we decided to extend existing management information formats/languages (first WSOL and then WS-Policy4MASC) and corresponding management middleware (WSOI and MASC, respectively), instead of developing a completely new format/language or extending the existing works on context management. This is because there have been more academic works and industrial products on Web service management than on context management for Web services. The corresponding expertise, experience, languages, and tools (including, but not limited to our own work related to WSOL/WSOI and WS-Policy4MASC) could be reused with our approach. Prior to our study of addition of context, WSOL and WS-Policy4MASC already addressed for QoS metrics questions that are similar to those we are discussing here for context properties. In addition, WSOI and MASC middleware contained appropriate support to measure these QoS metrics, transfer their values, evaluate relevant QoS constraints, and adapt service-oriented system compositions. These existing QoS management infrastructure solutions could be extended for processing of context information relatively easily.

Fourth, instead of building a limited set of context property types into the specification language or allowing definition of context property types together with (i.e., in the same files as) other management-related definitions, we decided to outsource definitions of context property types into external ontologies. While we provide some simple formats for such ontological definitions, these external ontologies can be, in principle, defined in any ontological language. This is consistent with the way how we define QoS metric types. The main benefit of this solution is the balance between flexibility/extensibility and complexity of the specification language for management information. Various existing ontologies that define different types of context properties could be reused to some extent (having in mind the differences between definitions of the term "context").

2. How to formally specify when, where, how, for which parties (e.g., provider, consumer) and by which parties (e.g., provider, consumer, some independent/third party) the context monitoring is performed, as well as when and how values of context properties are transferred between various parties?

As mentioned above, our approach is based on the recognition that specification of management information (including context information) must be unambiguous, detailed, precise, and in a well-defined format that can be interpreted by software. Therefore, our languages (WSOL and WS-Policy4MASC) enable specification of all the necessary details, usually in XML attributes of special actions for monitoring and data transfer. (When complexity of a particular description is so high that it cannot be specified within an XML attribute, XML elements are used.) For example, information about the party that performs monitoring and information about the party for which context is monitored is specified in such attributes (in a general case, these two parties need not be the same, e.g., context could be monitored for a provider, but monitored by an independent third party). To reduce complexity of specifications, the most common situations are specified as default values of XML attributes and elements. When it comes to definition of monitoring activities, our languages support both measurement and calculation (including estimation) of context properties. For example, geographic longitude and latitude are context properties that could be measured by a Global Positioning System (GPS) device attached to the mobile Web service, while country of location could be determined by providing geographic longitude and latitude to a conversion Web service. To specify when monitoring (as well as transfer of management information and all other management activities) happens, our languages define

various events (WS-Policy4MASC has much richer support in this regard than WSOL) and also enable definition of complex schedules. Our languages also support various mechanisms for transfer of management information. The default is piggybacking into SOAP headers, but special push and pull operations can also be specified, as discussed in (Tosic, Pagurek, Patel, Esfandiari, & Ma, 2005).

3. How to specify various ways in which context properties influence operation of service-oriented systems (particularly provider services), monitoring of service-oriented systems, and dynamic adaptation of service compositions?

In different contexts, a service-oriented system might require different inputs or initial conditions, provide different results, provide different QoS, bill different prices and monetary penalties, use different management third parties, or perform different adaptation actions (such as replacing some activities or services in a service composition with appropriate alternatives). In our work (WS-Policy4MASC is much more powerful than WSOL in this regard), there are two groups of solutions, discussed in the following paragraphs:

a. values of context properties can be used in expressions to specify their influences, and
b. event notifications about context changes can be used to trigger adaptation activities.

Our languages enable detailed and powerful specification of various expressions. These expressions can manipulate information in different data types (Boolean, arithmetic, arithmetic-with-unit, string, time) and can have different purpose (e.g., description of conditions to be met, description of monetary prices/penalties to be paid and other utilities, description of probability of something occurring, filtering/limiting applicability of other constructs). Our work enables specification of expressions that limit provided service functionality only to particular values of context properties. In this way, behavior of the service-oriented system can differ in different contexts. For example, a post-condition (modeled in WS-Policy4MASC as a goal policy assertion) of the truck-tracking Web service could state that a Web service operation returns speed of the truck in kilometers/hour in Canada or in miles/hour in the USA. Analogously, expressions enable limiting monitoring and control (including adaptation) activities only to particular values of context properties. For example, it is possible to specify for the truck-tracking Web service that monitoring of availability performed by a particular independent third party is performed only in Canada (e.g., because this third party is hosted by a wireless network provider that operates only in Canada). In such a case, constructs that limit acceptable values for the monitored availability and that prescribe billing of prices or penalties related to this availability or specify what to do when these availability guarantees are not met are all relevant only in Canada. An important special case of such influence of context is when different adaptation actions are performed in different contexts. It is also possible to limit the expected values of context properties in expressions. This helps in fault detection. For example, if the truck-tracking Web service is attached to a truck that is supposed to drive only in Canada and the USA and suddenly the context property for location of this truck-tracking Web service states that the location is in the middle of the Indian Ocean, something is wrong (e.g., the GPS device is faulty) and many of the regular management activities will be meaningless before the cause of this fault is determined and corrected. In some (relatively rare) situations, it might be useful to only check in a particular expression whether a context property is monitored (and then do something based on this Boolean value) without limiting the value of the context property, e.g., because the details of context-sensitivity are described in another, related, construct. Our work also supports these situations.

A crucial aspect of our work (particularly in WS-Policy4MASC) is specification of adaptation actions to be executed when context changes. The expressions discussed above are passive in determining context changes (in the sense that they do not discover context changes until they are evaluated). Therefore, our work also enables active event notification about context changes. When such a notification arrives, the management middleware undertakes the required management operations. These event notifications can be raised by the management middleware itself or they can be external. An example internal management middleware event for the truck-tracking Web service is the change of country from Canada to the USA. It is determined by evaluating expressions specified in our languages and when it happens, it automatically triggers execution of other management actions (e.g., described in WS-Policy4MASC action policy assertions), such as reconfiguring the Web service to use wireless network for the USA instead of the wireless network for Canada, to switch payments from CAD$ to US$, and/or to switch from the metric to the imperial (US) system of measures. An example of an external event is notification that temperature of the freezer in a truck that transports perishable goods (e.g., food) is above some limit prescribed by safety standards. When this external event is raised, the format of the information that the truck-tracking Web service sends to its consumers changes, to highlight the urgency of the situation.

4. How can specification of context properties be used for discovery and selection of appropriate service-oriented systems and their QoS?

In our approach, SLAs or policies are advertised in an extended Universal Description, Discovery, and Integration (UDDI) directory, as additions to the Web Services Description

Language (WSDL) functional specifications. Since values of QoS metrics and context properties change much more often than functional characteristics, SLAs/policies are published not in WSDL extensions but as separate UDDI tModels. In addition to storage of supplementary information, the extended UDDI directory also contains improved operations for publication and search. After a set of services satisfying required functional characteristics is determined during a search, SLAs/policies (including values of context properties) are used for narrowing the selection. Further details about this solution are outside of the scope of this book chapter, but note that a prototype extension of UDDI for WS-Policy4MASC policies was designed, implemented, and tested in (Liu, 2008) and will be presented in another publication. (Unfortunately, there was no analogous work for WSOL.)

Compared to the approaches that specify context properties separately from the other management information, our approach has higher complexity (and this is its main weakness). Rich and powerful management information specification languages (e.g., our WSOL and WS-Policy4MASC) are complex, both in terms of syntax and semantics. This complexity has design-time and run-time aspects. During design-time, the power and generality of the language can lead to verbosity. The complexity of language processing during run-time is related to (and, to some extent, causes) the overall complexity of the corresponding management middleware (e.g., our WSOI and MASC). The use of such management middleware can sometimes incur overhead (e.g., additional use of memory, processing, battery and other resources; higher response times) that might not be acceptable, particularly in mobile service-oriented systems with limited resources. While our solutions might not be appropriate in some cases when only simple specification of context with no (or very simple) other management aspects is needed and resources are scarce, in most other situations the benefits of our approach

significantly outweigh the problems caused by higher complexity.

WS-POLICY4MASC IMPLEMENTATION OF CONTEXT MODELING AND ITS EVALUATION

To enable specification of the conceptual solutions presented in the previous section, WS-Policy-4MASC has a number of constructs, specified through XML elements and attributes in the language grammar. We will particularly emphasize the new constructs added in WS-Policy4MASC version 0.9 that directly support specification of context-related information. (Karunaratne, 2008) contains the precise XML Schema and illustrative examples for these new WS-Policy4MASC constructs, while this book chapter will provide summary, explanations, and one example highlighting many of our solutions to general readership. The example that we will present is related to management of the truck tracking mobile Web service mentioned earlier. Figures 2 through 7 show some aspects of WS-Policy4MASC support for context-sensitivity in this example and we will discuss them in the following paragraphs. Please note that the complete WS-Policy4MASC file for this example contains some additional information (e.g., namespace definitions), that we omitted for brevity. Furthermore, this WS-Policy4MASC file is accompanied by a WS-PolicyAttachment file, as explained and illustrated in (Tosic, Erradi, & Maheshwari, 2007). The omitted aspects are not crucial for understanding the WS-Policy4MASC modeling of context-related concepts.

The most important feature of the WS-Policy4MASC 0.9 support for context is the new construct "MonitoredContextProperty" for specification of monitored context properties. This includes not only directly monitored context properties (e.g., geographic latitude and longitude), but also complex context properties (e.g., country of location) calculated from other context

Figure 2. The truck-tracking Example: Definitions of monitored context properties for current longitude and current country

```
<masc-cp:MonitoredContextProperty MASCID="CurrentLongitude"
PropertyType="xs:decimal" PropertyUnit="measurementOntology:Degree-Decimal-
Minus180toPlus180">
  <masc-om:OntologicalMeaning OntologicalDefinition="contextOntology:GeographicLongitude-
WestIsNegative" />
</masc-cp:MonitoredContextProperty>
…
<!-- Definition of geographic latitude is similar to the definition of geographic longitude, so it is
omitted for brevity -->
…
<masc-cp:MonitoredContextProperty MASCID="CurrentCountry"
PropertyType="xs:string" PropertyUnit="masc-cn:MASC_NO_UNIT">
  <masc-om:OntologicalMeaning OntologicalDefinition="contextOntology:CountryOfLocation" />
</masc-cp:MonitoredContextProperty>
```

properties. Since our approach is to specify context properties analogously to other management information (particularly QoS metrics), this new construct has somewhat similar syntax to the construct "MonitoredDataItem" shown in Figure 1, but the semantics are different. Note that "MonitoredContextProperty" can be used wherever "MonitoredDataItem" can be used (this required modifications of some other WS-Policy-4MASC constructs, as summarized later in this section). Among other attributes and sub-elements, the "MonitoredContextProperty" element contains definition of the data type and, if applicable, unit type of the context property, as well as a reference to an external ontological definition of the monitored context property. The party (e.g., provider, consumer) or other scope (e.g., particular operation) for which the context property is monitored is determined by the WS-PolicyAttachment scope to which this particular "MonitoredContextProperty" construct is attached.

Figure 2 shows example WS-Policy4MASC definitions of two context properties. "Current-Longitude" is defined as a real (i.e., decimal, float) number associated with the unit "Degree-Decimal-Minus180toPlus180" (defined in the ontology determined by the namespace "measurementOntology") and representing the ontological concept "GeographicLongitude-WestIsNegative" (defined

in the ontology determined by the namespace "contextOntology"). "CurrentCountry" is defined as a string associated with no unit and representing the ontological concept "CountryOfLocation" (defined in the ontology determined by the namespace "contextOntology").

To specify the details necessary for monitoring and inter-party transfer of context properties, WS-Policy4MASC version 0.9 extended the existing constructs "MonitoredDataCollection" and "MonitoredDataTransfer", so that they could be used not only for QoS metrics, but also context properties. Both of these constructs are actions that can be specified in action policy assertions. The "MonitoredDataCollection" action references a context property that is monitored and specifies how its measurement or calculation is performed, where this measurement is performed (the default is within the party that performs monitoring), and whether the monitored values are transferred using piggybacking in SOAP headers (which is the default mode of transfer of monitored values). If push/pull operations for transfer of monitored values are used in addition to (or instead of) SOAP headers, then the "MonitoredDataTransfer" action should also be specified. The latter construct references a set of context properties to be transferred together and specifies to which party they are transferred, the type of data transfer

Figure 3. The truck-tracking example: Definitions of actions and action groups for calculation and transfer of the context property for current country

```
<masc-ap:MonitoredDataCollection MASCID="LocationDataCalculation"
PassedInSOAPHeaders="false">
 <masc-cp:MonitoredContextPropertyRef To="tns:CurrentCountry" />
 <masc-ap:ConfigurationData>
  <masc-ex:ExternalOperationCall CallID="CountryFromCoordinates" Service="conversion-
wsdl:ConversionService" PortOrPortType="conversion-wsdl:GeographicConversion"
Operation="conversion-wsdl:CountryFromLongitudeAndLatitude">
   <masc-ex:CallList>
    <masc-cp:MonitoredContextPropertyRef To="tns:CurrentLongitude" />
    <masc-cp:MonitoredContextPropertyRef To="tns:CurrentLatitude" />
   </masc-ex:CallList>
  </masc-ex:ExternalOperationCall>
  <masc-ex:StringExpression>
   <masc-ex:ExternalOperationResult CallID="tns:CountryFromCoordinates"
ResultPartName="conversion-wsdl:Country" />
  </masc-ex:StringExpression>
 </masc-ap:ConfigurationData>
 </masc-ap:MonitoredDataCollection>
...
<masc-ap:MonitoredDataTransfer MASCID="LocationDataTransfer"
TransferPartner="masc-cn:MASC_WSORCHESTRATOR" TransferType="push">
 <masc-cp:MonitoredContextPropertyRef To="tns:CurrentCountry" />
 </masc-ap:MonitoredDataTransfer>
...
<masc-ap:ActionGroup MASCID="LocationData-CollectionAndTransfer">
 <masc-ap:MonitoredDataCollectionRef To="tns:LocationDataCalculation" />
 <masc-ap:MonitoredDataTransferRef To="tns:LocationDataTransfer" />
</masc-ap:ActionGroup>
```

(e.g., push or pull), and the particular operation (in a particular endpoint/port of a particular Web service) used for this data transfer. The information on which party (e.g., orchestrator, provider, or consumer) performs monitoring or from which data is transferred is specified in an attribute of the action policy assertion that contains the "MonitoredDataCollection" and "Monitored-DataTransfer" actions. The information about the conditions that have to be satisfied for monitoring or transfer of context property values are specified in the "When" construct referenced by the action policy assertion. These conditions list states in which the actions could be executed, events (possibly periodic events generated from complex schedules) that could trigger execution of these actions, and optional filtering Boolean conditions that make that the actions are executed only if these conditions are satisfied. In the same action policy assertion, multiple "MonitoredDataCollec-

tion" and "MonitoredDataTransfer" actions can be specified, but then they all have to have the same execution conditions and to share the same party that is responsible for management activities.

Figure 3 shows example WS-Policy4MASC constructs for collection (in this case, calculation) and transfer of the context property "CurrentCountry". The "MonitoredDataCollection" construct "LocationDataCalculation" states that "CurrentCountry" is calculated as the result of providing the context properties "CurrentLongitude" and "CurrentLatitude" to the operation "CountryFromLongitudeAndLatitude" (specified in the external WSDL file determined by the namespace "conversion-wsdl") and that it is not passed in SOAP headers. (Monitoring of "CurrentLongitude" and "CurrentLatitude" is not defined in Figure 3, but these values could be obtained from a GPS device.) The "Monitored-DataTransfer" construct "LocationDataTransfer" states that the context property "CurrentCountry" is transferred to the orchestrator ("MASC_ WSORCHESTRATOR" is a special constant) using a predefined push-type operation. Since these actions are contained in the action group "LocationData-CollectionAndTransfer" (shown in Figure 3), which is used in the action policy assertion "MonitorCurrentCountry" (shown in Figure 5) for which management party is the provider ("MASC_WSPROVIDER"), this means that calculation of "CurrentCountry" is performed by the provider and that the provider transfers (i.e., pushes) the calculated value of "CurrentCountry" (to the orchestrator, as mentioned above).

To specify influence of context properties on operation of the managed service-oriented systems, monitoring activities, and dynamic adaptation activities, we had to only slightly modify specification of expressions and to add one new event type. WS-Policy4MASC 0.9 contains a very powerful and detailed specification of Boolean, arithmetic, arithmetic-with-unit, string, and time expressions. It is based on the WSOL specification of expressions, summarized in (Tosic, Pagurek, Patel, Esfandiari, & Ma, 2005). As shown in Figure 1, WS-Policy4MASC Boolean expressions are specified within filtering Boolean conditions of the "When" construct or within goal policy assertions. Arithmetic-with-unit expressions are specified within business value metrics that are within utility policy assertions and could be used for specification of various limits for policy conflict resolution strategies in meta-policy assertions, while arithmetic expressions are specified within probability policy assertions. Additionally (and this is not shown in Figure 1), Boolean expressions can contain comparisons of the other types of expressions (e.g., a comparison of a monitored context property with the arithmetic-with-unit data type with a constant or expression with the arithmetic-with-unit data type). Particularly important is the use of context properties in Boolean expressions within filtering conditions that are part of the "When" construct, because they limit

applicability of WS-Policy4MASC policy assertions only to a particular context. For example, use of such a filtering condition within a "When" construct for an action policy assertion leads to execution of actions (e.g., adaptations) in different contexts. To support such use of context properties, we enabled that monitored context properties can be referenced as parameters in all types of expressions (since different context properties could have different data types) and added the Boolean operator "IsMonitoredContextProperty" checking whether a context property is monitored. To support notification about changes in context properties, we added the new event type "MonitoredContextPropertyChanged", which references a particular monitored context property. Using this event type, it is possible to use a change in a monitored context property to trigger evaluation of a goal policy assertion, execution of an action policy assertion, and calculation of a utility (or probability) policy assertion.

Figure 4 shows definition of the "MonitoredContextPropertyChanged" event notifying about updates of "CurrentLongitude". The same figure also defines the "When" construct that is satisfied when geographic longitude or geographic latitude is updated. This "When" construct does not have a filtering condition, which means that it is executed whenever one of the specified events is triggered (and the MASC system is in the executing state).

Figure 5 shows how WS-Policy4MASC enables specification that a change of the context property "CurrentLongitude" or "CurrentLatitude" triggering the "When" construct "LongitudeOrLatitudeUpdated" (defined in Figure 4) results in re-calculation and transfer of the context property "CurrentCountry" through the action group "LocationData-CollectionAndTransfer" (defined in Figure 3).

Figure 6 shows how the context property "CurrentCountry" is used within the Boolean expression "IsCurrentCountryUSA" that specifies a filtering condition of the "When" construct "CountryUpdatedToUSA". In this Boolean

Figure 4. The truck-tracking example: Definitions of the event notifying about updates of the context property for current longitude and the "when" construct that defines the situation when either current longitude or current latitude is updated

```
<masc-se:EventDefinition MASCID="LongitudeUpdated">
 <masc-se:MonitoredContextPropertyChanged ContextPropertyID ="tns:CurrentLongitude" />
</masc-se:EventDefinition>
...
<!-- Definitions of events for notification of updates of geographic latitude and current country is
analogous to the definition of the event for geographic longitude, so it is omitted for brevity -->
...
<masc-se:When MASCID="LongitudeOrLatitudeUpdated">
 <masc-se:AllowedStates>
  <masc-se:StateRef To="tns:MASC_EXECUTING"/>
 </masc-se:AllowedStates>
 <masc-se:PossibleTriggerEvents>
  <masc-se:EventRef To="tns:LongitudeUpdated"/>
  <masc-se:EventRef To="tns:LatitudeUpdated"/>
 </masc-se:PossibleTriggerEvents>
</masc-se:When>
```

expression, "CurrentCountry" is compared for equality with the string constant "USA". Only if this condition is satisfied (and the value for the "CurrentCountry" context property was updated and the MASC system is in the executing state), the "When" construct is satisfied. This means that in any country other than the USA, this "When" construct cannot be satisfied.

Figure 7 shows how the context-sensitive "When" construct "CountryUpdatedToUSA" (defined in Figure 6) limits evaluation of the goal policy assertion "MaxSpeedInUSA" only to the USA. In this case, the Boolean expression "UpperLimitOfValidCurrentSpeed" contained by the goal policy assertion "MaxSpeedInUSA" limits the current speed of the tracked truck to 65.00 miles/hour (this speed is returned by an operation of the truck-trucking mobile Web service). How-

ever, the main point in Figure 7 is the reference to the "When" construct "CountryUpdatedToU-SA" with the above-mentioned filtering condition that limits applicability to the USA. There could be an analogous Boolean expression, "When" construct, and goal policy assertion limiting truck's speed to 100 kilometers/hour when the truck is in Canada. Then, change of value in the context property "CurrentCountry" automatically affects which of these two goal policy assertions is evaluated.

To verify and validate our conceptual solutions related to modeling of context for management of service-oriented systems, we built these concepts into our languages (first WSOL and then WS-Policy4MASC) and middleware (WSOI and only to some extent MASC). The implementation, verification, and validation of our

Figure 5. The truck-tracking example: Definition of the action policy assertion for calculation and transfer of the context property for current country

```
<masc-ap:ActionPolicyAssertion MASCID="MonitorCurrentCountry" ManagementParty="masc-
cn:MASC_WSPROVIDER">
  <masc-se:WhenRef To="tns:LongitudeOrLatitudeUpdated"/>
  <masc-ap:ActionGroupRef To="tns:LocationData-CollectionAndTransfer"/>
</masc-ap:ActionPolicyAssertion>
```

Figure 6. The truck-tracking example: Definition of the "when" construct that defines the situation when current country is updated to the string "USA"

```
<masc-se:When MASCID="CountryUpdatedToUSA">
 <masc-se:AllowedStates>
  <masc-se:StateRef To="tns:MASC_EXECUTING"/>
 </masc-se:AllowedStates>
 <masc-se:PossibleTriggerEvents>
  <masc-se:EventRef To="tns:CountryUpdated"/>
 </masc-se:PossibleTriggerEvents>
 <!-- The following Boolean expression is the filtering condition that the new value of the context
property for current country must be "USA" -->
 <masc-ex:BooleanExpression MASCID="IsCountryUSA">
  <masc-ex:StringComparator Type="Equal" />
  <masc-cp:MonitoredContextPropertyRef To="tns:CurrentCountry" />
  <masc-ex:StringConstant Value="USA" />
 </masc-ex:BooleanExpression>
</masc-se:When>
```

specification-related solutions in WSOL version 1.4 were discussed in (Tosic, Lutfiyya, & Tang, 2006a), while implementation and validation of our middleware-related solutions in WSOI version 3.0 were presented in (Tosic, Lutfiyya, & Tang, 2006b). We will here summarize our work on evaluation of recent context-related solutions based on WS-Policy4MASC. To verify feasibility and implementability of the new WS-Policy4MASC constructs discussed above, we defined or modified relevant WS-Policy4MASC

schemas and checked their syntax correctness. In addition, we thoroughly studied required modifications of the corresponding MASC middleware that uses WS-Policy4MASC for management of service-oriented systems. The MASC version described in (Erradi, Tosic, & Maheshwari, 2007) supported WS-Policy4MASC version 0.8, so only implementation of the recent WS-Policy4MASC version 0.9 is needed. Due to the similarities in WS-Policy4MASC modeling of QoS metrics and context properties, a lot of previously existing

Figure 7. The truck-tracking example: Definition of the boolean expression and the referencing goal policy assertion to limit value of the monitored data item for current speed in the USA

```
<!-- Definition the monitored data item "CurrentSpeed" is omitted for brevity. In essence, current
speed is returned by an operation of the truck-trucking mobile Web service and uses measurement
units of the current country of location (e.g., the imperial system for the USA, the metric system for
Canada). -->
...
<masc-ex:BooleanExpression MASCID="UpperLimitOfValidCurrentSpeed">
 <masc-ex:ArithmeticWitUnitComparator Type="LessOrEqual"/>
 <masc-ex:MonitoredDataItemRef To="tns:CurrentSpeed"/>
 <masc-ex:ArithmeticWitUnitConstant>
   <masc-ex:ArithmeticValue>65.00</masc-ex:ArithmeticValue>
   <masc-ex:Unit OntologicalType="measurementOntology:MilesPerHour"/>
 </masc-ex:ArithmeticWitUnitConstant>
</masc-ex:BooleanExpression>
...
<masc-gp:GoalPolicyAssertion MASCID="MaxSpeedInUSA" ResponsibleParty="masc-
cn:MASC_WSPROVIDER" ManagementParty="masc-cn:MASC_WSPROVIDER">
 <masc-se:WhenRef To="tns:CountryUpdatedToUSA"/>
 <masc-ex:BooleanExpressionRef To="tns:UpperLimitOfValidCurrentSpeed"/>
</masc-gp:GoalPolicyAssertion>
```

MASC code can be reused to deal with context. The most important modification required from the MASC middleware extension is to update the management information model to store, process, and communicate context information. While we have not yet implemented it fully (due to the unfortunate lack of C#/.NET programmers in our current team), we thoroughly checked the detailed design that there are no issues with implementability. To validate usefulness of the proposed WS-Policy4MASC improvements, we explored several hypothetical case studies (e.g., the truck tracking Web service) for which we developed example WS-Policy4MASC files and checked their syntax and semantic correctness. We rejected several potential improvements that required too complex modifications of related service-oriented system middleware tools or for which we could not find in our case studies convincing examples of usefulness. The fact that we used a similar approach to verification and validation of implementation of some of these conceptual solutions in WSOL/WSOI strengthens our conclusions that these conceptual solutions are feasible/implementable and useful.

FUTURE TRENDS

The area of context-sensitive operation and context management for service-oriented systems executing in mobile devices is an important research trend. As the number and diversity of mobile devices (e.g., mobile/cell phones, PDAs, laptops) grows rapidly, the number of mobile consumer and provider Web services increases, along with diversity of context properties relevant for their operation. Therefore, the importance of this research area will continue to increase in the near future.

Due to the huge diversity of definitions of the term "context", this is a very broad research area. We believe that it is important to more clearly characterize the area and its research problems by agreeing on a definition of the term "context". (Otherwise, this term will become an empty marketing buzzword, used at will for promotion of whatever is put for sale.) Note that definition of the term "context" directly impacts definition/specification/description of individual context properties (attributes), which directly impacts what can be done in and achieved by monitoring and control activities. In this book chapter, we provided our broad definition and narrow definition of the term "context", appropriate from the viewpoint of IT system management. However, we invite the readers to discuss and improve our proposal, so that we together can find a terminological solution appropriate for the broader community.

An important research sub-area is how to integrate context specification and management into (Web) service management systems that deal with various management activities and various types of service-oriented systems (some of which are mobile, but the majority of which are non-mobile). This sub-area is the focus of this research chapter. While we made important progress towards addressing the identified challenges, many open issues remain, both for the broader community and for our research program, as outlined below.

The main challenges for the broader research community are in the area of control of service-oriented systems, taking into consideration various context properties. Dynamic (run-time) adaptation to changes in context is a particularly important and fruitful topic for future research. Ideally, such dynamic adaptation would be with minimal human involvement, because knowledgeable humans are not always available, might react too slowly, or are too expensive. More precisely, humans would only set high-level goals and rules (e.g., in the form of policies) and not detailed programs how to react to each particular situation, because many situations might not be predictable when the software is written. This is the ideal of self-management of IT systems, also popularized through the autonomic computing initiative (Kephart & Chess, 2003). However, it is important that the management system optimizes business value metrics (e.g., profit, customer satisfaction) in addition to technical QoS metrics (e.g., response time, availability). This is because business value metrics are more important to business users than technical QoS metrics. Unfortunately, the past practice has shown that mapping between technical and business models and metrics is difficult. For example, higher availability need not lead to increases in business profits. The goal of business-driven IT management (BDIM) (Bartolini, Sahai, & Sauve, 2007) is to determine such mappings and leverage them to make run-time IT system management decisions that maximize business value. For example, it tries to quantify impact on business profits of increased/decreased availability. Our work on WS-Policy4MASC and the corresponding MASC middleware contains unique support for autonomic business-driven management of service-oriented systems (Tosic, Erradi, & Maheshwari, 2007). However, many additional adaptation algorithms for dynamic adaptation to various changes (including, but not limited, changes in context) can be developed. These additional algorithms can use and, if needed, extend WS-Policy4MASC for specification of diverse management policies and other management information (including information related to context).

Another set of challenges for the broader research community are in the area of service selection and composition, taking into consideration context information. There are many open issues here. One of them is that historical information about QoS metrics from past contexts might not be fully appropriate for the new context of the composition. For example, historical average and maximum response time of a service located in Toronto, Canada that had up to 1000 concurrent customer invocations from Canada might not be relevant when this service is composed with services located in Sydney, Australia and is expected to receive up to 5000 concurrent invocations from Australia. Another open issue is that lightweight mashups of services (the popularity of which rap-

idly increases) might lack contractual composition information that is very useful (if not necessary) for management, leading to additional management challenges. Finally, we note the open issue of better integration of ontologies, Semantic Web technologies, and service intelligence research results into IT system management, both for service selection and composition and for control of service-oriented systems.

The long-term objective of our own research program is a powerful management system for service-oriented systems executing in diverse environments, ranging from embedded systems to mobile devices to desktop computers to specialized servers to cloud/utility/grid computing systems. In the short term, we are particularly focused on providing innovative solutions for autonomic business-driven management of service-oriented systems and business processes they implement. The work presented in this book chapter is an important step towards our goal. However, we have been building upon the presented results (and WS-Policy4MASC in general) by developing new algorithms for advanced (Web) service management and business process management, particularly in the area of dynamic adaptation. We also want to perform additional implementation and evaluation of our solutions. In this respect, we are searching for industrial partners interested in application of our research results on real-life scenarios.

CONCLUSION

Many recent research projects and papers (particularly in mobile computing) are related to context modeling, processing, and/or management. They explored the concept of context in various circumstances and from various viewpoints. However, they used many different definitions of the term "context". We found that these definitions cover several groups of concepts that have considerably different nature and that must be differentiated for successful IT system management (monitoring and control) activities. Therefore, we decided to provide two definitions of the term "context". In the broad sense, context is (any and every) information that characterizes situation of the (managed) system. On the other hand, in the narrow sense, context is information about external run-time circumstances that characterize situation of the (managed) system and influence its operation (i.e., execution, behavior), but are outside its direct control. In this book chapter, we have focused on context in the narrow sense. Context-sensitivity means taking into consideration the influence of context on operation and management of the managed system. It is particularly important for mobile systems, because location and characteristics of the surrounding environment are context properties that can considerably influence operation and management. Context-sensitivity is also important for operation and management of mobile (and also non-mobile) service-oriented systems, but this area is not yet explored thoroughly. In different contexts, a service-oriented system might require different inputs or initial conditions, provide different results, provide different QoS, bill different prices and monetary penalties, use different management third parties, or perform different adaptation actions.

Specification of monitored context properties and their influence on operation of service-oriented systems and on management activities is a prerequisite for context-sensitivity. In spite of many recent related works, context specification for a management system performing various management activities and used by various types of service-oriented systems was not addressed adequately prior to our research.

Our approach to providing context-sensitive operation and management of service-oriented systems is based on extending existing management information specification languages and corresponding management middleware. This supports compatibility between management of mobile service-oriented systems and manage-

ment of the other service-oriented systems. Due to the similarities between processing and use of context properties and processing and use of QoS metrics, we decided to model context properties analogously to QoS metrics. However, due to the semantic differences between context properties and QoS metrics (e.g., the fact that the managed system is not responsible for values of context properties, but is at least partially responsible for values of QoS metrics), context properties are modeled as a distinct concept. While our specifications of monitored context properties are well-defined, detailed, and precise (so that they can be used for management activities), their meaning is defined in external reusable ontologies. To formally specify when, where, how, for which parties and by which parties the context monitoring is performed, as well as when and how values of context properties are transferred between various parties, our approach provides special actions for monitoring (measurement or calculation) and transfer of values of context properties. The necessary details are captured in attributes (or sub-elements) of these actions. To formally specify various ways in which context properties influence operation, monitoring, and control (particularly dynamic adaptation) of service-oriented systems, we enabled that values of context properties can be used in various expressions and provided events that notify about context changes and, subsequently, trigger adaptation activities.

While these are the major strengths of our approach, its main weakness is additional complexity (compared to the approaches that specify context properties separately from the other management information). The generality, expressive power, and richness of management information specification languages cause some complexity. This complexity has design-time and run-time aspects. During design-time, there is a need to specify various aspects and there can be some verbosity. (Our WS-Policy4MASC example in Figure 2 through Figure 7 shows some verbosity.

While most constructs in WS-Policy4MASC are optional, there are some constructs, such as the "When" construct, that are usually necessary for specification of context and its influences.) The complexity of language processing during run-time is related to (and, to some extent, causes) the overall complexity of the corresponding management middleware. The use of such middleware can incur overhead (e.g., additional use of memory, processing, battery and other resources; higher response times) that might not be acceptable, particularly in mobile service-oriented systems with limited resources. Thus, our solutions might not be appropriate in cases when only simple specification of context with no (or very simple) other management aspects is needed and the resources are scarce. Nevertheless, in most situations the strengths of our approach significantly outweigh its weaknesses.

We implemented our solutions for specification of context properties and related management activities in the WS-Policy4MASC language, which extends the industrial standard WS-Policy with powerful constructs for formal specification of information necessary for run-time management (e.g., dynamic adaptation) of service-oriented systems. These WS-Policy4MASC constructs include goal policy assertions, action policy assertions, utility policy assertions, probability policy assertions, meta-policy assertions, as well as a number of auxiliary constructs specifying ontological meaning, monitored QoS metrics, states, state transitions, schedules, events, scopes, and various types of expression (Boolean, arithmetic, arithmetic-with-unit, string, time/date/duration).

To enable specification of the conceptual solutions for modeling of context and related information, the recent WS-Policy4MASC version 0.9 added or extended several constructs, such as the new "MonitoredContextProperty" specification of context properties, the extended "ManagementDataCollection" and "ManagementDataTransfer" actions, extensions to all types of expressions, the new Boolean operator "IsMonitoredContextProperty", and the new event type "MonitoredContextPropertyChanged". Particularly important is the use of context properties in Boolean expressions within filtering conditions that are part of the "When" construct, because they limit applicability of WS-Policy4MASC policy assertions only to a particular context. Also important is the use of the event type "MonitoredContextPropertyChanged" to trigger evaluation of goal policy assertions, execution of action policy assertions (e.g., performing dynamic adaptation), and calculation of utility (or probability) policy assertions. All these new or extended constructs increase usefulness of WS-Policy4MASC for management of mobile service-oriented systems. To verify feasibility and implementability of the new WS-Policy4MASC constructs, we checked their syntactical correctness and thoroughly studied required modifications of the MASC middleware that uses WS-Policy4MASC for management of service-oriented systems. To validate usefulness of the proposed WS-Policy4MASC improvements, we explored several hypothetical case studies (e.g., the truck tracking mobile Web service). We plan additional implementation and evaluation of our solutions, hopefully on real-life scenarios.

ACKNOWLEDGMENT

NICTA is funded by the Australian Government as represented by the Department of Broadband, Communications and the Digital Economy and the Australian Research Council through the ICT Centre of Excellence program. The initial stages of the research project on specification of context for management of service-oriented systems (but not the WS-Policy4MASC specifics) were performed while Vladimir Tosic was an NSERC (Natural Sciences and Engineering Research Council of Canada) post-doctoral fellow at the University of Western Ontario. Hanan Lutfiyya and Yazhe Tang contributed to these stages. Earlier versions (up to 0.8) of WS-Policy4MASC were developed within a research project sponsored by the Australian Research Council (ARC) and Microsoft Australia. Abdelkarim Erradi and Piyush Maheshwari contributed to this early work on WS-Policy4MASC.

REFERENCES

W3C Web Services Policy Working Group. (2007). *Web Services Policy 1.5 – Framework*. W3C Recommendation. Published September 4, 2007. Retrieved April 10, 2009, from http://www.w3.org/TR/ws-policy/

Amundsen, S. L., & Eliassen, F. (2008). A resource and context model for mobile middleware. *Personal and Ubiquitous Computing, 12*(2), 143–153. doi:10.1007/s00779-006-0105-4

Baldauf, M., Dustdar, S., & Rosenberg, F. (2007). A Survey on Context-aware Systems. *International Journal of Ad Hoc Ubiquitous Computing, 2*(4), 263–277. doi:10.1504/IJAHUC.2007.014070

Bartolini, C., Sahai, A., & Sauve, J. P. (Eds.). (2007). *Proceedings of the Second IEEE/IFIP Workshop on Business-Driven IT Management, BDIM'07*. Piscataway, USA: IEEE Press.

Chen, G., & Kotz, D. (2000). *A Survey of Context-Aware Mobile Computing Research*. Technical Report. UMI Order Number: TR2000-381. Dartmouth College, USA. Retrieved April 10, 2009, from http://www.cs.dartmouth.edu/~dfk/papers/chen-survey-tr.pdf

Chen, I. Y. L., Yang, S. J. H., Huang, J. J. S., & Lan, B. C. W. (2006). Ubiquitous Provision of Context Aware Web Services. In *Proceedings of the 2006 IEEE International Conference on Services Computing Services Computing* (pp. 60-68). Los Alamitos, USA: IEEE-CS Press.

Dey, A. K. (2001). Understanding and Using Context. *Personal and Ubiquitous Computing, 5*(1), 4–7. doi:10.1007/s007790170019

Erradi, A., Tosic, V., & Maheshwari, P. (2007). MASC -. NET-Based Middleware for Adaptive Composite Web Services. In *Proceedings of the 2007 IEEE International Conference on Web Services* (pp. 727-734). Los Alamitos, USA: IEEE-CS Press.

Farlex. (2009). *Context – Definition of Context by the Free Online Dictionary, Thesaurus, and Encyclopedia*. Retrieved April 10, 2009, from http://www.thefreedictionary.com/context

Forstadius, J., Lassila, O., & Seppanen, T. (2005). RDF-Based Model for Context-Aware Reasoning in Rich Service Environment. In *Proceedings of the 2nd Workshop on Context Modeling and Reasoning at PerCom'05* (pp. 15-19). Los Alamitos, USA: IEEE-CS Press.

Herssens, C., Faulkner, S., & Jureta, I. J. (2008). Context-Driven Autonomic Adaptation of SLA. In *Proceedings of the 6th international Conference on Service-Oriented Computing* (pp. 362-377). Berlin, Germany: Springer.

Karunaratne, R. P. (2008). *Analysis of Methods for Improving IT Support for Business*. Undergraduate Thesis B Report, School of Computer Science and Engineering, University of New South Wales, Australia, October 2008.

Keller, A., & Ludwig, H. (2003). The WSLA Framework: Specifying and Monitoring Service Level Agreements for Web Services. [New York: Plenum Publishing.]. *Journal of Network and Systems Management, 11*(1), 57–81. doi:10.1023/A:1022445108617

Kephart, J. O., & Chess, D. M. (2003). The Vision of Autonomic Computing. [Los Alamitos, USA: IEEE-CS Press.]. *Computer, 36*(1), 41–50. doi:10.1109/MC.2003.1160055

Little, M. (2007). WS-CAF: Contexts, Coordination and Transactions for Web Services. In R. Meersman and Z. Tari et al. (Eds.), *On the Move to Meaningful Internet Systems 2007: CoopIS, DOA, ODBASE, GADA, and IS* (LNCS 4803, pp. 439-453).

Liu, A. (2008). *Extending Service-Oriented Middleware for Business-Driven IT Management*. Undergraduate Thesis B Report, School of Computer Science and Engineering, University of New South Wales, Australia, October 2008.

Ludwig, H., Dan, A., & Kearney, R. (2004). Cremona: An Architecture and Library for Creation and Monitoring of WS-Agreements. In *Proceedings of the 2nd International Conference on Service Oriented Computing* (pp. 65-74). New York: ACM.

Rong, W., Liu, K., & Liang, L. (2008). Association Rule Based Context Modeling for Web Service Discovery. In *Proceedings of the 10th IEEE Conference on E-Commerce and E-Services* (pp. 299-304). Los Alamitos, USA: IEEE-CS Press.

Sheng, Q. Z., & Benatallah, B. (2005). ContextUML: a UML-based modeling language for model-driven development of context-aware Web services. In *Proceedings of the 2005 International Conference on Mobile Business* (pp. 206-212). Los Alamitos, USA: IEEE-CS Press.

Spanoudakis, G., Mahbub, K., & Zisman, A. (2007). A Platform for Context Aware Runtime Web Service Discovery. In *Proceedings of the 2007 IEEE International Conference on Web Services* (pp. 233-240). Los Alamitos, USA: IEEE-CS Press.

Strang, T., & Linnhoff-Popien, C. (2004). A Context Modeling Survey. In *Proceedings of the First International Workshop on Advanced Context Modeling, Reasoning, and Management* at UbiComp 2004 (pp. 33-40). Los Alamitos, USA: IEEE-CS Press.

Tosic, V. (2010). On Modeling and Maximizing Business Value for Autonomic Service-Oriented Systems. [IJSSOE]. *International Journal of Systems and Service-Oriented Engineering, 1*(1), 79–95.

Tosic, V., Erradi, A., & Maheshwari, P. (2007). WS-Policy4MASC - A WS-Policy Extension Used in the Manageable and Adaptable Service Compositions (MASC) Middleware. In *Proceedings of the 2007 IEEE Services Computing Conference* (pp. 458-465). Los Alamitos, USA: IEEE-CS Press.

Tosic, V., Lutfiyya, H., & Tang, Y. (2006a). Web Service Offerings Language (WSOL) Support for Context Management of Mobile/Embedded XML Web Services. In *Proceedings of the Advanced international Conference on Telecommunications and International Conference on internet and Web Applications and Services* (pp. 45-52). Los Alamitos, USA: IEEE-CS Press.

Tosic, V., Lutfiyya, H., & Tang, Y. (2006b). Extending Web Service Offerings Infrastructure (WSOI) for Management of Mobile/Embedded XML Web Services. In *Joint Proceedings of the 8th IEEE International Conference on E-Commerce Technology and 3rd IEEE International Conference on Enterprise Computing, E-Commerce and E-Services (CEC/EEE 2006), 3rd IEEE International Workshop on Mobile Commerce and Wireless Services (WMCS 2006), 2nd International Workshop on Business Service Networks and 2nd International Workshop on Service oriented Solutions for Cooperative Organizations* (pp. 571-578). Los Alamitos, USA: IEEE-CS Press.

Tosic, V., Pagurek, B., Patel, B., Esfandiari, B., & Ma, W. (2005). Management Applications of the Web service Offerings Language (WSOL). [Amsterdam: The Netherlands: Elsevier.]. *Information Systems, 30*(7), 564–586. doi:10.1016/j.is.2004.11.005

Wibisono, W., Zaslavsky, A., & Ling, S. (2008). Towards a Service-Oriented Approach for Managing Context in Mobile Environment. In *Proceedings of the 6th international Conference on Service-Oriented Computing* (LNCS 5364, pp. 210-224)

KEY TERMS AND DEFINITIONS

System Management: The process of monitoring and control of a system to ensure regular operation of the system and to handle run-time problems (e.g., faults, performance degradations).

Monitoring: The process of determining the state of a system, e.g., by measuring or calculating various quality of service (QoS) metrics, determining presence of faults, evaluating satisfaction of requirements and guarantees, and calculating monetary amounts to be paid.

Control: The process of run-time modification (e.g., re-configuration) of a system to ensure its regular operation, in spite of external changes or internal run-time problems (e.g., faults, performance degradations).

Quality of Service (QoS): A: group of measures of how well (e.g., how quickly, how reliably) a system performs its operations.

QoS Metric: A particular measure of QoS, such as response time, throughput, or availability.

Context (Broad Meaning): Information that characterizes situation of a system, such as geographic location, past interactions with other systems, and past availability.

Context (Narrow Meaning): Information about external run-time circumstances (e.g., geographic location of a mobile system, events that come from outside, preferences of system's consumers) that characterize situation of a system and influence its operation, but are outside its direct control.

Context Property: A particular attribute/ aspect of context, such as country of location or network latency between the monitored system and external systems.

Policy: A collection of high-level, implementation-independent goals and/or rules that describe what should be achieved by management (e.g., specify limits for response time).

Policy Assertion: The atomic unit for policy specification in the Web Services Policy Framework (WS-Policy) industrial standard.

Chapter 10
A Case Study on Service Oriented Enterprise Interoperability in Automobile Supply Chain

Yong Zhang
Shandong University, China

Shijun Liu
Shandong University, China

Yuchang Jiao
IBM, China

Yuqing Sun
Shandong University, China

ABSTRACT

Interoperability is an important issue in the supply chain management (SCM) systems that highly influence the productivity, especially in such complex automobile domain that many supplies take part in the activities and requirements are dynamically changed according to the market. In order to keep ahead in the competitive market, each enterprise in the supply chain should keep efficient interoperability with its partners. However, it is difficult for all of them to update their SCM systems in real time for collaboration especially for some small suppliers due to the expensive maintenance and complex technologies. In this paper, we propose a service-oriented approach to solve the above problem by providing an integrated platform, where interoperability is considered as utility-like capability and delivered in the form of Software as a Service (SaaS). Each enterprise in a supply chain could establish the interoperation activities with other partners in this platform and thus they could efficiently collaborate. We illustrate in detail how two SaaS-typed applications interact with each other.

DOI: 10.4018/978-1-61520-819-7.ch010

INTRODUCTION

Global competition has compelled manufacturing companies to produce an ever increasing variety of products, in lower quantities, with higher quality, lower costs and within shorter production times. In line with this irreversible trend, a new pattern of inter-enterprise relationship is evolving. There is a tendency for large firms to evolve into loosely tied and decentralized federations or business units, making products and seeking alliances both within and outside the "consortium" to serve customers' demands to their best ability. The emergence of these "small firms" and the new pattern of inter-firm relationships will evolve into a new production paradigm - a virtual enterprise.

So the competitiveness of today's enterprise is to a large extent determined by its ability to seamlessly interoperate with others. Enterprise Interoperability (EI) has therefore become an important area of research to ensure the competitiveness and growth of enterprises (Yannis et al., 2008). In modern manufacturing field, such as automobile industry, an entire manufacturing process often cooperated by assembly factory and part suppliers. Agile Supply Chain Management increasingly becomes an effective and important measure to enhance competitive advantage of enterprises that needs the support of agile information system to integrate their supply chain more effectively and quickly (Tarokh et al., 2007). As auto manufacturers inexorably move their sourcing of components and low value-added operations offshore, to lower cost countries, so their supply chains increase in both distance and complexity. Many companies are faced with the challenge of providing an agile response to customers and yet operating a lean operation across an extended global supply chain. This is a challenge that needs a solution beyond the abilities of simply judgment, the telephone and spreadsheets (Ross, 2003).

The need to set up alliances among different types of enterprises quickly in order to benefit from market opportunities, are causing new types of problems, like interoperability, to appear in the enterprise. Enterprise interoperability issues in the automotive industry are important because the complexity of the product, the design process, and the industry magnifies the impact of interoperability problems while obscuring their solution. Choosing a framework is a necessary condition for facilitating interoperability engineering because they are representing best practices in the domain of interoperable systems engineering. According to the INTEROP NoE interoperability framework, three categories of interoperability barriers are identified: conceptual barriers, technological barriers, and organizational barriers. What's more, there are three basic ways to relate systems together to establish interoperations: integrated approach, unified approach, and federated approach (David Chen et al., 2008).

In this paper, our research work aims at developing a methodology that provides a guide on how to implement an interoperability solution in automotive supply chain management through a federated approach. More precisely the methodology allows establishing interoperability by: (1) constructing a virtual enterprise by identifying and involving various actors and stakeholders in the interoperability service platform; (2) dynamically composing available interoperability service utilities according to identified requirements; (3) evaluating and improving the interoperability solution in practice.

Under the guiding of this methodology, we design and develop a service platform, which is built on top of existing ICT infrastructure available in most of enterprises. In our platform, the interoperability services are delivered in the form of SaaS (Abhijit et al., 2007), which are cheap, fast, reliable, and without major integration efforts, so they can be invoked by enterprises on the fly in support of their business activities. The goal of the Platform is to provide a holistic solution enabling the collaborative supply chain management in a flexible and dynamic environment and especially to facilitate SMEs' participation to collaborative supply chain management processes.

BACKGROUND

Since the beginning of 2000s, research on enterprise interoperability has been emerging. Most related work is concerned with the elaboration of an enterprise interoperability framework, such as LISI, IDEAS, AIF, EIF, etc. In the field of enterprise interoperability, it is worth noting the first significant initiative: the LISI (levels of information systems interoperability) approach developed by C4ISR Architecture Working Group (AWG) during 1997. The purpose of LISI is to provide the US Department of Defense (DoD) with a maturity model and a process for determining joint interoperability needs, assessing the ability of the information systems to meet those needs, and selecting pragmatic solutions and a transition path for achieving higher states of capability and interoperability (David Chen et al., 2008).

The IDEAS interoperability framework was developed by IDEAS project on the basis of ECMA/NIST Toaster Model, ISO 19101, and ISO 19119 augmented through the quality attributes. The framework also intended to reflect the view that Interoperability is achieved on multiple levels: inter-enterprise coordination, business process integration, semantic application integration, syntactical application integration and physical integration. The ATHENA interoperability framework (AIF) is structured into three levels and based on sources of results and usage of the framework. The ATHENA interoperability framework and IDEAS interoperability framework were considered complementary. At each level of AIF, one can use the IDEAS interoperability framework to structure interoperability issues into three layers (business, knowledge and ICT) and a semantic dimension. Comparing the AIF with ISO 15704 GERAM framework shows a tentative mapping of GERAM components to the ATHENA interoperability framework (AIF).

This paper followed the enterprise interoperability framework developed within the frame of INTEROP Network of Excellence (NoE). The purpose of this framework is to define the research domain of enterprise interoperability and help to identify and structure the knowledge of the domain. It has been considered that enterprises systems are not interoperable because there are barriers to interoperability. Barriers are incompatibilities of various kinds and at various enterprise levels. The incompatibilities obstruct the sharing of information and prevent from exchanging services. There exist common barriers to all enterprises whatever the sector of activities and size.

Research on interoperability is not only a matter of removing barriers but also in the way in which these barriers are removed. Generally speaking, there are three basic ways to relate entities (systems) together to establish interoperations (C.J. Petrie, 1992; ISO 14258, 1999).

Integrated approach: There exists a common format for all models. This format must be as detailed as models. The common format is not necessarily a standard but must be agreed by all parties to elaborate models and build systems.

Unified approach: There exists a common format but only at a meta-level. This meta-model is not an executable entity as it is in the integrated approach but provides a means for semantic equivalence to allow mapping between models.

Federated approach: There is no common format. To establish interoperability, parties must accommodate on the fly. Using a federated approach implies that no partner imposes its models, languages and methods of work.

In the NoE interoperability framework, there many research challenges, just like Interoperability service utility. The delivery model of interoperability service is a key problem to be considered. Software as a Service (SaaS) is a new delivery model for software, which lowers the cost of development, customization, deployment and operation of a software application to support multi-tenants over the Internet. Software delivered in a SaaS model is no longer run exclusively for one customer at a customer's premise but run at a service provider and accessed via the Internet. In contrast to traditional "on-premise" software that is deployed and run in a data center at the customer's premise, SaaS Software is run at a SaaS hosting provider and can be accessed over a network by the software user. SaaS offers a set of advantages for software customers: Instead of being forced to build and maintain large data centers and hosting a big amount of middleware to run applications, companies consume IT-Services in the SaaS model just like they would use any other utility such as electricity or water.

This paper proposed an enterprise interoperability service platform, which is used to remove the barriers between enterprises. In this platform, interoperability is considered to be a utility-like capability and delivered in the form of SaaS. This paper introduces the detailed architecture framework of interoperability services and proposes an interactive framework which is used to establish interoperability between SaaS applications.

VIRTUAL ENTERPRISES AND THE SUPPORTING PLATFORM

Virtual Enterprises in Auto Industry

The virtual enterprise (V.E.) concept is one of the most important ways to raise the agility and competitiveness of a manufacturing enterprise (D. Wang et al., 2001). Under this concept a master company develops its products by using the manufacturing resources of external partners. In the process of designing and manufacturing an automobile, many individuals and organizations exchange product data. The design and manufacturing process involves many divisions within the original equipment manufacturer (OEM), many first-tier suppliers, a number of second-tier and

sub-tier suppliers. This exchange of data supports the process of concurrent engineering and design, allowing these organizations to work together to improve the performance and manufacturability of a product and to advance the competitiveness of the industry.

Figure 1 shows a typical structure of the supply chain in automotive industry. As shown in Figure 1, the automotive supply chain consists of four primary elements: original equipment manufacturers (OEMs), first-tier suppliers, sub-tier suppliers, raw and processed materials suppliers. However, individual companies may operate in several different positions in the supply chain. A company may work for many customers and function as a first-tier supplier on one project and a sub tier supplier on other projects. Generally speaking, there mainly exist three different kinds of virtual enterprises in automobile industry.

The first kind of V.E. is the most common and standard one. In this kind of V.E., an OEM is the unique master, and a number of suppliers serve it. The relationship among them is very simple because there is no intersection in the organization. However, in the second kind of V.E., the relationship is more complicated, because intersections appear among V.E.'s boundaries. One supplier may serve several masters. As a result, they will exchange information with different OEMs.

The third kind of V.E., is the most complicated one. In the service platform, all the enterprise users could apply for interoperability services, so it potentially allows a "double-role" situation. In other words, the master of a V.E., may be a supplier in another V.E... Just take an engine manufacture enterprise for example, it can be master of a V.E., and get outsourcing parts to produce engines; meanwhile, it may play the role of a supplier to serve other OEMs.

As is well known that, enterprise interoperability is very important for the competitiveness and growth of enterprises. Members of the auto industry generally acknowledge that imperfect

Figure 1. Typical structure of the supply chain in automotive industry

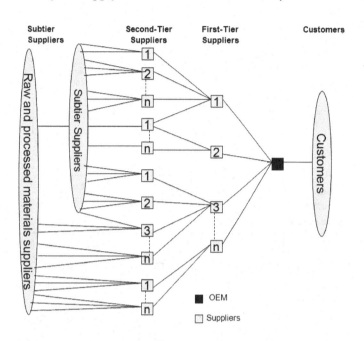

interoperability is an important and expensive problem. However, SMEs are still far behind in the reform of supply chain management due to their small IT budgets, crude process standards with little visibility data to enable them to share and compare with trading partners in a virtual enterprise.

In order to resolve this problem, a service platform is designed, and many interoperability services are offered. With the help of this platform, a virtual enterprise can be constructed online easily, and interoperability can also be established more efficiently. In the service platform, construction of virtual enterprises is a prerequisite to use these interoperability services. All the stakeholders have to register to be users of the platform, if they want to use the interoperability service utilities to support their business activities. The OEM users have authorization to create a virtual enterprise. They can choose appropriate suppliers from all the registered users to supply the parts/ materials they need for normal production. After the OEM gathering all the suppliers it needs, a virtual enterprise is constructed. Then, master of

the V.E. could apply for services such as SBM service and APO service. After been approved by the platform, the master could use them with the other members of V.E. to establish interoperability easily and quickly.

Architecture of Interoperability Service Platform

According to the methodology mentioned above, we design and develop a service platform, which is used to deliver interoperability service utilities easily and quickly. Both the assembly factory and the supplier should first register to be users of this platform, where they can negotiate for goods and services. After the establishing of a virtual enterprise in our platform, the master of the V.E. could apply for the authorization to use these services, such as SBM and APO.

The design of the platform is based on the SOA principle; all the functions are implemented as services, including web services and software as a service. The architecture of our platform is shown in figure 2, which has 5 different layers.

Figure 2. Architecture of the interoperability service platform

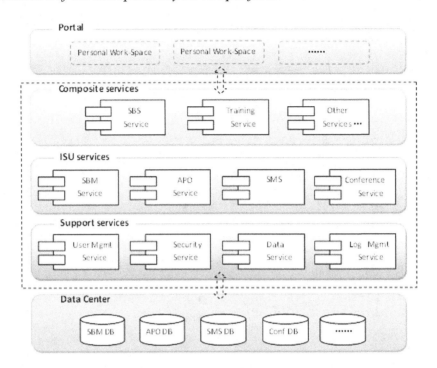

The bottom of the architecture is the data center of our platform. There are data bases for all kinds of important data needed in the normal execution of the platform. Portal is the presentation layer of the service platform, and the use of the platform is organized in a way of "personal work-space". That's to say, when the user logs in our platform, he will work in his self-customized workspace to support the business activities. If the user is from a part supplier, he can get the orders from his assembly factory, and deliver the materials on time. Support service layer is basic and fundamental layer in the platform. In this layer, it contains many services which are used to support the basic function of our platform, such as user management service, security service, data synchronization service, log service and so on. All the interoperability services are based on these support services.

Interoperability services layer is the most important one in our platform. As the platform is designed to support the auto supply chain management, the interoperability service utilities are the

core functions auto manufacturer enterprises will use to enhance the interoperability between stakeholders. In the ISU platform, it provides several widely used services, which are delivered in the form of SaaS. They are SBM service, APO service, SMS service and conference service etc. In real world, SBM service and APO service will directly influence the production of enterprises, while the SMS service and conference service are often used to support daily business activities that are not very important.

To build agile supply chain management for automobile industry, SBM provides a cooperative environment of supply business for assembly factory and its suppliers, where the assembly factory is in the center of the business. SBM will help the assembly factory to deal with businesses related to suppliers such as bill inquiry, inventory management, and payment management, etc.

Advanced Planning and Optimization (APO) is very important in the automobile industry, because it is at the leading edge of manufacturing management technology. The appeal of APO to manufacturers is obvious, because companies can optimize their supply chains to reduce costs, improve product margins, lower inventories, and increase manufacturing throughput. APO necessitates deciding when to build each order, in what operation sequence, and with what machines to meet the required due dates.

In real world, most of the SMEs can't afford the expensive software systems with the same function of SBM and APO. Therefore, the goal of the platform is to facilitate SMEs' participation to collaborative supply chain management processes by invoking SBM service and APO service on the fly. At present, SBM service and APO service are the most important services in the platform used to improve interoperability between enterprises. They will be introduced in the following sections.

The composite services layer of the architecture is more complex than the ISU services layer. In automobile supply chain management, SBM and APO are often used together to support the important business activities. Dynamically composing available interoperability service utilities according to identified requirements is the key step to construct a new application. Therefore, a composite services layer is designed to deal with the complicated business requirements. This paper will introduce an interactive framework used to establish interoperability between two services: SBM and APO.

Business Scenario

In order to introduce the platform in a detailed way, we give the following business scenario. An automobile manufacturer (named F) has its own CAPP software system which is used to support its daily business activities and improve efficiency of the supply chain management. During execution, production department makes daily production plans, and these plans will be imported into CAPP system. Then CAPP system decomposes these plans and gets concrete parts/materials needed according to the BOM. Compared with the inventory, CAPP will generate daily procurement plans. According to these procurement plans, workers in procurement department will call the corresponding suppliers to deliver parts/materials on time to ensure normal production. If some of these suppliers can't supply on time, the workers will get some alternative suppliers to fill the gap. When suppliers deliver parts/materials to company F, they have to go to procurement department first to print procurement orders through CAPP system, and then deliver goods to warehouse together with the printed orders. As a result, there is usually a long queue in the office of procurement department waiting to print procurement orders. When suppliers go to finance department to get some financial information, they also have to wait a long time.

In this scenario, efficiency of the supply chain management needs to be improved immediately, as all the information can be read from the inner software system, but they can't be shared with suppliers. In a word, company F needs an information platform to share all the important data with its hundreds of suppliers to enhance the interoperability with these stakeholders.

However, with the help of our interoperability services platform, company F could address these issues more easily. First of all, Company F and its suppliers could register to be users of the platform, and then a corresponding V.E. could be constructed easily online. Secondly, they can use the interoperability services offered by the platform to establish interoperability among these stakeholders instead of developing a new solution from scratch. Finally, company F enhances efficiency of their supply chain management by importing the third-party SBM service to decrease its IT investment and operational cost. Meanwhile, the suppliers could use the APO service and SBM service together to automatically calculate their replenishment capacities.

SBM SERVICE IN THE SOFTWARE AS A SERVICE MODEL

To build agile supply chain for automobile industry, a system named Supply Business Management (SBM) was developed. SBM is an interoperability service utility which is delivered in the form of SaaS on the service platform. The SaaS vision focuses on separating the possession and ownership of software from its use. Delivering software's functionality as a set of distributed services that can be configured and bound at delivery time can overcome many current limitations constraining software use, deployment, and evolution. At present, the SBM service is widely used by many assembly factories that have their powerful inner software systems but have no information platform to share all the important data with their hundreds of suppliers.

Architecture Framework of SBM Service

Figure 3 shows an architectural framework of the Supply Business Services in Software as a Service model. This framework provides the capability of hosting multi-tenants using a single application instance supported by the same set of computing backend servers. It consists of a Web server, a Database server and an Application server. The presentation and customization modules of the application are deployed in a Web server. The Security, Directory, Metadata and Shared services, the business services of the application are deployed in the Application server. The Database server contains a central user account database, a central tenant metadata database. However, there are several polices to design the data architecture of the business data for multi-tenants. In our design, we used the shared database with different schemas.

In real world, business rules of automobile assembly factories are complicated and different from each other. Therefore, SBM service may not

Figure 3. Architecture framework of SBM service

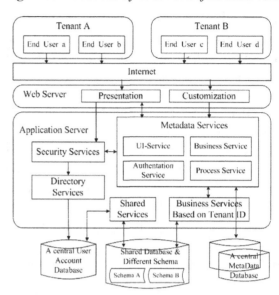

be suitable for all of them. So we provide the function of customization to deal with various conditions, in the form of metadata services. All the customized information will be written in corresponding formats in the central tenant metadata database. Actually, there are many kinds of metadata services in SBM service: UI service, authorization service, process service, and the business logic service.

The logo and menus can be customized configured in the UI metadata service; roles of users and authorization of all kinds of operations are configured in the authorization service. What's more, all the business rules are configured in the business logic service. As a result, with these metadata, an SBM instance can be customized by the master of a V.E. It has to be addressed that, before the master of V.E. is approved to use SBM service, SLA (service level agreements) should be contracted, such as the maximal concurrent users on line and the response time of querying 1 million records etc.

With the support of SBM service, assembly factory could enhance and improve interoperability with its suppliers with little IT investment and operational cost, instead of developing a new solution from scratch.

Functions of SBM Service

SBM provides a cooperative environment of supply business for assembly factory and suppliers. At the beginning, company F will use a data synchronization service to synchronize all the important data it wants to share with these suppliers. Data synchronization service is one of the support services provided in our platform, which is used to synchronize important data from inner systems of an enterprise to the platform. During execution, we have to synchronize the production data to the database of SBM. This is a precondition to use SBM service.

With the help of SBM service, assembly factory can share production related information easily with its hundreds of suppliers. SBM provides several services to support the business activities, such as plan service, order service, finance service, quality service, notice service, inventory service etc. Using the plan service, assembly factory could publish its procurement plans to suppliers to guide their production and shipping. There are mainly three kinds of purchase plans, including monthly plans, weekly plans, and daily plans. Order service is the most important function in SBM. Assembly factory allocates orders to its suppliers according to the pre-defined quota standard. The decomposed orders are published immediately to corresponding suppliers. Then, the suppliers will print orders online and shipping the parts/materials directly to warehouse. They will never wait a long time in procurement department to print the orders. Finance service publishes all the financial information to suppliers, such as general ledger arrearages, quality compensation etc. Quality service gives all the quality related data, such as quality inspection, sampling inspection etc. Inventory service allows suppliers to get the accurate inventory in assembly factory. According to the inventory, suppliers can get the

information of already used materials, and carry out the distribution.

In order to serve all kinds of assembly factories, the SBM service is designed and realized flexibly, which provides the function of customization. That is to say, users of SBM could customize the service and use it in a DIY way.

INTEROPERABILITY BETWEEN SBM AND APO

An integrated family of (enterprise) systems must, of necessity, be interoperable, but interoperable systems need not be integrated. Integration is much more difficult to solve, while interoperability is more of a technical issue (C.J. Petrie, 1992). In the service platform, SBM and APO are delivered in the form of SaaS. However, SBM and APO usually have to be used together to fulfill some special requirements. An interactive framework is proposed to establish the interoperability between two SaaS applications.

APO and SBM are both SaaS application. After being composed, APO acts as a function module of SBM. All users cannot realize that their operations are implemented in a third party application. This is a seamless composition. Compared with other solutions in services composition, our composition works exist in presentation layer, process layer and data layer, which will be introduced in the following sections.

Requirements of Interoperability

In the scenario mentioned above, with the help of SBM service, company F could share the important information synchronously with its suppliers. In SBM service, information flow is only from company F to its suppliers: company F publishes its procurement plans to its suppliers, who then determine whether they have enough capacities to satisfy such demands. However, company F knows nothing about the capacities of its suppliers.

Actually, almost none of its suppliers have such kinds of software to support their calculations on production planning and scheduling, so they have to deal with such heavy tasks manually, which are not only time-consuming, but also lead to imprecise results.

To address such issues, company F plans to enhance efficiency of its supply chain management by compositing SBM and APO together to help suppliers automatically calculate their replenishment capacities. APO is a set of packaged services that provides strong capabilities for advanced production planning and optimization through explosion or implosion.

After the composition, suppliers can get the procurement plans through SBM service and directly invoke the APO service to calculate the production planning and optimization. What's more, with the help of APO, suppliers can feedback on line to the assembly factory whether they can supply the needed parts/materials on time.

In this improved scenario, the interoperability is established by the following steps:

1. Production department of company F makes daily production planning and imports these plans into the CAPP system;
2. Then CAPP system will decompose these plans and get concrete parts/materials needed according to the BOM. Compared with the inventory, CAPP will generate the daily procurement plans;
3. The suppliers get corresponding procurement plans published throw services in SBM, and then calculate the advanced planning and optimization through the APO service which is invoked in SBM;
4. APO returns the results to the suppliers, who then make decisions based on the implosion results and send a response to procurement department to feedback whether they can supply on time. Then the suppliers prepare to produce the required parts/materials;

5. The procurement department collects responses from all the suppliers. If there are some suppliers that can't completely fulfill the initial procurement plans, it will then try to find some alternative suppliers to fill the gap;
6. In some special situations where no alternative suppliers could be found, production department of company F has to adjust its production plans.

With the help of SBM service and APO service, suppliers can share the information of company F easily; moreover, they can calculate their production planning and optimization automatically based on the interoperability between SBM and APO.

Interactive Framework

As shown in Figure 4, the composition is implemented on three layers: presentation layer, function layer and data layer. As presentation layer, we design EWidget model and implement web UI driven flow based on the model. The green bevels are the implemented instances of EWidget model. These instances are deployed on to the UI layer of SBM. All the authorized users can visit these widgets to carry out business operations. As function layer we provide all the functions as web service which encapsulated by SURROGATE, then the surrogates can be composed into business flow. We extend the surrogate by adding identity module into it to solve the authentication and authorization problems. Rectangle in Figure 4 represents the web services exposed in APO and SBM. Each exposed web service has a corresponding surrogate. Users can define their own business flow by combine different surrogate together. Composition on data layer runs through presentation layer and function layer. Besides that we designed a data synchronizing tool. We also design a service coordination mechanism based

Figure 4. Interactive framework

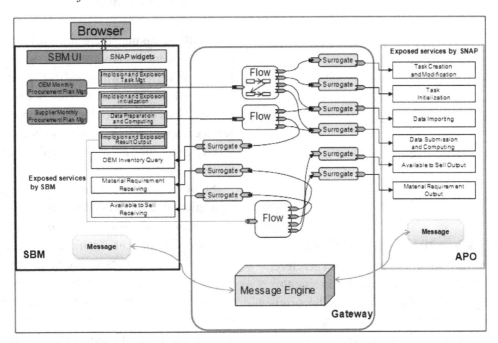

on message notification as shown in the bottom part of Figure 4.

Architecture of EWidget Model

As shown in Figure 4, the APO cannot appear as a self governed system. So an extended UI widget model-EWidget was designed. EWidget is the point that people used to access information and services through SBM even the real information and services are implemented in APO. Widget is an instance of EWidget. Each widget contains one application function. Several widgets can be composed to an application to act as the UI of a workflow. EWidget defines property used for exchanging information between different widgets.

According to the EWidget model, the original web pages of APO have been converted into widgets. After that all the widgets can be embedded into web pages of SBM. When composing APO with SBM, each widget corresponds to different business operation. As users move from one widget to another driven by business flow, the whole business process will be finished step by step. Different widget corresponds to different data structure. The business data is transferred from one widget to another, from widget to APO, from widget to SBM. The widget plays an important role during the executing of the process. EWidget model calls remote service, but the popular browsers prohibit calling service from remote host on the web. So we add the DELEGATE module to it to conquer this problem.

Figure 5 shows the architecture of EWidget model, which lies in both presentation layer and business logic layer. The size, layout and initial variables of a EWidget can be defined in its properties which are used in the exchanging of information. EWidget can support the invoking of remote services through DELEGATE. {op1, op2,…, opn} defines the operations which can be customized by application designers. EWidget model extends Dojo toolkit, which is written in JavaScript and XML. In EWidget model, the invoking of remote services is needed to execute business process. However, most of the popular

Figure 5. Architecture of EWidget model

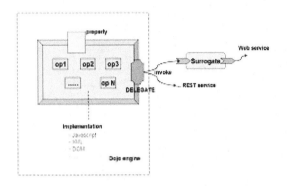

browsers, such as IE and Firefox, prohibit the cross-domain invoking of web services. Therefore, we import the DELEGATE module to solve this problem. According to the EWidget model, original web pages of APO could be converted into widgets that can be embedded into pages of SBM.

Each widget stands for a unique function. The whole process will be fulfilled by traversing from one widget to another according to the business rules. At the same time, each widget deals with a certain kind of data structure, and the business data will be transferred from one widget to another, from APO to SBM.

Service Connection

Generally speaking, there are various services in a heterogeneous environment; web service is just one of them. How to identify them and make them work together is an issue need to be addressed. This paper provides solutions including service authentication, service authorization and service connection according to different business requirements.

Service surrogate extended from SCA provides a programming model which is used to construct applications and solutions based on SOA. SCA (Service Component Architecture) is a model that aims to encompass a wide range of technologies for service components and for the access methods used to connect them. Component is the basic unit of Service Component Architecture, as shown in Figure 6. Component is a paragraph of codes that provide special functions. As to access methods, SCA compositions support various communication and service access technologies such as web service, messaging system and RPC (Remote Procedure Call). The original definition of SCA Component defines the implementation, exposure and invoking mechanism of services. However, it cannot fulfill our requirements for interoperability, such as service authorization and service authentication.

Figure 6. Definition of surrogate based on SCA component

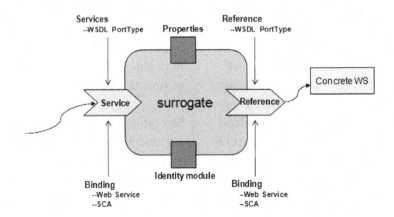

SCA provides service flow definition mechanism to finish complex business automatically. It is the same as the extended SCA component. SCA describes the content and linkage of an application in assemblies called composites. Composites can contain components, services, references, property declarations, plus the wiring that describes the connections between these elements. Composites can group and link components built from different implementation technologies, allowing appropriate technologies to be used for each business task.

This paper extends SCA Component by adding the Identity Module to monitor and process SOAP messages based on WS-Security. As is shown in Figure 6, the extended SCA Component is named "surrogate". In common situation, SBM and APO manage their users separately. So the detailed solution of service connection is:

1. Encapsulating the related web services with SCA Component.
2. Process the identity information in the identity module. A mapping table for users should be maintained in the ISU platform. The table stores the mapping relationship of SBM users and APO users. The role and authorization will not be changed and still be managed by SBM and APO. When an authorized user, such as Bob logs in SBM and invokes web services provided by APO, the authentication process will be activated. Firstly, Identity Module will insert Bob's identity information into SOAP head; then the gateway will capture the message and find the corresponding user of Bob in the mapping table. If succeed, the new user_id certified by APO will be inserted into SOAP head to invoke the services exposed by APO. The return process is the same.

Service Coordination

Service coordination is often used to support a number of applications, including those that need to reach consistent agreement on the outcome of distributed transactions. In order to ensure the interoperability between SBM service and APO service, this paper proposes a Message Notification based service coordination technology, which is driven by business rules. We design and implement a tool named Message Engine in dependence on Apache Kandula2 project, which provides an open-source implementation of WS-Coordination, WS-Atomic Transaction and WS-Business Activity.

Message Engine not only enables an application service to create a context needed to propagate an activity to other services but also enables the coordination of transactions among web services. As shown in Figure 7, with the help of the Message Engine, the whole process of service coordination based on Message Notification is carried out by the following steps:

1. Configuring the Message Q of SBM service and APO service;
2. Registering the Message Q of SBM to Message Engine;
3. Users log in SBM service and then activate a business process;
4. Web services involved in the process are invoked and Message Q of APO is registered to Message Engine;
5. Message Q in APO invokes the completed () function automatically after the execution;
6. Message Engine invokes the complete () function of SBM to notify the end of the process;
7. On receiving the notification, the whole process ends;
8. Notifying APO the whole process ends.

Figure 7. Service coordination based on message notification

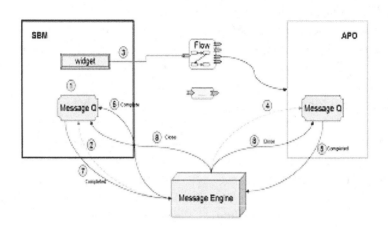

With the help of these technologies, interoperability between SBM and APO can be established to fulfill the requirement of making them work together to enhance the efficiency of supply chain management.

CONCLUSION AND FUTURE WORK

This paper proposed a methodology that provides a guide on how to establish interoperability between enterprises through a federated approach. Under the guide of this methodology, the paper designed and realized an interoperability service platform to enhance the interoperability and efficiency of the supply chain management in automobile industry. The paper introduced the architecture of service platform and the application of SBM service and APO service. Moreover, the paper proposed an interactive framework to establish the interoperability between SBM service and APO service.

However, there are only several interoperability service utilities in the platform and not enough to support the whole process of supply chain management. In the future, we will design and develop more services for automobile industry. What's more, there are many grand challenges in the research of enterprise interoperability, such

as "Future Internet and Enterprise Systems", "Knowledge-Oriented Collaboration and Semantic Interoperability" etc.; we will focus on these key issues.

REFERENCES

Charalabidis, Y., Gionis, G., Hermann, K.M., & Martinez, C. (2008, Feb). *Enterprise Interoperability Research Roadmap.*

Chen, D., & Doumeingts, G. (2008). Architectures for enterprise integration and interoperability-Past, present and future. *Computers in Industry, I*(59), 647–659. doi:10.1016/j.compind.2007.12.016

Dubey, A., & Wagle, D. (2007, May). *Delivering software as a service.* Paper presented at the McKinsey Quarterly, Web exclusive.

ISO 14258. (1999, April). *Industrial Automation Systems—Concepts and Rules for Enterprise Models.* ISO TC184/SC5/WG1.

Panetto, H., & Molina, A. (2008). Enterprise integration and interoperability in manufacturing systems: Trends and issues. *Computers in Industry, I*(59), 641–646. doi:10.1016/j.compind.2007.12.010

Petrie, C. J. (Ed.). (1992). *Enterprise Integration Modeling*. Cambridge, MA: The MIT Press.

Ross, A. (2003). Creating agile supply chains. *Manufacturing Engineering*, *82*(6), 18–21. doi:10.1049/me:20030603

Tarokh, M. J., Ghahremanloo, H., & Karami, M. (2007, Aug). *Agility in Auto Dealers SCM*. Paper presented at the IEEE International Conference on Service Operations and Logistics, and Informatics.

Wang, D., Yung, K. L., & Ip, W. H. (2001). A heuristic genetic algorithm for subcontractor selection in a global manufacturing environment. *IEEE Transactions on Systems, Man and Cybernetics. Part C, Applications and Reviews*, *31*(2), 189–198. doi:10.1109/5326.941842

KEY TERMS AND DEFINITIONS

Enterprise Interoperability: The Enterprise Interoperability qualifies the faculty of Enterprise to establish a partnership activity (in product design, organization of the activities of production, supply chains piloting) in a efficient and competitive way in an environment of unstable market. Also, inside a company, the need in interoperability of the various services is very generally identified.

Software as a Service: Software as a Service is a model of software deployment whereby a provider licenses an application to customers for use as a service on demand. SaaS software vendors may host the application on their own web servers or download the application to the consumer device, disabling it after use or after the on-demand contract expires. The on-demand function may be handled internally to share licenses within a firm or by a third-party application service provider (ASP) sharing licenses between firms.

Supply Chain Management: Supply chain management (SCM) is the management of a network of interconnected businesses involved in the ultimate provision of product and service packages required by end customers. Supply Chain Management spans all movement and storage of raw materials, work-in-process inventory, and finished goods from point of origin to point of consumption.

Virtual Enterprise: A Virtual Enterprise (VE) is a temporary alliance of enterprises that come together to share skills or core competencies and resources in order to better respond to business opportunities, and whose cooperation is supported by computer networks. It is a manifestation of Collaborative Networks and Distributed Collaborative Working.

Service Oriented Architecture (SOA): In computing, service-oriented architecture (SOA) provides a set of principles or governing concepts used during phases of systems development and integration. Such architecture will package functionality as interoperable services. Several different organizations may integrate or use such services — software modules provided as a service — even if their respective client systems are substantially different. It is an attempt to develop yet another means for software module integration. Rather than defining an API, SOA defines the interface in terms of protocols and functionality. An endpoint is the entry point to such an SOA implementation.

Chapter 11
Car Navigation System Using Genetic Algorithm Processor

Masaya Yoshikawa
Meijo University, Japan

ABSTRACT

Recently, car navigation systems that support safe and comfortable driving have been used widely. This chapter proposes a new car navigation system which enables the provision of the following three services: (1) the route search service including unspecified stopover points, (2) the route search service for traveling through sightseeing spots and considering sightseeing time, and (3) the quick response using dedicated hardware. Moreover, the proposed car navigation system is implemented on a field programmable gate array, and its validity is verified by several evaluative experiments using actual map information.

INTRODUCTION

The automobile industry has become a communication tool facilitating the movement of people as well as providing a means of transport. In particular, car navigational systems that support safe and comfortable driving are becoming more and more sophisticated. When a car navigation system was first put into practical use, its function was only to display maps using a CD-ROM. Later, however, technological progress made it possible to build various functions and services, such as voice guidance service and traffic congestion in-

formation displays, into car navigation systems. Generally, the main role of car navigation systems is a route search from a specified starting point to a final destination.

General car navigation systems use the Dijkstra algorithm (DA) (Fujita, *et al.*, 2003) for route search. Although the DA can obtain the shortest route between two points represented on a graph, it cannot obtain the shortest route within an allowable processing time when a problem's scale becomes large. Moreover, the DA cannot search for a route that includes multiple unspecified transit points, or search for a route considering time spent at a transit point.

DOI: 10.4018/978-1-61520-819-7.ch011

However, users of car navigation systems, drivers, desire that a route search can be performed in consideration of several unspecified stopover points (transit points) before reaching their final destination. In real life, for instance, a driver deposits mail at a post office and supplies oil to his car on a gas station before arriving at his final destination. In this case, the post and gas station are not necessarily specified, and a short travel route from the starting point to the final destination, including several stopover points, is desirable.

On the other hand, convenient travel involves an efficient route through sightseeing spots within a limited time. Namely, if a route search can consider transit points (sightseeing spots) and sojourn times (sightseeing times), the car navigation system will be convenient for drivers.

This chapter proposes a new car navigation system that enables a route search that includes multiple unspecified transit points and considers time spent at transit spots. The proposed car navigation system uses a genetic algorithm (GA) (Goldberg, 1989 and, Holland, 1992) as its basic algorithm, which is based on technologically modeling biological evolutionary process; and it has a powerful searching ability for combinatorial optimization problems. However, because a GA is a multi-points search algorithm, it has an inherent processing time problem. This chapter introduces dedicated hardware for a GA to realize high-speed processing. Moreover, the proposed car navigation system is implemented on the field programmable gate array (FPGA), and its validity is verified by several evaluation experiments using actual map information.

The organization of this chapter is as follows: Section 2 briefly surveys the researches in terms of route search algorithms using GA and dedicated GA hardware. Section 3 explains the base route planning algorithm in the car navigation system. Section 4 discusses dedicated hardware of the proposed car navigation system. Section 5 reports the experiments, and Section 6 summarizes and concludes the chapter.

RELATED STUDIES

Kanoh, *et al*. (2000) and Chakraborty, *et al.* (2005) have studied a route search using a GA. Kanoh *et al.*(2000) introduced virus operators into a route search, and created a route search algorithm that includes unspecified stopover points. They proved its validity by evaluative experiments. Chakraborty, *et al.*(2005) proposed a multi-objective route search algorithm containing a shortest route search and minimum turning. However, these studies of a route search using a GA were always based on software processing.

On the other hand, examples of dedicated hardware for a GA have been reported by Imai, *et al.* (2002) and Scott, *et al.* (1995). Imai *et al.*(2002) created the architecture of a parallel GA and, by estimating the number of processing steps, they expected high-speed processing to be realized in the dedicated hardware. The dedicated hardware's processing speed could be several dozen times faster than that of software. Scott *et al.* (1995) developed a hardware-based GA and demonstrated its superiority to software in speed and solution quality.

However, these studies of dedicated hardware aimed to solve small and simple problems, and no studies have been reported on practical problems such as a car navigation system. Thus, car navigation systems using dedicated hardware for a GA, which enable two types of route searches, have not been studied.

ROUTE SEARCH ALGORITHM

This chapter proposes a route search algorithm using a GA as the basic algorithm, and aimed to realize the following two route searches: (1) a route search including unspecified stopover points, and (2) a route search for traveling through sightseeing spots.

Route Search Including Unspecified Stopover Points

Regarding a route search including unspecified stopover points (transit points), a route starting at a house, stopping at a post and gas station, and reaching a company is proposed as a concrete example. In this case, multiple posts and gas stations exist, and the post and gas station to stop at are not necessarily specified. Moreover, the order of stopover points is not predetermined; that is, either from a post to a gas station or from a gas station to a post is allowed. In this route search, the specific stopover point is selected from multiple stopover points (multiple posts or gas stations existed). Simultaneously, the shortest route is obtained from the starting point to the final destination via the selected stopover points. Hereinafter, this route search is referred to as the stopover mode. The stopover mode's concrete processing procedure is shown in Figure 1, where the part enclosed by the solid line expresses the processing flow of the stopover mode. It is described below.

First, an initial individual group (population) is generated in the initialization. Generally, an individual expresses a solution in a GA. In the proposed technique's method of coding individuals, an individual consists of the stopover points, which are arranged in the travel order. Figure 2 shows an example of coding.

Next, crossover processing is performed on two arbitrarily selected individuals, and the individual with the lower evaluation value is eliminated. Here, each individual is evaluated based on the travel route including stopover points, and the Manhattan distance between these points is used to approximate the distance between the stopover points. Regarding the crossover, a crossover developed based on a one-point crossover and another developed based on a uniform crossover, are both changed over appropriately. Here, the former is called the modified one-point crossover and the latter is called the modified uniform crossover. Figures 3 and 4 show examples of the

Figure 1. Example of the stopover mode's processing procedure

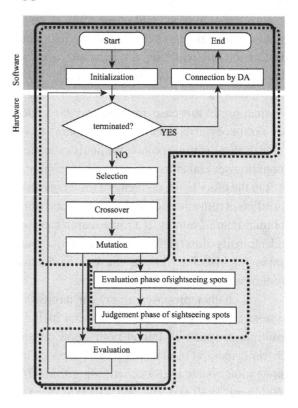

Figure 2. Example of coding

Post (P) : $P_{(1)}, P_{(2)}, \dots, P_{(i)}$

Coffee shop (C) : $C_{(1)}, C_{(2)}, \dots, C_{(j)}$

Gas station (G) : $G_{(1)}, G_{(2)}, \dots, G_{(k)}$

(1) Candidates

| Locus | 1 | 2 | 3 |

Gene $\{ P_{(2)}, G_{(5)}, C_{(1)} \}$

(2) Individual

Figure 3. Example of the modified one-point crossover

Parent (A) $\{ G_{(2)}, P_{(2)}, C_{(3)} \}$

Parent (B) $\{ P_{(1)}, G_{(1)}, C_{(2)} \}$

↓ Selected (P)

Child (a) $\{ G_{(2)}, \boxed{P_{(1)}}, C_{(3)} \}$

Child (b) $\{ \boxed{P_{(2)}}, G_{(1)}, C_{(2)} \}$

Figure 4. Example of the modified uniform crossover

Figure 4. Example of the modified uniform crossover

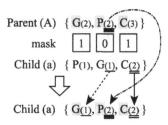

modified one-point and the modified uniform crossovers, respectively.

In the modified one-point crossover, a new individual is generated by exchanging a stopover point for another stopover point of the same type. In other words, the type of stopover point is selected first, and two stopover points corresponding to the selected type between two parent individuals are exchanged. Consequently, two new individuals are generated. In Figure 3, a post is selected; and exchanging post (2) in parent (A) for post (1) in parent (B) generated children (a) and (b).

In the modified uniform crossover, a parent individual is denoted as the standard individual (parent (A)), and child (a), which inheriting the standard individual's travel order of stopover points, is generated. Specifically, the mask pattern 0/1 is arbitrarily generated first. Then, in the part where the mask pattern is 0, the standard individual's gene is inherited. In the part where the

mask pattern is 1, the gene of the stopover point of the same type is inherited by the other parent individual (parent individual (B)). In Figure 4, because the mask pattern is 101, the gas station that is the first stopover point (transit point) inherits the gas station of parent (B), which is gas station (1). Moreover, because the mask pattern of the post, which is the next transit point, is 0, it inherits post (2) of the standard individual. Furthermore, because the mask pattern of the coffee shop, which is the final transit point, is 1, it inherits coffee shop (2) of parent (B). Regarding child (b), genes that are not used by child (a) are inherited in the genetic order of the other parent, which is not the standard individual.

The proposed algorithm employed modified uniform crossover in early generations (initial stages of the search), in order to perform a global search mainly. Then the modified one-point crossover is employed as a local search in order to search for vicinity of optimal solutions after several generations have passed. Figure 5 shows an example of changing over these crossovers. In this figure, the vertical axis represents fitness (travel route) and the horizontal axis represents the number of generation.

Two types of mutation are also introduced into the proposed algorithm. One is a mutation in which the two stopover points' order is swapped (hereinafter, swap mutation), and the other is a mutation in which a stopover point is exchanged

Figure 5. Example of changing over two crossovers

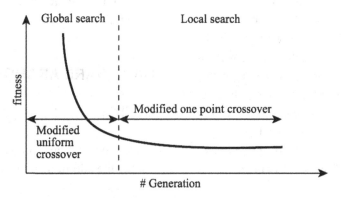

Figure 6. Examples of swap mutation

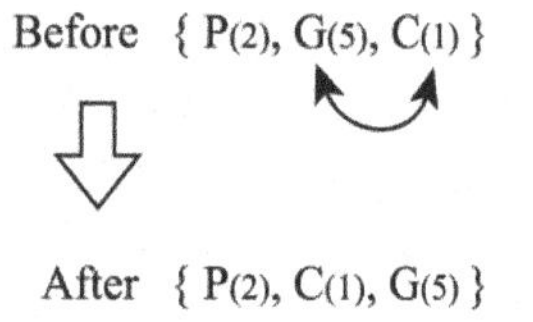

Before { P(2), G(5), C(1) }

⇩

After { P(2), C(1), G(5) }

Figure 7. Example of exchange mutation

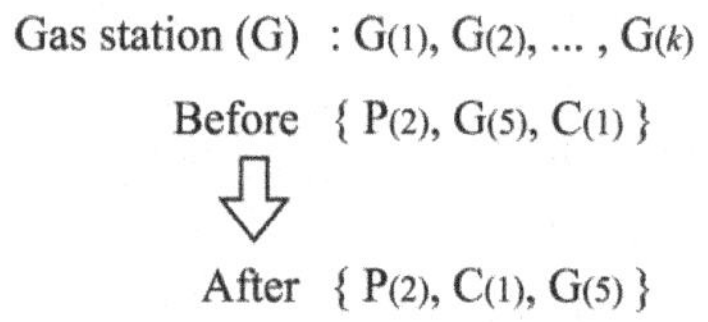

Gas station (G) : G(1), G(2), ... , G(k)

Before { P(2), G(5), C(1) }

⇩

After { P(2), C(1), G(5) }

for another one of the same type (hereinafter, exchange mutation). Figures 6 and 7 show examples of swap and exchange mutations, respectively.

The proposed algorithm does not generate lethal genes during the operation of either crossover or mutation, when generating new individuals. In the stopover mode, the travel order of the stopover points is obtained by GA and the partial route between the stopover points is connected by using the DA; and subsequently, the final route is determined.

Route Search for Traveling Through Sightseeing Spots

As the preconditions of a route search for traveling through sightseeing spots, multiple sightseeing spots exist; and the sightseeing time (required sojourn time) and the recommendation level (value) are evaluated for each sightseeing spot.

This route search method obtains the route in such a way that the sum of the values is maximized within a predetermined time (restricted time). Hereinafter, this route search is referred to as the sightseeing mode. The concrete processing procedure of the sightseeing mode is shown in Figure 1, where the part enclosed by the dotted line expresses the processing flow of the sightseeing mode. For initialization, selection, evaluation, crossover, and mutation, the same processing as that of the stopover mode is employed. Moreover, the sightseeing spots in the sightseeing mode correspond to the stopover points in the stopover mode.

The sightseeing mode consists of two phases, an evaluation phase of the sightseeing spots and

a judgement phase of sightseeing spots. In the evaluation phase of the sightseeing spots, the sum of the values of sightseeing spots visited and the time required to travel through sightseeing spots are calculated. The time required to travel through sightseeing spots (necessary time) is the sum of the sightseeing time and the travel time. The travel time is calculated by adding a weight to the route's distance, so the travel time is in proportion to the distance required for the route to travel through sightseeing spots. In the judgement phase of sightseeing spots, the number of sightseeing spots is increased or decreased depending on the necessary time and the restricted time. When the necessary time calculated by evaluating sightseeing spots is within the restricted time, a sightseeing spot is arbitrarily added to the route. When the necessary time exceeds the restricted time, a sightseeing spot is arbitrarily removed. Figures 8 shows examples of adding and removing a sightseeing spot.

Moreover, the partial route between the stopover points is connected by using the DA, similar to the stopover mode. Hierarchically combining the GA and the DA can reduce a problem's scale, and two route searches can be performed, which have not been achieved by conventional car navigation systems.

HARDWARE ARCHITECTURE

Coding

In the proposed car navigation system, in order to enable the addition and removal of a sightseeing

Figure 8. Example of adding and removing a sightseeing spot

Value	12	5	8	10
Time	30	20	15	18
Name	Aquarium	Casino	Tower	Zoo

(1) Candidates

Before { Tower, Zoo, Aquarium } (Total time 63)

⇩

After { Tower, Casino, Zoo, Aquarium } (Total time 83)

(2) Addition

Before { Tower, Casino, Zoo, Aquarium } (Total time 83)

⇩

After { Casino, Zoo, Aquarium } (Total time 68)

(3) Deletion

spot, the variable-length list structure is employed as the genetic structure. Figure 9 shows a coding example in the hardware.

The proposed architecture treats an individual as data 24 bits wide and 64 bits long. Of the initial 24 bits, 8 bits are assigned to identify the data, 8 bits are assigned to the individual number, and 8 bits are assigned to the individual's length (the length of the data). Of the next 24 bits, 8 bits are assigned to the sum of the values and 16 bits are assigned to the sum of the costs.

Here, the sum of the values is used only in the sightseeing mode. The sum of the costs stores the travel route in the stopover mode, and it stores the sum of the travel route and the values of the sightseeing spots in the sightseeing mode. Then 24 bits are assigned to hold the information on either the stopover point or the sightseeing spot. Here, 6 bits are assigned to the number of the stopover point (or the sightseeing spot), 4 bits are assigned to the type of the stopover point, 6 bits are assigned to the sightseeing time, and 8 bits are assigned to the value of the sightseeing spot. However, the information on sightseeing time and the value of the sightseeing spot is not used in the stopover mode. On the contrary, the

Figure 9. Example of a coding in the hardware

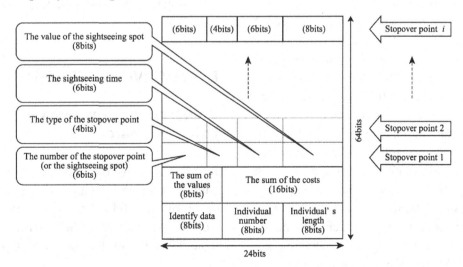

Figure 10. The proposed car navigation system

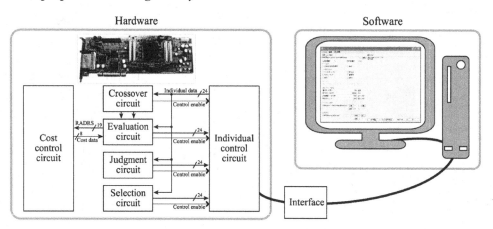

information on the type of stopover point is not used in the sightseeing mode.

Circuit Configuration

Figure 10 shows the proposed car navigation system. The dedicated hardware of which consists of the individual control circuit, the evaluation circuit, the selection circuit, the crossover circuit, the judgement circuit, and the interface.

The concrete processing flow of the proposed car navigation system can be explained as follows:

1. Initial individuals are generated by a PC (software processing).
2. The initial population (individual group) generated is stored in the internal memory of the individual control circuit through the interface circuit. This internal memory holds the data of all the individuals. Therefore, the individual control circuit controls not only the reading and writing of the individual, but also the generation of the population.
3. The parameters are also sent to each circuit through the interface circuit.
4. In the stopover mode, the individual is read from the individual control circuit; and the crossover, mutation, and evaluation are repeatedly performed. The crossover and

mutation are performed in the crossover circuit.

5. In the sightseeing mode, a sightseeing spot is added (removed) after performing the crossover and mutation, and then evaluation is performed. The judgement about the necessary time and restricted time required for the addition/removal of a sightseeing spot, is performed in the judgement circuit.
6. When both modes satisfy the termination conditions, the individual with the highest evaluation value (elite individual) is sent to the PC.
7. The PC calculates each partial route between stopover points (sightseeing spots) using the DA.

EVALUATIVE EXPERIMENTS

Comparative Experiments Using Software

In order to verify the route search algorithm's validity, comparative experiments are performed using software. Table 1 shows the information of stopover points used in the experiments. In this table, "6 types * 30" for the type of stopover point means that each stopover point is classified as one of 6 types, and each type has 30 stopover points.

First, in order to verify the proposed crossover technique's validity, comparative experiments are performed using the following four types of crossover methods: (1) modified one-point crossover, (2) modified uniform crossover, (3) from the modified one-point crossover to the modified uniform crossover, and (4) from the modified uniform crossover to the one-point crossover. Here, (3) and (4) are the crossover methods in which crossovers are changed over after a certain number of generations have passed, and (4) is the proposed technique. Table 2 shows the experimental results. All experiments uses data of 6 types * 30, and these are performed 10 times. As this table shows, the proposed technique shows the highest performance.

Next, in order to evaluate the stopover mode, three cases are compared; the starting point and final destination are the same in all cases, but two cases have stopover points and the other does not. Table 3 shows the experimental results.

Compared to the case without stopover points, the travel route length increased by only 0.8% and 3.2% in the cases with three and six types of stopover points, respectively. Therefore, the proposed algorithm enables a route search for traveling through stopover points without taking a roundabout way.

Comparative Experiments Using Hardware

In order to verify the proposed hardware's validity, it is described by Verilog-HDL and implemented on the FPGA (Xilinx Virtex-II). The clock frequency is 33MHz. Table 4 shows the proposed hardware's circuit scale.

First, in order to verify the hardware's performance, it is compared with software. The software processing run on a PC (CPU: Pentium IV 2.66GHz, Memory 1Gbyte). Table 5 shows the comparison results of run time.

Table 1. Information of stopover points

Data	Types of stopover points
3 types * 30	Coffee shop, Convenience store, Gas station
6 types * 30	Coffee shop, Convenience store, Gas station, Post, Bank,, Hospital

Table 2. Experimental results to evaluate the proposed crossover technique

Crossover method	Best (The shortest travel route length)	Average of 10 times
(1)	12548	12548
(2)	12643	13237
(3)	12296	13121
(4) Proposed	12256	12844

Table 3. Experimental results to evaluate the stopover mode

Case	Data	The travel route length
(1)	Without stopover points	12005
(2)	3 types * 30	12105
(3)	6 types * 30	12393

Table 4. Circuit scale

Name of block	Used	Available	Utilization
# slices	27709	33792	82%
# 4 input LUTs	21828	67584	32%
# bounded IOBs	39	1104	35%
# TBUFs	116	16896	1%
# BRAMs	1	144	0%
# GCLKs	1	16	6%

Table 5. Comparison results of run time

Data	Software [sec]	Hardware [sec]	Improvement (times)
3 types * 30	6.0	2.6	2.6
6 types * 30	8.1	4.0	2.0

Table 6. Communication overheads of software and hardware

Data	Communication time [sec]
3 types * 30	$1.47 * 10^{-2}$
6 types * 30	$8.07 * 10^{-2}$

Next, the communication time is measured in order to verify the communication overheads of software and hardware. Table 6 shows the measurement results.

As shown in Tables 5 and 6, even if the communication overhead result, the processing speed in the hardware is faster than that in the software. Moreover, although this experiment used an operating frequency of 33 MHz because of the FPGA's restrictions, if a faster FPGA or an application-specific integrated circuit (ASIC) are used, the processing speed becomes faster.

Figures 11, 12, and 13 show the routes obtained by the proposed architecture. Figures 11 and 12 show the results obtained by the stopover mode. Figure 13 shows the results obtained by the sightseeing mode. As shown in these figures, each route search of the stopover and sightseeing modes is effective.

CONCLUSION

This chapter proposed a new car navigational system based on a GA. The proposed car navigation system realized two route searches, a route search including unspecified stopover points and a route search for traveling through sightseeing spots and considering sightseeing time. Moreover, in order to solve the GA's processing time problem, dedicated hardware is newly introduced, consequently realizing high-speed processing. Furthermore,

Figure 11. Routing result with three kinds of the stopover points

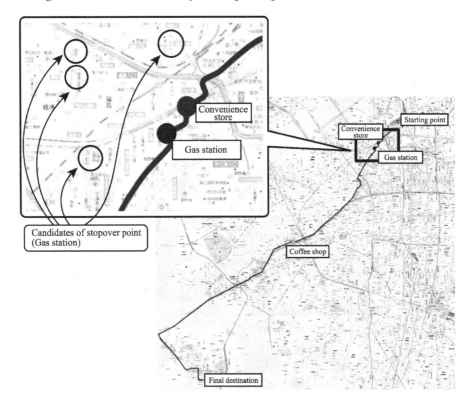

Figure 12. Routing result with six kinds of the stopover points

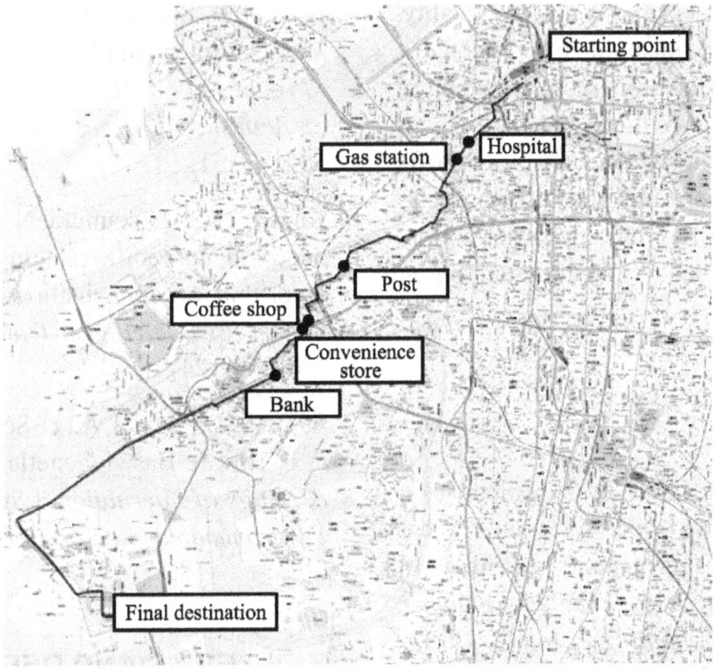

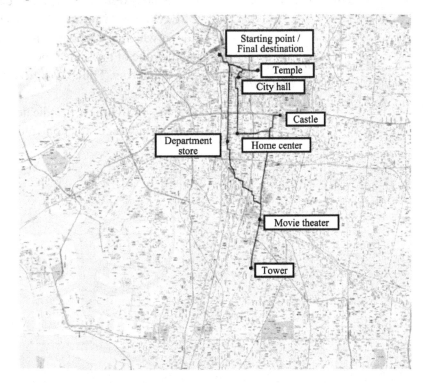

Figure 13. Routing result of the sightseeing mode

implementing the proposed car navigation system to the FPGA verified its validity and practicality.

Our future work is to incorporate traffic congestion information into the proposed car navigation system. Achieving this requires developing both a route search technique that considers traffic congestion information, and dedicated hardware that can cope with traffic congestion information, which changes minute by minute (changing at very short intervals).

REFERENCES

Chakraborty, B., Maeda, T., & Chakraborty, G. (2005). Multiobjective route selection for car navigation system using genetic algorithm. In *Proceedings of the 2005 IEEE Mid-Summer Workshop on Soft Computing in Industrial Applications* (pp.190-195).

Fujita, Y., Nakamura, Y., & Shiller, Z. (2203). Dual Dijkstra Search for paths with different topologies. In *Proceedings of IEEE International Conference on Robotics and Automation* (Vol. 3, pp. 3359-3364).

Goldberg, D. E. (1989). *Genetic algorithms in search optimization, and machine learning. Addison Wesley. Holland, J. (1992). Adaptation in Natural Artificial Systems*. Cambridge, MA: MIT Press.

Imai, T., Yoshikawa, M., Terai, H., & Yamauchi, H. (2002). Scalable GA-Processor Architecture and Its Implementation of Processor Element. In . *Proceedings of IEEE International Conference on Acoustics, Speech, and Signal Processing, 3*, 3148–3151.

Kanoh, H., & Nakamura, N. (2000). Route guidance with unspecified staging posts using genetic algorithm for car navigation systems. In *Proceedings of IEEE Intelligent Transportation Systems*, (pp. 119-124).

Scott, S. D., Samal, A., & Seth, S. (1995). HGA: A Hardware-Based Genetic Algorithm. In *Proceedings of International Symposium on Field-Programmable Gate Array* (pp. 53-59).

KEY TERMS AND DEFINITIONS

Stopover Point: It indicates transit point such as coffee shop, gas station, and mail box.

Swap Mutation: It indicates a mutation in which the two stopover points' order is swapped.

Exchange Mutation: It indicates is a mutation in which a stopover point is exchanged for another one of the same type.

Sightseeing Time: It indicates the required sojourn time.

Elite Individual: It indicates the individual with the highest evaluation value.

Chapter 12

Process–Oriented Information Modeling and Exchange Paradigm for the Support of Complex after Sales Services with Mobile Technologies:
A Case Study in the German Machine and Plant Construction Industry

Nadine Blinn
Hamburg University, Germany

Markus Nüttgens
Hamburg University, Germany

Thorsten Dollmann
German Research Center for Artificial Intelligence (DFKI) Saarland University, Germany

Oliver Thomas
University of Osnabrueck, Germany

Peter Loos
German Research Center for Artificial Intelligence (DFKI) Saarland University, Germany

Michael Schlicker
INTERACTIVE Software Solutions GmbH, Germany

ABSTRACT

As technical products become more complex, the related technical customer services also do. The required information to accomplish technical customer services are dynamic, complex and at the same time business critical for the success of the services. This chapter deals with the process-oriented integration of product development and service documentation for the support of technical customer services (TCS) in

DOI: 10.4018/978-1-61520-819-7.ch012

machine and plant construction, illustrated on the example of the heating, air conditioning and sanitary engineering (HAS) branch. Both using mobile application systems and creating a product service system can increase the efficiency of procedures in service provision. The development and provision of the product service system calls for an interdisciplinary perspective. The problem, as well as the solution on the basis of hybrid added value, the structure of the product service system, the IT-concept and the implementation of the service process modeling will be discussed in detail in this article. In conclusion, the concept presented here will be explained in a practical use case.

INTRODUCTION

Problem and Challenges

Value-added partnerships in the machine and plant construction industry are an established tool for reducing costs and increasing efficiency. They are especially used in areas of branches where customer service is provided for serially produced products over a large geographical area. A separation of tasks occurs here between manufacturers and independent customer service organizations. They also act as resellers and represent the only contact to the customer (multi-level distribution channel). However, today breaches in the flow of information still accompany the division of tasks along the value-added chain. This separates product and product-related services and thus, leaves enormous improvement potential unrealized.

With approximately 965,000 employees, the machine and plant construction industry is the largest industry in Germany (VDMA, 2008). Today, companies address the increasing competition in this field by way of customer retention. The manufacturers' central aspect here is the expansion and improvement of their service offers, especially in technical customer services (TCS), which can be seen as the interface between the production and the use of the products (Bolumole et al., 2006; Czepiel, 1980; Harris, 2007; LaLonde, 1976; Peel, 1987; Sterling & Lambert, 1989). The manufacturers own service organizations are not the only ones acting in this branch, but also outsourced small and medium-sized enterprises and trade and repair businesses, which carry out inspections and maintenance work needed within

the product's life cycle (Willerding, 1987). To adequately fulfill the tasks connected with these services, a technical customer service team must be provided with the right "mix of information". The central problem here is to determine the scope, moment and detailing of the decision-relevant information (Sawy & Bowles, 2003; Timm, 2005). Current approaches for the support of TCS often fail due to the increased complexity of the machines and the need for the representation of service processes connected with this. The result is faulty start-up, maintenance and repair work and thus, extended machine down times, which, in the end, result in higher costs for the customer and market deficits for the manufacturer.

The field of heating, air conditioning and sanitary engineering (HAS) is ideal for achieving trend-setting research results in regard to the problem, objective and approach. On the one hand, manufacturers in this field produce sophisticated, technically complex products, and on the other hand, TCS is carried out, for the most part, by trade and repair businesses and service organizations from the HAS trade (Hoppe & Sander, 1996) (cp. Figure 1). The diversity of maintenance objects from the HAS branch confronts the TCS to very different challenges, for example, the repair of defective cisterns or the repair of operational faults within complex heat generation plants (Bundesinstitut für Berufsbildung, 2004; Haines, 2006; MacQuiston, 2005). Different challenges for the technical customer services in the HAS branch are seen by the manufacturer, the trade and repair businesses and the customer service technicians. Products from the HAS branch are provided to the market predominately through the approximately

Figure 1. Status quo of the value-added chain in the HAS branch

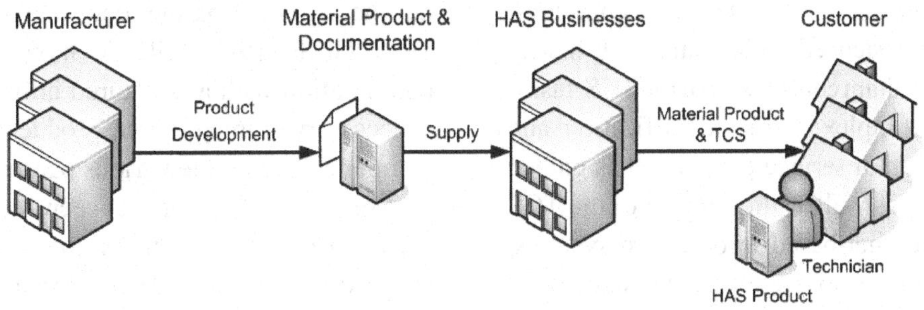

50,000 specialized HAS enterprises and their approximately 300,000 employees in Germany. The TCS is rendered by the manufacturer's customer service team or service partners selected by the manufacturer or specialized HAS enterprises (Hoppe & Sander, 1996; Willerding, 1987). The challenge for manufacturers in the field of TCS consists in communicating repair and product knowledge to the respective customer service organizations. Thus, training is provided for customer service technicians, telephone support set up for carrying out repairs via call centers and technical documents are made available, whether in paper or electronic form, for example on CD-ROM. For manufacturers, this challenge is extremely time-consuming with regard to the provision and transfer of this knowledge. Thus, in some businesses, more and more jobs for consultants are being created, in order to manage the increasing demand for repair information. Despite these high expenses on the part of the manufacturers, many mistakes are still made by the TCS. On the one hand, the defective maintenance and repair work results in extra costs for the manufacturer for additional services (for example: warranties, guarantees, goodwill) that cannot be allocated to the customer. And on the other hand, the manufacturer runs the risk of losing important market shares due to customer dissatisfaction.

HAS trade and repair businesses must also differentiate themselves from their competitors, keep existing customers and win new customers

(MacQuiston, 2005). This takes place more and more over the TCS. The challenge for HAS businesses in the field of TCS is that they must use products from different manufacturers and filter out the right information for certain repair situations from the abundance of information provided by manufacturers (Howell et al., 2005) (cp. Figure 1). It is not only difficult, but also cost-intensive for the trade and repair businesses to balance out the wide-range of knowledge from the customer service technicians, transfer this information to adequate repair tasks and compensate for the loss of knowledge in a company due to the retirement of experienced employees. In analogy to the argumentation of the manufacturer's perspective, extra costs also result for the HAS businesses from additional customer service assignments.

The way the HAS trade works has changed from the function-oriented division of labor to a more process-oriented view. The entire customer order process has become a main focus – especially in TCS. The customer service technician renders his services more or less "solo", on location; i. e., he is responsible for carrying out his work correctly and identifying and procuring the spare parts required. The successful execution of the repair – and with it, the economic success of the HAS company – is considerably affected by the effectiveness and efficiency of the work done. The main problem for the customer service technicians is however, the large number of manufacturers and products to be serviced. Even experienced customer service technicians, let alone inexperienced technicians, can hardly manage the resultant complexity of the TCS-tasks. Due to this complexity, the identification and optimum design of service processes has gained in importance, as well as the support of the TCS by mobile, internet-based information systems, which allow the customer service technicians to access the most current service information at any time and at any place (Isaac & Leclerq, 2006).

Background

Bundles of physical products and services are being seen more and more in an integrated manner (Engelhardt et al., 1993; Eppen et al., 1991; Freiden et al., 1998; Herrmann et al.; Ovans, 1997; Shostack, 1977). In doing so, the different scientific disciplines focus on diverse aspects and accordingly, use their own terminology. Thus for example, in business literature, there are the terms 'compack' (complex package) (Bressand et al., 1989), 'service system' (Haischer et al., 2001; Kingman Brundage, 1989; Tax & Stuart, 1997) and 'servitization' (Vandermerwe & Rada, 2007) – in addition to the already mentioned 'bundle'. In engineering the terms 'covalent product' (Weber et al.; 2002) 'servicification' or 'post mass production paradigm' (Sakao & Shimomura, 2007; Tomiyama, 2002) are used. In information systems research the term 'hybrid product' has established (Botta & Thomas, 2002; Karapidis, 2005; Pahl, 2007; Thomas et al., 2007; Vonderembse et al., 2006). The term 'product-service system' (PSS) was coined by the field of engineering science (Evans et al., 2007; Krucken & Meroni, 2006; Manzini et al., 2001; Mont, 2004; Morelli, 2002; Sterling & Lambert, 1989). Important for this article is the fact that bundles of products and services are often not put together by a single company, but rather divided up and offered by several partners in a value-added network. Such value-added networks are already the topic of a large number of scientific studies, especially under the aspect of partner coordination (Castells, 1996; Jarillo, 1988; Miles & Snow, 1978). Tight coordination with a structured information flow is necessary to integrate the products and service components from the various partners.

Mutual cooperation between the companies active in the steps of the value-added chain is referred to as a value-added partnership. It is a vertical cooperation generally established for a longer period of time (e.g. Lapiedra et al., 2004). The cooperation partners are not linked institutionally, but rather act and decide independently for the partnership. However, a value-added partnership goes beyond a vertical cooperation in so far as the coordination of the cross-company service provision is planned and organized by all of the partners together. This gives the outward impression of a self-contained competitive unit.

Up to now, value-added partnerships in the machine and plant construction industry have been studied under the aspect of supply chain management (SCM) as supply cooperation between manufacturers and their subcontractors (Lambert, 2006; Vomderembse et al., 2006). Through strategies such as Efficient Consumer Response (ECR) and measures like CRP (Continuous Replenishment), JMI (Jointly Managed Inventory) or CPFR (Collaborative Planning, Forecasting and Replenishment) reductions in production costs should be achieved and passed on to the customer, in order to use the price to differentiate oneself from competitors. Approaches to value-added partnerships on the sales side however, often make the customer a value-added partner, for example within the framework of customer integration and customer participation especially in the area of service provision. The customer's ability to provide the sub-services outsourced to him can however, not be assumed in the case of technical customer services: the customer needs a complete solution made up of technical services, as well as product-related customer services (Czepiel, 1980; Harris, 2007; LaLonde, 1976; Peel, 1987; Sterling

& Lambert, 1989). It is the reselling customer service organization that defines the degree of integration of this product-service system.

Currently, many new business models for promoting the integration of production and customer service with the end customer as the focus are being created. While for example, classic models assume that the end customer buys the product and customer service separately, the investment risk resulting from unplanned malfunctions and failures is met by build-operate-transfer models. However, all of the approaches can be classified under two mainstreams ("Make-or-Buy") with regard to the value-added chain: in a single-level distribution channel the manufacturer himself operates his or her own regionally limited or worldwide service networks and organizes the corresponding service products and provision himself; in a multi-level distribution channel the manufacturer cooperates with product-independent customer service providers without a nation or worldwide service network. At the same time, these customer service providers act as technical customer service providers, consultants and resellers for the customer.

HYBRID ADDED VALUE AS A STIMULUS FOR INNOVATION

Approach

The main idea of this approach is to increase efficiency for the TCS in machine and plant construction. To do so, a methodology for the development of product service systems was developed based on the integrated process-oriented examination of product development and service documentation and such a product service system was prototypically implemented using the HAS branch as an example. The research results can be generally applied to the machine and plant construction industry and allow the "hybridization" of existing, as well as future technical products.

The technical products of the machine and plant construction industry and their documentation are the material components of the product service system. Existing or future technical plants become product service systems by realizing services for the development, provision, use and revision of integrated service process descriptions, which cover the complete life cycle of the service process documentation. In addition, an information system must allow the cost-efficient collection and modeling of relevant service information at the manufacturers. Service organizations should be able to access this information mobile. Two important implications of the approach described above are:

- Through the integrated design of a new product service system, TCS-requirements for the customer-oriented start-up, maintenance and repair of machines and plants can be guaranteed and the efficiency of procedures in the TCS increased.
- By coupling product development, documentation, TCS, process consulting and modern information technology at an early stage, product service systems are created, which for the first time, describe the life cycle of integrated process-oriented product and service information at the manufacturers with justifiable expenses and effort.

The scenario in Figure 2 shows the result of the PIPE project for hybrid added value in machine and plant construction. It can be seen as an extension of the status quo for the value-added chain in the HAS branch. There are two cycles which contribute to the continual improvement of the product service system and in doing so, first to the improvement of product development on the part of the manufacturer and second, to the improvement of service offers on the part of HAS businesses (cp. Figure 2). The first cycle exists between the design process of the new product

Figure 2. Hybrid added value with the PIPE concept

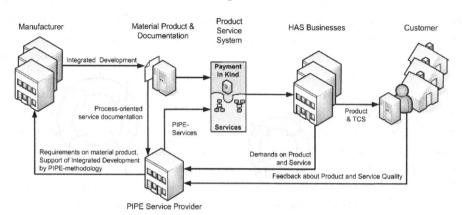

service system by the PIPE service provider and both of the feedback processes from the HAS businesses (cp. Figure 2, right). The feedback relates on the one hand, to the requirements of the HAS businesses to the components of the product service systems and, on the other hand, to the evaluation of the actual quality of the components rendered by the HAS businesses using the product service system, which is additionally evaluated by the end customer.

The second cycle exists between the manufacturers and the PIPE service provider, to whom the manufacturers send the documentation of the plants, as well as basic information pertaining to service processes (cp. Figure 2, left). In the opposite direction, the PIPE service provider first passes on feedback from the HAS businesses to the manufacturer and second, supports the product development on the manufacturer's side using the PIPE methodology. This results in the process-oriented integration of product development and service documentation, which can be used to improve the TCS in machine and plant construction.

Structure of the Product Service System

The product service system to be created consists of several service components in addition to

the material components (for example: heating systems). These are thematically centered on the service documentation and divided up into four sections:

- The first section comprises all of the services connected with the service process modeling: the development of a modeling method, the creation of the actual service process models according to this method and tests for the quality assurance of these models.

- The second section focuses on the application of the service process models, especially the mobile use, and thus provision of mobile services for the TCS. This means their provision for online-access via a network, as well as their offline-access via a stand-alone application on CD-ROM, for example for situations where network access is not available at the maintenance site. The transfer of service process models comprises, in   addition to transporting information, their suitable conversion – the display of a PDA for example requires a higher reduction level of information as a desktop PC. A request-response-protocol is also conceivable. Thus, one could only transfer the parts of the required process and so, response times are shorter than those for transferring an entire model. Altogether, technical implementation details are highly dependent both on user preferences and the technological platform, so only principal restrictions are taken into account for design decisions at this early stage of development, for example smaller screens and less computing power in handhelds compared to laptops or even stationary computers, or lower bandwidth but higher on-site availability of mobile internet access via GPRS, EDGE or UMTS.

- The third section comprises the controlling of the service processes. The goal here is to reveal room for improvement in service processes and identify construction-related weaknesses in the technical plant itself (an indication for such a weak spot is for example, an accumulation of repairs on a certain assembly group). The basis for the controlling is an assessment scheme, which gives TCS-employees structured feedback that can be integrated into the product life cycle of the plant and the process life cycle of the service process.

- The fourth section addresses the economical benefit of the service processes by developing and maintaining a business model with several components. Its core is a cooperation model that outlines the economic interaction of the participating parties, for example HAS manufacturers, TCS organizations and their technician service process model developers, and the portal provider who runs the central service process repository. In doing so, the business model accommodates their economical interests. Further components are the identification of an adaptation to new forms of applications for the service process models (for example: their use in training programs), as well as the provision of tools for marketing. Moreover the increased amount of information which is available about each piece of the attended HAS equipment could allow for a more precise prediction of failures or a more detailed planning of necessary maintenance work to avoid failures. Thus the total cost of ownership of HAS equipment could be calculated more precisely, allowing for comprehensive product-service bundles ("warm dwelling") which could be offered at reasonable prices to the customers instead of separate product and service ("heating and TCS when necessary"), where at least amount and costs of service are rather difficult to predict.

This hybrid approach emphasizes the interdisciplinary component of the PIPE project and combines different topics with each other in an innovative fashion. The business process modeling acts as the methodological basis of the service process modeling. The technical product development represents the basis of the service process models with regards to content. The field of research for mobile application systems is closely connected to the mobile application and controlling of service process models by the TCS on site. The schema of the hybrid added value is especially reflected in the connection of the product and service process life cycles.

IT-Design

The PIPE system-architecture displayed in Figure 3 is the basis for the use of process modeling for mobile application systems in the field of technical customer services. It supports the creation, provision and controlling of the immaterial outputs in the product service system.

The service process models and services connected with this, such as the creation, maintenance, application and controlling are the focus of the product service system. The architecture's core is a repository for service process descriptions and links to connected master data (for example:

Figure 3. PIPE system architecture

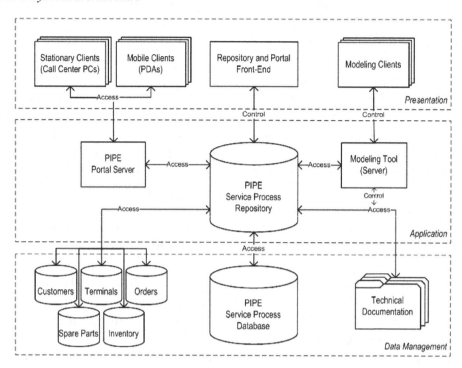

customers, devices, parts etc.), as well as technical documentation available in unstructured form (for example, in the form of PDF-files). This repository combines the heterogeneous data sources in a process-oriented view and thus, establishes the technical foundation for the services outlined in Section Structure of the product service system.

Other components, set around the repository, support the execution of the PIPE services. The creation and maintenance of models in the repository is locally realized over a client-server-application, which allows several model developers to access the central modeling server over their respective clients at the same time. The modeling server supports the concurrency of different modeling processes by controlling the simultaneous access to resources by locking and unlocking. The bonding of technical documents in the models is also controlled by the modeling system.

Application and controlling are supported over a portal server with the various clients, mobile or

stationary access. Through this, the portal server takes over the communication with the clients in two directions. From the repository to the client, a search mechanism is implemented in the portal server that allows a client to search and select a service process model. Then the selected model is converted according to the client's requirements and transported to the client by the portal server. The service process is then visualized and interactively supported by the client. In the other direction, from the client to the repository, the portal server receives controlling data from the client and integrates it into the repository. The repository and the portal server are configured and controlled over an integrated front-end.

Implementation and Realization

This section deals with the technical implementation of the introduced concepts. We will focus on the service processes, which constitute the core of the hybrid approach and thus, that of the system

Figure 4. Modeling technical plants with functions and service processes

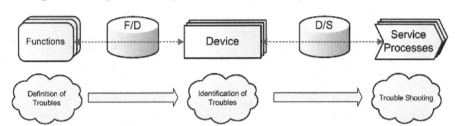

architecture. In the following, the structuring of the service processes and their placement in the total concept will be emphasized.

The main idea of the service process modeling, on which the PIPE approach is based, is the differentiation between function, assembly and service processes in technical plants. The functions, as well as the service processes of a technical plant are directly connected with their assembly. Figure 4 shows how this connection is represented and used in PIPE by defining the malfunction on the basis of the function structure, identifying the assembly groups relevant for the fulfillment of the function and recommending the appropriate service processes.

Functions. The modeling of functions in a technical plant is the basis for the definition of malfunctions, defined as "function failures". Unlike the definitions of possible malfunctions, the functions of a technical plant can be specified and – as discussed in detail in the next section – assigned to technical assembly groups, which are ultimately the center of reference for the work done by the TCS teams.

The modeling of a function of a technical plant in process logic is not aim leading. The identification of a malfunction in the process flow of the plant may help in organizing the diagnostic steps ("from front to back along the water conduit"), it is however, not relevant for the definition of the malfunction (the organization of the diagnostic steps is recommended to the user by the PIPE system, on the basis of, for example, the empirically calculated failure probability of the individual

functions or the respective cost estimates.). It makes more sense to classify functions and assign their respective sub-functions. This allows a localization of the malfunction efficiently and by doing so, narrow down the general malfunction of the function "heat water" to the sub-functions "operate burner" and "burn heating oil". The diagnosis of the malfunction is thus simplified by specifying a few, clearly defined alternatives, which are, in addition, easy to verify ("Heating output reduced", "Development of smoke").

Assembly groups: The technical arrangement of the plant into different assembly groups is followed by the functional arrangement (cp. Figure 5, right). It results from the technical product development, where first, simple component parts are manufactured and then put together in several steps to form more complicated assembly groups (the technical arrangement of a product can be seen as a given in industrial manufacturing, because for example, the disposing of materials takes place over the respective parts lists).

The connection of assembly groups with functions takes place on the basis of technical task sharing – an assembly group is assigned to the functions it is necessary for. The objective here is to identify the assembly groups that come into question as a cause for the malfunction. This results in a m:n-relationship between assembly groups and functions. The m:n-relations between functions and assembly groups are represented as 1:1-relations in Figure 5 due to reasons of clarity. In addition, a tree structure was used for the classification of functions and assembly groups.

Figure 5. Relations between assembly groups and service processes

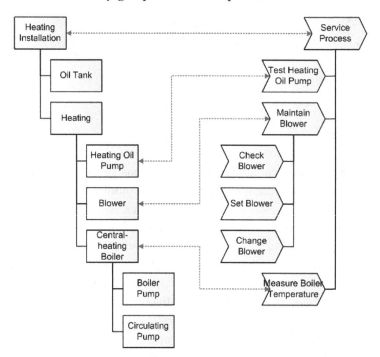

Other approaches are also conceivable here, for example m:n-relations between the functions resp. assembly groups.

Service processes: The objective of the malfunction diagnosis is fault repair, which is achieved by executing service processes on the assembly groups of the technical plant. This is made possible by connecting service processes with assembly groups on different levels (cp. Figure 5). The combination of several assembly groups results in functions, which exceed the sum of the individual functions in an assembly group – a heater can, for example, heat water, which is something that none of its assembly groups can do alone. Analogue to this, new service processes result from the construction of assembly groups. These apply to the interaction of the individual components. Therefore, the hierarchical arrangement of service processes and sub-processes is also intended here, as described for example in (Scheer et al., 2005). The composition of an assembly group does not lead to the adoption of the processes of its components, but rather makes it possible to complement new processes.

If, with the structuring of functions described above, assembly groups as possible carriers of the malfunction are identified, measures for their repair can be selected and carried out via the connection with the service processes. In doing so, the linkage of assembly groups and processes is also represented as a m:n-relation. The existence of several service processes for an assembly group (1:n) is obvious, but it is also possible for a generic service process ("Turn off electricity") to be used on several assembly groups (m:1).

APPLICATION SCENARIO "HOT WATER IS NOT HOT"

In the following, a realistic mobile application scenario will illustrate the approach represented above. The scenario describes a malfunction in a heating device for hot water, which is found to be faulty on site, at the customers. The starting point for the scenario is the fault "Hot water is not hot", i. e. there is a malfunction in the device that affects its functioning so that the water in the device is not heated as intended (the scenario is based on a heating device of a nameable German manufacturer). The processing of this repair procedure makes high demands on the TCS, because almost any part of the heating system could be the cause of the problem. This scenario is therefore ideally suited for demonstrating the general feasibility of the approach described in the third section. In addition, we will outline in the following how the PIPE system architecture from section IT-design and the implementation in section implementation and realization are used in the application scenario.

Preparation for Troubleshooting

As a preparatory measure, the manufacturer must first make the necessary service process information for the faulty device available over the PIPE repository (cp. Figure 3). The function, product and service process structure (cp. section implementation and realization), as well as the service process models created using the modeling software and connected to the relevant technical documents (for example: spread sheets and exploded views) belong to the service information. The service process displayed in Figure 6 is the result of this scenario.

The event-driven process chain (EPC) is used as a modeling language here (Keller et al., 1992). The model has 28 functions on the top-most hierarchy level. Due to lack of space, Figure 6 only shows a section of the model. The model construction was based on the identification of the parts of the heating device, which could be the cause of the problem. Eight parts were identified and ordered depending on their processing order for repair. Each part was mapped to testing, as well as to testing and change-functions. Functions for

collecting general device and plant data, which could for example, allude to the registration of hot water leakage or the analysis of the flow pressure on a gas connection, were added to the repair process.

Troubleshooting

The guiding theme of the project PIPE is to help the TCS to repair the malfunction described above quickly and efficiently. To do this, the customer service technician receives a mobile terminal (PDA, notebook). Thus, he can access the service process repository via the PIPE portal server (cp. Figure 7). The troubleshooting is divided up into two phases: the identification of the device, as well as the diagnosis and repair of the malfunction.

Identification of the defective device. In step one, the customer service technician identifies the faulty device. This can take place mobile on-site, because device-specific documents must no longer be brought along for the preparation of the TCS-assignment. The TCS is given a library of service information via online-access to the PIPE repository. This dispenses with the time-consuming identification of the device by the customer via telephone or by the HAS business on the basis of old bills. In addition, service documents in paper form must no longer be managed, searched and transported. After the device type is identified it is taken up in the context of the dialogue with the PIPE server, so that only the information relevant for the device is automatically visible for all subsequent TCS operations.

Diagnosis and Troubleshooting. After identifying the device, its product, function and service process structure is made available to the customer service technician via his mobile terminal (cp. Figure 7). Now the diagnostic process for the malfunction begins as described in Section Implementation and Realization: the parts of the heating device eligible for causing the selected malfunction are identified based on the function that

Figure 6. EPC-Model "Troubleshooting: Hot water is not hot" (Section)

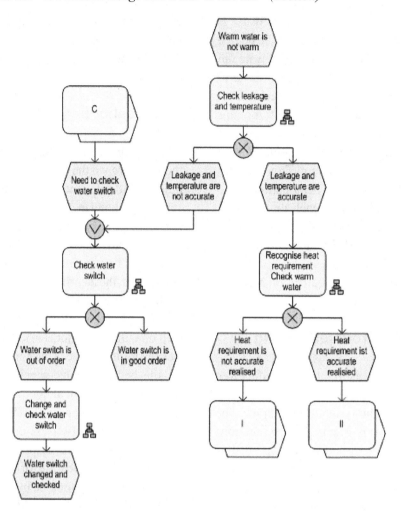

failed – this process is displayed in summarized form in Figure 6. The order of the diagnostic steps can, for example be determined dynamically by the empirical analysis of failure probability or the effort for the diagnostic steps. The customer service technician always has, however, the possibility to leave the recommended diagnostic procedure. This can, for example, be necessary if a malfunction in the system is not clearly mapped or not registered. In this case, no service process models are available, but technical documents can still be accessed for the individual assembly groups.

Post Processing the Troubleshooting

After the repair of the malfunction, an evaluation of the IT-support by the customer service technician is intended. Feedback won here is integrated into the repository via the PIPE portal server for example, through the constant maintenance of meta-data from the service process models. The manufacturer can later consult the aggregated feedback pertaining his devices to improve his service processes. If for example, the failure probability of a certain assembly group is significantly high, then a change in its construction can be considered.

Figure 7. Mobile application "Interactive Service Portal"

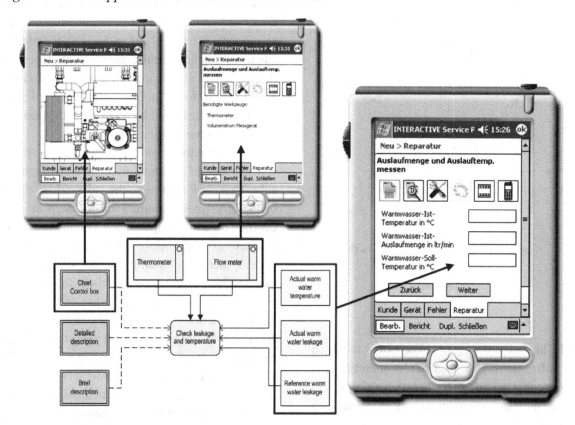

EVALUATION AND DISCUSSION

Attainable qualitative and quantitative benefits of the approach can be deduced from approaches evaluating the efficiency of IT investments (Mertens, 2006). They can be separated into cost reduction (personnel costs, communication costs), economy of time (throughput time, information retrieval, information transmission) and information value enhancement (availability, up-to-dateness, data analysis). A return in investment can only be assigned to solutions like PIPE if its appliance enhances the supported business processes – the information provision itself isn't of avail.

The approach presented here is evaluated with regard to the increase in benefit generated by it and its practical relevance. In terms of its benefits, the implications based on four qualitative attributes represented in Figure 8 should be studied. They result from the intensification of the information exchange in the value-added partnership. The degree of the information exchange (right axis) between the partners pertains to the amount and extent of the service information for the customer service organization, as well as the information about the service work carried out for the manufacturer. The more comprehensive the exchange, the stronger is the effect of the information on the product and service quality (top axis). The curve of quality growth levels off with an increase in the amount of information, as by degrees information saturation occurs. The effort made by the value-added partners for setting up and maintaining the cooperation (bottom axis) also depends disproportionately on the degree of the information exchanged: the creation of the organizational and IT- requirements for the information exchange initially remain independent

Figure 8. Implications of the intensification of the value-added partnership

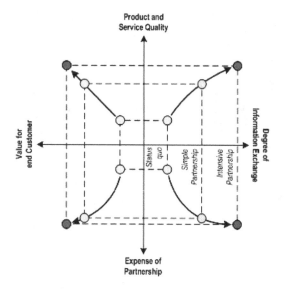

of the intensity of their use. The extent to which this infrastructure is used hardly increases the effort so that the difference between a simple and a more intense partnership is only marginal with regard to effort.

The benefit of the various value-added partnerships for the end-customer is derived on the left axis from the qualitative parameters already mentioned. It depends directly on the product and service quality and is therefore symbolized in the upper left-hand quadrant by a linear relationship. Thus, in the lower left-hand quadrant a qualitative cost-benefit-estimate results, which shows that the customer benefit is disproportionately high to the effort. If a direct connection is made between the customer benefit, customer satisfaction and economic success of the value-added partners then two conclusions can be made: (1) Even a weak exchange of information leads to a considerable increase in benefit, (2) Further intensification of the exchange causes disproportionately high additional benefits. With regard to its transfer to practice, the solution developed in PIPE was first evaluated with regard to customer service within the framework of an empirical survey carried out

nationwide in 2007 in the HAS-branch including factory, as well as product-independent customer service providers (N=129). In doing so, the current situation in technical customer service with regard to the tools available and their use was studied, requirements for a mobile, interactive solution like the one designed by PIPE and the general need for it were explicitly inquired.

In expert interviews it became clear that there is also a lack of information on the manufacturer side. Thus, task sharing in the value-added chain of the HAS-manufacturers allows them to concentrate on core competencies, namely the management of their supply network, as well as the development and manufacturing of technical devices; however it separates them from the use of the products from an IT point of view. The information arising here on the constructive and service technical improvement potential for their products reaches the manufacturers at best in fragments via the factory customer service department or via irregular and unstructured communication with the customer service organization, so that here the development of the solution presented is also being followed with much interest.

In a second step, a process benchmarking by use of a field study was performed to evaluate the developed application system. Potential end users were confronted with special defect characteristics of a specific prepared device. Additionally different utilities were made available. The comparison of the different process flows allows to identify the benefit of the system.

The reference processes where agreed with the manufacturer and represent the ideal paths for the repairing processes. This process models are used by the tool. To have a comparability in matters of time and proceeding, the usage of the PIPE tool was contrasted to the process variants "without aids" (problem solution based on education and work experience) and "with manufacturer information" (manuals, catalogs, training guide and hotline). Probands of the experiment have been scholars of master classes of the sector education and single domain experts, and in each case processing one defect characteristic with the tool and another defect characteristic with another guidance variant. In sum 59 process instances were collected and analyzed. Answers of the individuals express that more than half of the processors estimate the expenditure of process time as faster and much faster, although the IT-supported variants weren't significantly faster at all. At the same time, 84% of the service processors rate the quality of the result by using the tool as better or much better in contrast to processing without the tool and as easement for their work (85%). At large, examining e.g. the first specific defect characteristic, a much smaller part of the process instances was aborted (6%) in contrast to the usage of no or only the traditional aids (75% respectively 25%). A further observation is the reduction of the time and effort for information retrieval in relation to the amount of work in successful cases. While this quota is more than 40% using the traditional aids, this value dwindled to 13% when using the tool. The participants of the field study express the assistance of the tool in particular in a subjective time reduction for accessing actual manufacturer data and an optimal failure retrieval with markers and indicators. In sum the experiment circumstantiated the theses in terms of information value enhancement and temporal benefits. A monetary consideration could be deduced or rather needs further qualitative analyses.

SUMMARY AND OUTLOOK

In this article, improvement potential with regard to the cross-company flow of information in value-added networks was identified based on an analysis of value-added chains in the machine and plant construction industry. An approach was derived from this, concretized in a conceptual IT-architecture and exemplified on a use case from operational practice. The main aspect was the coordinated, IT-supported exchange of informa-

tion along the value-added chain. The concluding evaluation of the concept shows that this approach is in high demand.

The question as to whether a solution is a physical product, services rendered or a combination of both will become more and more difficult to answer in the future and takes a back seat in importance – the borders between products and services have become blurred. Therefore, our central challenge in the future is to design adequate information systems for product-service systems engineering.

ACKNOWLEDGMENT

This work was supported by the BMBF (German Federal Ministry of Education and Research) in the context "Innovation with Service Provision" (promotional reference: 01FD0623).

REFERENCES

Bolumole, Y.A., Knemeyer, A.M., & Lambert, D.M. (2006). *The customer service management process*. Sarasota, FL: Supply Chain Management Institute.

Botta, C., & Thomas, O. (2002). New Requirements on the Support of the Product Development Process. In R. Mosca, F. Tonelli & S. Pozzi Cotto (Eds.), *Proceedings of the 4th International Conference on: The Modern Information Technology in the Innovation Processes of the Industrial Enterprises, MITIP 2002, Savona, Italy, 27.-29. June 2002* (pp. 107-111). Genoa, Italy: Edizioni Culturali Internazionali Genova.

Bressand, A., Distler, C., & Nicolaidis, K. (1989). Networks at the Heart of the Service Economy . In Bressand, A., & Nicolaidis, K. (Eds.), *Strategic trends in services: an inquiry into the global service economy* (pp. 17–32). New York: Harper & Row.

Bundesinstitut für Berufsbildung. (2004). *Anlagenmechaniker/-in für Sanitär-, Heizungs- und Klimatechnik - ein neuer Name oder mehr? Neuordnung*. Bielefeld: Bertelsmann.

Castells, M. (1996). *The rise of the network society*. Cambridge, MA: Blackwell.

Czepiel, J. A. (1980). *Managing customer satisfaction in consumer service businesses*. Cambridge, MA: Marketing Science Institute.

Engelhardt, W. H., Kleinaltenkamp, M., & Reckenfelderbäumer, M. (1993). Leistungsbündel als Absatzobjekte: Ein Ansatz zur Überwindung der Dichotomie von Sach- und Dienstleistungen. *Zeitschrift für betriebswirtschaftliche. Forschung, 45*(5), 395–426.

Eppen, G. D., Hanson, W. A., & Martin, R. K. (1991). Bundling: new products, new markets, low risk. *Sloan Management Review, 32*(4), 7–14.

Evans, S., Partidário, P. J., & Lambert, J. (2007). Industrialization as a key element of sustainable product-service solutions. *International Journal of Production Research, 45*(18), 4225–4246. doi:10.1080/00207540701449999

Freiden, J., Goldsmith, R., Takacs, S., & Hofacker, C. (1998). Information as a product: not goods, not services. *Marketing Intelligence & Planning, 16*, 210–220. doi:10.1108/02634509810217327

Haines, R. W. (2006). *Control Systems for Heating, Ventilating, and Air Conditioning* (6th ed.). New York: Springer, New York

Haischer, M., Bullinger, H.-J., & Fähnrich, K.-P. (2001). Assessment and Design of Service Systems. In G. Salvendy (Ed.), *Handbook of Industrial Engineering: Technology and Operations Management* (3rd ed., pp. 634–650). New York: John Wiley & Sons. doi:10.1002/9780470172339.ch22

Harris, E. K. (2007). *Customer service, a practical approach* (4th ed.). Upper Saddle River, N.J: Pearson Prentice Hall.

Herrmann, A., Huber, F., & Coulter, R. H. (1997). Product and service bundling decisions and their effects on purchase intention. *Pricing Strategy and Practice, 5*, 99–107. doi:10.1108/09684909710171873

Hoppe, M. & Sander, M. (1996). SHK - eine Branche im Wandel. *Sanitär + Heizungstechnik, 61*(3), 38-46.

Howell, R. H., Sauer, H. J., & Coad, W. J. (2005). *Principles of heating ventilating and air conditioning*. Atlanta, GA: American Society of Heating, Refrigerating and Air Conditioning Engineers.

Isaac, H., & Leclercq, A. (2006). Give me a mobile phone, and I will work harder! Assessing the value of mobile technologies in organizations: an exploratory research. In *International Conference on Mobile Business* (p. 18). ICMB 2006, Los Alamitos, CA: IEEE Computer Society.

Jarillo, J. C. (1988). On strategic networks. *Strategic Management Journal, 9*(1), 31–41. doi:. doi:10.1002/smj.4250090104

Karapidis, A. (2005). Service Management in Production Companies. In G. Zülch, H. Jagdev, & P. Stock (Eds.), *Integrating Human Aspects in Production Management* (pp. 375–385). Boston, MA: Springer. doi:10.1007/0-387-23078-5_29

Keller, G., Nüttgens, M., & Scheer, A.-W. (1992). Semantische Prozeßmodellierung auf der Grundlage Ereignisgesteuerter Prozeßketten (EPK) . In Scheer, A.-W. (Ed.), *Veröffentlichungen des Instituts für Wirtschaftsinformatik, No. 89*. Saarbrücken: Universität des Saarlandes.

Kingman-Brundage, J. (1989). The ABCs of Service System Blueprinting. In M.J. Bitner, & L.A. Crosby (Eds.), *Designing a winning service strategy: 7th Annual Service Marketing Conference proceedings*. Chicago, IL: American Marketing Association.

Krucken, L., & Meroni, A. (2006). Building stakeholder networks to develop and deliver product-service-systems: practical experiences on elaborating pro-active materials for communication. *Journal of Cleaner Production, 14*(17), 1502–1508. doi:10.1016/j.jclepro.2006.01.026

LaLonde, B. J. (1976). *Customer service: meaning and measurement.* Chicago, IL: National Council of Physical Distribution Management.

Lambert, D. M. (2006). *Supply chain management, processes, partnerships, performance* (2nd ed.). Sarasota, FL: Supply Chain Management Institute.

Lapiedra, R., Smithson, S., Alegre, J., & Chiva, R. (2004). Role of information systems on the business network formation process: an empirical analysis of the automotive sector. *Journal of Enterprise Information Management, 17*(3), 219–228. doi:10.1108/17410390410531461

MacQuiston, F. C. (2005). *Heating, ventilating, and air conditioning: analysis and design* (6th ed.). Hoboken, NJ: John Wiley & Sons.

Manzini, E., Vezzoli, C., & Clark, G. (2001). Product-Service Systems: Using an Existing Concept as a New Approach to Sustainability. *Journal of Desert Research, 1*(2).

Mertens, P. (2006). Moden und Nachhaltigkeit in der Wirtschaftsinformatik. *Handbuch der Modernen Datenverarbeitung - Praxis der Wirtschaftsinformatik, 42*(250), 109-118.

Miles, R. E., & Snow, C. C. (1978). *Organizational strategy, structure, and process.* New York: McGraw-Hill.

Mont, O. (2004). *Product-service systems, panacea or myth?* Lund: IIIEE Dissertations.

Morelli, N. (2002). Designing Product/Service Systems: A Methodological Exploration. *Design Issues, 18*(3), 3–17. doi:10.1162/074793602320223253

Ovans, A. (1997). Make a bundle bundling. *Harvard Business Review, 75*(6), 18–20.

Pahl, V. (2007). Research and Development for a Sustainable Services Sector. In D. Spath & K. P. Fähnrich (Eds.), *Advances in Services Innovations* (pp. 279–288). Berlin: Springer. doi:10.1007/978-3-540-29860-1_14

Peel, M. (1987). *Customer service: how to achieve total customer satisfaction.* London: Kogan Page.

Sakao, T., & Shimomura, Y. (2007). Service CAD System to Support Servicification of Manufactures. In *Advances in Life Cycle Engineering for Sustainable Manufacturing Businesses: Proceedings of the 14th CIRP Conference on Life Cycle Engineering.* Waseda University, Tokyo, Japan, (pp. 143-148) June 11th-13th. London: Springer.

Sawy, O. A. E., & Bowles, G. (2003). *Information technology and customer service.* Oxford: Butterworth-Heineman.

Scheer, A.-W., Thomas, O., & Adam, O. (2005). Process Modeling Using Event-driven Process Chains. In M. Dumas, W.M.P. van der Aalst, & A.H.M ter Hofstede (Eds.), *Process-aware Information Systems: Bridging People and Software through Process Technology* (pp. 119-145), Hoboken, NJ: Wiley.

Shostack, L. G. (1977). Breaking Free from Product Marketing. *Journal of Marketing, 41*(2), 73–80. doi:.doi:10.2307/1250637

Sterling, J. U., & Lambert, D. M. (1989). Customer service research, past, present and future. *International journal of physical distribution & materials management, 19*(2), 2-23.

Tax, S. S., & Stuart, I. (1997). Designing and Implementing New Services: The Challenges of Integrating Service Systems. *Journal of Retailing, 73*(1), 105–134. doi:10.1016/S0022-4359(97)90017-8

Thomas, O., Walter, P., & Loos, P. (2008). Design and Usage of an Engineering Methodology for Product-Service Systems. *Journal of Desert Research*, 7(2), 177–195. doi:10.1504/JDR.2008.020854

Thomas, O., Walter, P., Loos, P., Nüttgens, M., & Schlicker, M. (2007). Mobile Technologies for Efficient Service Processes: A Case Study in the German Machine and Plant Construction Industry. In *Proceedings of the 13th Americas Conference on Information Systems*: August 09-12, Keystone, Colorado, USA. Atlanta, GA: AIS.

Timm, P. R. (2005). *Technology and customer service: profitable relationship building; loyalty, satisfaction, organizational success.* Upper Saddle River, NJ: Pearson Prentice Hall.

Tomiyama, T. (2002). Service Engineering to Intensify Service Contents in Product Life Cycles. Japan *ECP Newsletter,* 19.

Vandermerwe, S., & Rada, J. F. (2007). Servitization of Business: Adding Value by Adding Services. *European Management Journal*, 6(4), 314–324. doi:10.1016/0263-2373(88)90033-3

Vonderembse, M. A., Uppal, M., Huang, S. H., & Dismukes, J. P. (2006). Designing supply chains: Towards theory development. *International Journal of Production Economics*, 100(2), 223–238. doi:10.1016/j.ijpe.2004.11.014

Weber, C., Pohl, M., Steinbach, M., & Botta, C. (2002). Diskussion der Probleme bei der integrierten Betrachtung von Sach- und Dienstleistungen - "Kovalente Produkte"". In: 13. Symposium "Design for X", Neukirchen/Erlangen 10.-11.10.2002: Tagungsband (pp. 61-70). Friedrich-Alexander-Universität Erlangen-Nürnberg.

Willerding, T. (1987). Gestaltungsmöglichkeiten der Kooperation im technischen Kundendienst zwischen Hersteller und Handel. Bochum: Studienverlag Brockmeyer VDMA (2008). Maschinenbau in Zahl und Bild 2008. Mühlheim am Main: reuffurth.

KEY TERMS AND DEFINITIONS

PIPE: Is the acronym for „Prozessorientierte Integration von Produktentwicklung und Servicedokumentation zur Unterstützung des technischen Kundendienstes" (german). Hence PIPE deals with the process-oriented integration of product development and service documentation for the support of technical customer services (TCS) in machine and plant construction

PIPE Service Provider: Organization in the PIPE concept. The PIPE service provider is an independent organization, which also provides consulting services for the manufacturer in connection with the development and operation of their portals and represents the central coordination of the various manufacturer portals and the value-added partnership.

Chapter 13
Online-Oriented Service Quality:
An Aspect of Multichannel Retailing

Samar I. Swaid
Philander Smith College, USA

Rolf T. Wigand
University of Arkansas at Little Rock, USA

ABSTRACT

Equipped with advancements in technology, multichannel retailers design multichannel servicing systems to meet their customers' needs. A notable practice by multichannel shoppers is the online-oriented shopping, where shoppers search, purchase and pay online, while they go offline for products pickup/ returns. Once multichannel retailers understand how shoppers evaluate service quality in the setting of online-oriented shopping, better servicing systems can be designed. This chapter is dedicated to understand how service quality is evaluated in online-oriented shopping. Because customer satisfaction is paramount, a service quality model incorporates customer satisfaction as an outcome. As this study is the first of its types focusing on service quality in the setting of "buy online, pickup in-store", traditional retailers can consider our findings as guidelines of advancing into the online world. As such, pure online retailers can benefit from our findings in understanding the impact of establishing a physical presence on service quality models and customer satisfaction.

INTRODUCTION

Services sector is one of the main sectors of industrialized nations' economy. According to the US National Academy of Engineering (as cited in Spohrer et al., 2007), the service sector accounts for more than 80% of the US gross domestic product and is projected to account for most of

DOI: 10.4018/978-1-61520-819-7.ch013

the US job growth (Hefley, 2008). The growth of service sectors benefitted from a large workforce number comprised of workers from the disciplines of science, engineering and management (Spohrer et al., 2007), while applying the information technology as its main infrastructure (Hefley, 2008) and businesses processes as its vehicle creating servicing systems. Unlike manufacturing depending completely on the manufacturer, servicing systems need both the collaboration of the service provider and service client in creating value (Tieng and Berg as cited in Spohrere et al., 2007).

One type of servicing systems that evolved and become innovative is the Multichannel Retailing Servicing Systems (MRSS). Multichannel retailing servicing systems (MRSS) refer to servicing systems that enable searching, purchasing and delivery of products and services via alternative channels. As the behavior of online shoppers' is transforming from a uni-channel shopper to multi-channel shopper (Lennstrand et al., 2002; Forrester 2007), retailers who developed MRSS enabling smooth shopping experiences across channels are the real winners. In this chapter, we focus on multichannel retailing[1], through which single retailers adopt coordination strategies between web (online) channel and store (offline) channel. In this sense, multichannel retailers integrate both channels onto unified customer-centric servicing systems allowing shoppers to move in both directions. However, based on attributes of market structure, infrastructure capabilities and customer segments (Müller-Lankenau et al., 2004; Prasarnphanich and Gillenson, 2003; Saeed et al., 2003) MRSS differ. Some retailers chose to split their web business from the rest of their operations and operate each as a separate entity. The splitting-channel strategy (Müller-Lankenau et al., 2004) has been witnessed by the U.S. book retailer Barnes & Nobles at the early stages of the Internet era. On the other hand, other multichannel retailers opted to integrate their channels. According to Steinfield et al. (2005), multichannel integration can be classified into either information integration or logistical integration. Information integration allows customers to locate the nearest store, check inventory, order and make payments, and manage online accounts. Logistical integration refers to providing a single front that enables customers to pick up their order and make product returns through channels of their choice. Regardless of the opted for strategy of channel integration, retailers need to develop MRSS that enable their shoppers to shop smoothly. According to industry

reports and academic research, the most common and adopted practice of multichannel strategies is the logistical integration (Forrester, 2007, 2009; Goersch 2002; Lee and Whang, 2001; Saeed et al., 2003; Steinfield et al., 2005). Increasingly, online shoppers are witnessed to practice purchasing online and utilizing a physical store/touch-point for the purchase collection and purchase returns. Such shoppers take the advantage of the availability of alternative channels for purchase collections and returns to decrease monetary and non-monetary costs of their transaction (e.g., time, effort and psychological cost) (Hoffman and Novak, 1996). In this setting of online-oriented shopping – buying online and going offline for purchase collection and returns-- take the advantages of the interactive format of the web, the information intense and the personalized recommendations provided online, while acquiring an immediate access for their purchases. On the retailers' side, offering added-value services of purchase pickup and returns brings a number of advantages such as cross-selling, service innovations, flexibility and cost efficiencies (Bitner et al., 2000; Steinfield et al., 2005). For customers, offering "buy online, pickup/return in-store" resulted in enhanced perceived value, increased perceived control, reduced perceived risk and improved trust (Prasarnphanich and Gillenson, 2003; Steinfield et al., 2005; Goersch, 2002). Pioneer multichannel retailers such as Sears, JCPenney, Target, Wal-Mart, Staples, Best Buy, Barnes & Nobles, Grainger, Old Navy, Gap, Nordstrom, Tiffany's, Home Depot, ACE Hardware, Lowes, and O'Reilly Auto Parts adopt such practices to improve their businesses (James, 2008; Prasarnphanich and Gillenson, 2003; RetailerNetGroup, 2009; Reuters, 2009).

Although an extensive review of scholarly work and industry reports focused on multichannel strategies (Adelaar et al., 2001; Muller-Lankenau et al., 2004; Forrester, 2006b; 2007; Prasarnphanich and Gillenson, 2003; Jupiter 2007), multichannel integration advantageous (Lee and Whang, 2001; Goersch, 2002; Steinfield et al.,

2001), multichannel customer behavior (Forrester, 2006a, 2007; Teltzrow et al., 2003), service quality in multichannel environments has been rarely researched (Sousa and Voss, 2004). We are interested in exploring how online shoppers evaluate service quality in the complicated setting of "buy online, pickup/return in-store"? and what are the relationships between service quality on the aggregate and the individual-dimension levels?

As more evidence is gained on the increasing number of retailers who are moving toward offering "buy online, pickup in-store" (Berman and Thelen 2004; InternetRetailer, 2007; Forrester, 2009), and the numerous challenges multichannel retailers are confronted with this study is dedicated to focus on service quality in the setting on Multichannel Retailing Servicing Systems (MRSS) Specifically, in this chapter, we aim to achieve the following objectives:

- Objective 1: Understand how shoppers evaluate service quality in the setting of "buy online, pickup/return in-store"
- Objective 2: Explore the relationships among the dimensions of service quality and variables of customer satisfaction.

We believe that pursuing the above mentioned objectives will add to scholarly knowledge and will assist managers in designing an effective MRSS.

The rest of the chapter is structured as follows. First, we discuss channel choice in multichannel settings. Second, we discuss prior research on e-service quality since the current study extends the research model of e-service quality to suit the setting of online-oriented shopping. Third, we discuss the research model and hypotheses development. Next, we present the analytical work. Fifth, results and findings are discussed. Finally, based on our findings we present implications and acknowledge the limitations of the current study. As this study is the first of its types that focuses on service quality in the setting of "buy online, pickup in-store", traditional retailers can consider

our findings as guidelines when advancing into the online world. As such, pure online retailers can benefit from our findings in understanding the impact of establishing a physical presence on service quality models and customer satisfaction. For multichannel retailers, the current chapter provides them with an instrument to assess their service quality attributes in the setting of "buy online, pickup/return in-store".

BACKGROUND

It is likely that multi-channel customers switch from one channel to another when using Multichannel Retailing Servicing System (MRSS). According to a study by Forrester (2007), multichannel customers have come to expect a seamless multichannel experience. Therefore, providing a consistent experience for customers has come to be critical and demands developing customer-centric servicing systems. On the retailer side, multichannel integration increases customer's awareness of the retailers and its offerings, reduces operation cost, enables differentiation through value-added services (Goersch, 2002) and influences customer spending and loyalty (Forrester, 2007, 2009; Retailer Daily, 2008). A study by McKinsey found that multichannel retailers need about $5 to bring an existing customer online, whereas an e-retailer needs to spend an average $45 for acquiring a customer (as cited in Goersch, 2002). In addition, multi-channel integration influences customer spending and loyalty (Forrester, 2009; Retailer Daily, 2008).

Multi-Channel Customer Channel Choice

Based on research in cognitive science and marketing, shoppers demonstrate diverse behavior when shopping in multichannel environments. As explained by Sousa and Voss (2006, p. 358) "it may be up to a customer to decide on the combination of channels to employ in engaging in a particular service instance". Generally, in MRSS, two multi-channel shopping behaviors can be recognized: the online-oriented shopping and the offline-oriented shopping.

Online-Oriented Shopping

Research on behavior of online shopping suggests that online shoppers are goal-driven shoppers who seek to do their task with the use of as little effort as necessary reducing monetary and non-monetary costs (Hoffman and Novak, 1996). In the setting of online shopping, issues of delayed product collection, paying shipping costs and difficulty of returning online purchases form some of the barriers to online shopping (Prasarnphanich aqnd Gillenson 2003; Teltzrow et al. 2003). As a result, innovative retailers developed multichannel servicing systems that enable their shoppers to shop online and pickup/return their purchase using store or offline touch-point (e.g., Sears, JCPenney, Target, Wal-Mart, Staples, Barnes & Nobles, Grainger, Old Navy, Gap, Nordstrom, Tiffany's, The Limited, Lands' End, O'Reily Auto Parts, ACE Hardware and Home Depot) (Prasarnphanich and Gillenson, 2003; RetailerNetGroup, 2009; Reuters, 2009). As such, pure Internet retailers adopted offering added-value services of in-store pickup/return for online shoppers. For example, the strategic alliance between GroceryWorks.co and Safeway enables customers to buy online and pick products from a physical store of Safeway (Prasarnphanich and Gillenson, 2003).

This transformation of online-shoppers behavior from a single-channel behavior to the online-oriented shopping has been explained by features of: (1) web-based elements of the servicing systems and (2) physical elements of the servicing systems. Web-based elements of the servicing systems refers to the interactivity of the web, the functionality of the search engines, comparison features, 24/7 accessibility, wide products selection and special promotions. On the other hand, the

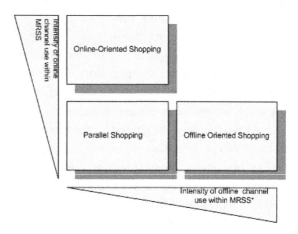

*Figure 1. Customer behavior in multichannel setting (*MRSS: Multichannel Retailing Servicing Systems)*

physical elements of the servicing systems refer to the extent alternative channels *complement* the functionality of the web channel (Sousa and Voss, 2006). Although offering online shoppers the use of physical stores for product collection and returns is encouraged, managing service quality in such complicated setting becomes a challenging issue.

Offline-Oriented Shopping

Some shoppers are very tied to traditional stores. However, they use the web for information searching, price comparison features and store location mapping. Forrester (2007) found that 51% of today's shoppers incorporate the web onto their shopping transaction for information search and decision making, but go offline for product order. According to "The State of Retailing Online 2006," retailers reported that 22% of their offline sales were influenced by the web. Such shoppers value the depth of information found online, but overwhelmingly prefer the offline experience (Forrester, 2007). We term this segment of multichannel shopping behavior, offline-oriented shopping (see Figure 1).

Service Quality in the Setting of Online-Oriented Shopping

Service quality has long been found to be an elusive construct that is difficult to comprehend and measure (Cronion and Taylor, 1992). Research on traditional service quality has relied extensively on the model of the SERVQUAL (Parasuaraman et al., 1988). The SERVQUAL model is based on the gap function between perceptions and expectations and comprises five dimensions: reliability, responsiveness, assurance, empathy and tangibles. Reliability is generally defined as the ability to deliver the promised service dependably and accurately. Responsiveness is the willingness to help customers and provide prompt services. Assurance can be described as the ability of the company and its employees to inspire confidence and trust. Empathy is the individualized attention and caring the firm provides its customers. Tangibles are defined as the physical facilities, equipment and appearance of personnel (Parasuraman et al., 1988). Although the SERVQUAL instrument has been developed empirically focusing on "high touch-low tech" environments (Bitner et al., 2000), the model was used to evaluate service quality in technology-based environments. For example, Iwaarden, Wiele, Ball and Millen (2004) using the SERVQUAL model conducted their research identifying the five dimensions of online service quality: fast access, easy navigation on the website, presentation of complete overview of the order before a final purchase decision, assurance and simple registration process. The established instrument draws upon the SERVQUAL model, however, the study focuses primarily on the technical quality of the website. Another study by Barnes and Vidgen (2002) applied the SERVQUAL model as its starting point found that online service quality can be measured on: usability, design, information, trust and empathy. Also, this study focused solely on web interactivity and technical quality, therefore, customer service was not integrated in research models. Other studies developed new scales that focused exclusively on the setting of online services. For example, Wolfinbarger and Gilly (2003) developed a scale to measure service quality using factors of website design, reliability/fulfillment, privacy/security and customer service. Although the study applied qualitative as well a quantitative study, some of the developed measures do not show strong face validity (Parasuraman et al., 2005). Following this stream of research, Parasuraman, Zeithaml and Malhotra (2005) developed two scales: E-S-Qual (efficiency, system availability, fulfillment and privacy) and the E-RecS-Qual (responsiveness, compensation and contact.). The E-S-Qual scale measures the quality of core services quality dimensions consisting of efficiency, fulfillment, system availability and privacy, while E-RecS-QUAL is for measuring quality of service recovery that includes responsiveness, compensation and contact". The e-RecS-QUAL is used when customers face "nonroutine encounters" such as dealing with customer problems. Despite the systematic process in establishing and validating the two scales, we stress our concern that responsiveness factor in "responding promptly to customer questions" should be included in core service quality measures. Offering after-sale services and support reduce insecurity and signals unobservable process quality (Bauer et al., 2006).

The aforementioned research on service quality in online environments, online service quality illustrates that models of service quality in online-oriented shopping is virtually absent in the literature. Thus far, the focus has been on service quality as channel-specific perspective (Sousa and Voss, 2006), which fails to consider quality attributes when customers interact with service providers through several channels. The next section attempts to develop a conceptual model to measure service quality in the setting of online-oriented service quality.

RESEARCH MODEL

Our conceptual model builds on existing research on online service quality. We define service quality in online-oriented shopping as the overall perception of quality of service experienced by customers encompassing the online channel and the complementary use of the offline channel supporting the online purchase transaction.

Antecedents of Service Quality in Online-Oriented Shopping

The first objective of our chapter is to adequately conceptualize service quality by considering the formation of the perception of service quality across all moments of contact with the service provider (Sousa and Voss, 2006). We follow the recommendation of Voss's (2003) by reformulating and extending the SERVQUAL model to assess service quality in online-oriented shopping.

Website Design

The graphical style of the website is equivalent to the tangible dimension of service quality in traditional facilities (Zeithaml et al., 2000). Attractive websites that generate pleasure and enjoyment while shopping influence the overall service quality and customer's satisfaction (Wolfinbarger and Gilly, 2003). Rationally, we suggest that website design influences the overall service quality and, rationally, customer satisfaction.

Website Usability

As service consumption in the online-oriented servicing system is initiated using the web, quality attributes of the website influences overall service quality (Parasuraman et al., 2005; Loiacono et al., 2007; Wolfinbarger and Gilly, 2003). Prior research on technology adoption found that user perception of usefulness and ease of use determines the adoption of new systems (Davis, 1989; 1993; Venkatesh and Davis, 2000). Moreover, research on human-computer interaction suggests that the ease to use website that is powered with search engines, comparison capabilities, navigation structure and attractive graphic style influences the usage of web-based servicing systems (Hoque and Loshe, 1999).

Information Quality

The quality of information contained in the website appears to be critical to the success of e-businesses (Montoya-Weiss et al., 2003). Information content of the website includes materials of product description, order status and corporate policies. Research on information quality suggests attributes of information utility, information accuracy and information timeliness as measures of information quality (e.g., Deshpande and Zaltman, 1982). Consistent with prior research, we propose that information quality positively influences of the overall service quality.

Reliability

Reliability in traditional stores is defined as "the ability to perform the promised service dependably and accurately (Parasuraman et al., 1988, p. 23). In online shopping, as well as in online-oriented shopping, reliability can be translated into the proper functioning of the website and delivery of product and services as promised (Zeithaml et al., 2002).

Responsiveness

Shoppers expect websites to respond to their inquiries and questions. Responsiveness represents the extent the website responds promptly to the shoppers' questions and inquiries using automated agents and human representatives.

Assurance

Studies on online service quality found that assurance is one of the important drivers of loyalty intentions (e.g., Parasuraman et al., 2005; Swaid and Wigand, 2009; Wolfinbarger and Gilly, 2003) and a crucial factor in transactional buyer-seller environments and especially these that lack face-to-face interaction (Reichheld and Schefter 2000). Assurance is the customer perception of the confidence and trust toward the website (Gefen, 2002); Zeithaml et al. (2002) included the dimension of security and privacy, which involve the "degree to which the customer believes the site is safe from intrusion and personal information is protected" (p. 16). In this chapter, we believe assurance should be defined broader than just privacy and security to translate to all cues websites signal that inspire confidence and trust.

Personalization

It has been argued that personalization is one of the most important drivers to online shopping. Personalization is strongly related to the empathy dimension in the SERVQUAL model, as websites offer individualized attention, personalized recommendations and the ability to customize the website to the shoppers' preferences (Zeithaml et al., 2002). For example, the San Francisco-based Due Maternity has four stores in addition to the web site. The DueMaternity.com gathers online shopper data by asking shoppers to register. The customer-centric data is sorted by the customers' due date and used to send personalized promotions accordingly before and after the baby is born.

Logistical Integration

Sousa and Voss (2006) define integration quality as "the ability to provide customers with a seamless service experience across multiple channels"

(p. 365). In multichannel servicing systems where customers can receive their products at home or opt picking up their products from a store, logistical integration is a must. In addition, multichannel servicing systems need integrated logistics when customers buy online and choose to return their purchase to a store. This dimension is necessary as online-oriented shoppers use the web for product search and order placement, while they go offline – store or touchpoint- for product collection and/or returns. Such behavior, requires consistency of interaction across channels (Sousa and Voss, 2006). In this chapter we define logistical integration as the extent the multichannel servicing system enables online shoppers to pickup/return their purchase using the offline store/touch-point.

Based on the aforementioned dimensions of service quality in the setting of online-oriented setting, we propose the following:

H1: Service quality in an online-oriented shopping is composed of website design, website usability, information quality, reliability, responsiveness, assurance, personalization, logistical integration quality.

Quality and Satisfaction

Studies on customer satisfaction show the potential influence of satisfaction on customer behavioral intentions and thereby customer retention (Cronion and Taylor, 1992). Satisfied customers are less expensive and promote positive word-of-mouth that is even more affective than advertising in print or mass media channels (Bhattacherjee, 2001). Research on online service quality suggests that customer satisfaction is influenced by the quality of services provided (e.g., Wolfinbarger and Gilly, 2003) and affects the participants' motivation to stay with the channel (Montoya-Weiss et al., 2003). According to Oliver, customer satisfaction is " … a judgment that a product or service feature or the

Figure 2. Research model

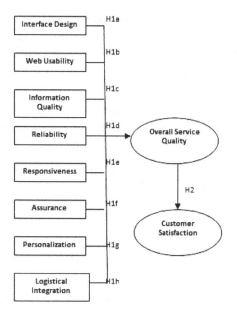

product or service itself, provided (or is providing) a pleasurable level of consumption-related fulfillment, including levels of over fulfillment" (Oliver, 1997, p. 13). Rationally, we suggest that the perception of service quality influences customer satisfaction on the aggregate and the dimensional level (see Figure 2).

H2: The perception of service quality influences customer satisfaction.

The Study

In this study we followed the framework suggested by Churchill (1979) in constructing multi-dimensional scales. The process begins by conceptualizing proposed constructs. Second, constructs are operationalized using reliable and valid measures adapted from existing literature where possible. Nonexistent measures are developed using focus group research. Third, items are purified using factor analysis and reliability analysis. Forth, measures are verified by conducting another round of statistical analysis. At the second phase of statistical analysis, we apply

structural analysis. Finally, the scale is tested in terms of reliability and validity.

Phase 1: Focus Group Research

As the study incorporates dimensions of integration quality, it was necessary to compile a pool of items that best represent this dimension. The targeted population of our study included customers actively using the web for product purchase and picked/returned their online purchase using a physical store, making them true online-oriented shoppers. Two focus groups were conducted with 18 subjects; each session lasted about two hours. The qualitative research facilitated the development of measures of the logistical integration construct. Surprisingly, focus group research output suggests that integration quality is perceived as two dimensions. Online-oriented shoppers differentiate between factors of: integrated-pickup and integrated-returns. Integrated-pickup refers to the extent the web facilitates online shoppers to pickup their online purchase from a physical outlet. Specifically, customers care about enabling them to pickup their purchase from a number of locations, sending notification emails when products are ready to be picked up and finding the product at a store when picked up. As such, the construct of integrated-returns refers to the extent the web enables and facilitates returning online purchase to a physical store. In particular, focus group participants indicated that it is important to be able to return their online purchase easily to physical stores and refunding their payments accurately (see Table 1 for items generated).

Phase 2: An Empirical Study

Measures of online service quality were adopted from prior research, while factors of integration quality items were generated from our focus group research (see Table 1). Multi-item variables of overall service quality and customer satisfaction were adopted from Wolfinbarger and Gilly (2003).

Table 1. Items of logistical integration dimensions

Dimension	Items	References
Integrated-returns	1. The website's return policy allows me to return products to a physical outlet 2. I can return my items to store 3. I can return my items easily 4. The website offers me a number of locations where I can return my items 5. The website offers me to return my items with no cost 6. The website gives me enough of a time window to return my products 7. The website issue a credit to the credit card used 8. The website has detailed instructions for in-store returns 9. The website offers in-store returns options for most of the displayed products	Focus group research
Integrated-pickup	1. The website offers me in-store pickup 2. The website offers me a number of locations where I can pick up my items 3. A store-pick-up notification email is sent to me within 24 hours of placing my order 4. I found my items ready to be picked up from the selected outlet/location 5. The credit card is charged when I pick up my items 6. The website has detailed instructions for in-store pickups 7. The website offers in-store pickup options for most of the displayed	Focus group research

All items were measured using seven-point Likert-type scales ranging from (1) strongly disagree to (7) strongly agree. A filtering question was included in the survey to target the appropriate populations of online-oriented shoppers.

As college students are the most active web users (Jupiter, 2004) and about 81% of college students have made an online purchase (EMarketer, 2009), students of a mid-size university were invited to participate. Subjects that have experienced buying online and using physical store/touch-point for online purchase pickup/returns were targeted. Following Churchill's (1979) recommendations for instrument construction, the obtained sample (N= 307) was partitioned randomly onto two datasets. One dataset is used for items factor analysis, while the second dataset is used to assess the reliability and validity of the developed instrument.

Analysis and Results

At the first phase, research hypotheses were tested using Exploratory Factor Analysis (EFA) to identify factors of service quality in the setting of online-oriented shopping. At the second phase,

we applied Structural Equation Modeling (SEM) to test research hypotheses.

Exploratory Factor Analysis (EFA) was applied using the principal axis factoring as an extraction method and Varimax method was used for rotation. Factor analysis resulted in identifying a factor solution of eight factors: website usability (the extent to which the website is well-structured and easy to navigate), information quality (the extent to which the website offers high content quality), reliability (the extent to which the website performs services as promised), responsiveness (the extent to which it is possible to get a quick response and needed help using automated and human factors), assurance (the extent to which the website conveys trust and confidence), personalization (the extent to which the website provides individualized attention), integrated-pickup (the extent to which the shoppers perceive ease of picking-up their online purchase using physical store/touch-points) and integrated-returns (the extent to which the shoppers perceive ease of returning their online purchase using physical store/touch-points) (see Table 2). Before incorporating the identified factors in hypotheses testing, it is

Table 2. Results of exploratory factor analysis

Construct/ Measure	Factor Loading(a)	Construct Reliability
Information Quality		.915
IQ1: Accurate and relevant information	.934	
IQ2: Current and timely information	.897	
IQ5: Appropriate format of information	.882	
IQ6: Easy to understand information	.873	
IQ3: Rich in detail	.866	
IQ4: Fit-to-task information	.851	
Reliability		.869
REL1: promises fulfillment	.883	
REL2: Sending order confirmation emails	.876	
REL3: Sending order cancellation and returns	.862	
REL4: Performing service right the first time	.760	
REL5: Availability of order tracking details	.718	
REL6: Availability of the website	.702	
Responsiveness		.889
RES1: Providing prompt customer service	.835	
RES2: Dealing with customer complaints	.801	
RES3: Website addresses are included in all existing documentation, publicity and advertising channel	.788	
RES4: Relevant, accurate, and appropriate email responses to customer requirements	.745	
RES5: Showing sincere interest in resolving problems	.733	
Assurance		.894
ASS1: Availability of security policy	.921	
ASS2: Availability of privacy policy	.884	
ASS3: External validation of trustworthiness	.797	
ASS4: Good reputation of e-retailer	.782	
Website Usability		.881
US1: Attractiveness of website	.779	
US2: Consistent and standardized navigation	.787	
US3: Scrolling through pages is kept to minimum.	.765	
US4: Appropriate use of graphics and animation	.742	
Personalization		.862
PERS1: Providing personal attention	.912	
PERS2: Enabling ordering personalized products	.888	
PERS3 Understanding customers needs	.879	
Integrated-Returns		.836
RET1: Offering a number of locations for item returns	.766	
RET2: Ease of returning items	.798	
RET3: No costs for returning online items	.892	
RET4: Issuing a credit to the credit card used	.731	
RET5: Offering in-store return option for most of the displayed products.	.841	
Integrated-Pickup		.828
PICK1: Offering number of locations for items pickup	.733	
PICK2: Sending a notification email within 24 hours of placing order	.825	
PICK3: Designing a separate counter/site for items pickup	.876	
PICK4: Picking up items has been done smoothly and speedy	.776	
PICK5: Findings items ready to be picked up as expected	.668	

necessary to test the reliability and validity of the developed measures.

Reliability of measures was tested using Cronbach's alpha (Nunnally and Bernstein, 1994). Obtained reliability values of the measures exceeded the cut-off value of 0.80 indicating strong reliability (Nunnally and Bernstein, 1994).

Validity of scales was assessed considering convergent validity and discriminant validity. All items loaded on its factors with factor loading exceeding 0.70 indicating convergent validity (Bagozzi and Yi, 1988). Discriminant validity was assessed using the confidence interval test. None of the calculated confidence intervals included the value of one suggesting the discriminant validity of scales (Hatcher, 1994). The nomological validity of the scale was assessed by examining the relationships among the dimensions of service quality and the well established dependent variable of overall-service quality and customer satisfaction as shown next.

After ensuring the reliability and validity for developed scales, we can proceed in hypotheses testing. a two-step process was followed in conducting Structural Equation Modeling (SEM) (Anderson and Gerbing, 1988). First, a measurement model was developed by conducting confirmatory factor analysis to ensure the stability of the factor solution. Second, a theoretical model was compiled to test research hypotheses. The measurement model included independent variables of factors of service quality and the dependent variables of overall-service quality and customer satisfaction. The model evaluated for goodness-of-fit using indices of the normed chi-square (Ratio of the chi-square to the degrees of freedom), Goodness of Fit Index (GFI), Bentler's Comparative Fit Index (CFI), the Bentler & Bonett Non-Normed Fit Index (NNFI) and the Root Mean Square Error of Approximation (RMSEA) (Hatcher, 1994). Normed chi-square was 2.0 less than 3.0 as suggested by Bagozzi and Yi (1988). The value of GFI was 0.98 indicating a good fit (Bagozzi & Yi, 1988), while both of the CFI test and the NNFI test were 0.97, respectively, exceeding the cut-off value of 0.90 indicating (Hair et al., 1998). The value of the RMSEA was .048 less than the value of .05 as suggested by Hatcher (1994).

Next, the theoretical model is developed that consists of the relationships among latent factors of service quality and dependent variables of overall service quality and customer satisfaction. The theoretical model was assessed using the goodness-of-fit indices of Normed chi-square, GFI, CFI, NNFI, Adjusted Goodness of Fit index (AGFI), the Parsimony Ratio (PR) and the parsimonious normed-fit index (PNFI) (Hatcher, 1994) (see Figure 3). The normed chi-square was 2.12 less than the cut-off value of 3.0, while the GFI value was 0.94 greater than the cut-off value of 0.90. CFI and NNFI were 0.92 indicating a good ft. The parsimony of the model was assessed using the AGFI, PR and the PNFI (Hatcher, 1994). The AGFI was 0.89 slightly below the 0.90, while the PR ratio was 0.74 and PNFI was 0.71. Both values are greater than the 0.50 limit (Hatcher, 1994). In addition, value of RMSEA was 0.049 less than the value of 0.05 (Hatcher, 1994).

As shown in Figure 3, factors of service quality influence significantly the perception of overall service quality and customer satisfaction.

On the aggregate level, the perception of overall service quality affects significantly customer satisfaction with a coefficient of 0.39. As shown in Figure 2, reliability and assurance perceptions

Figure 3. Results of Structural Analysis

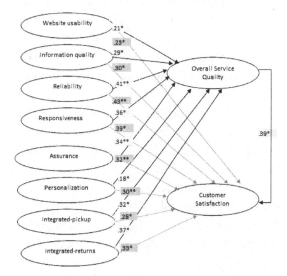

are the most important factors influencing overall service quality. It is also important to note that factors of integration quality affect overall service quality even more than technology-based factors such as website usability. The findings also show that customer satisfaction is positively improved by the perception of reliability, responsiveness and assurance. Customer satisfaction is positively influenced by the perception of integrated pickup and integrated returns having the first to have more effect.

FUTURE TRENDS

Shoppers in multichannel setting are demanding of a seamless shopping experience across channels. Equipped with advancements in technology, multichannel retailers design multichannel servicing systems that meet their customers' needs. A notable practice by multichannel shoppers is the online-oriented shopping, where shoppers search, purchase and pay online, while they go to stores for products pickup and returns. Once multichannel retailers understand how shoppers evaluate service quality in the setting of online-oriented shopping, better servicing systems can be designed. This chapter is dedicated to understand how service quality is evaluated in online-oriented shopping. Because customer satisfaction is paramount, a service quality model incorporates customer satisfaction as an outcome. We explored the effect of service quality on customer satisfaction on the dimensional level. However, further research is needed to understand service quality in multichannel retailing servicing systems. For example, offering in-store payment is highly valued by multichannel shoppers (Teltzrow et al., 2003) and is expected to reduce the perceived risk associated with online shopping (Steinfield et al., 2005). Additional research may also include the construct of loyalty. Loyalty is an important outcome in online service quality models (Para-

suraman et al., 2005; Swaid and Wigand, 2007). A fruitful area of research is considering different types of loyalty (preference loyalty, loyalty under increased pricing and complaining behavior) (Swaid and Wigand, 2009) to test the relationships among service quality and customer loyalty considering the dimensionality of both concepts. In this study we used samples of college students. Also including individual differences may shed light on additional findings. Moreover, the current study was conducted without controlling for demographic variables. A report by Media Audit (2008) finds that online shopping by minorities is increasing. Therefore, it would be beneficial to consider the perspectives of the other populations such as African Americans, Asians and Hispanics on quality of service. As computing and information technologies support the development of innovative servicing systems, more customized services can be offered considering the different types of customer behaviors.

CONCLUSION

Previous research on multichannel service quality has left two important issues virtually unaddressed. First, no appropriate metrics have been established for the assessment of the quality of service in the setting of online-oriented shopping. Second, studies addressing the relationships between service quality and satisfaction in multichannel servicing systems are rare. In this chapter, we present a research model to understand how online-oriented shoppers evaluate service quality. In conducting this work, scales were proposed, empirically tested and validated. Because of the unique characteristics of multichannel servicing systems in general, and the online-oriented servicing system in particular, we have included qualitative feedback from focus group research to understand attributes of integration quality. Our findings indicate that it is important to consider the different components of virtual quality and integration quality. Elements of virtual quality are a well-organized website that is attractive, rich information that helps in making informed decision, clear privacy and security that inspires a sense of confidence and personalized offerings and recommendation. Such elements are important in technology-based environments because it should replace the sales person and the physical surroundings of traditional stores (as cited in Montoya-Weiss et al., 2003). In addition, websites should be responsive to shoppers' questions and needs promptly. Using advanced technologies, retailers can offer click-to-chat or click-to-call features enabling their customers to speak with customer service representatives. Our findings reveal that effective servicing systems should adapt transactions to the customer's needs. Collecting customer-centric data that is enabled by advanced technologies should be adapted to shoppers' behavior and preferences. As the case in traditional service quality, reliability is the most important factor that influences the perception of service quality and satisfaction. Websites that do not crash and offer products and services as promised indicate the technical reliability of the service.

More importantly, our findings indicate that online shoppers value the choice of ordering items online and picking up these purchases at a nearby store. Online shoppers favor this practice as a means of avoiding shipping charges. Websites that enable locating nearby stores inform shoppers when product is ready for pickup encourage customers' satisfaction and thereby are expected to influence their loyalty. This indicates that the retailer's database not only needs to be integrated, but also requires an efficient logistics system to enable a smooth purchase transaction. Retailers also should not underestimate the importance of reverse logistics to customers. Therefore, multichannel retailers are encouraged to use the complementary effect of channels in designing multichannel servicing systems as these complementary effects encourage using one channel in favor of the other.

The attainment of service management has become a pivotal concern for service managers. This chapter is dedicated to understand the concept of service quality considering the subjective variability of customers in multichannel retailing.

REFERENCES

Anderson, J., & Gerbing, D. (1988). Structural Equation Modeling in Practice: A Review and Recommended Two-Step Approach. *Psychological Bulletin*, *103*(3), 411–423. doi:10.1037/0033-2909.103.3.411

Bagozzi, R., & Yi, Y. (1988). On the Evaluation of Structural Equation Models. *Journal of the Academy of Marketing Science*, *16*(1), 74–94. doi:10.1007/BF02723327

Barnes, S., & Vidgen, R. (2002). An Integrative Approach to the Assessment of E-Commerce Quality. *Journal of Electronic Commerce Research*, *3*(2), 114–127.

Bauer, H., Falk, T., & Hammerschmidt, M. (2006). eTransQual: A Transaction Process-based Approach for Capturing Service Quality in Online Shopping. *Journal of Business Research*, *59*, 866–875. doi:10.1016/j.jbusres.2006.01.021

Berman, B., & Thelen, S. (2004). A Guide to Developing and Managing a Well-integrated Multichannel Retail Strategy. *International Journal of Retail and Distribution Management*, *32*(3), 147–156. doi:10.1108/09590550410524939

Bhattacherjee, A. (2001). Understanding Information Systems Continuance: An Expectation-Confirmation Model. *Management Information Systems Quarterly*, *25*(3), 351–370. doi:10.2307/3250921

Birgelen, M., Jong, A., & Ruyter, K. (2006). Multichannel service retailing: The Effects of Channel Performance Satisfaction on Behavioral Intentions. *Journal of Retailing*, *82*(4), 367–377. doi:10.1016/j.jretai.2006.08.010

Bitner, J., Brown, S., & Meuter, M. (2000). Technology Infusion in Service Encounters. *Journal of the Academy of Marketing Science, 28*, 138–149. doi:10.1177/0092070300281013

Churchill, G. (1979). A Paradigm for Developing Better Measures of Marketing Constructs. *JMR, Journal of Marketing Research, 16*(1), 64–73. doi:10.2307/3150876

Cronin, J., & Taylor, S. (1992). Measuring Service Quality: A Reexamination and Extension. *Journal of Marketing, 56*, 55–68. doi:10.2307/1252296

Davis, F. (1989). Perceived Usefulness, Ease of Use and User Acceptance of Information Technology. *Management Information Systems Quarterly, 13*(3), 319–339. doi:10.2307/249008

Davis, F. (1993). User Acceptance of Information Technology: Systems Characteristics, User Perceptions and Behavioral Impacts. *International Journal of Man-Machine Studies, 38*(3), 475–487. doi:10.1006/imms.1993.1022

Deshpande, R., & Zaltman, G. (1982). Factors Affecting the Use of Market Research Information: A Path Analysis. *JMR, Journal of Marketing Research, 19*(February), 14–31. doi:10.2307/3151527

EMarketer. (2009). College Students Online: Driving Change in Internet and Mobile Usage. Retrieved October 30, 2009 from http://www.emarketer.com/Report.aspx?code=emarketer_2000524

Forrester. (2006a). Trends 2006: Multichannel retail. Retrieved October 30, 2009 from http://www.forrester.com/Research/Documents

Forrester. (2006b). Best Practices in Multichannel Retailing. Retrieved October 30, 2009 from http://www.forrester.com/Research/Documents

Forrester. (2007). Trends 2007: Multichannel Retal. Retrieved October 30, 2009 from http://www.forrester.com/Research/Documents

Forrester. 2009. Multichannel: In-Store Pickup Gains Importance. Retrieved October 30, 2009 from http://www.forrester.com/Research/Document/Excerpt/0,7211,48133,00.html

Gefen, D. (2002a). Customer loyalty in e-commerce. *Journal of the Association for Information Systems, 3*(1), 27–51.

Goersch, D. (2002). Multi-channel integration and its implications for retail web sites. Retrieved October 30, 2009 from http://is2.lse.ac.uk/asp/aspecis/20020015.pdf

Hair, J., Tatham, R., Anderson, R., & Black, W. (1998). *Multivariate Data Analysis* (5th ed.). Englewood Cliffs, NJ: Prentice-Hall.

Hatcher, L. (1994). *A Step-by-Step Approach to Using the SAS System for Factor and Structural Equation Modeling.* Cary, NC: The SAS Institute.

Hefley, W. (2008). Service Science: A Key Driver of the 21st Century Prosperity. Retrieved October 30, 2009 from http://www.itif.org/files/BHefley-Summary.pdf

Hoffman, D., & Novak, T. (1996). Marketing in Hypermedia Computer-Mediated Environments: Conceptual Foundations. *Journal of Marketing, 80*(4), 50–68. doi:10.2307/1251841

Hoque, Y., & Lohse, G. (1999). An Information Search Cost Perspective for Designing Interfaces for Electronic Commerce. *JMR, Journal of Marketing Research, 36*(3), 387–394. doi:10.2307/3152084

InternetRetailer. (2007). More Merchants are Mastering Buy Online/Pick-Up In-Store. Retrieved October 30, 2009 from http://www.internetretailer.com/dailyNews.asp?id=23384

Iwaarden, J., Wiele, T., Ball, L., & Millen, R. (2004). Perceptions about the Quality of Web Sites: A Survey among Students at Northeastern and Eastern University. *Information & Management, 41*, 947–959. doi:10.1016/j.im.2003.10.002

James, A. (2008). Nordstrom lets you buy online, pick up at the store. Retrieved October 30, 2009 from http://www.seattlepi.com/business/363901_nordstrom21.html

Jupiter. (2007). Trends 2007: Multichannel Retailer. Retrieved October 30, 2009 from www.forrester.com/Research/Documents

Jupiter Research. (2004). Concept report from JupiterMedia: New York, December 30, 2004, In Collier & Bienstock. (2006). Measuring service quality in e-retailing. *Journal of Service Research*, *8*(3), 260–275.

Lee, H., & Whang, S. (2001). Winning the Last Mile of E-Commerce. *MIT Sloan Management Review*, *42*(4), 4–62.

Lennstrand, B., Persson, C., & Wikström, S. (2002). E-commerce in a Multi-Channel Retailing Context." *ITS 14th Biennial Conference*, August 18-21, 2002, Seoul, Korea.

Loiacono, E., Watson, R., & Goodhue, D. (2007). WebQual: An Instrument for Consumer Evaluation of Web Sites. *International Journal of Electronic Commerce*, *11*(3), 51–87. doi:10.2753/JEC1086-4415110302

MediaAudit. 2008. Online Shopping By Minorities Increase. Retrieved October 30, 2009 from http://ecommerce-news.internetretailer.com/search?p=Q&ts=custom2&isort=date&mainresult=mt_inrg_f&w=customer+service&x=10&y=10=

Montoya-Weiss, M., Voss, G., & Grewel, D. (2003). Determinants of Online Channel Use and Overall Satisfaction with a Rational, Multichannel Service Provider. *Journal of the Academy of Marketing Science*, *31*(4), 448–458. doi:10.1177/0092070303254408

Müller-Lankenau, C., Klein, S., & Wehmeyer, K. 2004. Developing a Framework for Multi-Channel Strategies: An Analysis of Cases from the Grocery Retailing Industry. In *Proceedings the 17th Bled Electronic Commerce Conference*. Bled, Slovenia, June 21-23.

Nunnally, C., & Bernstein, I. (1994). *Psychometric Theory* (3rd ed.). New York: McGraw-Hill.

Oliver, R. (1980). A Cognitive Model for the Antecedents and Consequences of Satisfaction. *JMR, Journal of Marketing Research*, *17*(4), 460–469. doi:10.2307/3150499

Oliver, R. (1997). *Satisfaction: A Behavioral Perspective on the Consumer*. New York: McGraw-Hill.

Parasuraman, A., Zeithaml, V., & Berry, L. (1988). SERVQUAL: A Multi-Item Scale for Measuring Consumer Perception of Service Quality. *Journal of Retailing*, *64*, 2–40.

Parasuraman, A., Zeithaml, V., & Malhotra, A. (2005). E-S-Qual: A Multiple-Item Scale for Assessing Electronic Service Quality. *Journal of Service Research*, *7*(3), 213–233. doi:10.1177/1094670504271156

Pastore, M. (2000). US college students use net for shopping. Retrieved October 30, 2009 from http://www.clickz.com/stats/sectors/demographics/article.php/432631

Prasarnphanich, P., & Gillenson, M. (2003). The Hybrid Clicks and Bricks Business Model. *Communications of the ACM*, *46*(12), 178–185. doi:10.1145/953460.953498

Reichheld, F., & Schefter, P. (2000). E-loyalty: Your secret weapon on the Web. *Harvard Business Review*, *78*(4), 105–113.

Retailer Daily. 2008. Multi-Channel Holiday Shoppers Prefer Web to In-Store. Retrieved October 30, 2009 from http://www.retailerdaily.com/entry/first-time-ever-multi-channel-holiday-shoppers-prefer-web-to-in-store/

RetailerNetGroup. (2009). The new alternative channels: From site to store. Retrieved October 30, 2009 from http://archive.constantcontact.com/fs028/1102142477435/archive/1102649159680.html

Reuters (2009). O'Reilly Auto Parts Introduces Buy Online, Pick Up In Store. Retrieved October 30, 2009 from http://www.reuters.com/article/pressRelease/idUS244274+21-Apr-2009+BW20090421

Saeed, K., Grover, V., & Hwang, Y. (2003). Creating synergy with a click and mortar approach. *Communications of the ACM, 46*(12), 206–212. doi:10.1145/953460.953501

Sousa, R., & Voss, C. (2006). Service Quality in Multichannel Services Employing Virtual Channels. *Journal of Service Research, 8*(4), 356–371. doi:10.1177/1094670506286324

Spohrer, J., Maglio, P., Baily, J., & Gruhl, D. (2007). Steps toward a Science of Service Systems. *Computer, 40*(1), 71–77. doi:10.1109/MC.2007.33

Steinfield, C., Adelaar, T., & Fang, L. (2005). Click and Mortar Strategies Viewed from the Web: A Content Analysis of Features Illustrating Integration Between Retailers' Online and Offline Presence. *Electronic Markets, 15*(3), 199–212. doi:10.1080/10196780500208632

Steinfield, C., Mahler, A., & Bauer, J. (1999b). Electronic Commerce and the Local Merchant: Opportunities for synergy between physical and web presence. *Electronic Markets, 9*(1/2), 51–57.

Swaid, S., & Wigand, R. (2009). Measuring the Quality of E-Service: Scale Development and Initial Validation. *Journal of Electronic Commerce Research, 10*(1), 13–28.

Teller, C., Kotzab, H., & Grant, D. (2006). The consumer direct services revolution in grocery retailing: An exploratory investigation. *Managing Service Quality, 16*(1), 78–96. doi:10.1108/09604520610639973

Teltzrow, M., Günther, O., & Pohle, C. (2003). Analyzing Consumer Behavior at Retailers with Hybrid Distribution Channels - A Trust Perspective. *ACM International Conference Proceedings. 5th International Conference of Electronic Commerce*, Pittsburgh, Pennsylvania.

Venkatesh, V., & Davis, F. (2000). A Theoretical Extension of the Technology Acceptance Model: Four Longitudinal Field Studies. *Management Science, 46*(2), 186–204. doi:10.1287/mnsc.46.2.186.11926

Voss, C. (2003). Rethinking Paradigms of Service: Service in a Virtual Environment. *International Journal of Operations & Production Management, 23*(1), 88–104. doi:10.1108/01443570310453271

Wolfinbarger, M., & Gilly, M. (2003). E-TailQ: Dimensionalizing, Measuring and Predicting Etail Quality. *Journal of Retailing, 27*, 183–198. doi:10.1016/S0022-4359(03)00034-4

Woodall, R., Colby, C. & Parasuraman A. (2007). *E-volution to Revolution*, 29-34.

Zeithaml, V., Parasuraman, A., & Malhorta, A. (2000). A Conceptual Framework for Understanding E-Service Quality: Implications for Future Research and Managerial Practice. *Marketing Science Institute (MSI)*, Report # 00-115.

Zeithaml, V., Parasuraman, A., & Malhotra, A. (2002). Service quality delivery through the Web sites: A critical review of extant knowledge. *Journal of the Academy of Marketing Science, 30*(4), 362–375. doi:10.1177/009207002236911

Zhang, X., & Prybutok, V. (2005). A Consumer Perceptive of E-Service Quality. *IEEE Transactions on Engineering Management, 52*(4), 461–477. doi:10.1109/TEM.2005.856568

ENDNOTE

[1] Other terms referring to multichannel are click-and-mortar, hybrid ecommerce, bricks-and-clicks and cyber-enhanced retailing.

261

Chapter 14
Business Models for Insurance of Business Web Services

Liu Wenyin
City University of Hong Kong, China & CityU-USTC Advanced Research Institute, China

An Liu
University of Science & Technology of China, China & City University of Hong Kong, China & CityU-USTC Advanced Research Institute, China

Qing Li
City University of Hong Kong, China & CityU-USTC Advanced Research Institute, China

Liusheng Huang
University of Science & Technology of China, China & CityU-USTC Advanced Research Institute, China

ABSTRACT

A new business—insurance on business Web services—is proposed. As more and more Web services will be developed to fulfill the ever increasing needs of e-Business, the e-marketplace for Web services will soon be established. However, the qualities of these business Web services are unknown without real experiences and users can hardly make decisions on service selection. We propose that insurance can help build trust in the market of Web services. In this chapter, we propose three insurance models for business Web services and enabling technologies, including quality description, reputation scheme, transaction analysis, etc. We believe that the insurance of business Web services will help service competition and hence boost the development of more and more business Web services, and the software industry at large.

INTRODUCTION

Electronic Business, or e-Business, is the business that can be conducted via computers and software over information networks. It is a revolutionary business paradigm that has emerged with the ad-

vent of the Internet era. It is currently transforming the commercial world. E-Business features automatic information transfer on the Web and automatic information processing at the nodes of the Web, known as Web servers. Software applications are playing critical roles in automating these tasks. Currently, software applications on the Web can deliver a wide variety of solutions to

DOI: 10.4018/978-1-61520-819-7.ch014

address a wide variety of customer and business needs. Electronic purchase orders, payments, negotiations, collaborative work, stock trading, are just a few examples of these applications in e-Business.

What a server can provide can be called services in general. Hence, traditionally, what a Web server can provide has also been called Web services. However, just in the recent several years, Web services have been mainly used to refer to those platform-neutral, self-describing software components that implement business functions and can be automatically discovered and engaged with other Web components to complete complex tasks over the Internet. In other words, Web services are just software components that are networked—instead of applications that are networked. The Web services approach can greatly simplify B2B collaboration and provides a new model for the way businesses share their data and systems. By packaging business processes as software components, Web services will drive much of the still-to-be-developed e-business landscape. Web services will be the main driver of e-business as more business processes are transformed into software elements. Most of such Web services that implement core functions of business will be delivered to customers with service charge and we refer to this kind of Web services as business Web services. Gartner says that the market of software as a service (SaaS) will reach $9.6 billion in 2009, a 21.9 percent increase from 2008 revenue of $6.6 billion, and will show consistent growth through 2013 when worldwide SaaS revenue will total $16 billion for the enterprise application markets. Therefore, in the remaining parts of this paper, we also mean "business Web services" when we talk about "Web services", if it is not clearly specified.

Many experts have highly evaluated the impact of Web services, which will fundamentally transform Web-based applications by enabling them to participate more broadly as an integrated component to an e-Business solution. As pointed out by

Alexander Linden, research director for Gartner, Web services will facilitate much faster software development and integration, enable businesses to become more agile, and help them focus on their core competencies (Coursey, 2001). Gartner had predicted that software Web services will be the next big business IT trend, picking up speed soon. Several companies have already seen the potential commercial opportunities and have invested largely on the Web services infrastructures, which can facilitate the development, delivery, and integration of Web services. For instances, Microsoft has already released their Web service platform, known as Microsoft.NET (http://www.microsoft.com/net/); Sun Microsystems has also launched their own counterpart project, which is named Sun Open Net Environment, or in short, Sun ONE (http://www.sun.com/sunone/), to compete with Microsoft.NET. Other big companies also join this competition, including IBM Web Services Toolkit (http://www.alphaworks.ibm.com/tech/webservicestoolkit/) and HP Web Service Platform (http://www.bluestone.com/products/hp_web_services/).

Actually, competition will not be limited on Web services platforms. The Web service technologies can also bring competition among different Web services and service providers (Cheng, Chang & Zhang, 2007). It can be expected that, with the facilities of advanced Web service technologies, more and more Web services of various functions will be developed, deployed, published soon on the Web and users will have more opportunities to choose among these services. The factors that may affect a user's decision on service selection (from the service marketplace) include service price and quality (we use the term "quality" in this paper to refer to the general performance of Web services, including security, stability, correctness, accuracy, responsive speed, and information processing speed, etc). Just like other kind of services, people have to make tradeoffs between price and quality (Liu et al., 2008). Some services with the same functions or qualities may ask for different prices, which may not be worthy of (or matching) their qualities. It is quite hard for a user to choose a service provider and its service from available ones (of the same or similar kinds). Actually, users may require different levels of qualities of services for different purposes of businesses and different qualities of services should deserve different prices. For those critical businesses, users usually are willing to pay a higher price for a more reliable service, and for non-critical businesses, a moderate quality with a lower price is more preferable.

However, users are usually unable to know the qualities of these services in detail before really using them. They usually get to know these services and their qualities from their providers' own reports or advertisements. No objective, third-party, independent report is currently available. Sometimes, quality of service is more critical in the success of a business since potential lost due to quality of service is risky (Kokash & D'Andrea, 2007). Losses caused by the software services can be huge, depending on the role of the services in the entire business. Similar to hardware devices and equipments, software products or services also cannot be technically and completely guaranteed to function as expected all the time. Hence, the customers of these software products and services are suffering some critical losses while benefiting from their functionalities. Actually, Standish Group has reported that software bugs have cost US companies about 100 billion dollars in 2001. And that does not include the cost of losing angry customers. A concrete example is that, eBay Inc. had ever suffered a 22-hour outage of its E-commerce Web site, traced to a bug in the Solaris operating system (product of Sun Microsystems) that corrupted information in an Oracle database. Sun CEO Scott McNealy had acknowledged a known bug that caused the problem. Due to the impossibility of complete testing (Liu, Jia & Au, 2002), no matter how many time spent on software testing, we cannot test all inputs or all combinations of inputs. This even does

not include the case of potential problems of the complicated Internet environment, which makes the testing more difficult. Hence, the situation of buggy software or services is very likely to stay for a long period of time.

Before the quality of a service (or the potential risk due to service failure) is completely known, insurance of Web services is absolutely one means among the others to increase the service quality in some sense, at least in the sense that customers can trust the service quality more, though additional cost may be needed. Web service providers can also use insurance to survive the coming fierce competition. Thus, it is necessary for insurance companies to step into this area and cover the insurance of Web services, which will become a new prosperous business to greatly help and push the development and pervasion of insured Web services. We define an insured business Web service as a Web service with a service charge, whose service quality, including operation correctness, response time, and other quantitative performance, is insured such that any deteriorated quality/performance causing any kind of loss from its clients can result in a claim for compensation.

THE STATE OF THE ART OF SOFTWARE INSURANCE

The insurance industry began in the middle of 19th century as the engineering insurance emerged with the advent of steam power (Daley, 1999). After that, it took more than one hundred years for the insurance industry to get full development. In the last half century, especially, in the last 20 years, insurance has been expanded to many new areas, e.g., medical insurance and liability insurance, and has become more and more popular in our daily lives and works.

However, software, as either products or services, has constantly been out of from the policy coverage of insurance companies. As Voas (Voas, 1999) pointed out, the reason is that the insurers do not have enough time to collect sufficient historical data for actuaries to estimate premium before a software product becomes obsolete. Another reason is that the intrinsic software quality is usually not guaranteed. For example, it was estimated that the well-known Y2K problem might have needed 300~600 billion dollars for the massive repair effort, which might be beyond the capability of the entire insurance industry. The high risk of software mishap has kept insurers away from this area. Only in recent years, several companies (SpamEater. Net, 2004; Voas, 1999) began to offer insurance on certain types of software/service hazards, such as security breach. A general framework for insurance for such cyber-risks has been discussed by Gordon et al. (Gordon et al., 2003). However, the compensation is usually in fixed amounts and the coverage is too limited. Users can hardly benefit from such insurance.

THE SIGNIFICANCE OF INSURANCE ON WEB SERVICES

Sriram et al. (Sriram et al., 2001) have predicted that more and more commercial off-the-shelf software component will be developed and put on the market for search and integration. To fulfill the ever increasing needs of e-Business, the e-marketplace for Web services will soon be established. It means that someday there will also be a wide variety of Web services available and e-Business systems can automatically search from the market for those that will meet their requirements. Actually, there are already some Web services available (e.g., at www.xmethods.com), which have been developed on several different platforms.

However, whatever the market type, the key barrier to entry is trust (Norris, 2000). People especially do not trust those automatic systems they had never experienced before. Linketscher and Child (Linketscher & Child, 2001) have found that users would be nervous relinquishing total control to such systems from the outset. They

would like to be able to develop a relationship with the system over time and when trust has been established, to increase delegation and reduce their monitoring of the system. We believe that providing insurance on these systems (or Web services) can help reduce the initial mistrust (or doubt) of their users and gradually establish such trust. Once their reputations have been built, they can also help reduce the insurance premium and eventually benefit the system owners or the service providers.

BUSINESS MODELS OF INSURANCE OF BUSINESS WEB SERVICES

Figure 1 is the working model of Web services. In such a model, a Web service is registered in a Web service directory and its client searches from the directory, and requests the service and binds (calls) it within itself. Currently, this working model is supported by the following three core technologies: Web Services Description Languages (WSDL); Universal Description, Discovery and Integration (UDDI); and the Simple Object Access Protocol (SOAP). WSDL is a language that programmers can use to describe the programmatic interfaces of the Web services. UDDI lets Web services register their characteristics with a registry so that other Web applications can look them up. SOAP provides the means for communication between Web services and client applications.

We propose three business models for insurance of Web services: service provider insurance,

Figure 1. The working model of Web services

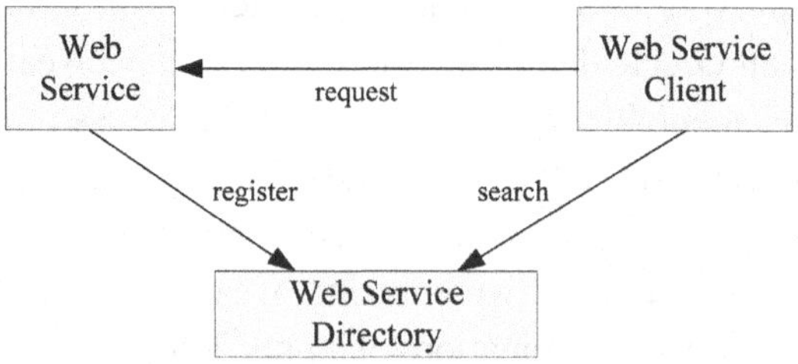

Figure 2. The business model for service provider insurance

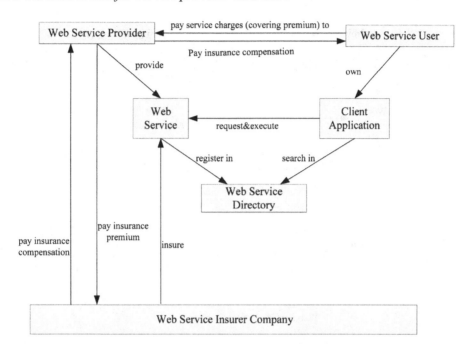

service user insurance and service agent insurance. Figure 2 shows the relationship among stakeholders in the service provider insurance model. In this model, the service provider requests insurance for his service in total from the insurance company. Once a service user/client claims for compensation, the provider first claims and obtains the compensation from the insurance company and then pays to the service user/client. In this case, the service charge includes the premium paid to the insurance company.

Figure 3 shows the relationship among stakeholders in the service user insurance model. In this model, the service user/client requests insurance for this service as individual from the insurance company. The service user should claims for compensation from the insurance company directly once a loss happens. In this case, the service charge requested by the service provider can be lower since it should not include the premium. But the insurance company might need to estimate the insurance premium for each individual case of the applications of this Web service.

Figure 4 illustrates the relationship among the stakeholders in the service agent insurance model. In this model, a new party---web service agent is introduced. Unlike the above two models, web service user and web service provider do not communicate directly in the service agent model but through a web service agent. This is based on the observation that the web service user may not be familiar with the provider. When a user decides to purchase a web service, the information obtained by searching the web service directory is not enough. He would probably need to pay a lot of effort to investigate the details of the service provider and compare between different vendors. In this situation, a delegated web service agent is useful. The web service agent is supposed to be familiar with the web service market and know the advantage and disadvantage of each provider. Hence, when the user raises his requirements, the web service agent is able to provide the user with a good suggestion and specific training for the user to consume the web service. Since the web service agent has a profound insight on the mar-

Figure 3. The business model for service user insurance

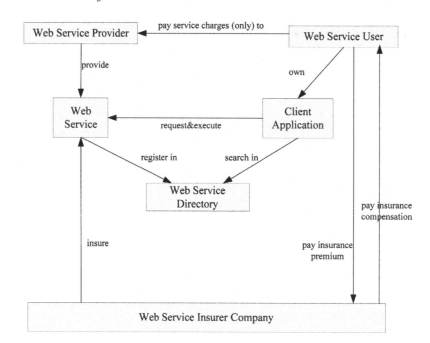

ket, it can better estimate the risk of using specific web service and buy the suitable insurance accordingly for the user. The process is transparent to the user. The user just needs to provide his requirements, pay the service charges (which includes the premium, and service charge of web service and agent), and receive compensation from the agent if any problem occurs. In other words, the web service agent plays a role similar to the retailer between the factory and the user,

Figure 4. The business model for service agent insurance

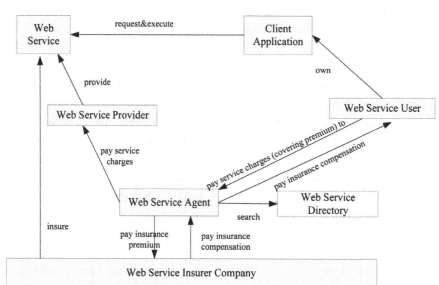

and the consulting firm between the market and the client.

Each model may be suitable for certain types of services. The service provider insurance model is more suitable for those services focusing on calculation and generation of data in a core business solution. The providers of such services are responsible for the correctness, speed, and other internally responsible qualities of these services. Hence, it is the liability of service providers to buy insurance on such services. For example, a service provider can buy insurance on his security service, such as a 128-bit encryption scheme, which will need billions of years to test all the keys to break the code. Although it can also be very lucky to find the key on the first attempt, this possibility is very low (e.g., a billionth per year in this case), and the insurance company can estimate on the premium based on this possibility.

The service user insurance model is more suitable for those services focusing on communication, delivery of data, and other externally dependent functionalities. The quality of such services can hardly be controlled by the providers. E.g., the delivery of data can be delayed due to network congestion. Since the data channel is public and involves more factors and can hardly be guaranteed by few providers, users can buy insurance on such services for themselves. Actually, current software insurance practices are mainly of this model.

The service agent model is more suitable for those large services which have plenteous budget and require high quality. Generally, in large software projects, investigation to the market to choose a suitable middleware may be crucial to the final quality and cost of the whole project. By delegating this as well as the insurance affair to a professional agent, the web service user can focus on his own affair. Furthermore, as a third party, the web service agent can provide an objective to the web service quality, which has strong influence on how much insurance that the user should buy in his optimal case.

CASE STUDIES

In this section, we use three Web services as examples to show how insurance can help Web services serve users better. They are services that can help filter computer viruses, filter spams from emails sent to users, and outsource software components.

Virus Data Update Service

The first example service is related to anti-virus software. In order to do virus scan and cleaning, the software (or its end user) should frequently download the virus update files (DAT files) in order to know what viruses are and what not. Usually the DAT files are owned by the same software company (e.g., McAfee or Symantec). Now in the Web service model, the DAT files can be provided as an online Web service by a provider independent to all anti-virus software companies. The DAT service provider can focus on this service and hence can do it much better, e.g., provide very quicker update when a new virus emerges. It is quite possible since it can focus all its efforts on this matter. Then all anti-virus software can call this online Web service when they want to do virus scan. Suppose the service is called VirusUp2date (it is just a coincidence if this name has been used by some company). In order to compete with other similar services, VirusUp2date guarantees no virus infections (due to late update of virus data files or unavailability) to end users if they pay a monthly fee (say at $19.99). If a data loss due to this reason happens, VirusUp2date promises to pay $1,000 each time to the end user. Actually, the monthly service fee ($19.99) has already included a premium and hence in overall the VirusUp2date service provider can still make a big amount of money even though it may pay some compensation to some early virus victims. The effect is similar if the service provider pays these premiums to an insurance company and if this insurance company trusts this provider. Actually, this scenario follows the business model of service provider insurance. The effect of the service user insurance model is similar but the end users should pay premiums to and claim compensations from the insurance company directly. One of the key issues here is how to know the exact reason of the data loss since there is another stakeholder got involved—the independent anti-virus software. Is it due to service or due to the anti-virus software? The operating system should keep a log of the usage such that the exact reason should be identified. Another issue is how the insurance companies trust the reliability of the service. In the earlier stage of this service, it may be a good idea for the provider to pay the loss to the end users. At a later stage, after sufficient data are collected, the insurance company can calculate a more reasonable premium value for this service and its compensation scheme and then insure this service.

Spam Filtering Service

The second example service is related to spam filtering. Spam, or junk mail, refers to unsolicited commercial e-mail (UCE) and unsolicited bulk e-mail (UBE), e.g., unsolicited advertisements. Spam spreads everywhere on the Internet nowadays and create problems to most of the e-mail users. Although e-mail companies and standards bodies are trying to work on new ways to deal with this problem, receiving junk mail is still unavoidable with today's e-mail standards and technology. All parties are trying their best to cut down the number of spam. Hence, anti-spam is also a good business. Actually, some companies, including SpamEater.Net, have already provided services for spam filtering. It charges a monthly fee to end users (or enterprise users) for filtering the spam from the emails sent to the users bypassing its server. However the accuracy cannot be 100%. For example, SpamEater.Net claims that they can catch more than 96% spam with a less than 1% false alarm (i.e., wrongly filter out a good email) rate. SpamEater.Net has already noticed this

problem and promise to refund back the money paid if the user is not satisfied with the anti-spam effect within 30 days. This is a kind of insurance in some sense. However, if they are confident in their accuracy, they may still make an insurance scheme, like 1$ payback for each wrong spam identification or even higher for those caused bigger loss or inconvenience. By doing so, the users may want to continue with this service. Another spam filtering service, SpamAssasin (SpamAssasin, 2009), does not really remove suspected spam. Instead, it just labels it with a likelihood tag. The email reader at the client (user) side can do the final action to these suspected emails. Since the accuracy is not 100%. The end user can also do necessary actions to manually check those emails with lower likelihood. In this sense, if an insurance scheme is applied, the risk is not high and therefore the premium can be much lower for each wrongly identified email. But the overall monthly service fee should also be lower since the end user may have to conduct manual check and hence reduce his/her productivity.

Software Components Outsourcing Services

Nowadays, outsourcing has become a very popular way to software development due to the large laboring expense differences between different countries and areas. According to the statistics studies by the marketing researchers, the US IT offshore outsourcing market is growing in a rate of 14.4% annually and will nearly double to 14.7 billion dollars by year 2009 (IDC, 2005), and it is reported (Global Outsourcing Report, 2005) that three quarters of US companies outsourced some or all their information technology activities in year 2004, and this percentage is expected to increase furthermore in 2005. Nearly three quarters of the international software outsourcing companies expect to grow their revenues by 11% within the next 12 months (ComputerWeekly, 2005). Web service, as a platform neutral technology, is a very convenient and reliable framework to the outsourcing industry. The whole software project can be divided into several functional components by the development company, and some of them could be outsourced, which could be implemented in web service technology. Since the web service technology has few requirements on caller components, such a way can utilize many existing software modules, without consideration of their platforms. For example, there may be some existing modules in Linux and using web service technology can reduce the migration/re-development cost greatly. Furthermore, the whole infrastructure, e.g., the hardware, of the components could be outsourced. In such a software development process, every task could be much more specialized, and dispatched to an experienced or low cost company. The developing efficiency could be boosted while the cost could be reduced. However, web service components also bring the risk into the whole project. The quality of outsourced components is beyond the control of the project development company, and there may be some interoperability bugs between the distributed components. Though the full system testing could fix the bugs within and between components and reduce the risk, it is not sufficient to guarantee the overall quality. In this situation, the web service insurance of component outsourcing could be introduced to further guarantee the quality of the whole product, such that the project development company can be compensated in case of any individual or interoperability problem occurs.

KEY TECHNOLOGIES FOR INSURANCE OF BUSINESS WEB SERVICE

In either model, the key technologies are how to estimate the premium for an insured Web service and how to determine the loss and compensation due to this service. Other related technologies, including how to test/evaluate Web services qualities, how to improve Web services qualities, and how to build and manage the reputation record of Web services, are also important in the insurance business of Web services.

How to estimate premium? Although the role of a Web service in a business solution can also affect the premium, we focus on the influence of the quality of service in this paper. As we mentioned before that the reason why insurance companies do not want to get involved in software insurance is that the insurers do not have enough time to collect sufficient historical data for actuaries to estimate premium before a software product becomes obsolete. While in the case of Web services, they will not expire since they will frequently be upgraded and maintained as the same services. Through a period of time in service, the reputation of the services can be built. Currently, most Web services are generally not concerned about the level of quality of service presented to their users/client. However, the quality of service that is experienced by its users will become a dominant factor for the success of a business Web service. First of all, the principle quality attributes these users can perceive include those related to the "responsiveness" of the service, i.e., the service availability and timeliness. A service that is frequently unavailable may have the effect of tarnishing the reputation of the service provider or result in loss of opportunity. Secondly, security level of the services is also a reputation. Those websites frequently be hacked will definitely lose reputations. Finally, other qualities, including functionality correctness and stabilities, caused by software bugs can also affect the reputation of a service. Hence, Web service quality test/evaluation is a key technology for insurance of Web services. For example, active monitoring and user feedbacks could be used to evaluate non-deterministic qualities such as service availability and timeliness (Liu, Ngu & Zhang, 2004; Jurca, Binder & Faltings, 2007) Related technologies that could help users experience better services, e.g., work load balancing and exception notification of Web services (Liu, Jia & Au, 2002), are also useful in the insurance business of Web services.

Insurance premium can also be set differently at different times, like temporal fares for telephone systems. Some service can guarantee more immediate response at non-busy period, e.g., in weekends; but others may heavily rely on human supports, which are more expensive in weekends. Either they can change such service prices or they can change the insurance premium.

How to determine loss and compensation? Every transaction of the Web service execution, including the situation of the environment, e.g., input/output, time, network status, etc., should be logged such that the execution of this service can be repeated. Once a claim on loss compensation happens, the cause of such loss can be found through transaction analysis and the loss and compensation can then be calculated according to related insurance terms. For example, Liu et al. (2008) proposed a methodology to predict the expected loss and profit of service-oriented business applications. Moreover, transaction analysis can also help find other quality problems of the Web services. Currently, since there is no exercise of such insurance compensation, there should be much research work to do in this aspect for the insurance business of Web services.

How to build and manage a reputation record of (insured) business Web services? A historical record of users' rating can help. A mechanism similar to Platform for Internet Content Selection (PICS) can also help. For new services, third party testing can also help build initial quality rating. The insurance company can also hold a website like www.methodx.com and rate all services for users to look up and choose among them. The original quality level claimed by the service providers can also be used to compare with the real qualities and reputations. Both the quality level (in all aspects) and the reputation should be included into the description of services. Currently, WSDL and UDDI specifications do not support QoS description and query, but they provide extension

mechanisms that can be used to advertise QoS. For example, service providers can attach execution price to the operation elements in the WSDL to specify how much the service consumer should pay to the service provider when invoking these operations. In addition, UDDI can be extended to support publish and query QoS (Zhou et al., 2004). However, these approaches need to modify WSDL and UDDI. To follow the design strategy, separation of concern, which is widely accepted in the service oriented architecture, some other approaches are proposed recently. For example, Web services agreement specification (Andrieux et al., 2007) is a piece of work that allows service providers to advertize QoS separately.

We hope that the future versions of WSDL, UDDI, and SOAP can also include or help automation of contract signing, accepting the insurance terms and prices, negotiations, payment, fulfillment reputation records, etc. In this case, decision on service selection can also be automated.

CONCLUSION

We have proposed the insurance on business Web services as a new business, which can help both to build trust in the e-marketplace of business Web services and to ensure lossless e-Business. Three insurance models for business Web services—service provider insurance, service user insurance and service agent insurance—have been proposed. Their enabling technologies, including reputation scheme, quality description, transaction analysis, have been discussed. We believe that the insurance of business Web services will help service competition and hence boost the development of more and more business Web services, and the software industry at large.

To further promote business Web services and the software industry at large and reduce the risk of e-Business (including risks of both service providers and services customers), we also advocate the impact of governments and legislatures on

Web service insurance and Web service qualities. The governments' attitudes to the Y2K problem have successfully helped the world pass that time smoothly. We hope they can help again in the insurance of business Web services.

REFERENCES

Andrieux, A., Czajkowski, K., Dan, A., Keahey, K., Ludwig, H., Nakata, T., et al. (2007). Web services agreement specification (WS-Agreement). http://www.ogf.org/documents/GFD.107.pdf

Cheng, S., Chang, C. K., & Zhang, L.-J. (2007). Towards competitive web service market. In *Proceedings of International Workshop on Future Trends of Distributed Computing Systems* (pp. 213-219).

ComputerWeekly. (2005). UK jobs to benefit from outsourcing growth. Retrieved from http://www.computerweekly.com/Article138576.htm?src=rssNews

Coursey, D. (2001). The four biggest biz-tech trends of the coming decade. ZDNet/AnchorDesk, http://www.zdnet.com/anchordesk/stories/story/0,10738,2816779,00.html

Daley, A. (1999). Towards safer electrical installations: The insurer's view. In *Proceedings of IEE Colloquium on toward safer electrical installations - learning the lessons* (pp. 1-6).

Global Outsourcing Report. (2005). Release of the Global Outsourcing Report. Retrieved from http://pdfserver.prweb.com/pdfdownload/220341/pr.pdf

Gordon, L. A., Loeb, M. P., & Sohail, T. (2003). A framework for insurance for cyber-risk management. *Communications of the ACM, 46*(3), 81–85. doi:10.1145/636772.636774

IDC. (2005). US off shoring to double to $14.7 billion by 2009. Retrieved from http://www.financialexpress.com/fe_full_story.php?content_id=102877

Jurca, R., Binder, W., & Faltings, B. (2007). Reliable QoS Monitoring based on client feedback. In *Proceedings of International Conference on World Wide Web* (pp. 1003-1011).

Kaner, C. (1997). The impossibility of complete testing. *Software QA, 4*(4), 28–44.

Kokash, N., & D'Andrea, V. (2007). Evaluating quality of web services: a risk-driven approach. In *Proceedings of International Conference on Business Information Systems* (pp. 180-194).

Linketscher, N., & Child, M. (2001). Trust issues and user reactions to e-services and e-marketplaces: a customer survey. In *Proceedings of 12th International Workshop on Database and Expert Systems Applications* (pp. 752-756).

Liu, A., Li, Q., Huang, L., & Liu, H. (2008). Building profit-aware service-oriented business applications. In *Proceedings of the International Conference on Web Services* (pp. 489-496).

Liu, W., Jia, W., & Au, P. O. (2002). Add exception notification mechanism to Web services. In *Proceedings of International Conference on Algorithms & Architectures for Parallel Processing* (pp. 483-488).

Liu, Y., Ngu, A., & Zeng, L. (2004). QoS computation and policing in dynamic web service selection. In *Proceedings of the International Conference on World Wide Web* (pp. 66-73).

Muse, D. (2001). Gartner says Web services coming soon. *Internetnews/ASP News*, Oct. 10, (http://www.internetnews.com/asp-news/article/0,3411_901271,00.html).

Norris, M. (2000). Survival in the eBusiness jungle. *Software Focus, 1*(1), 23–26. doi:10.1002/1529-7950(200009)1:1<23::AID-SWF4>3.0.CO;2-A

PICS. (Platform for Internet Content Selection (PICS)). Retrieved from http://www.w3.org/PICS/

Rossi, M. A. (2001). Stand alone e-commerce market survey. *IRMI Expert Commentary*. Retrieved from http://www.irmi.com/expert/articles/rossi004chart.asp

SpamAssasin. (2009). Retrieved from http://spamassassin.apache.org/

SpamEater. Net (2009). Retrieved from http://www.spameater.net.

Sriram, S., Kumar, A., Gupta, D., & Jalote, P. (2001). ComponentXchange: a software component marketplace on the Internet. In *Proceedings of the International Conference on World Wide Web* (pp. 1098-1099).

Voas, J. (1999). The cold realities of software insurance. *IT Professional*, *1*(1), 71–72. doi:10.1109/6294.774795

Zhou, C., Chia, L.-T., & Lee, B.-S. (2004). QoS-aware and federated enhancement for UDDI. *International Journal of Web Services Research*, *1*(2), 58–85.

Compilation of References

Abowd, G. D., Dey, A. K., Brown, P. J., Davies, N., Smith, M., & Steggles, P. (1999). *Towards a Better Understanding of Context and Context-Awareness* (pp. 304–307). Handheld and Ubiquitous Computing.

Agrawal, R., & Srikant, R. (1994). Fast algorithms for mining association rules in large databases. In *Proc. of International Very Large Databases Conference* (pp. 589–598).

Albanese, M., Capasso, P., Picariello, A., & Rinaldi, A. M. (2005). Information Retrieval from the Web: An Interactive Paradigm. In *Advances in Multimedia Information Systems* (LNCS 3665, pp. 17-32). Heidelberg: Springer.

Almeida, J. P. A., Iacob, M.-E., Jonkers, H., & Quartel, D. A. C. (2006). *Model-Driven Development of Context-Aware Services* (pp. 213–227). Distributed Applications and Interoperable Systems.

Alonso, G., Casati, F., Kuno, H., & Machiraju, V. (2004). *Web Services: Concepts, Architectures and Applications*. Berlin: Springer-Verlag.

Amundsen, S. L., & Eliassen, F. (2008). A resource and context model for mobile middleware. *Personal and Ubiquitous Computing, 12*(2), 143–153. doi:10.1007/s00779-006-0105-4

Amyot, D., Becha, H., Bræk, R., & Rossebø, J. E. Y. (2008). *Next Generation Service Engineering. ITU-T Innovations in NGN Kaleidoscope Conference* (pp. 195-202). IEEE Computer Society.

Anderson, J., & Gerbing, D. (1988). Structural Equation Modeling in Practice: A Review and Recommended Two-Step Approach. *Psychological Bulletin, 103*(3), 411–423. doi:10.1037/0033-2909.103.3.411

Andrews, T., Curbera, F., Dholakia, H., Goland, Y., Klein, J., Leymann, F., et al. (2003). *Business Process Execution Language for Web Services (BPEL4WS) 1.1*.

Andrieux, A., Czajkowski, K., Dan, A., Keahey, K., Ludwig, H., Nakata, T., et al. (2007). Web services agreement specification (WS-Agreement). http://www.ogf.org/documents/GFD.107.pdf

Apache Tomcat. (n.d.). Retrieved from http://tomcat.apache.org/

Apache. (2009). Java API to Access Microsoft Format Files. Retrieved from http://poi.apache.org/

APQC (American Productivity & Quality Center). (2010). Process Classification Framework. Retrieved from http://www.apqc.org

ARIS EPC. (n.d.). Retrieved February 10, 2009, from the ARIS EPC Wiki: http://en.wikipedia.org/wiki/Event-driven_process_chain.

Arkin, A., Askary, S., Fordin, S., Jekeli, W., Kawaguchi, K., Orchard, D., et al. (2002). *Web Service Choreography Interface (WSCI) 1.0*.

Athanasopoulos, D., Zarras, A., & Issarny, V. (2009). Towards the Maintenance of Service Oriented Software. In *Proceedings of the 3rd CSMR Workshop on Software Quality and Maintenance (SQM'09)*.

Atkinson, M., DeRoure, D., Alistair Dunlop, A., et al. (2004). Web service grids: An evolutionary approach. *UK e-Science Technical Report Series*. Retrieved July 6, 2009 from http://www.nesc.ac.uk/technical_papers/UKeS-2004-05.pdf

Axis (n.d.). Retrieved from http://ws.apache.org/axis/index.html

Baader, F., Calvanese, D., McGuinness, D. L., Nardi, D., & Patel-Schneider, P. (2003). *The description logic handbook: theory, implementation and applications.* Cambridge: Cambridge University Press.

Bagozzi, R., & Yi, Y. (1988). On the Evaluation of Structural Equation Models. *Journal of the Academy of Marketing Science, 16*(1), 74–94. doi:10.1007/BF02723327

Baldauf, M., Dustdar, S., & Rosenberg, F. (2007). A Survey on Context-aware Systems. *International Journal of Ad Hoc Ubiquitous Computing, 2*(4), 263–277. doi:10.1504/IJAHUC.2007.014070

Barbara, D., Garcia-Molina, H., & Porter, D. (1992). The management of probabilistic data. *IEEE Transactions on Knowledge and Data Engineering, 4*(5), 487–50. doi:10.1109/69.166990

Barnes, S., & Vidgen, R. (2002). An Integrative Approach to the Assessment of E-Commerce Quality. *Journal of Electronic Commerce Research, 3*(2), 114–127.

Bartolini, C., Sahai, A., & Sauve, J. P. (Eds.). (2007). *Proceedings of the Second IEEE/IFIP Workshop on Business-Driven IT Management, BDIM'07.* Piscataway, USA: IEEE Press.

Bastida, L. (2008). A Methodology for Dynamic Service Composition. *International Conference on Composition-Based Software Systems* (pp. 33-42).

Bauer, H., Falk, T., & Hammerschmidt, M. (2006). eTransQual: A Transaction Process-based Approach for Capturing Service Quality in Online Shopping. *Journal of Business Research, 59*, 866–875. doi:10.1016/j.jbusres.2006.01.021

Bell, M. (2008). *Introduction to Service-Oriented Modeling. Service-Oriented Modeling: Service Analysis, Design, and Architecture.* Wiley & Sons.

Ben Mokhtar, S., Kaul, A., Georgantas, N., & Issarny, V. (2006). Efficient Semantic Service Discovery in Pervasive Computing Environments. In *Proceedings of the 7th ACM/IFIP/USENIX International Middleware Conference (MIDDLEWARE'06)* (LNCS 4290, pp. 240-259).

Benatallah, B., Reza, H., & Nezhad, M. (2006, July/August). A model-driven framework for web services life-cycle management. *IEEE Internet Computing,* 55–63. doi:10.1109/MIC.2006.87

Bennett, K., et al. (2000). Service-Based Software: the Future for Flexible Software. In *Proceedings of the Seventh Asia-Pacific Software Engineering Conference.* IEEE Press.

Berardi, D., Calvanese, D., DeGiacomo, G., Lenzerini, M., & Mecella, M. (2005). Automatic Service Composition Based on Behavioral Descriptions. *International Journal of Cooperative Information Systems, 14*(4), 333–376. doi:10.1142/S0218843005001201

Berman, B., & Thelen, S. (2004). A Guide to Developing and Managing a Well-integrated Multi-channel Retail Strategy. *International Journal of Retail and Distribution Management, 32*(3), 147–156. doi:10.1108/09590550410524939

Bezdek, J. (1974). Cluster validity with fuzzy sets. *Journal of Cybernetics, 3*(3), 58–73. doi:10.1080/01969727308546047

Bhattacherjee, A. (2001). Understanding Information Systems Continuance: An Expectation-Confirmation Model. *Management Information Systems Quarterly, 25*(3), 351–370. doi:10.2307/3250921

Bhiri, S., Godart, C., & Perrin, O. (2005). *Reliable Web Services Composition using a Transactional Approach.* Paper presented at the 2005 IEEE International Conference on e-Technology, e-Commerce, and e-Services (EEE 2005), Hong Kong, China.

Bhiri, S., Perrin, O., & Godart, C. (2005). *Ensuring Required Failure Atomicity of Composite Web Services.* Paper presented at the Proceedings of the 14th international conference on World Wide Web, WWW 2005, Chiba, Japan.

Bidan, C., Issarny, V., Saridakis, T., & Zarras, A. (1998). A Dynamic Reconfiguration Service for CORBA. In *Proceedings of the 4th IEEE International Conference on Configurable Distributed Systems* (pp. 35-42).

Bieberstein, N. (2005). *Service-Oriented Architecture (SOA) Compass: Business Value, Planning, and Enterprise Roadmap.* IBM Press.

Birgelen, M., Jong, A., & Ruyter, K. (2006). Multi-channel service retailing: The Effects of Channel Performance Satisfaction on Behavioral Intentions. *Journal of Retailing, 82*(4), 367–377. doi:10.1016/j.jretai.2006.08.010

Bitner, J., Brown, S., & Meuter, M. (2000). Technology Infusion in Service Encounters. *Journal of the Academy of Marketing Science*, *28*, 138–149. doi:10.1177/0092070300281013

Blair, G. S., Blair, L., Issarny, V., Tuma, P., & Zarras, A. (2000). The Role of Software Architecture in Constraining Adaptation in Component-Based Middleware Platforms. In *Proceedings of the 2nd ACM/IFIP/USENIX International Middleware Conference (MIDDLEWARE'00)* (pp. 164-184).

Bodie, Z. (2004). *Essentials of Investments* (5th ed.). New York: McGraw-Hill/Irwin.

Bolumole, Y. A., Knemeyer, A. M., & Lambert, D. M. (2006). *The customer service management process*. Sarasota, FL: Supply Chain Management Institute.

Botta, C., & Thomas, O. (2002). New Requirements on the Support of the Product Development Process. In R. Mosca, F. Tonelli & S. Pozzi Cotto (Eds.), *Proceedings of the 4th International Conference on: The Modern Information Technology in the Innovation Processes of the Industrial Enterprises, MITIP 2002, Savona, Italy, 27.-29. June 2002* (pp. 107-111). Genoa, Italy: Edizioni Culturali Internazionali Genova.

Bræk, R., & Haugen, Ø. (1993). *Engineering Real Time Systems*. Hemel Hempstead: Prentice Hall.

Bressand, A., Distler, C., & Nicolaidis, K. (1989). Networks at the Heart of the Service Economy. In Bressand, A., & Nicolaidis, K. (Eds.), *Strategic trends in services: an inquiry into the global service economy* (pp. 17–32). New York: Harper & Row.

Broll, G., Hubmann, H., Prezerakos, G. N., Kapitsaki, G., & Salsano, S. (2007). *Modeling Context Information for Realizing Simple Mobile Services* (pp. 1–5). Mobile and Wireless Communications Summit.

Bucchiarone, A., & Gnesi, S. (2006). A survey on services composition languages and models. In *Proceedings of the International Workshop on Web Services – Modeling and Testing* (Web service-MaTe 2006), Palermo, Sicily, June 9 (pp.51-63).

Bundesinstitut für Berufsbildung. (2004). *Anlagenmechaniker/-in für Sanitär-, Heizungs- und Klimatechnik - ein neuer Name oder mehr? Neuordnung*. Bielefeld: Bertelsmann.

Burlton, R. (2001). *Business Process Management: Profiting From Process*. Sams.

Burstien, M. (2005). A semantic Web services architecture. *IEEE Internet Computing*, *9*(5), 72–81. doi:10.1109/MIC.2005.96

Cabrera, L. F., Copeland, G., Feingold, M., Freund, R. W., Freund, T., & Johnson, J. (2003). *Web Services Coordination*. WS-Coordination.

Cabrera, L. F., Copeland, G., Feingold, M., Freund, R. W., Freund, T., & Johnson, J. (2005). *Web Services Atomic Transaction*. WS-AtomicTransaction.

Cabrera, L. F., Copeland, G., Feingold, M., Freund, R. W., Freund, T., & Joyce, S. (2005). *Web Services Business Activity Framework*. WS-BusinessActivity.

Cardoso, J., & Sheth, A. (2006). *Semantic Web Services, Processes and Applications*. Springer. doi:10.1007/978-0-387-34685-4

Castejón, H. N. (2008). *Collaborations in Service Engineering*. PhD thesis, Norwegian University of Science and Technology, Trondheim, Norway.

Castejón, H. N., & Bræk, R. (2005). *Dynamic Role Binding in a Service Oriented Architecture*. International Federation for Information Processing 190.

Castejón, H. N., & Bræk, R. (2006). A collaboration-based approach to service specification and detection of implied scenarios. *5th Int. Workshop on Scenarios and State Machines: Models, Algorithms and Tools (SCESM'06)* (pp. 37-43). ACM Press.

Castejón, H. N., Bochmann, G., & Bræk, R. (2007). Realizability of collaboration-based service specifications. *14th Asia-Pacific Software Engineering Conference* (pp. 73-80). IEEE CS.

Castells, M. (1996). *The rise of the network society*. Cambridge, MA: Blackwell.

Cavallo, R., & Pittarelli, M. (1987). The theory of probabilistic databases. In *Proceedings of the 13th International Conference on Very Large Data Bases* (pp. 71-81).

Celentano, A., Faralli, S., & Pittarello, F. (2008). *The Situation Lens: Looking into Personal Service Composition* (pp. 165–174). ER Workshops.

Chaffey, D. (2007). *E-Business and E-Commerce Management* (3rd ed.). Harlow, UK: Prentice Hall.

Chakraborty, B., Maeda, T., & Chakraborty, G. (2005). Multiobjective route selection for car navigation system using genetic algorithm. In *Proceedings of the 2005 IEEE Mid-Summer Workshop on Soft Computing in Industrial Applications* (pp.190-195).

Chang, J. F. (2005). *Business Process Management Systems: Strategy and Implementation.* Auerbach Publications. doi:10.1201/9781420031362

Charalabidis, Y., Gionis, G., Hermann, K.M., & Martinez, C. (2008, Feb). *Enterprise Interoperability Research Roadmap.*

Chen, H. (2003). Digital government: technologies and practices. *Decision Support Systems, 34*(3), 223–227. doi:10.1016/S0167-9236(02)00118-5

Chen, D., & Doumeingts, G. (2008). Architectures for enterprise integration and interoperability-Past, present and future. *Computers in Industry, I*(59), 647–659. doi:10.1016/j.compind.2007.12.016

Chen, G., & Kotz, D. (2000). *A Survey of Context-Aware Mobile Computing Research.* Technical Report. UMI Order Number: TR2000-381. Dartmouth College, USA. Retrieved April 10, 2009, from http://www.cs.dartmouth.edu/~dfk/papers/chen-survey-tr.pdf

Chen, I. Y. L., Yang, S. J. H., Huang, J. J. S., & Lan, B. C. W. (2006). Ubiquitous Provision of Context Aware Web Services. In *Proceedings of the 2006 IEEE International Conference on Services Computing Services Computing* (pp. 60-68). Los Alamitos, USA: IEEE-CS Press.

Cheng, R., & Su, S. Yang, F., & Li, Y. (2006). Using case-based reasoning to support web service composition. In V.N. Alexandrov et al. (Eds.), *ICCS 2006, Part IV* (LNCS 3994, pp. pp. 87-94). Berlin, Heidelberg: Springer-Verlag.

Cheng, S., Chang, C. K., & Zhang, L.-J. (2007). Towards competitive web service market. In *Proceedings of International Workshop on Future Trends of Distributed Computing Systems* (pp. 213-219).

Choi, S., Kim, H., Jang, H., Kim, J., Kim, S. M., & Song, J. (2008). A framework for ensuring consistency of Web Services Transactions. *Information and Software Technology, 50*(7-8), 684–696. doi:10.1016/j.infsof.2007.07.001

Chui, C. K., Kao, B., & Hung, E. (2007). Mining frequent itemsets from uncertain data. In *Proc. of the 11th Pacific-Asia Conference on Knowledge Discovery and Data Mining (PAKDD-2007).*

Churchill, G. (1979). A Paradigm for Developing Better Measures of Marketing Constructs. *JMR, Journal of Marketing Research, 16*(1), 64–73. doi:10.2307/3150876

ComputerWeekly. (2005). UK jobs to benefit from outsourcing growth. Retrieved from http://www.computerweekly.com/Article138576.htm?src=rssNews

Coursey, D. (2001). The four biggest biz-tech trends of the coming decade. ZDNet/AnchorDesk, http://www.zdnet.com/anchordesk/stories/story/0,10738,2816779,00.html

Cronin, J., & Taylor, S. (1992). Measuring Service Quality: A Reexamination and Extension. *Journal of Marketing, 56,* 55–68. doi:10.2307/1252296

Curtis, B. (1992). Process Modeling. [ACM Press.]. *Communications of the ACM, 35,* 75–90. doi:10.1145/130994.130998

Czepiel, J. A. (1980). *Managing customer satisfaction in consumer service businesses.* Cambridge, MA: Marketing Science Institute.

Daley, A. (1999). Towards safer electrical installations: The insurer's view. In *Proceedings of IEE Colloquium on toward safer electrical installations - learning the lessons* (pp. 1-6).

Dan, A., Kuebler, D., & Davis, D. (2004). Web services on demand: WSLA-driven automated management. *IBM Systems Journal, 43*(1), 136–158. doi:10.1147/sj.431.0136

Dang, J., Hedayati, A., Hampel, K., & Toklu, C. (2008). An ontological framework for adaptive medical workflow. *Journal of Biomedical Informatics, 41*(5), 829–836. doi:10.1016/j.jbi.2008.05.012

Davenport, T. (1993). *Process Innovation: Reengineering Work Through Information Technology.* Boston: Harvard Business School Press.

Davenport, T., & Short, J. (1990). The New Industrial Engineering: Information Technology and Business Process Redesign. *MIT Sloan Management Review, Summer 1990,* 11-27. MIT Press.

Davis, F. (1989). Perceived Usefulness, Ease of Use and User Acceptance of Information Technology. *Management Information Systems Quarterly*, *13*(3), 319–339. doi:10.2307/249008

Davis, F. (1993). User Acceptance of Information Technology: Systems Characteristics, User Perceptions and Behavioral Impacts. *International Journal of Man-Machine Studies*, *38*(3), 475–487. doi:10.1006/imms.1993.1022

Deitel, H. M., Deitel, P. J., DuWadt, B., & Trees, L. K. (2004). *Web Services: A technical Introduction*. Upper Saddle River, NJ: Prentice Hall.

Dekhtyar, A., Ross, R., & Subrahmanian, V. (2001). Probabilistic temporal databases, I. [TODS]. *ACM Transactions on Database Systems*, *26*(1). doi:10.1145/383734.383736

Deshpande, R., & Zaltman, G. (1982). Factors Affecting the Use of Market Research Information: A Path Analysis. *JMR, Journal of Marketing Research*, *19*(February), 14–31. doi:10.2307/3151527

Dey, D., & Sarkar, S. (1996). A probabilistic relational model and algebra. [TODS]. *ACM Transactions on Database Systems*, *21*(3), 339–369. doi:10.1145/232753.232796

Dey, A. K. (2001). Understanding and Using Context. *Personal and Ubiquitous Computing*, *5*(1), 4–7. doi:10.1007/s007790170019

Dietz, J. L. G. (2008). Advances in Enterprise Engineering. In *Proceedings of the 4th International Workshop CIAO! and the 4th International Workshop EOMAS*, held at CAiSE 2008, June 16-17, 2008. Montpellier, France.

Dubey, A., & Wagle, D. (2007, May). *Delivering software as a service*. Paper presented at the McKinsey Quarterly, Web exclusive.

Dustdar, S., & Schreiner, W. (2005). A survey on web services composition. *International Journal Web and Grid Services*, *1*(1), 1–30. doi:10.1504/IJWGS.2005.007545

Dustdar, S., & Schreiner, W. (2005). A survey on web services composition. *International Journal of Web and Grid Services*, 1-30.

Eiter, T., Lu, J., Lukasiewicz, T., & Subrahmanian, V. (2001). Probabilistic object bases. *ACM Transactions on Database Systems*, *26*(3), 264–312. doi:10.1145/502030.502031

EMarketer. (2009). College Students Online: Driving Change in Internet and Mobile Usage. Retrieved October 30, 2009 from http://www.emarketer.com/Report.aspx?code=emarketer_2000524

Engelhardt, W. H., Kleinaltenkamp, M., & Reckenfelderbäumer, M. (1993). Leistungsbündel als Absatzobjekte: Ein Ansatz zur Überwindung der Dichotomie von Sach- und Dienstleistungen. *Zeitschrift für betriebswirtschaftliche. Forschung*, *45*(5), 395–426.

Eppen, G. D., Hanson, W. A., & Martin, R. K. (1991). Bundling: new products, new markets, low risk. *Sloan Management Review*, *32*(4), 7–14.

Erl, T. (2006). *Service-Oriented Architecture (SOA): Concepts, Technology, and Design*. Upper Saddle River, NJ: Prentice Hall.

Erl, T. (2005). *Service-Oriented Architecture: Concepts, Technology, and Design*. Upper Saddle River: Prentice Hall PTR.

Erradi, A., Tosic, V., & Maheshwari, P. (2007). MASC -. NET-Based Middleware for Adaptive Composite Web Services. In *Proceedings of the 2007 IEEE International Conference on Web Services* (pp. 727-734). Los Alamitos, USA: IEEE-CS Press.

Ester, M., Kriegel, H., Sander, J., & Xu, X. (1996). A density-based algorithm for discovering clusters in large spatial databases with noise. In *Proc. of 2nd Int'l Conf. on Knowledge Discovery and Data Mining*, (pp. 226-231).

Evans, S., Partidário, P. J., & Lambert, J. (2007). Industrialization as a key element of sustainable product-service solutions. *International Journal of Production Research*, *45*(18), 4225–4246. doi:. doi:10.1080/00207540701449999

Farlex. (2009). *Context – Definition of Context by the Free Online Dictionary, Thesaurus, and Encyclopedia*. Retrieved April 10, 2009, from http://www.thefreedictionary.com/context

Feng, B., Hu, G., Zhao, K., & Yi, J. (2006). Research and realization on self-feeding back Chinese words segmentation system. [in Chinese]. *Computer Technology and Development*, *16*(5), 7–9.

Ferris, C., & Farrell, J. (2003). What are web services? *Communications of the ACM, 46*(6), 31. doi:10.1145/777313.777335

Finin, T., Ding, L., Pan, R., Joshi, A., Kolari, P., Java, A., & Peng, Y. (2005). Swoogle: searching for knowledge on the semantic web. In *Proc. of the 20th National Conference on Artificial Intelligence and the 17th Innovative Applications of Artificial Intelligence Conference, Pittsburgh, Pennsylvania,* 1682-1683. Retrieved March 10, 2007, from https://www.aaai.org/Papers/AAAI/2005/ISD05-007.pdf

Floch, J., & Bræk, R. (2000). Towards Dynamic Composition of Hybrid Communication Services. *International Conference on Intelligence in Networks* (pp. 73-92).

Foo, S., & Li, H. (2004). Chinese word segmentation and its effect on information retrieval. *Information Processing & Management, 40*(1), 161–190. doi:10.1016/S0306-4573(02)00079-1

Forrester. (2006a). Trends 2006: Multichannel retail. Retrieved October 30, 2009 from http://www.forrester.com/Research/Documents

Forrester. (2006b). Best Practices in Multichannel Retailing. Retrieved October 30, 2009 from http://www.forrester.com/Research/Documents

Forrester. (2007). Trends 2007: Multichannel Retal. Retrieved October 30, 2009 from http://www.forrester.com/Research/Documents

Forrester. 2009. Multichannel: In-Store Pickup Gains Importance. Retrieved October 30, 2009 from http://www.forrester.com/Research/Document/Excerpt/0,7211,48133,00.html

Forstadius, J., Lassila, O., & Seppanen, T. (2005). RDF-Based Model for Context-Aware Reasoning in Rich Service Environment. In *Proceedings of the 2nd Workshop on Context Modeling and Reasoning* at PerCom'05 (pp. 15-19). Los Alamitos, USA: IEEE-CS Press.

Fredj, M., Georgantas, N., Issarny, V., & Zarras, A. (2008). Dynamic Service Substitution in Service-Oriented Architectures. In *Proceedings of the IEEE International Conference on Services Computing (SCC'08)* (pp. 101-104).

Freiden, J., Goldsmith, R., Takacs, S., & Hofacker, C. (1998). Information as a product: not goods, not services. *Marketing Intelligence & Planning, 16,* 210–220. doi:. doi:10.1108/02634509810217327

Freitas, F. L. G., & Bittencourt, G. (2000). Cognitive multi-agent systems for integrated information retrieval and extraction over the Web. In *Advances in Artificial Intelligence* (LNCS 1952, pp. 310 -319). Heidelberg: Springer.

Fu, G., Kit, C., & Webster, J. J. (2008). Chinese word segmentation as morpheme-based lexical chunking. *Information Sciences, 178*(9), 2282–2296.

Fujita, Y., Nakamura, Y., & Shiller, Z. (2203). Dual Dijkstra Search for paths with different topologies. In *Proceedings of IEEE International Conference on Robotics and Automation* (Vol. 3, pp. 3359-3364).

Garcia, D. Z. G., & de Toledo, M. B. F. (2006). A web service architecture providing QoS management. In *Proceedings of the Fourth Latin American Web Congress* (LA-Web '06) (pp. 189-198).

Garcia-Molina, H., & Salem, K. (1987). *Sagas.* Paper presented at the Proceedings of the Association for Computing Machinery Special Interest Group on Management of Data 1987 Annual Conference, San Francisco, California.

Gefen, D. (2002a). Customer loyalty in e-commerce. *Journal of the Association for Information Systems, 3*(1), 27–51.

Gillot, J.-N. (2008). *The Complete Guide to Business Process Management.* BookSurge Publishing.

Gisolfi, D. (2001). Web services architect: Part 1: An introduction to dynamic e-business. Retrieved July 8, 2009 from http://www.ibm.com/developerworks/webservices/library/ws-arc1

Glatard, T., Montagnat, J., Emsellem, D., & Lingrand, D. (2008). A service-oriented architecture enabling dynamic service grouping for optimizing distributed workflow execution. *Future Generation Computer Systems, 24*(7), 720–730. doi:10.1016/j.future.2008.02.011

Global Outsourcing Report. (2005). Release of the Global Outsourcing Report. Retrieved from http://pdfserver.prweb.com/pdfdownload/220341/pr.pdf

Goersch, D. (2002). Multi-channel integration and its implications for retail web sites. Retrieved October 30, 2009 from http://is2.lse.ac.uk/asp/aspecis/20020015.pdf

Goldberg, D. E. (1989). *Genetic algorithms in search optimization, and machine learning. Addison Wesley. Holland, J. (1992). Adaptation in Natural Artificial Systems.* Cambridge, MA: MIT Press.

Gómez-Pérez, A. (1998). Knowledge sharing and reuse. In Liebowitz, J. (Ed.), *The Handbook on Expert systems*. CRC Press.

Gordon, L. A., Loeb, M. P., & Sohail, T. (2003). A framework for insurance for cyber-risk management. *Communications of the ACM, 46*(3), 81–85. doi:10.1145/636772.636774

Gottschalk, K., et al. (2000). Web Services architecture overview. Retrieved July 15, 2009 from http://www.ibm.com/developerworks/webservices/library/w-ovr

Goudarzi, K. M., & Kramer, J. (1996). Maintaining Node Consistency in the Face of Dynamic Change. In *Proceedings of the 3rd IEEE International Conference on Configurable Distributed Systems* (pp. 62-69).

Gracia, J., Trillo, R., Espinoza, M., & Mena, E. (2006). Querying the web: a multiontology disambiguation method. In *Proc. of the 6th Int'l Conf. on Web Engineering* (pp. 241-248). Palo Alto, California: ACM.

Gray, J., & Reuter, A. (1993). *Transaction Processing: Concepts and Techniques*. Morgan Kaufmann.

Gray, J. (1981). *The Transaction Concept: Virtues and Limitations (Invited Paper).* Paper presented at the Very Large Data Bases, 7th International Conference, Cannes, France, Proceedings.

Grefen, P. W. P. J. (2002). *Transactional Workflows or Workflow Transactions?* Paper presented at the DEXA '02: Proceedings of the 13th International Conference on Database and Expert Systems Applications, London, UK.

Gruber, T. R. (1993b). A translation approach to portable ontology specification. *Knowledge Acquisition, 5*(2), 199–220. doi:10.1006/knac.1993.1008

Gruber, T. R. (1993a). *Toward principles for the design of ontologies used for knowledge sharing.* Paper presented at the International Workshop on Formal Ontology, Padova, Italy.

Guarino, N., Masolo, C., Vetere, G., & Council, N. R. (1999). OntoSeek: content-based access to the web. *IEEE Intelligent Systems, 14*(3), 70–80. doi:10.1109/5254.769887

Guha, R., McCool, R., & Miller, E. (2003). Semantic search. In *Proc. of the 12th Int'l Conf. on World Wide Web* (pp. 700-709). Hungary: Budapest: ACM.

Guidi, C., Lucchi, R., & Mazzara, M. (2007). A Formal Framework for Web Services Coordination. *Electronic Notes in Theoretical Computer Science, 180*(2), 55–70. doi:10.1016/j.entcs.2006.10.046

Guruge, A. (2004). *Web Services: Theory and Practice*. Amsterdam: Elsevier Inc.

Haines, R. W. (2006). *Control Systems for Heating, Ventilating, and Air Conditioning* (6th ed.). New York: Springer, New York

Hair, J., Tatham, R., Anderson, R., & Black, W. (1998). *Multivariate Data Analysis* (5th ed.). Englewood Cliffs, NJ: Prentice-Hall.

Haischer, M., Bullinger, H.-J., & Fähnrich, K.-P. (2001). Assessment and Design of Service Systems. In G. Salvendy (Ed.), *Handbook of Industrial Engineering: Technology and Operations Management* (3rd ed., pp. 634–650). New York: John Wiley & Sons. doi:10.1002/9780470172339.ch22

Halpin, T. (2001). *Information modeling and relational databases, from conceptual analysis to logical design.* California: Morgan Kaufmann.

Hammer, M. (1990). Reengineering Work: Don't Automate, Obliterate. *Harvard Business Review*, (July/August): 104–112.

Hammer, M., & Champy, J. (1993). *Reengineering the Corporation: A Manifesto for Business Revolution.* Harper Business.

Han, J., Pei, J., & Yin, Y. (2000). Mining frequent patterns without candidate generation. In *Proc. of ACM SIGMOD* (pp. 1–12).

Harris, E. K. (2007). *Customer service, a practical approach* (4th ed.). Upper Saddle River, N.J: Pearson Prentice Hall.

Hatcher, L. (1994). *A Step-by-Step Approach to Using the SAS System for Factor and Structural Equation Modeling.* Cary, NC: The SAS Institute.

Hauptmann, S., & Wasel, J. (1996) On-line Maintenance with On-the-y Software Replacement. In *Proceedings of the 3rd IEEE International Conference on Configurable Distributed Systems* (pp. 70-80).

Hefley, W. (2008). Service Science: A Key Driver of the 21st Century Prosperity. Retrieved October 30, 2009 from http://www.itif.org/files/BHefleySummary.pdf

Henderson-Sellers, B., & Giorgini, P. (Eds.). (2005). *Agent-Oriented Methodologies.* Hershey, PA: Idea Group Publishing.

Herrmann, A., Huber, F., & Coulter, R. H. (1997). Product and service bundling decisions and their effects on purchase intention. *Pricing Strategy and Practice, 5,* 99–107. doi:.doi:10.1108/09684909710171873

Herssens, C., Faulkner, S., & Jureta, I. J. (2008). Context-Driven Autonomic Adaptation of SLA. In *Proceedings of the 6th international Conference on Service-Oriented Computing* (pp. 362-377). Berlin, Germany: Springer.

Hinneburg, A., & Keim, D. (1999). Optimal grid-clustering: towards breaking the curse of dimensionality in high-dimensional clustering. In *Proc. of the 25th VLDB Conf.,* (pp. 506-517).

Hirakawa, M., & Hewagamage, K. P. (2001). Situated Computing: A Paradigm for the Mobile User-Interaction with Multimedia Sources. *Annals of Software Engineering, 12*(1), 213–239. doi:10.1023/A:1013395612527

Hoffman, K. D. (2003). Marketing + MIS = E-Services. *Communications of the ACM, 46*(6), 53–55. doi:10.1145/777313.777340

Hoffman, D., & Novak, T. (1996). Marketing in Hypermedia Computer-Mediated Environments: Conceptual Foundations. *Journal of Marketing, 80*(4), 50–68. doi:10.2307/1251841

Hofmeister, C., & Purtilo, J. M. (1993). Dynamic Recon_guration in Distributed Systems: Adapting Software Modules for Replacement. In *Proceedings of the 13th IEEE International Conference on Distributed Computing Systems* (pp. 101-110).

Holtkamp, B., & Wojciechowski, M. (2007). Experiences with Situation Aware Service Provision. *International Conference on Grid and Cooperative Computing* (pp. 863-870).

Hoppe, M. & Sander, M. (1996). SHK - eine Branche im Wandel. *Sanitär + Heizungstechnik, 61*(3), 38-46.

Hoque, Y., & Lohse, G. (1999). An Information Search Cost Perspective for Designing Interfaces for Electronic Commerce. *JMR, Journal of Marketing Research, 36*(3), 387–394. doi:10.2307/3152084

Howell, R. H., Sauer, H. J., & Coad, W. J. (2005). *Principles of heating ventilating and air conditioning.* Atlanta, GA: American Society of Heating, Refrigerating and Air Conditioning Engineers.

Hung, E., & Cheung, D. (2002). Parallel mining of outliers in large database. [DAPD]. *Distributed and Parallel Databases, 12,* 5–26. doi:10.1023/A:1015608814486

Hung, E., Getoor, L., & Subrahmanian, V. (2007). Probabilistic Interval XML. [TOCL]. *ACM Transactions on Computational Logic, 8*(4), 1–38. doi:10.1145/1276920.1276926

Hung, E. (2009). Probabilistic XML. In Aggarwal, C. C. (Ed.), *Managing and Mining Uncertain Data.* Springer. doi:10.1007/978-0-387-09690-2_12

Hung, E. (2005). *Managing Uncertainty and Ontologies in Databases.* Unpublished doctoral dissertation, University of Maryland, College Park.

Hung, E., & Xiao, L. (2008). An efficient representation model of distance distribution between two uncertain objects. In *Proc. of IEEE First Pacific-Asia Workshop on Web Mining and Web-based Application 2008 (WMWA'08), in conjunction with the 12th Pacific-Asia Conference on Knowledge Discovery and Data Mining (PAKDD-2008),* Osaka, Japan.

Hung, E., Getoor, L., & Subrahmanian, V. (2003a). Probabilistic Interval XML. In *Proc. of International Conference on Database Theory (ICDT),* Siena, Italy.

Hung, E., Getoor, L., & Subrahmanian, V. (2003b). PXML: A Probabilistic Semistructured Data Model and Algebra. In *Proceedings of the 19th International Conference on Data Engineering (ICDE)* (pp. 467-478).

Hung, P. C. K., Li, H., & Jeng, J. J. (2004). Web service negotiation: An overview of research issues. In *Proc of 37th Hawaii Intl Conf on System Sciences* (pp. 1-10).

Hybertson, D. W. (2009). *Model-Oriented Systems Engineering Science: a Unifying Framework for Traditional and Complex Systems*. Auerbach Publications.

IBM. (2005). *Component Business Modeling*. Retrieved from http://www-1.ibm.com/services/us/bcs/html/bcs_componentmodeling.html

IBM. Microsoft Corporation, & BEA (2002). Business Process Execution Language for Web Service (BPEL4WS) v.1.0. Retrieved from http://www.ibm.com/developerworks/webservices/library/ws-bpel/

ICWS. (2009). http://conferences.computer.org/icws/2009/.

IDC. (2005). US offshoring to double to $14.7 billion by 2009. Retrieved from http://www.financialexpress.com/fe_full_story.php?content_id=102877

Imai, T., Yoshikawa, M., Terai, H., & Yamauchi, H. (2002). Scalable GA-Processor Architecture and Its Implementation of Processor Element. In. *Proceedings of IEEE International Conference on Acoustics, Speech, and Signal Processing, 3,* 3148–3151.

InternetRetailer. (2007). More Merchants are Mastering Buy Online/Pick-Up In-Store. Retrieved October 30, 2009 from http://www.internetretailer.com/dailyNews.asp?id=23384

Isaac, H., & Leclercq, A. (2006). Give me a mobile phone, and I will work harder! Assessing the value of mobile technologies in organizations: an exploratory research. In *International Conference on Mobile Business* (p. 18). ICMB 2006, Los Alamitos, CA: IEEE Computer Society.

ISO 14258. (1999, April). *Industrial Automation Systems—Concepts and Rules for Enterprise Models.* ISO TC184/SC5/WG1.

Iwaarden, J., Wiele, T., Ball, L., & Millen, R. (2004). Perceptions about the Quality of Web Sites: A Survey among Students at Northeastern and Eastern University. *Information & Management, 41,* 947–959. doi:10.1016/j.im.2003.10.002

Jackson, J., & McIver, R. (2004). *Microeconomics* (7th ed.). Australia: McGraw-Hill.

Jain, A., Murty, M., & Flynn, P. (1999). Data clustering: A review. *ACM Computing Surveys, 31*(3), 264–323. doi:10.1145/331499.331504

James, A. (2008). Nordstrom lets you buy online, pick up at the store. Retrieved October 30, 2009 from http://www.seattlepi.com/business/363901_nordstrom21.html

Jarillo, J. C. (1988). On strategic networks. *Strategic Management Journal, 9*(1), 31–41. doi:.doi:10.1002/smj.4250090104

Jarrar, M., & Meersman, R. (2008). Ontology engineering - the Dogma approach. In Dillon, T., Chang, E., Meersman, R., & Sycara, K. (Eds.), *Advances in Web Semantics I* (pp. 7–34). Berlin, Germany: Springer.

Jeston, J., & Nelis, J. (2006). *Business Process Management: Practical Guidelines to Successful Implementations.* Butterworth-Heinemann.

Johansson, H. J. (1993). *Business Process Reengineering: BreakPoint Strategies for Market Dominance.* John Wiley & Sons.

Jørstad, I., & Do, V. T. (2007). A Framework and Tool for Personalisation of Mobile Services Using Semantic Web. *International Conference on Mobile Data Management* (pp. 402-406).

Jupiter Research. (2004). Concept report from JupiterMedia: New York, December 30, 2004, In Collier & Bienstock. (2006). Measuring service quality in e-retailing. *Journal of Service Research, 8*(3), 260–275.

Jupiter. (2007). Trends 2007: Multichannel Retailer. Retrieved October 30, 2009 from www.forrester.com/Research/Documents

Jurca, R., Binder, W., & Faltings, B. (2007). Reliable QoS Monitoring based on client feedback. In *Proceedings of International Conference on World Wide Web* (pp. 1003-1011).

Kaner, C. (1997). The impossibility of complete testing. *Software QA, 4*(4), 28–44.

Kanoh, H., & Nakamura, N. (2000). Route guidance with unspecified staging posts using genetic algorithm for car navigation systems. In *Proceedings of IEEE Intelligent Transportation Systems*, (pp. 119-124).

Karapidis, A. (2005). Service Management in Production Companies. In G. Zülch, H. Jagdev, & P. Stock (Eds.), *Integrating Human Aspects in Production Management* (pp. 375–385). Boston, MA: Springer. doi:10.1007/0-387-23078-5_29

Karunaratne, R. P. (2008). *Analysis of Methods for Improving IT Support for Business*. Undergraduate Thesis B Report, School of Computer Science and Engineering, University of New South Wales, Australia, October 2008.

Ke, W., & Wei, K. K. (2004). Successful e-government in Singapore. *Communications of the ACM, 47*(6), 95–99. doi:10.1145/990680.990687

Keeney, J., & Cahill, V. (2003). Chisel: A Policy-Driven, Context-Aware, Dynamic Adaptation Framework. *International Workshop on Policies for Distributed Systems and Networks* (pp. 3-14).

Keller, A., & Ludwig, H. (2003). The WSLA Framework: Specifying and Monitoring Service Level Agreements for Web Services. [New York: Plenum Publishing.]. *Journal of Network and Systems Management, 11*(1), 57–81. doi:10.1023/A:1022445108617

Keller, G., Nüttgens, M., & Scheer, A.-W. (1992). Semantische Prozeßmodellierung auf der Grundlage Ereignisgesteuerter Prozeßketten (EPK). In Scheer, A.-W. (Ed.), *Veröffentlichungen des Instituts für Wirtschaftsinformatik, No. 89*. Saarbrücken: Universität des Saarlandes.

Kephart, J. O., & Chess, D. M. (2003). The Vision of Autonomic Computing. [Los Alamitos, USA: IEEE-CS Press.]. *Computer, 36*(1), 41–50. doi:10.1109/MC.2003.1160055

Kingman-Brundage, J. (1989). The ABCs of Service System Blueprinting. In M.J. Bitner, & L.A. Crosby (Eds.), *Designing a winning service strategy: 7th Annual Service Marketing Conference proceedings*. Chicago, IL: American Marketing Association.

Köhler, J., Philippi, S., Specht, M., & Rüegg, A. (2006). Ontology based text indexing and querying for the semantic web. *Knowledge-Based Systems, 19*(8), 744–754. doi:10.1016/j.knosys.2006.04.015

Kokash, N., & D'Andrea, V. (2007). Evaluating quality of web services: a risk-driven approach. In *Proceedings of International Conference on Business Information Systems* (pp. 180-194).

Kon, F., Cost, F., Blair, G., & Campbell, R. H. (2002). The Case of Reective Middleware. *Communications of the ACM, 45*(6), 33–38. doi:10.1145/508448.508470

Kraaijenbrink, J. (2002). Centralization revisited? Problems on implementing integrated service delivery in The Netherlands. In R. Traunmüller, & K. Lenk (Eds.), *Electronic Government, 1st International Conference, EGOV 2002, Aix-en-Provence, France, September 2 - September 5, 2002, Proceedings* (pp. 10-17). Berlin, Germany: Springer.

Kraemer, F. A., Bræk, R., & Herrmann, P. (2009). *Compositional Service Engineering with Arctis*. Telektronikk.

Kraemer, F. A. (2007). Arctis and Ramses: Toole Suites for Rapid Service Engineering. Norsk informatikkonferanse.

Kramer, J., & Magee, J. (1985). Dynamic Configuration for Distributed Systems. *IEEE Transactions on Software Engineering, 11*(4), 424–436. doi:10.1109/TSE.1985.232231

Kramer, J., & Magee, J. (1990). The Evolving Philosophers Problem: Dynamic Change Management. *IEEE Transactions on Software Engineering, 16*(11), 1293–1306. doi:10.1109/32.60317

Kreger, H. (2001). Web services conceptual architecture (WSCA 1.0), IBM Software Group. Retrieved March 28, 2009, from http://www.cs.uoi.gr/~zarras/mdw-ws/WebServicesConceptualArchitectu2.pdf

Kriegel, H., & Pfeifle, M. (2005a). Density-based clustering of uncertain data. In *Proc. 11th Int. Conf. on Knowledge Discovery and Data Mining (KDD'05)* (pp. 672-677).

Kriegel, H., & Pfeifle, M. (2005b). Hierarchical density-based clustering of uncertain data. In *Proc. 5th IEEE Int. Conf. on Data Mining (ICDM'05)*.

Krucken, L., & Meroni, A. (2006). Building stakeholder networks to develop and deliver product-service-systems: practical experiences on elaborating proactive materials for communication. *Journal of Cleaner Production, 14*(17), 1502–1508. doi:.doi:10.1016/j.jclepro.2006.01.026

Kruse, P. M., Naujoks, A., Röesner, D., & Kunze, M. (2005). Clever search: a wordnet based wrapper for internet search engines. In *Proc. of the 2nd GermaNet Workshop: Applications of GermaNet II*. Bonn, Germany: Arxiv preprint.

Kwon, O. B. (2003). Meta web service: building web-based open decision support system based on web services. *Expert Systems with Applications, 24*, 375–389. doi:10.1016/S0957-4174(02)00187-2

Ladner, R. (2008). Soft computing techniques for web service brokering. *Soft Computing, 12*, 1089–1098. doi:10.1007/s00500-008-0277-0

Lakshmanan, V., Leone, N., Ross, R., & Subrahmanian, V. (1997). Probview: A flexible probabilistic database system. *ACM Transactions on Database Systems, 22*(3), 419–469. doi:10.1145/261124.261131

LaLonde, B. J. (1976). *Customer service: meaning and measurement*. Chicago, IL: National Council of Physical Distribution Management.

Lambert, D. M. (2006). *Supply chain management, processes, partnerships, performance* (2nd ed.). Sarasota, FL: Supply Chain Management Institute.

Langley, P., Iba, W., & Thompson, K. (1992). An analysis of bayesian classifiers. In *Proc. of the 10th National Conf. on Artificial Intelligence* (pp. 223-228).

Lapiedra, R., Smithson, S., Alegre, J., & Chiva, R. (2004). Role of information systems on the business network formation process: an empirical analysis of the automotive sector. *Journal of Enterprise Information Management, 17*(3), 219–228. doi:.doi:10.1108/17410390410531461

Lee, J. (2005). Model-Driven Business Transformation and Semantic Web. *Communications of the ACM, 48*(12). doi:10.1145/1101779.1101813

Lee, J. (2006). Ontology Management for Large-Scale Enterprise Systems. *Journal of Electronic Commerce Research and Applications, 5*(3).

Lee, H., & Whang, S. (2001). Winning the Last Mile of E-Commerce. *MIT Sloan Management Review, 42*(4), 4–62.

Lennstrand, B., Persson, C., & Wikström, S. (2002). E-commerce in a Multi-Channel Retailing Context." *ITS 14th Biennial Conference*, August 18-21, 2002, Seoul, Korea.

Lewis, D., Keeney, J., & Sullivan, D. O. (2006). *Policy-based Management for Resource-Specific Semantic Services*. Workshop on Distributed Autonomous Network Management Systems.

Leymann, F. (2003). Web Services: Distributed Applications without Limits: An Outline. In *Proceedings Database Systems for Business, Technology and Web BTW*, Leipzig, Germany, Feb 26 – 28, 2003, Springer. Retrieved April 1, 2208, from http://doesen0.informatik.uni-leipzig.de/proceedings/paper/keynote-leymann.pdf

Li, L., Liu, C., & Wang, J. (2007). *Deriving Transactional Properties of Composite Web Services*. Paper presented at the IEEE International Conference on Web Services, Salt Lake City, Utah, USA.

Li, Y., Hung, E., Chung, K., & Huang, J. (2008). Building a decision cluster classification model for high dimensional data by a variable weighting k-means method. In *Proc. of the Twenty-First Australasian Joint Conference on Artificial Intelligence*, Auckland.

Limthanmaphon, B., & Zhang, Y. (2003). Web service composition with case-based reasoning. In *ACM Intl Conf Proc Series (Vol. 143), Proc. 14th Australasian Database Conf*, Adelaide, Australia (pp. 201-208).

Linketscher, N., & Child, M. (2001). Trust issues and user reactions to e-services and e-marketplaces: a customer survey. In *Proceedings of 12th International Workshop on Database and Expert Systems Applications* (pp. 752-756).

Little, M. (2003). Transactions and Web Services. *Communications of the ACM, 46*(10), 49–54. doi:10.1145/944217.944237

Little, M. (2007). WS-CAF: Contexts, Coordination and Transactions for Web Services. In R. Meersman and Z. Tari et al. (Eds.), *On the Move to Meaningful Internet Systems 2007: CoopIS, DOA, ODBASE, GADA, and IS* (LNCS 4803, pp. 439-453).

Little, M., & Freund, T. (2003). *A Comparison of Web Services Transaction Protocols*.

Liu, C., & Zhao, X. (2008). Towards Flexible Compensation for Business Transactions in Web Service Environment. *Journal on Service Oriented Computing and Applications, 2*(2-3), 79–91. doi:10.1007/s11761-008-0024-5

Liu, A. (2008). *Extending Service-Oriented Middleware for Business-Driven IT Management*. Undergraduate Thesis B Report, School of Computer Science and Engineering, University of New South Wales, Australia, October 2008.

Liu, A., Li, Q., Huang, L., & Liu, H. (2008). Building profit-aware service-oriented business applications. In *Proceedings of the International Conference on Web Services* (pp. 489-496).

Liu, S. (2005). *A model-theoretic semantics for XML and its applications*. Unpublished doctoral dissertation (in Chinese), Beijing University, Beijing, China.

Liu, W., Jia, W., & Au, P. O. (2002). Add exception notification mechanism to Web services. In *Proceedings of International Conference on Algorithms & Architectures for Parallel Processing* (pp. 483-488).

Liu, Y., Ngu, A., & Zeng, L. (2004). QoS computation and policing in dynamic web service selection. In *Proceedings of the International Conference on World Wide Web* (pp. 66-73).

Loiacono, E., Watson, R., & Goodhue, D. (2007). WebQual: An Instrument for Consumer Evaluation of Web Sites. *International Journal of Electronic Commerce*, *11*(3), 51–87. doi:10.2753/JEC1086-4415110302

Ludwig, H., Dan, A., & Kearney, R. (2004). Cremona: An Architecture and Library for Creation and Monitoring of WS-Agreements. In *Proceedings of the 2nd International Conference on Service Oriented Computing* (pp. 65-74). New York: ACM.

MacQuiston, F. C. (2005). *Heating, ventilating, and air conditioning: analysis and design* (6th ed.). Hoboken, NJ: John Wiley & Sons.

Malhotra, Y. (1998). Business Process Redesign: An Overview. *IEEE Engineering Management Review*, *26*(3).

Malone, T. W., & Crowston, K. (1994). The interdisciplinary study of coordination. *ACM Computing Surveys*, *26*(1), 87–119. doi:10.1145/174666.174668

Manzini, E., Vezzoli, C., & Clark, G. (2001). Product-Service Systems: Using an Existing Concept as a New Approach to Sustainability. *Journal of Desert Research*, *1*(2).

MediaAudit. 2008. Online Shopping By Minorities Increase. Retrieved October 30, 2009 from http://ecommerce-news.internetretailer.com/search?p=Q&ts=custom2&isort=date&mainresult=mt_inrg_f&w=customer+service&x=10&y=10=

Mehrotra, S., Rastogi, R., Korth, H. F., & Silberschatz, A. (1992). *A Transaction Model for Multidatabase Systems*. Paper presented at the ICDCS.

Melliar-Smith, P. M., & Moser, L. E. (2007). Achieving Atomicity for Web Services Using Commutativity of Actions. *J. Universal Computer Science*, *13*(8), 1094–1109.

Melloul, L., & Fox, A. (2004). Reusable Functional Composition Patterns for Web Services. In *Proceedings of the IEEE International Conference on Web Services (ICWS' 04)* (pp. 498-506).

Mertens, P. (2006). Moden und Nachhaltigkeit in der Wirtschaftsinformatik. *Handbuch der Modernen Datenverarbeitung - Praxis der Wirtschaftsinformatik*, *42*(250), 109-118.

Miles, R. E., & Snow, C. C. (1978). *Organizational strategy, structure, and process*. New York: McGraw-Hill.

Miller, G. (2005). NET vs. J2EE. *Communications of the ACM*, *48*(7), 64–67.

Miller, R., & Yang, Y. (1997). Association rules over interval data. In *Proc. 1997 ACM-SIGMOD '97*.

Minsky, N., Ungureanu, V., Wang, W., & Zhang, J. (1996). Building Reconfiguration Primitives into the Law of a System. In *Proceedings of the 3rd IEEE International Conference on Configurable Distributed Systems* (pp. 62-69).

Moldovan, D. I., & Mihalcea, R. (2000). Using WordNet and lexical operators to improve internet searches. *IEEE Internet Computing*, *4*(1), 34–43. doi:10.1109/4236.815847

Mont, O. (2004). *Product-service systems, panacea or myth?* Lund: IIIEE Dissertations.

Montoya-Weiss, M., Voss, G., & Grewel, D. (2003). Determinants of Online Channel Use and Overall Satisfaction with a Rational, Multichannel Service Provider. *Journal of the Academy of Marketing Science*, *31*(4), 448–458. doi:10.1177/0092070303254408

Morelli, N. (2002). Designing Product/Service Systems: A Methodological Exploration. *Design Issues, 18*(3), 3–17. doi:.doi:10.1162/074793602320223253

Motahari Nezhad, H. R., Benatallah, B., Martens, A., Curbera, F., & Casati, F. (1996). SemiAutomated Adaptation of Service Interactions. In *Proceedings of the International World Wide Web Conference (WWW'07)* (pp. 993-1002).

Müller-Lankenau, C., Klein, S., & Wehmeyer, K. 2004. Developing a Framework for Multi-Channel Strategies: An Analysis of Cases from the Grocery Retailing Industry. In *Proceedings the 17th Bled Electronic Commerce Conference*. Bled, Slovenia, June 21-23.

Murthy, S. (1998). Automatic construction of decision trees from data: a multidisciplinary survey. *Data Mining and Knowledge Discovery, 2*(4), 345–389. doi:10.1023/A:1009744630224

Muse, D. (2001). Gartner says Web services coming soon. *Internetnews/ASP News*, Oct. 10, (http://www.internetnews.com/asp-news/article/0,3411_901271,00.html).

Nagypál, G., & Motik, B. (2003). A fuzzy model for representing uncertain, subjective and vague temporal knowledge in ontologies. In *On The Move to Meaningful Internet Systems 2003: CoopIS, DOA, and ODBASE* (LNCS 2888, pp. 906-923). Heidelberg: Springer.

Nahrstedt, K., & Balke, W.-T. (2004). A taxonomy for multimedia service composition. In *Proceedings of the 12th Annual ACM International Conference on Multimedia* (pp. 88-95).

Naing, M. M., Lim, E. P., & Goh, D. H. L. (2002). Ontology-based web annotation framework for hyper-Link structures. In *Proc. of the Int'l Workshop on Data Semantics in Web Information Systems (DASWIS'02)* (pp. 184-193). Singapore.

Narendra, N. C., & Orriens, B. (2006). Requirements-driven modeling of the web service execution and adaptation lifecycle. In S. Madria et al. (Eds.), *ICDCIT* (LNCS 4317, pp. 314-324).

Navigli, R., & Velardi, P. (2003). *An analysis of ontology-based query expansion strategies*. Paper presented at the International Workshop on Adaptive Text Extraction and Mining, Cavtat-Dubrovnik, Croatia.

Newcomer, E., & Lomow, G. (2005). *Understanding SOA with Web Services*. Addison Wesley.

Ngai, J., Kao, B., Cheng, R., Chau, M., Yip, K., & Chui, C. K. (2006). Efficient Clustering of Uncertain Data, in *Proc. of The 2006 IEEE International Conference on Data Mining* (pp. 436-445), Hong Kong.

Nierman, A., & Jagadish, H. (2002). ProTDB: Probabilistic data in xml. In *Proc. of the 28th VLDB Conference*, Hong Kong, China.

Norris, M. (2000). Survival in the eBusiness jungle. *Software Focus, 1*(1), 23–26. doi:10.1002/1529-7950(200009)1:1<23::AID-SWF4>3.0.CO;2-A

Nunnally, C., & Bernstein, I. (1994). *Psychometric Theory* (3rd ed.). New York: McGraw-Hill.

OASIS Business Transactions TC. (2004).

OASIS Web Services Composite Application Framework (WS-CAF) TC. (2004).

OASIS. (2004). Web Services Resource Properties (WS-ResourceProperties). Retrieved from http://docs.oasis-open.org/wsrf/2004/06/wsrf-WS- ResourceProperties-1.2-draft-04.pdf

Oliver, R. (1980). A Cognitive Model for the Antecedents and Consequences of Satisfaction. *JMR, Journal of Marketing Research, 17*(4), 460–469. doi:10.2307/3150499

Oliver, R. (1997). *Satisfaction: A Behavioral Perspective on the Consumer*. New York: McGraw- Hill.

OMG. (2006). *Business Process Modeling Notation (BPMN) Version 1.0 (OMG Final Adopted Specification)*. Needham, MA: Object Management Group.

OMG. (2009). *UML 2.2 Superstructure Specification, formal/2009-02-02*. Object Management Group.

Ould, M. (2005). *Business Process Management: A Rigorous Approach*. Meghan-Kiffer Press.

Ovans, A. (1997). Make a bundle bundling. *Harvard Business Review, 75*(6), 18–20.

Overbeek, S. J., van Bommel, P., & Proper, H. A. (2007). Visualizing formalisms with ORM models. In Meersman, R., Tari, Z., & Herrero, P. (Eds.), *On the Move to Meaningful Internet Systems 2007: OTM 2007 Workshops, Vilamoura, Portugal, November 25 - 30, 2007, Proceedings, Part I* (pp. 709–718). Berlin, Germany: Springer. doi:10.1007/978-3-540-76888-3_93

Pahl, V. (2007). Research and Development for a Sustainable Services Sector. In D. Spath & K. P. Fähnrich (Eds.), *Advances in Services Innovations* (pp. 279–288). Berlin: Springer. doi:10.1007/978-3-540-29860-1_14

Panetto, H., & Molina, A. (2008). Enterprise integration and interoperability in manufacturing systems: Trends and issues. *Computers in Industry, I*(59), 641–646. doi:10.1016/j.compind.2007.12.010

Papazoglou, M. P., Traverso, P., Dustdar, S., & Leymann, F. (2008). Service-Oriented Computing: a Research Roadmap. *International Journal of Cooperative Information Systems, 17*(2), 223–255. doi:10.1142/S0218843008001816

Papazoglou, M. P. (2003). Service -Oriented Computing: Concepts, Characteristics and Directions. In *Proceedings of 4th Intl Conf on Web Information Systems Engineering* (WISE2003) (pp. 3-12).

Papazoglou, M.P., Traverso, P, Dustdar, S. & et al. (2006). Service-oriented computing research roadmap. Retrieved April 4, 2009, from http:drops.dagstuhl.de/opus/volltexte/2006/524/

Parasuraman, A., Zeithaml, V., & Berry, L. (1988). SERVQUAL: A Multi-Item Scale for Measuring Consumer Perception of Service Quality. *Journal of Retailing, 64,* 2–40.

Parasuraman, A., Zeithaml, V., & Malhotra, A. (2005). E-S-Qual: A Multiple-Item Scale for Assessing Electronic Service Quality. *Journal of Service Research, 7*(3), 213–233. doi:10.1177/1094670504271156

Park, J., Chen, M., & Yu, P. (1995). An effective hash-based algorithm for mining association rules. In *Proc. of ACM SIGMOD* (pp. 175-186).

Pastore, M. (2000). US college students use net for shopping. Retrieved October 30, 2009 from http://www.clickz.com/stats/sectors/demographics/article.php/432631

Peel, M. (1987). *Customer service: how to achieve total customer satisfaction.* London: Kogan Page.

Petrie, C. J. (Ed.). (1992). *Enterprise Integration Modeling.* Cambridge, MA: The MIT Press.

Petrie, C., Genesereth, M., et al. (2003). Adding AI to web services. In L. van Elst, V. Dignum, & A. Abecker (Eds.), *AMKM 2003* (LNAI 2926, pp. 322-338).

Pfleeger, S. L., & Atlee, J. M. (2006). *Software Engineering: Theory and Practice* (3rd ed.). Beijing: Pearson Education, Inc.

PICS. (Platform for Internet Content Selection (PICS)). Retrieved from http://www.w3.org/PICS/

Pihlanto, P. (1994). The action-oriented approach and case study method in management studies. *Scandinavian Journal of Management, 10*(4), 369–382. doi:10.1016/0956-5221(94)90024-8

Poladian, V., Sousa, J. P., Garlan, D., & Shaw, M. (2004). Dynamic Configuration of Resource-Aware Services. In *Proceedings of the 26th IEEE-ACM-SIGPLAN International Conference on Software Engineering (ICSE'04)* (pp. 604-613).

Ponnekanti, S. R. (2004) Application-Service Interoperation Without Standardized Service Interfaces. In *Proceedings of the 1st IEEE International Conference on Pervasive Computing and Communications* (pp. 30-37).

Ponnekanti, S. R., & Fox, A. (2004). Interoperability Among Independently Evolving Web Services. In *Proceedings of the 5th ACM/IFIP/USENIX International Middleware Conference (MIDDLEWARE'04)* (pp. 331-351).

Ponzi, L., & Koenig, M. (2002). Knowledge Management: Another Management Fad? *Information Research, 8*(1).

Prasarnphanich, P., & Gillenson, M. (2003). The Hybrid Clicks and Bricks Business Model. *Communications of the ACM, 46*(12), 178–185. doi:10.1145/953460.953498

Pressman, R. S. (2001). *Software Engineering: A Practitioner's Approach* (5th ed.). Boston: McGraw-Hill.

Rainbird, M. (2004). Demand and supply chains: The value catalyst. *International Journal of Physical Distribution & Logistics Management, 34*(3/4), 230–250. doi:10.1108/09600030410533565

Reichheld, F., & Schefter, P. (2000). E-loyalty: Your secret weapon on the Web. *Harvard Business Review*, *78*(4), 105–113.

Reiff-Marganiec, S., & Turner, K. J. (2003). *A Policy Architecture for Enhancing and Controlling Features* (pp. 239–246). Feature Interactions in Telecommunications and Software Systems.

Retailer Daily. 2008. Multi-Channel Holiday Shoppers Prefer Web to In-Store. Retrieved October 30, 2009 from http://www.retailerdaily.com/entry/first-time-ever-multi-channel-holiday-shoppers-prefer-web-to-in-store/

RetailerNetGroup. (2009). The new alternative channels: From site to store. Retrieved October 30, 2009 from http://archive.constantcontact.com/fs028/1102142477435/archive/1102649159680.html

Reuters (2009). O'Reilly Auto Parts Introduces Buy Online, Pick Up In Store. Retrieved October 30, 2009 from http://www.reuters.com/article/pressRelease/idUS244274+21-Apr-2009+BW20090421

Rong, W., Liu, K., & Liang, L. (2008). Association Rule Based Context Modeling for Web Service Discovery. In *Proceedings of the 10th IEEE Conference on E-Commerce and E-Services* (pp. 299-304). Los Alamitos, USA: IEEE-CS Press.

Ross, R., Subrahmanian, V., & Grant, J. (2005). Aggregate operators in probabilistic databases. *Journal of the ACM*, *52*, 54–101. doi:10.1145/1044731.1044734

Ross, J. W. (2006). *Enterprise Architecture as Strategy: Creating a Foundation for Business Execution*. Harvard Business Review Press.

Ross, A. (2003). Creating agile supply chains. *Manufacturing Engineering*, *82*(6), 18–21. doi:10.1049/me:20030603

Rossebø, J. E. Y., & Bræk, R. (2006). A Policy-driven Approach to Dynamic Composition of Authentication and Authorization Patterns and Services. *Journal of Computers*, *1*(8), 13–26. doi:10.4304/jcp.1.8.13-26

Rossebø, J. E. Y., & Runde, R. K. (2008). *Specifying Service Composition Using UML 2.x and Composition Policies* (pp. 520–536). Model Driven Engineering Languages and Systems.

Rossi, M. A. (2001). Stand alone e-commerce market survey. *IRMI Expert Commentary*. Retrieved from http://www.irmi.com/expert/articles/rossi004chart.asp

Rust, R. T., & Kannan, P. K. (2003). E-service: A new paradigm for business in the electronic environment. *Communications of the ACM*, *46*(6), 37–42. doi:10.1145/777313.777336

Sabucedo, L. M. A., Rifón, L. E. A., Pérez, R. M., & Gago, J. M. S. (2009). Providing standard-oriented data models and interfaces to eGovernment services: A semantic-driven approach. *Computer Standards & Interfaces*, *31*(5), 1014–1027. doi:10.1016/j.csi.2008.09.042

Saeed, K., Grover, V., & Hwang, Y. (2003). Creating synergy with a click and mortar approach. *Communications of the ACM*, *46*(12), 206–212. doi:10.1145/953460.953501

Sakao, T., & Shimomura, Y. (2007). Service CAD System to Support Servicification of Manufactures. In *Advances in Life Cycle Engineering for Sustainable Manufacturing Businesses: Proceedings of the 14th CIRP Conference on Life Cycle Engineering*. Waseda University, Tokyo, Japan, (pp. 143-148)June 11th-13th. London: Springer.

Salatge, N., & Fabre, J. C. (2007). Fault Tolerance Connectors for Unreliable Web Services. In *Proceedings of the 37th Annual IEEE/IFIP International Conference on Dependable Systems and Networks* (pp. 51-60).

Sanders, R. T., Castejón, H. N., Kraemer, F. A., & Bræk, R. (2005). *Using UML 2.0 Collaborations for Compositional Service Specification* (pp. 460–475). Model Driven Engineering Languages and Systems.

Sawy, O. A. E., & Bowles, G. (2003). *Information technology and customer service*. Oxford: Butterworth-Heineman.

Scheer, A.-W., Thomas, O., & Adam, O. (2005). Process Modeling Using Event-driven Process Chains. In M. Dumas, W.M.P. van der Aalst, & A.H.M ter Hofstede (Eds.), *Process-aware Information Systems: Bridging People and Software through Process Technology* (pp. 119-145), Hoboken, NJ: Wiley.

Schmit, B. A., & Dustdar, S. (2005). Model-driven Development of Web service Transactions. *International Journal of Enterprise Modeling and Information Systems Architecure*, *1*(1).

Schneider, G. P. (2003). *Electronic Commerce* (4th ed.). Boston, MA: Thomson Course Technology.

Schuldt, H., Alonso, G., Beeri, C., & Schek, H.-J. r. (2002). Atomicity and Isolation for Transactional Processes. *ACM Transactions on Database Systems, 27*(1), 63–116. doi:10.1145/507234.507236

Scott, S. D., Samal, A., & Seth, S. (1995). HGA: A Hardware-Based Genetic Algorithm. In *Proceedings of International Symposium on Field-Programmable Gate Array* (pp. 53-59).

Sensoy, M., & Yolum, P. (2007). Ontology-Based Service Representation and Selection. *IEEE Transactions on Knowledge and Data Engineering*, 1102–1115. doi:10.1109/TKDE.2007.1045

Shah, U., Finin, T., Joshi, A., Cost, R. S., & Matfield, J. (2002). Information retrieval on the semantic web. In *Proc. of the 11th Int'l Conf. on Information and Knowledge Management* (pp. 461-468). New York: ACM.

Sheng, Q. Z., Benatallah, B., & Maamar, Z. (2008). User-centric services provisioning in wireless environments. *Communications of the ACM, 51*(11), 130–135. doi:10.1145/1400214.1400241

Sheng, Q. Z., & Benatallah, B. (2005). ContextUML: a UML-based modeling language for model-driven development of context-aware Web services. In *Proceedings of the 2005 International Conference on Mobile Business* (pp. 206-212). Los Alamitos, USA: IEEE-CS Press.

Sheth, A. (2003). Semantic web process lifecycle: Role of semantics in annotation, discovery, composition and orchestration. Invited Talk, WWW 2003 Workshop on E-Services and the Semantic Web, Budapest, Hungary, May 20.

Shostack, L. G. (1977). Breaking Free from Product Marketing. *Journal of Marketing, 41*(2), 73–80. doi:. doi:10.2307/1250637

Singh, M. P., & Huhns, M. N. (2005). *Service-oriented Computing: Semantics, Processes, and Agents.* Chichester: John Wiley & Sons, Ltd.

Smith, H. & Fingar, P. (2004). Business Process Management: The Third Wave. *Journal of Information Systems.* American Accounting Association (AAA).

Song, W., & Zhang, M. (2004). *Semantic Network.* Beijing: High Education Press. (in Chinese)

Sousa, R., & Voss, C. (2006). Service Quality in Multichannel Services Employing Virtual Channels. *Journal of Service Research, 8*(4), 356–371. doi:10.1177/1094670506286324

SpamAssasin. (2009). Retrieved from http://spamassasin.apache.org/

SpamEater. Net (2009). Retrieved from http://www.spameater.net.

Spanoudakis, G., Mahbub, K., & Zisman, A. (2007). A Platform for Context Aware Runtime Web Service Discovery. In *Proceedings of the 2007 IEEE International Conference on Web Services* (pp. 233-240). Los Alamitos, USA: IEEE-CS Press.

Spanyi, A. (2003). *Business Process Management Is a Team Sport: Play It to Win!* Anclote Press Imprint of Meghan-Kiffer Press.

Spohrer, J., Maglio, P., Baily, J., & Gruhl, D. (2007). Steps toward a Science of Service Systems. *Computer, 40*(1), 71–77. doi:10.1109/MC.2007.33

Srikant, R., & Agrawal, R. (1996). Mining quantitative association rules in large relational tables. In *Proc. of ACM SIGMOD* (pp. 1-12).

Sriram, S., Kumar, A., Gupta, D., & Jalote, P. (2001). ComponentXchange: a software component marketplace on the Internet. In *Proceedings of the International Conference on World Wide Web* (pp. 1098-1099).

Steinfield, C., Adelaar, T., & Fang, L. (2005). Click and Mortar Strategies Viewed from the Web: A Content Analysis of Features Illustrating Integration Between Retailers' Online and Offline Presence. *Electronic Markets, 15*(3), 199–212. doi:10.1080/10196780500208632

Steinfield, C., Mahler, A., & Bauer, J. (1999b). Electronic Commerce and the Local Merchant: Opportunities for synergy between physical and web presence. *Electronic Markets, 9*(1/2), 51–57.

Sterling, J. U., & Lambert, D. M. (1989). Customer service research, past, present and future. *International journal of physical distribution & materials management, 19*(2), 2-23.

Strang, T., & Linnhoff-Popien, C. (2004). A Context Modeling Survey. In *Proceedings of the First International Workshop on Advanced Context Modeling, Reasoning, and Management* at UbiComp 2004 (pp. 33-40). Los Alamitos, USA: IEEE-CS Press.

Sun, Z., & Finnie, G. (2004). *Intelligent Techniques in E-Commerce: A Case-based Reasoning Perspective.* Berlin, Heidelberg: Springer-Verlag.

Sun, Z., & Finnie, G. (2005). A unified logical model for CBR-based e-commerce systems. *International Journal of Intelligent Systems, 20*(1), 29–46. doi:10.1002/int.20052

Sun Microsystems. (2003). Web services life cycle: Managing enterprise Web services, White Paper. Retrieved December 18, 2008, from http://www.sun.com/software

Sun, Z., & Lau, S. K. (2007). Customer experience management in e-services. In J. Lu, D. Ruan, & G> Zhang (Eds.), *E-Service Intelligence: Methodologies*, Technologies and Applications (pp. 365-388). Berlin, Heidelberg: Springer-Verlag.

Swaid, S., & Wigand, R. (2009). Measuring the Quality of E-Service: Scale Development and Initial Validation. *Journal of Electronic Commerce Research, 10*(1), 13–28.

Szeto, C. C., & Hung, E. (2009). Mining outliers with faster cutoff update and space utilization. In *Proc. of the 13th Pacific-Asia Conference on Knowledge Discovery and Data Mining (PAKDD-2009)*, Bangkok, Thailand.

Taher, Y., Benslimane, D., Fauvet, M.-C., & Maamar, Z. (2006). Towards an Approach for Web Services Substitution. In *Proceedings of the 10th International Database Engineering and Applications Symposium* (pp. 166-173).

Talia, D. (2002). The open grid services architecture: Where the grid meets the web. *IEEE Internet Computing, 6*(6), 67–71. doi:10.1109/MIC.2002.1067739

Tang, X. F., Jiang, C. J., Ding, Z. J., & Wang, C. (2007). A Petri net-based semantic web services automatic composition method. [in Chinese]. *Journal of Software, 18*(12), 2991–3000.

Tarokh, M. J., Ghahremanloo, H., & Karami, M. (2007, Aug). *Agility in Auto Dealers SCM.* Paper presented at the IEEE International Conference on Service Operations and Logistics, and Informatics.

Tax, S. S., & Stuart, I. (1997). Designing and Implementing New Services: The Challenges of Integrating Service Systems. *Journal of Retailing, 73*(1), 105–134. doi:. doi:10.1016/S0022-4359(97)90017-8

Teller, C., Kotzab, H., & Grant, D. (2006). The consumer direct services revolution in grocery retailing: An exploratory investigation. *Managing Service Quality, 16*(1), 78–96. doi:10.1108/09604520610639973

Teltzrow, M., Günther, O., & Pohle, C. (2003). Analyzing Consumer Behavior at Retailers with Hybrid Distribution Channels - A Trust Perspective. *ACM International Conference Proceedings. 5th International Conference of Electronic Commerce*, Pittsburgh, Pennsylvania.

Tentative Hold Protocol Part 1: White Paper. *(2001).*

Tentative Hold Protocol Part 2: Technical Specification. *(2001).*

ter Hofstede, A. H. M., Proper, H. A., & van der Weide, Th. P. (1993). Formal definition of a conceptual language for the description and manipulation of information models. *Information Systems, 18*(7), 489–523. doi:10.1016/0306-4379(93)90004-K

ter Hofstede, A. H. M., & van der Weide, Th. P. (1993). Expressiveness in conceptual data modelling. *Data & Knowledge Engineering, 10*(1), 65–100. doi:10.1016/0169-023X(93)90020-P

Thomas, O., Walter, P., & Loos, P. (2008). Design and Usage of an Engineering Methodology for Product-Service Systems. *Journal of Desert Research, 7*(2), 177–195. doi:. doi:10.1504/JDR.2008.020854

Thomas, O., Walter, P., Loos, P., Nüttgens, M., & Schlicker, M. (2007). Mobile Technologies for Efficient Service Processes: A Case Study in the German Machine and Plant Construction Industry. In *Proceedings of the 13th Americas Conference on Information Systems*: August 09-12, Keystone, Colorado, USA. Atlanta, GA: AIS.

Timm, P. R. (2005). *Technology and customer service: profitable relationship building; loyalty, satisfaction, organizational success.* Upper Saddle River, NJ: Pearson Prentice Hall.

Tomiyama, T. (2002). Service Engineering to Intensify Service Contents in Product Life Cycles. Japan *ECP Newsletter,* 19.

Tosic, V. (2010). On Modeling and Maximizing Business Value for Autonomic Service-Oriented Systems. [IJSSOE]. *International Journal of Systems and Service-Oriented Engineering*, *1*(1), 79–95.

Tosic, V., Pagurek, B., Patel, B., Esfandiari, B., & Ma, W. (2005). Management Applications of the Web service Offerings Language (WSOL). [Amsterdam: The Netherlands: Elsevier.]. *Information Systems*, *30*(7), 564–586. doi:10.1016/j.is.2004.11.005

Tosic, V., Erradi, A., & Maheshwari, P. (2007). WS-Policy4MASC - A WS-Policy Extension Used in the Manageable and Adaptable Service Compositions (MASC) Middleware. In *Proceedings of the 2007 IEEE Services Computing Conference* (pp. 458-465). Los Alamitos, USA: IEEE-CS Press.

Tosic, V., Lutfiyya, H., & Tang, Y. (2006a). Web Service Offerings Language (WSOL) Support for Context Management of Mobile/Embedded XML Web Services. In *Proceedings of the Advanced international Conference on Telecommunications and International Conference on internet and Web Applications and Services* (pp. 45-52). Los Alamitos, USA: IEEE-CS Press.

Tosic, V., Lutfiyya, H., & Tang, Y. (2006b). Extending Web Service Offerings Infrastructure (WSOI) for Management of Mobile/Embedded XML Web Services. In *Joint Proceedings of the 8th IEEE International Conference on E-Commerce Technology and 3rd IEEE International Conference on Enterprise Computing, E-Commerce and E-Services (CEC/EEE 2006), 3rd IEEE International Workshop on Mobile Commerce and Wireless Services (WMCS 2006), 2nd International Workshop on Business Service Networks and 2nd International Workshop on Service oriented Solutions for Cooperative Organizations* (pp. 571-578). Los Alamitos, USA: IEEE-CS Press.

Tsalgatidou, A., & Pilioura, T. (2002). An overview of standards and related technology in web services. *Distributed and Parallel Databases*, *12*, 135–162. doi:10.1023/A:1016599017660

Vaculin, R., Wiesner, K., & Sycara, K. (2008). *Exception Handling and Recovery of Semantic Web Services.* Paper presented at the ICNS '08: Proceedings of the Fourth International Conference on Networking and Services, Washington, DC, USA.

Vallet, D., Fernández, M., & Castells, P. (2005). An ontology-based information retrieval model. In *The Semantic Web: Research and Applications* (LNCS 3532, pp. 455-470). Heidelberg: Springer.

van Bommel, P., ter Hofstede, A. H. M., & van der Weide, Th. P. (1991). Semantics and verification of object-role models. *Information Systems*, *16*(5), 471–495. doi:10.1016/0306-4379(91)90037-A

Van Der Aalst, W., Hofstede, A. T., Kiepuszewski, B., & Barros, A. (2003). Workflow Patterns. *Distributed and Parallel Databases*, *14*(3), 5–51. doi:10.1023/A:1022883727209

van der Aalst, W. M. P., et al. (2003). Business Process Management: A Survey. *Business Process Management, Proceedings of the First International Conference*. Springer Verlag.

van Gils, B. (2006). *Aptness on the Web*. Ph.D. thesis, Radboud University, Nijmegen, The Netherlands.

Vandermerwe, S., & Rada, J. F. (2007). Servitization of Business: Adding Value by Adding Services. *European Management Journal*, *6*(4), 314–324. doi:. doi:10.1016/0263-2373(88)90033-3

Vaquero, L. M. (2009). A Break in the Clouds: Toward a Cloud Definition. *ACM SIGCOMM Computer Communication Review*, *39*(1), 50–55. doi:10.1145/1496091.1496100

Venkatesh, V., & Davis, F. (2000). A Theoretical Extension of the Technology Acceptance Model: Four Longitudinal Field Studies. *Management Science*, *46*(2), 186–204. doi:10.1287/mnsc.46.2.186.11926

Voas, J. (1999). The cold realities of software insurance. *IT Professional*, *1*(1), 71–72. doi:10.1109/6294.774795

Vonderembse, M. A., Uppal, M., Huang, S. H., & Dismukes, J. P. (2006). Designing supply chains: Towards theory development. *International Journal of Production Economics*, *100*(2), 223–238. doi:.doi:10.1016/j.ijpe.2004.11.014

Voss, C. (2003). Rethinking Paradigms of Service: Service in a Virtual Environment. *International Journal of Operations & Production Management*, *23*(1), 88–104. doi:10.1108/01443570310453271

W3C (2004). Web service management: Service life cycle. Retrieved December 26, 2008, from http://www.w3.org/TR/2004/NOTE-web servicelc-20040211/

W3C (2004). Web Services Architecture. Retrieved from http://www.w3c.org/TR/ws-arch.

W3C (2007). Semantic Annotations for WSDL and XML Schema. Retrieved from http://www.w3c.org/TR/sawsdl.

W3C Web Services Policy Working Group. (2007). *Web Services Policy 1.5 – Framework*. W3C Recommendation. Published September 4, 2007. Retrieved April 10, 2009, from http://www.w3.org/TR/ws-policy/

Wang, M., Liu, J., Wang, H., Cheung, W. K., & Xie, X. (2008). On-demand e-supply chain integration: A multi-agent constraint-based approach. *Expert Systems with Applications*, *34*(4), 2683–2692. doi:10.1016/j.eswa.2007.05.041

Wang, H., Jiang, F., & Hou, L. W. (2005). Study on development process of semantic-oriented metadata model. [in Chinese]. *Information Science*, *23*(1), 95–101.

Wang, H., Jiang, F., & Hou, L. W. (2006). Checking problems of ontology-based metadata extended models. [in Chinese]. *Systems Engineering-theory & Practice*, *26*(10), 57–66.

Wang, X., & Du, L. (2003). Automatic segmentation of Chinese using overlaying ambiguity examining method and statistics language model. [in Chinese]. *Journal of Electronics and Information Technology*, *25*(9), 1168–1173.

Wang, D., Yung, K. L., & Ip, W. H. (2001). A heuristic genetic algorithm for subcontractor selection in a global manufacturing environment. *IEEE Transactions on Systems, Man and Cybernetics. Part C, Applications and Reviews*, *31*(2), 189–198. doi:10.1109/5326.941842

Wang, A. I., Sørensen, C.-F., Le, H. N., Ramampiaro, H., Nygård, M., & Conradi, R. (2008). From Scenarios to Requirements in Mobile Client-Server Systems. In Tiako, P. F. (Ed.), *Designing Software-Intensive Systems: Methods and Principles* (pp. 80–101). Hershey, PA: IGI Global.

Wang, H. (2004). *Research on the construction of metadata models based on ontology*. Unpublished doctoral dissertation (in Chinese), Shanghai Jiaotong University, Shanghai, China.

Wang, M., Cheung, W. K., Liu, J., Xie, X., & Lou, Z. (2006). E-service/process composition through multi-agent constraint management. In *Intl Conf on Business Process Management* (BPM 2006), Vienna, Austria (LNCS 4102, pp. 274-289).

Warren, I., & Sommerville, I. (1996). A Model for Dynamic Configuration which Preserves Application Integrity. In *Proceedings of the 3rd IEEE International Conference on Configurable Distributed Systems* (pp. 81-88).

Waters, D. (2006). Demand chain effectiveness-supply chain efficiencies: A role for enterprise information management. *Journal of Enterprise Information Management*, *19*(3), 246–261. doi:10.1108/17410390610658441

Web Services Transactions Specifications. (2005).

Weber, C., Pohl, M., Steinbach, M., & Botta, C. (2002). Diskussion der Probleme bei der integrierten Betrachtung von Sach- und Dienstleistungen - "Kovalente Produkte"". In: 13. Symposium "Design for X", Neukirchen/Erlangen 10.-11.10.2002: Tagungsband (pp. 61-70). Friedrich-Alexander-Universität Erlangen-Nürnberg.

Weihl, W. E. (1988). Commutativity-Based Concurrency Control for Abstract Data Types. *IEEE Transactions on Computers*, *37*(12), 1488–1505. doi:10.1109/12.9728

Weiss, G. (Ed.). (1999). *Multiagent Systems: A modern approach to Distributed Artificial Intelligence*. Cambridge, MA: MIT Press.

Wibisono, W., Zaslavsky, A., & Ling, S. (2008). Towards a Service-Oriented Approach for Managing Context in Mobile Environment. In *Proceedings of the 6th international Conference on Service-Oriented Computing* (LNCS 5364, pp. 210-224)

Widom, J., & Ceri, S. (1996). *Active Database Systems: Triggers and Rules For Advanced Database Processing*. Morgan Kaufmann.

Wiki (2009). Retrieved April 2, 2009, from http://en.wikipedia.org/wiki/Demand_(economics).

Wilkinson, N. (2005). *Managerial Economics: A Problem-Solving Approach*. Cambridge: Cambridge University Press.

Willerding, T. (1987). Gestaltungsmöglichkeiten der Kooperation im technischen Kundendienst zwischen Hersteller und Handel. Bochum: Studienverlag Brockmeyer VDMA (2008). Maschinenbau in Zahl und Bild 2008. Mühlheim am Main: reuffurth.

Wolfinbarger, M., & Gilly, M. (2003). E-TailQ: Dimensionalizing, Measuring and Predicting Etail Quality. *Journal of Retailing, 27*, 183–198. doi:10.1016/S0022-4359(03)00034-4

Wong, W. K., Cheung, D. W., Hung, E., Kao, B., & Mamoulis, N. (2007). Security in outsourcing of association rule mining. In *Proc. of the 33rd International Conference on Very Large Data Bases (VLDB)*, University of Vienna, Austria.

Wong, W. K., Cheung, D. W., Hung, E., Kao, B., & Mamoulis, N. (2009). An audit environment for outsourcing of frequent itemset mining. In *Proceedings of the VLDB Endowment (PVLDB)*, 2.

Wong, W. K., Cheung, D. W., Hung, E., & Liu, H. (2008). Protecting privacy in incremental maintenance for distributed association rule mining. In *Proc. of the 12th Pacific-Asia Conference on Knowledge Discovery and Data Mining (PAKDD2008)*, Osaka, Japan.

Woodall, R., Colby, C. & Parasuraman A. (2007). *E-volution to Revolution*, 29-34.

WordNet 3.0 (2006). Princeton University. Retrieved from http://wordnet.princeton.edu/

Wu, P., Fekete, A., & Rohm, U. (2008). The Efficacy of Commutativity-Based Semantic Locking in a Real-World Application. *IEEE Transactions on Knowledge and Data Engineering, 20*(3), 427–431. doi:10.1109/TKDE.2007.190728

Wu, C., & Chang, E. (2005). A conceptual architecture of distributed web services for service ecosystems. In S. Dascalu (Ed.), *18th International Conf on Computer Applications in Industry and Engineering* (CAINE 2005) (pp. 209-214).

Xiao, L., Hung, E., & Hung, R. Y. S. (in press). An Efficient Representation Model of Distance Distribution Between Uncertain Objects. *Computational Intelligence*.

Xiao, L., & Hung, E. (2007). An efficient distance calculation method for uncertain objects. In *Proc. of 2007 IEEE Symposium on Computational Intelligence and Data Mining (CIDM)*, Honolulu, Hawaii, USA.

Xiao, L., & Hung, E. (2008). Clustering web-search results using transduction-based relevance model. In *Proc. of IEEE First Pacific-Asia Workshop on Web Mining and Web-based Application 2008 (WMWA'08), in conjunction with the 12th Pacific-Asia Conference on Knowledge Discovery and Data Mining (PAKDD2008)*, Osaka, Japan.

Xu, C. (2007). *Web service match based on ontology reasoning*. Unpublished doctoral dissertation (in Chinese), Ocean University of China, Qingdao, China.

Yang, J., & Papazoglou, M. (2004). Service Components for Managing the Lifecycle of Service Compositions. *Information Systems, 29*(2), 97–125. doi:10.1016/S0306-4379(03)00051-6

Yao, Y., Yang, F., & Su, S. (2006). Flexible decision making in web services negotiation. In J. Euzenat & J. Domingue (Eds.), *AIMSA 2006* (LNAI 4183, pp. 108-117).

Yau Stephen, S., & Liu, J. (2006). Incorporating Situation Awareness in Service Specifications. *International Symposium on Object-Oriented Real-Time Distributed Computing* (pp. 287-294).

Yu, C., Wang, H., & Luo, Y. (2006). Extended ontology model and ontology checking based on description logics. In Wang et al. (Eds.), *Fuzzy Systems and Knowledge Discovery: Vol. 4223. Artificial Intelligence* (pp. 607-610). Heidelberg: Springer.

Yuan, S.-T., & Lu, M.-R. (2009). An value-centric event driven model and architecture: a case study of adaptive complement of SOA for distributed care service delivery. *Expert Systems with Applications, 36*(2), 3671–3694. doi:10.1016/j.eswa.2008.02.024

Yuan, L., Li, Z., & Chen, S. (2008). Ontology-Based Annotation for Deep Web Data. [in Chinese]. *Journal of Software, 19*(2), 237–245. doi:10.3724/SP.J.1001.2008.00237

Zacarias, M., Pinto, H. S., Magalhães, R., & Tribolet, J. (in press). A 'context-aware' and agent-centric perspective for the alignment between individuals and organizations. *Information Systems*.

Zarras, A., Fredj, M., Georgantas, N., & Issarny, V. (2006). Engineering Reconfigurable Distributed Software Systems: Issues Arising for Pervasive Computing. In *Rigorous Development of Complex Fault-Tolerant Systems* (LNCS 4157, pp. 364-386).

Zeithaml, V., Parasuraman, A., & Malhotra, A. (2002). Service quality delivery through the Web sites: A critical review of extant knowledge. *Journal of the Academy of Marketing Science*, *30*(4), 362–375. doi:10.1177/009207002236911

Zeithaml, V., Parasuraman, A., & Malhorta, A. (2000). A Conceptual Framework for Understanding E-Service Quality: Implications for Future Research and Managerial Practice. *Marketing Science Institute (MSI)*, Report # 00-115.

Zghal, H. B., Aufaure, M. A., & Mustapha, N. B. (2007). A model-driven approach of ontological components for on-line semantic web information retrieval. *Journal of Web Engineering*, *6*(4), 309–336.

Zhang, M., Lu, Z., & Zou, C. (2004). A Chinese word segmentation based on language situation in processing ambiguous words. *Information Sciences*, *162*(3-4), 275–285. doi:10.1016/j.ins.2003.09.010

Zhang, X., & Prybutok, V. (2005). A Consumer Perceptive of E-Service Quality. *IEEE Transactions on Engineering Management*, *52*(4), 461–477. doi:10.1109/TEM.2005.856568

Zhang, L. J., & Jeckle, M. (2003). The next big thing: Web services composition. In M. Jeckle & L.J. Zhang (Eds.), *ICWS-Europe* (LNCS 2853, pp. 1-10).

Zhang, M., & Ma, J. (2009). An approach to Chinese word sense disambiguation based on HowNet. *Computer Technology and Development (in Chinese)*, *19*(2), 9-11, 15.

Zhao, W., Moser, L. E., & Melliar-Smith, P. M. (2008). A Reservation-Based Extended Transaction Protocol. *IEEE Transactions on Parallel and Distributed Systems*, *19*(2), 188–203. doi:10.1109/TPDS.2007.70727

Zhou, C., Chia, L.-T., & Lee, B.-S. (2004). QoS-aware and federated enhancement for UDDI. *International Journal of Web Services Research*, *1*(2), 58–85.

Zhu, D., Li, Y., Shi, J., Xu, Y., & Shen, W. (2009). A service-oriented city portal framework and collaborative development platform. *Information Sciences*, *179*(15), 2606–2617. doi:10.1016/j.ins.2009.01.038

About the Contributors

Ho-fung Leung is currently a full Professor in Computer Science and Engineering, The Chinese University of Hong Kong. He has been active in research on intelligent agents, multi-agent systems, game theory, and semantic web, and has published close to 150 papers in these areas. Professor Leung has served on the program committee of many conferences. He is a member of the planning committee of PRIMA and a senior PC member of AAMAS'08. He is currently serving on the program committees of CEC'08 & EEE'08, EDOC 2008, ICMLC 2008, IDPT 2008, ISEAT 2008, M2AS'08, SAC 2008 (PL Track) and SLAECE 2008. He was the chairperson of ACM (Hong Kong Chapter) in 1998. Professor Leung is a Senior Member of ACM, a Senior Member of the IEEE, and a Chartered Fellow of the BCS. He is a Chartered Engineer registered by the ECUK and is awarded the designation of Chartered Scientist by the Science Council, UK. Professor Leung received his BSc and M.Phil. degrees in Computer Science from The Chinese University of Hong Kong, and his PhD degree in Computing from Imperial College of Science, Technology and Medicine, University of London. He is an Associate Editor of the International Journal on Systems and Service-Oriented Engineering.

Dickson K.W. Chiu received the BSc (Hons.) degree in Computer Studies from the University of Hong Kong in 1987. He received the MSc (1994) and the PhD (2000) degrees in Computer Science from the Hong Kong University of Science and Technology (HKUST). He started his own computer company while studying part-time. He has also taught at several universities in Hong Kong. His research interest is in service computing with a cross-disciplinary approach, involving workflows, software engineering, information technologies, agents, information system management, security, and databases. The results have been widely published in over 120 papers in international journals and conference proceedings (most of them have been indexed by SCI, SCI-E, EI, and SSCI), including many practical master and undergraduate project results. He received a best paper award in the *37th Hawaii International Conference on System Sciences* in 2004. He is the founding Editor-in-chief of the *International Journal on Systems and Service-Oriented Engineering* and serves in the editorial boards of several international journals. He co-founded several international workshops and co-edited several journal special issues. He also served as a program committee member for over 70 international conferences and workshops. He is a *Senior Member* of both the ACM and the IEEE, and a *life member* of the Hong Kong Computer Society.

Patrick C. K. Hung is an Associate Professor at the Faculty of Business and Information Technology in UOIT and an Adjunct Assistant Professor at the Department of Electrical and Computer Engineering in University of Waterloo. Patrick is currently collaborating with Boeing Phantom Works (Seattle, USA) and Bell Canada on security- and privacy-related research projects, and he has filed two US patent applications on "Mobile Network Dynamic Workflow Exception Handling System." In addition, Patrick is also cooperating on Web services composition research projects with Southeast University in China. Patrick has been serving as a panelist of the Small Business Innovation Research and Small Business Technology Transfer programs of the National Science Foundation (NSF) in the States since 2000. He is an executive committee member of the IEEE Computer Society's Technical Steering Committee for Services Computing, a steering member of EDOC "Enterprise Computing," and an associate editor/editorial board member/guest editor in several international journals such as the IEEE Transactions on Services Computing, International Journal of Web Services Research (JWSR), International journal of Business Process and Integration Management (IJBPIM), and the International Journal on Systems and Service-Oriented Engineering.

* * *

Rama Akkiraju is a senior technical staff member at IBM Research labs in New York. She has 14 years of experience in the topics ranging from agent-based decision support systems, electronic market places, business transformation analytics, and business process integration technologies. Rama has co-authored 5 book chapters, and over 35 technical papers published in peer-reviewed journals and conferences. She holds a masters degree in computer science and an MBA from New York University, Stern School of Business. Rama graduated at the top of the MBA class in 2004 and received a gold medal of honor from the university.

Nadine Blinn is researcher and PhD candidate at the chair for Information Systems focusing business standard software and information management at University of Hamburg. Her research activities include business process management, information management, service science (particularly T-KIBS) and product service systems.

Patrick van Bommel received his Master degree in computer science in 1990, and the degree of PhD in mathematics and computer science, from the Radboud University Nijmegen, the Netherlands in 1995. He is currently assistant professor at the Radboud University. His main research interests include information modelling, where the focus is foundations of models and their transformations in order to establish theoretical properties and practical tools. Contact him at P.vanBommel@cs.ru.nl.

Rolv Bræk is professor in systems development at the Norwegian University of Science and Technology (NTNU), Department of Telematics, Trondheim. He has extensive industrial experience as systems designer, project manager and technical manager for the telecommunication industry working with specification, design and implementation of fault tolerant and distributed computer systems including the operating systems and application software. He also developed the SDL Oriented Methodology, SOM, with supporting tools and that were applied on several industrial projects. He has written textbooks and numerous publications in the area of industrial formal methods and tools. Currently his main research interest is methods, tools and platform support for rapid and incremental service engineering based on UML 2.0 collaborations.

Rong Zeng Cao holds a PhD degree from the Harbin Institute of Technology and has been a research staff member at IBM Research - China since 2003. His area of expertise is operation research, with a particular interest in service science and the use of analytics and optimization for business problems, such as pricing, planning and risk management.

Humberto Nicolás Castejón received the MSc degree in telecommunications from the Polytechnic University of Valencia, Spain, in 2000 and the PhD degree in telematics from the Norwegian University of Science and Technology, Norway, in 2008. Prior to enrolling on his PhD studies he worked at Telenor R&I from 2000 to 2002. From 2009 he is research scientist at Telenor GBD&R. His research interests include model-driven development of service-based systems, lightweight validation methods, and policy-based service adaptation and personalization.

Wei Ding is the senior manager of the Business Analytics & Optimization team at IBM Research - China. She received her PhD degree in management science from Harbin Institute of Technology. Her research interests include analytics & optimization technology, business value analysis, model driven business transformation technology.

Dong Dong is an Associate Professor in computer science and technology and the Deputy Head of the School of Computer Science and Technology, College of Mathematics and Information Science, Hebei Normal University, China. He holds a BSci from Hebei Normal University, a master degree of computer science from Asian Institute of Technology (Thailand) and a master degree of software engineering (MEng) from Beijing University of Technology, China. He has over 20 refereed journal and conference publications and five textbooks on information technology applications, algorithms and programming. His research interests include information systems, web based information systems, web intelligence and intelligent computing. He is a member of the China Computer Federation. His email is donald.ddong@gmail.com.

Thorsten Dollmann is researcher and PhD candidate at the Institute for Information Systems (IWi) at the German Research Institute for Artificial Intelligence (DFKI). He studied business administration and computer science at Saarland University and completed his degrees 2005 (Dipl.-Kfm.) and 2006 (Dipl.-Inform.). His research activities include business process management and automation of business processes.

Manel Fredj got her PhD in computer science from the University of Pierre et Marie Curie—Paris VI, in 2009. She is currently pursuing her post doc at CEA Saclay. Her research interests relate to middleware support for distributed system reconfiguration, based on the service-oriented paradigm. Further information about Manel's research interest and her publications can be obtained from http://www-rocq.inria.fr/who/Manel.Fredj/

Nikolaos Georgantas received his PhD in 2001 in Electrical and Computer Engineering from the National Technical University of Athens. He is currently researcher at INRIA with the ARLES research group. His research interests relate to distributed systems, middleware, ubiquitous computing systems and service & network architectures for telecommunication systems. He is or has been involved in a number of European projects and several industrial collaborations.

Liusheng Huang received the MS degree from the University of Science and Technology of China in 1988. He is currently a professor and Ph.D. supervisor at the University of Science and Technology of China. His research interests are in the areas of information security, distributed computing and high performance algorithms.

Edward Hung is an assistant professor at the Department of Computing, the Hong Kong Polytechnic University. He obtained his PhD degree from the Department of Computer Science, the University of Maryland, College Park (UMCP) in 2005. Edward's general research area is database, data mining, uncertainty reasoning and semantic web. He has seventeen conference papers, five journal articles and three book chapters related to data mining (for uncertain data, outsourcing, parallel system), outlier detection, classification, probabilistic ontology, RDF aggregates and view maintenance, recall improvement in XML queries by ontologies and similarities, probabilistic semistructured databases, data warehousing and E-commerce.

Valerie Issarny received her PhD and "Habilitation à diriger des recherches" in computer science from the University of Rennes I, France, in 1991 and 1997 respectively. She currently holds a "Directrice de recherche" position at INRIA. Since 2002, she is the head of the INRIA ARLES research project-team at INRIA Paris-Rocquencourt. Her research interests relate to distributed systems, software engineering, service-oriented computing, mobile wireless systems and middleware. Further information about Valerie's research interests and her publications can be obtained from http://www-rocq.inria.fr/arles/members/issarny.html

Marijn Janssen is an associate professor in the Information and Communication Technology section of the Faculty of Technology, Policy, and Management at Delft University of Technology, the Netherlands. His research interests include business engineering, information integration, agent-based and service-oriented architectures, and designing the coordination of networked public and private organizations. He is also the director of the interdisciplinary SEPAM Master program. Janssen received his PhD in information systems from the Delft University of Technology. Contact him at m.f.w.h.a.janssen@tudelft.nl.

Yuchang Jiao received his master degree in software and theory from Shandong University in 2008. He is currently working at IBM China SOA Design Center, Beijing, China. His current research interests include Service Oriented Architecture, services computing and virtualization technologies.

Shun Jiang holds both bachelor and master degree of computer science from Beijing University of Posts and Telecommunications and has been a research staff member at IBM Research - China since 2006. His area of expertise is architecture design\programming models, with a particular interest in business modeling, service pricing, and financial risk management.

Rasangi Karunaratne is currently completing a combined Bachelors degree in Bioinformatics and Financial Economics at UNSW. She recently completed her honours thesis supervised by Dr. Vladimir

Tosic, on the topic "Analysis of Methods for Improving IT support for Business" with a focus on Business Driven IT Management and WS-Policy4MASC. She currently also holds a professional position in the IT industry.

Hien Nam Le is currently working as a research scientist at the Department of Telematics, Norwegian University of Science and Technology (NTNU). He received the BSc in computer science from LaTrobe University, Australia, and master degree in information technology from University of Queensland, Australia in 1996 and 2001, respectively. He received his PhD in computer science in 2006 from Norwegian University of Science and Technology (NTNU), Norway. His research interests include mobile databases and transactions, component-based modelling and situated mobile services.

Juhnyoung Lee is a Research Staff Member at the IBM T. J. Watson Research Center in New York. He is currently working in the Business Informatics group. He finished his PhD at the Department of Computer Science in the University of Virginia at Charlottesville in 1994. He received his BS and MS in Computer Science from Seoul National University in 1985 and 1987, respectively. Since joining IBM Research in 1997, Dr. Lee has worked on e-commerce intelligence, electronic marketplaces, decision support systems, semantic Web technologies, and ontology management systems. Before joining IBM, he was a researcher at Los Alamos National Lab in New Mexico and at Lexis-Nexis in Ohio. His current research interests include service engineering and management, business and IT modeling, and model-driven business transformation.

Peter Loos is director of the Institute for Information Systems (IWi) at the German Research Institute for Artificial Intelligence (DFKI) and head of the chair for Business Administration and Information Systems at Saarland University. His research activities include business process management, information modelling, enterprise systems, software development as well as implementation of information systems. In 1997, Prof. Loos received the venia legendi in business administration. Prof. Loos has written several books, contributed to 30 books and published more than 100 papers in journals and proceedings

Li Li received her PhD degree with major in computing from Swinburne University of Technology, Melbourne, Victoria, Australia, in 2006. She has published more than 40 papers in journals and refereed conferences. Her research interests include service-oriented computing, semantic Web, ontology engineering and multi-agent systems.

Qing Li received the B.Eng. degree from Hunan University, Changsha, China, and the MSc and PhD degrees from the University of Southern California, Los Angeles, all in computer science. He is currently a professor at the City University of Hong Kong. His research interests include database modeling, multimedia retrieval and management, web services, and e-learning systems. He is a senior member of the IEEE.

An Liu received the PhD degrees from the University of Science and Technology of China, Hefei, China, and the City University of Hong Kong, Hong Kong, China, all in computer science. He is currently a lecturer at the University of Science and Technology of China. His research interests are in the area of service-oriented computing.

Chengfei Liu is a professor and the head of the Web and Data Engineering research group in Centre for Complex Software Systems and Services, Faculty of Information and Communication Technologies, Swinburne University of Technology, Australia. Prior to joining Swinburne in 2004, he taught at the University of South Australia and the University of Technology Sydney, and was a Research Scientist at Cooperative Research Centre for Distributed Systems Technology, Australia. He received the PhD degree in Computer Science from Nanjing University, China in 1988. His research interests cover XML data management, advanced database systems, workflows, and transaction management.

James N. K. Liu received the BSc (Hons) and M.Phil. degrees in mathematics and computational modeling from Murdoch University, Australia, in 1982 and 1987, respectively. He received the PhD degree in artificial intelligence from La Trobe University, Australia, in 1992. While working on the degree, he worked as a Computer Scientist at Defense Signal Directorate in Australia from 1988 till 1990. He joined the Aeronautical Research Laboratory of Defense Science and Technology Organization, Australia, as a Research Scientist in 1990. Now, Dr. Liu is an associate professor in the Department of Computing at the Hong Kong Polytechnic University. He has been session chairs for several recent international conferences including International Conference on Fuzzy Systems and Knowledge Discovery (FSKD'09), World Congress on Computational Intelligence (WCCI2008), and International Workshop on Reliability Issues of Knowledge Discovery (RIKD'06). His research interest includes forecasting technology, ontology modeling for content management, e-Learning systems, e-Commerce development and applications. Dr. Liu is a senior member of IEEE.

Shijun Liu is an associate professor of the School of computer science and technology at Shandong University, China. He earned his BS degrees in Oceanography from Ocean University of China, and MS and PhD degree in computer science from Shandong University. His teaching and research interests are focused on Service Computing, Networked Manufacturing, Computer Integrated Manufacturing System and Manufacturing Grid. He has published 2 books and over 50 papers in journals and conferences and obtained many academic awards including the Nation Scientific and Technological Progress Award in 2002.

Liu Wenyin (M¡¯99¨CSM¡¯02) received his B.Engg. and M.Engg. degrees in CS from the Tsinghua University, Beijing in 1988 and 1992 respectively, and his DSc from the Technion, Israel Institute of Technology in 1998. He had worked at Tsinghua as a faculty member for three years and at Microsoft Research China/Asia as a full time Researcher for another three years. He is now Asst Professor in Dept of CS at the City University of Hong Kong. Liu Wenyin played a major role in developing the MDUS system, which won First Place in the Dashed Line Recognition Contest in 1995. In 1997, he won a Third Prize in the ACM/IBM First International Java Programming Contest (ACM Quest for Java'97). In 2003, he was awarded the ICDAR Outstanding Young Researcher Award by IAPR for his significant impact in the research domain of graphics recognition, engineering drawings recognition, and performance evaluation. He is also TC10 chair of IAPR and a guest professor of University of Science and Technology of China (USTC). He is a senior member of IEEE and a member of the editorial board of the International Journal of Document Analysis and Recognition (IJDAR).

Qinghua Lu is presently a PhD student at the School of Computer Science and Engineering of the University of New South Wales. She started her PhD studies at UNSW/NICTA in March 2009. Her PhD topic is "Autonomic Business-driven Decision Making for Service Compositions" She is supervised by Prof. Ross Jeffery, Dr. Vladimir Tosic, and Dr. Jacky Wai Keung at NICTA.

Rakesh Mohan directs research in Industry Solutions at the IBM T.J. Watson Research Center, where he is a member of the Business Informatics department. Dr. Mohan is working on computational approaches to modeling and understanding businesses and solving business problems. This includes research on modeling and analyzing business strategy and operations, value networks, and the design, development and delivery of business solutions, especially for Packaged Applications and Financial Management.

Carl Nordman is an Associate Partner with IBM's Global Business Services (GBS) Institute for Business Value (IBV). Mr. Nordman leads the research group for Financial Management, which is responsible for conducting IBM's Market Research and Thought Leadership, such as the IBM Global CFO Survey. Mr. Nordman has 22 years of Financial Services Industry experience with clients in Banking, Investment Management and Insurance (P&C and HMO). Mr. Nordman's experience includes all aspects of Finance Transformation, including Process Analysis and Re-design, Organization Design and Shared Services Implementation, as well as managing the implementation of enabling Technologies such as Oracle and SAP. Mr. Nordman is also responsible, at IBM, for leading the development and rollout of IBM GBS Finance Transformation solutions and methods. Mr. Nordman has led these efforts globally, for IBM for the past 3 years, including the development and delivery of methods and practices, preparing and conducting Global Training initiatives within IBM and for clients, across the world and participating in IBM's 2008 Global CFO Study. Mr. Nordman has most recently participated in developing and rolling out IBM's GRC/Controls Integration solutions in the Oracle Service Line, through participation on the Oracle Tiger Team, as the GRC/Controls Integration Lead.

Markus Nüttgens is head of the chair for Information Systems focusing business standard software and information management at University of Hamburg. His research activities include business process management, information management, Information Systems in industries, service sector and government, open source/open access, IT governance, It outsourcing, IT-Entrepreneurship.

Sietse Overbeek is an assistant professor in the Information and Communication Technology section of the Faculty of Technology, Policy, and Management at Delft University of Technology, the Netherlands. His research interests include conceptual and formal modeling of information systems, ontology modeling, and service-oriented architectures. Overbeek received his PhD in computer science from the Radboud University Nijmegen, the Netherlands. He is a member of the ACM. Contact him at s.j.overbeek@tudelft.nl.

Siva Prashanth is a finance transformation consultant working on engagements within IBM's Global Delivery- Finance Management Systems practice. He has considerable consulting experience in the area of business modeling, finance transformation and Hyperion package solution consulting. Prior education includes post graduate degrees in Business Administration and Computer Applications. His outside interests include playing cricket and racquetball.

Judith E. Y. Rossebø, Senior Research Scientist, Telenor GBDR. She is also affiliated with The Norwegian University of Science and Technology. Prior to joining Telenor in October 2000, she worked three years as a systems engineer at Alcatel Telecom Norway and one year as an assistant professor teaching mathematics at the University of Tromsø. At Alcatel she worked with IN, and dimensioning, performance, dependability and traffic control in telecommunication networks. She received a Cand. Scient. degree in Mathematics from the University of Oslo (UiO) and a PhD in Telematics from the Norwegian University of Science and Technology (NTNU). At Telenor her research has encompassed service availability, authentication and authorization, crypto protocols, identity management, security modelling, threat and vulnerability analysis, Lawful Intercept, and security standardization. Since January 2003 she has been the Chairman of ETSI TISPAN WG7 Security. Her research interests include security in general; security issues in multimedia communications services, and in particular securing availability of services.

Michael Schlicker is managing partner of INTERACTIVE Software Solutions GmbH, Saarbruecken, Germany. INTERACTIVE Software Solutions is an international software and consulting company specialized in the development of interactive visualization systems and graphical user interfaces. In the future the innovative solution "Service information Management" will support in particular interactive modeling, communication, intuitive visualization and execution of complex after sales service processes in the Machine and Plant Construction industry by next generation user interfaces and mobile devices.

Yuqing Sun received her BSc, Master and PhD degrees in Computer Science from Shandong University, China. She is currently a professor in the School of Computer Science and Technology at Shandong University. She has been a visiting scholar at Hongkong University in Hongkong and at Purdue University in West Lafayette. Her research interests include access control model and technology, security policy, Web services, and workflow management. She has published more than thirty papers in refereed journals and in international conferences and symposia proceedings. She also reviews for international journals and serves on the program committees of many international conferences.

Zhaohao Sun is currently a senior lecturer in Information Systems at the Graduate School of Information technology and Mathematical Sciences, University of Ballarat, Australia, after working as a full professor of computer science and technology and the head of the School of Computer Science and Technology at Hebei Normal University, China for about two years. He is an expert of "China Education Informatization", selected by the Ministry of Education, China. Dr. Sun previously held academic positions at Hebei University, RWTH Aachen, TU Cottbus, Bond University and University of Wollongong and other universities. He has three books and over 90 refereed publications of journals, book chapters and conference proceedings. His current research interests include e-commerce, web services, case-based/experience-based reasoning, multiagent systems, web intelligence, service intelligence, service computing, intelligent computing, and experience management. He is a PC member for dozens of international conferences, and a reviewer for many international journals. He is an associate editor of

Journal of Intelligent and Fuzzy Systems. He is a member of the AIS and the IEEE. His email is z.sun@ballarat.edu.au or zhsun@ieee.org.

Ponn Janaarthanan Sundhararajan is a System Engineer in IBM India Global Service, Chennai, India. He is currently working as Application Developer. He has finished his Bachelor in Computer Science and Engineering in Madurai Kamaraj University 2004. Since 2007, he is working for IBM Global Services and Global Business Solution center as software engineer. His areas of interest include Java SOA and J2EE-based technology.

Samar Swaid is an Assistant Professor of Computer Science at Philander Smith College. Prior to being awarded the doctoral degree, she worked in the IT industry for 10 years. Her research interests are website quality, service quality, e-commerce, e-health and information systems adoption and implementation. Her work was published in a number of international and national conferences as well as in journals such as the Journal of Electronic Commerce Research.

Oliver Thomas studied business administration at the Saarland University. He has been the deputy head and a senior researcher of the Institute for Information Systems at the German Research Center for Artificial Intelligence (DFKI). His fields of research are business process management, enterprise modeling, soft computing and product-service systems. Oliver Thomas is a visiting associate professor at the Aoyama Gakuin University in Tokyo (Japan). He has a chair in information management and information systems at the Institute of Information Management and Corporate Governance, University of Osnabrueck, since 2009.

Chun hua Tian is a Research Staff Member at IBM Research, China. He received his PhD degree in Automation from Tsinghua University in 2004. His current research interests include system dynamics modeling and simulation, logistics and supply chain management, and rule-based optimization.

Vladimir Tosic is a Researcher at NICTA in Sydney, Australia; a Visiting Fellow at the University of New South Wales, Sydney, Australia; and an Adjunct Research Professor at the University of Western Ontario, London, Canada. He previously held several positions in industry and academia in Europe, Canada, and Australia. He completed his PhD degree at Carleton University, Ottawa, Canada and received many academic awards, including the 2001 Upsilon Pi Epsilon / IEEE Computer Society Award for Academic Excellence. Most of his peer-reviewed papers are on management of service-oriented systems, while his current research is focused on autonomic business-driven management. Further information is at: http://www.nicta.com.au/people/tosicv.

Hongwei Wang received the bachelor degree in information management and information systems from Dalian University of Technology, P.R. China, in 1996. He received the master degree in system engineering from Guangdong University of Technology, P.R. China, in 1999. His PhD degree in business intelligence was received from Shanghai Jiaotong University, P.R. China, in 2003. After the graduation, he worked as a senior analyst at the Shanghai Municipal Informatization Commission for half a year. Then, he joined the School of Economics and Management, Tongji University, Shanghai, P.R. China, in 2004, where he is now an associate professor. He has published technical papers on subjects in ontological modeling, business intelligence, and e-Commerce applications. He has been session chairs for several recent international conferences including FSKD'09, CDSIM'09. His current interests include business intelligent, affective computing in Chinese context, data mining, and Web-based information systems. Dr Wang is a member of AIS.

Junhu Wang is a senior lecturer at the School of Information and Communication Technology, Griffith University, Australia. Prior to his appointment at Griffith University in February 2003, he was a lecturer at Gippsland School of Computing and Information Technology, Monash University, Australia from September 2001 to February 2003. Dr. Junhu Wang received his PhD in Computer Science from Griffith University, Australia, in March 2003. His current research interest includes query transformation and query optimization, reasoning with database constraints, Keyword search over structured data, information extraction, as well as semantic web and web services.

Wei Wang is now a postgraduate student at the School of Management, Fudan University in Shanghai, P.R. China. He received his bachelor degree in information management and information systems from Tongji University, P.R. China, in 2007. His research focuses on ontology, semantic retrieval and E-commerce. His papers have appeared in Journal of Systems Engineering and Electronics, Logistics Technology, and IEEE: The International Conference on Management and Service Science (MASS2009).

Rolf T. Wigand is Maulden-Entergy Chair and Distinguished Professor of Information Science and Management at the University of Arkansas at Little Rock. He researches information management, electronic commerce and markets, vertical information systems standards development and the strategic deployment of information and communication technology. Current research on vertical IS standards in three industries (mortgage, retail, automotive supplies) as well as online gaming behavior is funded by the National Science Foundation.

John Yearwood is Professor of Informatics in the Graduate School of Information Technology and Mathematical Sciences and Director of the Centre for Informatics and Applied Optimization, University of Ballarat, Australia. His research spans areas of pattern recognition, argumentation, reasoning, decision support, web services and their applications. He has been chief investigator on a number of ARC projects in these areas. His work has involved the development of new algorithms and approaches to classification based on modern non-smooth optimization techniques, new frameworks for structured reasoning and their application in decision support and knowledge modelling. Some important outcomes relate to the use of text categorization techniques for detecting drugs responsible for adverse reactions. He is currently an ARC research fellow working in the area of argumentation and narrative structures. He is an associate editor for the Journal of Research and Practice in Information Technology. He has over 140 refereed journal and conference publications. His email is j.yearwood@ballarat.edu.au.

Masaya Yoshikawa is an associate professor of Department of Information Engineering at Meijo University, Nagoya, Japan. His research interests include Programmable logic, Parallel computing and Soft computing for VLSI CAD. He is a member of Institute of Electrical Electric of Japan (IEEJ), Information Processing Society of Japan (IPSJ), Institute of Systems, and Control and Information Engineers (ISCIE) and Institution of Electrical and Electric Engineering (IEEE). He is currently serving as the

Secretary of the IEEE Kansai Section MDC committee, the Steering Committee Member of IPSJ System LSI Design Methodology, and the Research Group Member of Educational Program for Electric Circuit in IEEJ. He received Industrial Technology Prize from ISCIE in 2007, and Best Paper Award from the Form on Information Technology 2003.

Apostolos Zarras received his BSc in Computer Science in 1994 from the Computer Science Department, University of Crete. From the same department he received his MSc in Distributed Systems and Computer Architecture. In 1999 he received his PhD in Distributed Systems and Software Architecture from the University of Rennes I. From 2004 until now he holds an assistant professor position at the Department of Computer Science of the University of Ioannina. Apostolos Zarras has published over 20 papers in international conferences, journals and magazines. He is currently a member of the IEEE computer society. His research interests include middleware, model-driven architecture development, quality analysis of software systems and pervasive computing.

Yong Zhang received his MS degree in software engineering from software college, Shandong University, china, in 2007. Currently, he is enrolled at the school of computer science and technology, also in Shandong University, as a PhD candidate working on services computing, grid computing. His current research interests are enterprise interoperability, software as a service and web service transactions.

Xiaohui Zhao is a research fellow in Faculty of Information and Communication Technologies, Swinburne University of Technology, Australia. He received his Bachelor and Master of Engineering degrees from Harbin Institute of Technology, Harbin, China, in 2001 and 2003, respectively, and his PhD degree from Swinburne University of Technology, Melbourne, Australia, in 2007, all in computer science. He has published around 30 peer-reviewed papers in international journals and conferences, and he has also organised a series of workshops and conferences. His research interests include business process management, pervasive computing, service-oriented computing, etc.

Index